ON BECOMING A CONSUMER

ON BECOMING
A CONSUMER

THE DEVELOPMENT OF CONSUMER BEHAVIOR PATTERNS IN CHILDHOOD

James U. McNeal

AMSTERDAM • BOSTON • HEIDELBERG • LONDON
NEW YORK • OXFORD • PARIS • SAN DIEGO
SAN FRANCISCO • SINGAPORE • SYDNEY • TOKYO
Butterworth-Heinemann is an imprint of Elsevier

ELSEVIER

Butterworth–Heinemann is an imprint of Elsevier
30 Corporate Drive, Suite 400, Burlington, MA 01803, USA
Linacre House, Jordan Hill, Oxford OX2 8DP, UK

 Recognizing the importance of preserving what has been written, Elsevier prints
its books on acid-free paper whenever possible.

Library of Congress Cataloging-in-Publication Data
McNeal, James U.
  On becoming a consumer : development of consumer behavior patterns in
childhood / author, James U. McNeal.
    p. cm.
  ISBN-13: 978-0-7506-8335-7
  ISBN-10: 0-7506-8335-X
  1. Consumer behavior—United States. 2. Child consumers—United States.
  I. Title.
  HF5415.33.U6.M386 2007
  658.8′3420830973—dc22

                                                          2006038018

British Library Cataloguing-in-Publication Data
A catalogue record for this book is available from the British Library.

ISBN 13: 978-0-7506-8335-7
ISBN 10: 0-7506-8335-X

For information on all Butterworth–Heinemann publications
visit our Web site at www.books.elsevier.com

Printed in the United States of America
07 08 09 10 11 10 9 8 7 6 5 4 3 2 1

TABLE OF CONTENTS

Part II ENVIRONMENTS IN WHICH CONSUMER BEHAVIOR PATTERNS DEVELOP

PREFACE: ON BECOMING A CONSUMER

It is expected that this book will serve as a supplemental text to undergraduate and graduate courses in consumer behavior (CB). All consumer behavior courses and their books focus on people's *being* consumers. This book should fit nicely on the front end of all those courses since its focus is on people's *becoming* consumers. The book should also serve as a stand-alone text for courses in children's consumer behavior (CCB), courses that also may be termed consumer development, developmental consumer psychology, and enculturation. It should serve, too, as a supplement to courses in consumer economics, consumer education, and economic psychology.

This book also should provide useful guidance for those millions of practitioners who target children of all ages. There is a lot of bad—improper and incorrect—marketing to children out there by both for-profit and not-for-profit organizations. The information and ideas in these pages will serve well those who read them carefully and apply them diligently.

In a way this book was started 40 years ago; my mid-1960s doctoral dissertation treated the topic of the development of consumer behavior patterns in childhood. I was interested at that time in describing the beginnings of consumer behavior patterns—a challenge presented to me from those who directed my joint program in marketing and psychology. To be specific, I started by pursuing an understanding of the beginnings of purchase behavior patterns. I had fallen in the trap that was/is common of consumer scientists, that is, equating consumer behavior with purchase behavior and pretty much disregarded preparation for purchase—prepurchase behavior—and use and disposal of those things purchased—postpurchase behavior. Thus, at that time period in my academic life, the notion of consumer development—the topic of this book—was mainly perceived as learning how to make independent purchases.

Gradually, I began to focus on the purchase behavior of parents on behalf of their children. While I was still taking a marketing perspective to consumer development, it was becoming more of a human development perspective—perhaps due to my coursework in developmental and clinical psychology. I was increasingly under the influence of Piaget, Erikson, and Freud—all three developmentalists and all three useful to theorizing about consumer development, although none would ever say that. All three would say that their theories were theories of human development, and I would answer that human development, at least in industrialized nations such as the United States, is, for the most part, consumer development. However, my interest was mainly in parental purchases that resulted from verbal requests of children and mostly those verbal requests made in the purchase setting. Thus, child-rearing theory, or what was becoming known as socialization and consumer socialization, also influenced my thinking and research. My thoughts about consumer development essentially were that language had to develop in order for there to be purchase requests, and there had to be purchase requests in order for there to be purchases. Consequently, my research focus often was on the "buy me," "get me," "gimme," and "can I have" statements of children and the results of such statements. I even began to construct some crude indexes of children's influences on their household purchases.

It took me many hours of thinking/researching/analyzing before these activities led me behind the action—behind the purchase requests that led to purchase behavior—to the actual genesis of consumer behavior patterns—an infant first discerning among products in his environment and in some manner expressing preferences for certain ones and using (consuming) them—according to his physical and mental development. It soon became clear to me that consumer behavior patterns begin shortly after birth and develop in tandem with physical/motor development and with cognitive development, and, in fact, I found the three so interrelated that they can be separated only for exposition's sake. Thus, I realized that consumer behavior cannot take place until there is adequate motor and cognitive development, but that these do not develop outside/without consumer behavior. Consumer behavior grows the body and the brain and the contents and abilities of each. For example, reaching for a toy mobile (CB) above the crib requires some motor and cognitive development on the infant's part, but the more reaching for the mobile, the more fostering of some motor and cognitive changes the infant gets.

Thus, it took me a long time of working (stumbling) backward—backtracking—to get to the beginnings of a consumer, to the beginnings of consumer behavior patterns that culminate in purchases. I guess it was one of those situations of not being able to see the forest (the complete consumer) for the trees (consumer acts). Another distraction or detriment to discovering the beginnings of consumer behavior patterns was my focus on products. Again, this was a result of my marketing training and teaching. With my marketing thinking, I often would linger for days on the analysis of children's consumption of certain food products, for example, and then turn my attention to their consumption of, say, clothing or play items. While this kind of brainstorming produced good information that eventually helped me to help organizations as a consultant, it didn't advance my thinking much regarding the development of consumer behavior patterns.

Further, looking for certain consumer behavior patterns within human behavior seemingly kept me from realizing that *most human behavior is consumer behavior*, at least in an advanced economy such as the United States. But it finally dawned on me that all those basic human behaviors we call *eating* and *sleeping*, *playing* and *studying*, *working* and *traveling* were really terms for consumer behavior, not just human behavior. It became increasingly clear to me, then, that consumer behavior was a constant in our society, that it was 24/7/360—it occurred all the time, every day and night, in every dimension of our lives. The baby asleep in her crib was behaving as a consumer—she was using (consuming) not only the crib but blankets, diapers, mobiles, and utilities while she slept—and when she woke she consumed more of these items plus food, toys, and other furniture such as her cradle, playpen, and chairs and tables. Thus, I finally realized that "life in these United States" was a forest of consumer behavior—not just a few trees on the commercial landscape—and it fortunately was growing more difficult for me to see the trees. Moreover, I began to realize that being a consumer—performing in the consumer role—was the nature of the human life that begins at birth and continues to death. In fact, I began to reason that many consumer behavior patterns may come with the wiring, that they may be genetic. That is, our parents may pass on to us such consumer behaviors as their cravings for sweets and salt, a desire to drink many liquids rather than just water that our bodies need, a desire to adorn our bodies with jewelry, and a desire to take risks. Studies published in the 1980s and today of the behavior patterns of identical twins raised apart appear to confirm this.

So, it became obvious to me that consumer behavior pervades our lives or, if you might, our lives are our consumer behavior patterns. When we invoke such terms as *working* and *vacationing*, we are talking about consumer behavior just as when we talk about someone going shopping or watching TV ads. All this nomenclature, in fact, tends to get in our way of seeing consumer behavior for what it is. When we say, "the baby is sleeping," we really mean that he is consuming a variety of products to rest his body and mind. Thus, it seems not only logical but imperative that we look carefully at the development of consumer behavior patterns since being a consumer is the most basic and the most prevalent of human behaviors and has much impact on our cognitive and motor development. And not unimportant, 24/7/360 consumer behavior explains the constant marketing—the 24/7/360 marketing—that parents and consumer advocates complain about but find absolutely necessary.

In the first chapter of this book, I introduce the term *tekram* to refer to each unit of consumer behavior. Amazingly, in spite of our lives being lives of thousands of consumer acts each day, we don't have a term for one unit of consumer behavior. The term *tekram* is *market* spelled backward and a logical term since each consumer act tends to designate a person as a member of one or more markets—the toy market, the teen market, the movie market, for instance. I do not have a single term to represent the many marketing acts that are in response to the many consumer acts—such as retailing, advertising, and packaging—except *selling*. So, when consumer protectionists complain, for example, about the great amount of advertising to children, they are complaining about selling.

One more basic point regarding distractions that kept me from seeing the big picture of consumer development was the focus of virtually all marketing and consumer behavior books and articles on people *being* consumers rather than or in addition to seeing people *becoming* consumers. For example, the marketing books that I studied and taught from discussed marketing to the upper-middle social class or middle-income class, or they talked about marketing to women or to Hispanics as if consumers are simply "out there," they are in-waiting by classification, rather than that they will be there, they are coming or, in essence, they are developing. There was virtually nothing said about growing customers—cradle-to-grave marketing—or perfecting perpetual markets—producing a steady stream of new customers that keep coming from their development in childhood. Such thinking has, for the most part, not yet become a normal part of marketing theory, much less of marketing practice.

Some premises or structural concepts have resulted from my years of researching consumer development, and these are presented in Chapter 1 and are threaded throughout subsequent chapters. They should be mentioned here in order to prepare the serious reader who goes from front to back:

1. Most human behavior is consumer behavior, at least in a developed economy/society such as the United States. That is, most roles such as working, worshipping, schooling, home making, recreating, on and on, consist mainly of consumer acts.
2. Human development, at least that in a developed economy/society, depends on consumer development. That is, consumer development does not take place except as a result of

    physical/motor development and cognitive development, but similarly, physical/motor and cognitive development do not occur except through their interactions with consumer development.

3. Consumer behavior throughout life is constant; it is 24/7/360. It occurs night and day, every day, in every dimension of life. For example, it does not shut down when we go to bed or go on vacation or seek tranquility; we continue to consume commercial objects just as we did before we undertook these actions.

4. There are many reasons to practice consumer behavior in addition to satisfying our bodily and personal needs. For instance, much of our consumer behavior is for the satisfaction of other consumers in our care.

5. Consumer behavior is the essence of a developed society. Production is the essence of an undeveloped society, and both consumer behavior and production behavior are essential for a person in a developing society. Consequently, enculturation—teaching our children how to function in our culture—is mainly teaching them consumer behavior patterns.

6. Consumer behavior is a directive to marketing and marketers. Our consumer behavior should determine what marketers offer and communicate about what they offer. From a socially responsible viewpoint, there is no reason for a profit or not-for-profit organization to offer people anything that does not fit with their consumer behavior patterns. Of course, as we will note, many business firms do not adhere to this principle and try to sell unwanted, harmful items to consumers through deception.

7. Consumer behavior patterns develop in stages that can be described and explained. It appears that consumer development begins at birth, or shortly after birth—after reflexes decline—and continues in orderly stages to at least around the age of 100 months when a person is at a level of competence to be considered a bona fide consumer—when a person can perform adequately in prepurchase, purchase, and postpurchase behavior. The stages are orderly, or invariant, in the sense that one must take place before the next one can. There is no skipping.

To explain these premises and the overall development of consumer behavior patterns—of consumers—the book has been structured as follows.

Chapter 1 attempts to put two basic concepts into perspective: consumer behavior and consumer development. Consumer behavior is explained as the most basic human behavior in an advanced economy/society such as the United States. Thus, consumer behavior is a function of the person and his environment. Consumer development is traced from birth to 100 months and shown to be intertwined with the development of mind and body. Then it is presented briefly as a five-stage concept.

Chapters 2 and 3 describe the two domains of the environment in which consumer behavior patterns develop. Chapter 2 treats the physical domain, which consists of objects, mostly commercial objects, and shows how it participates in consumer development. Chapter 3 considers the social domain of the consumer's environment by showing the various sets of people at various times who contribute to consumer development in childhood.

Chapters 4 and 5 focus on the personal development of the new human being and attempt to show how it is intricately related to consumer development. In Chapter 4, physical and motor development are described in stages, and each stage is related to consumer development by demonstrating how certain motor skills make certain consumer behavior patterns possible. Likewise, in Chapter 5, cognitive development, as seen through the theory and research of mainly Jean Piaget, is shown to be closely related to consumer development. An important point in both of these chapters is that mind and body development are interdependent, and both are interdependent with consumer development.

Chapters 6, 7, 8, 9, and 10 each treat one stage of consumer development. Chapter 6 discusses the first stage, the observation stage, in which the child first makes sensorimotor contact with commercial objects and forms preferences for some of them. Chapter 7, stage two, shows how the child through physical/motor development begins seeking and asking for preferred objects that have been discovered in the environment. Chapter 8 treats the third stage, selecting/taking, by showing that physical and mental development facilitates the taking of desired objects—taking them from the home setting, from playmates, and from the marketplace. In Chapter 9, the child is now old enough to attempt purchases of desired items with the help of a more experienced consumer such as a parent or older friend. Thus, the purchases are co-purchases in the sense that another party has to furnish certain types of assistance. Finally, Chapter 10 describes the independent purchase act by the child, a step that confirms the child as a bona fide consumer. Beyond this point in consumer development, the person as consumer will continue for life refining all the skills and knowledge that she has formulated in childhood to obtain satisfying commercial objects.

Chapters 11 and 12 step back and look at the role in consumer development of the two most influential parties in that development: parents and marketers. Chapter 11 goes through each stage of consumer development and highlights the role of parents in each. It shows that basic consumer behavior patterns such as product and brand preferences are learned mainly from parents—including preferences for good and for bad commercial objects. Chapter 12 parallels the preceding chapter by showing the role of marketers in each stage of consumer development. It makes a couple of important points: namely, that it is through parents that marketers gain headway into the lives of children consumers, and that marketers bring with them a lot of help for the new consumers but along with it come a lot of unethical practices.

A couple of other features to the book should be noted. Each chapter opens with a vignette of research dialogue related to the main topic of that chapter. In addition, each chapter contains photos of children performing in the consumer role that also illustrate features of the chapters. These photos, along with some editorial material, introduce consumer behavior in the Chinese culture to allow some comparison with the main topic of consumer behavior in the United States. Finally, in each chapter, an insert describes a current issue in consumer development, topics we read about in magazines and newspapers such as child abuse, shoplifting, and organized sports for children. These inserts are related to some part of the chapter topic and are intended to give the somewhat theoretical discussions some meaningful exposition. The issues may also serve as cases for the classroom.

There are some limitations that I should also mention. I have avoided theoretical jargon as much as possible while still presenting a developmental theory of consumer behavior. Also, I have tried to minimize citations that might get in the way of smooth reading. Both are accomplished to a great extent by relying heavily on my own research. I have attempted also to minimize the number of companies, brands, and people mentioned as compared to those in my previous books. The reason for this is that many readers of those other books incorrectly saw those mentions as endorsements rather than as examples at a point in time. Even where a business firm was criticized, some readers interpreted this to be an endorsement of competitors.

I have attempted to protect the identity of people named in the book. In no case do the names of consumers used in the vignettes and examples reflect the true names of those people, and often their locations have been masked. Also, names of people appearing in photos are not used. Credits for most of the photos are due specifically to Mariel Ma and Li Ying.

There are a couple of other people who have contributed directly and indirectly to the book that I would like to acknowledge. Dr. Chyon-Hwa Yeh, Senior Bio-Statistician at Procter & Gamble, provided much guidance in research notions and in quantitative analysis. Dr. Kara Chan at Hong Kong Baptist University directed several of the studies that provided information about Chinese children and their consumer behavior. Susan Sun, CEO of KinderPower (Beijing), assisted me in developing relations with schools in China. Qiuxiang Huang provided valuable assistance as my interpreter.

James Utah McNeal
College Station, Texas

PART I

INTRODUCTION

This first part of the book consists of one chapter in which the topic of consumer development is put into perspective. It establishes that consumer behavior is the most important role performed by human beings in a market-driven economy. It offers several reasons why the study of consumer behavior development is so important. It outlines the stages of consumer development, the topic of most of the book.

A Beijing third-grader drew this picture as part of a research project in which children were asked (in Chinese) to "Draw what comes to your mind when you think about going shopping." She illustrated herself and two friends shopping at the toy counter of a Beijing department store. She carefully drew a number of soft, cuddly creatures tending to demonstrate her femininity and nurturing qualities.

1

ON BECOMING A CONSUMER

Yulan Wang Becomes a Fast-Food Consumer

As part of the research described in the latter half of this book, a working mother and her fifth-grade daughter were interviewed in their Beijing apartment regarding parent-child buying habits. Here are some results of that recorded interview, providing a panorama of one child's consumer development.

When Yulan Wang was around four months old, her mother and father took her shopping with them for the first time in the Haidian District of Beijing. After purchasing some clothing for Yulan at Shang An department store, Mr. and Mrs. Wang took her to a nearby McDonald's where they purchased and shared a Happy Meal that consisted of a hamburger, fries, drink, ice cream, and a Snoopy action figure. Mrs. Wang told an interviewer that because she had her baby with her she chose McDonald's for a shopping break. The restaurant was her choice because of its cleanliness, including its clean restrooms, its no-smoking policy, its air conditioning, its well-lighted menu with its clearly stated prices, and the special food and fun for children—mentioned in that order. (It should be noted that the Wangs had several restaurant choices for their shopping break, including some within the department store, a busy fast-food noodle shop across the street, and a KFC next door.) While the Wangs consumed practically all of the Happy Meal themselves, they did give Yulan some ice cream—her first away from home—and, of course, the Snoopy toy that they took with them in the Happy Meal box. That was the first of many visits to a McDonald's for Yulan that later included a party visit for her first birthday, then for her second, and her third. Over a several-year period, Mrs. Wang estimated that Yulan received at least 20 different toys with purchases of food at the restaurant and still had some of them on a bookshelf at their apartment which Yulan was happy to show to the visiting interviewer.

When Yulan was able to walk at around 12 months, she walked to the McDonald's service counter holding her mom's hand, and by age two she was carrying some of the food to the table. Shortly after Yulan's fourth birthday, her mother gave her the money to pay for the meal, and Yulan actually put the money on the counter when her mother told her and then retrieved the change. (Mrs. Wang said that Yulan could not see the top of the counter but received assistance from a service person.) By the time Yulan was six, she could go to the counter at McDonald's, order a Happy Meal, specify what toy she wanted with it, pay for it, and carry the tray to the table where Mrs. Wang waited with excitement in her eyes and laughter on her face. Then the two of them, and sometimes Mr. Wang also, would enjoy the meal, the toy, and the event. That purchase of a Happy Meal was her last one as she "graduated" to adult offerings.

Part of these visits to McDonald's was due to Yulan's asking, even demanding, and part of them was due to the Wangs using the visits as an incentive to get Yulan to perform well at kindergarten and on reading and other educational tasks at home. When Yulan was in the second grade, she was permitted to go with other classmates to a McDonald's near her school once a week and purchase lunch with her own money. By the time she reached the fourth grade, Yulan regularly visited McDonald's with classmates for school lunch and after school, and sometimes on Saturday or Sunday morning with her parents, again, as a reward for school-related accomplishments. When asked what her favorite foods were at McDonald's, the fifth-grader replied, "Fries and Chicken McNuggets." Her mother noted that those two foods had been Yulan's favorites for years.

INTRODUCTION

These marketplace experiences of Yulan Wang represent a very thin slice of her consumer development, but they are quite similar to millions of other children in market-driven economies around the world, including urban China. Other episodes of consumer behavior could be described that might entail her visits with her parents to sit-down restaurants, clothing stores, and street markets in Beijing, whereas still others might represent the child's independent visits to some of the retail outlets she favored. But, what is omitted, and will be detailed in these pages, are the thousands of consumer acts performed daily by the child at home and at school—the substance of her consumer life, really the substance of her life in general. In a microcosm, though, this particular set of consumer events at a fast-food restaurant marks the early beginning of Yulan's consumer behavior patterns. Through research that produced this scenario and hundreds of others, we are provided a glimpse of the development of consumer behavior patterns in childhood that will be examined in this book.

This focus on Yulan's consumer development rather than, say, her development of work habits, her study habits, or her musical talents is intended because, as we will document, *consumer behavior represents the most important role a person will perform in life.* In fact, all the other roles she performs, such as student and worker, consist mainly of consumer behavior in different settings. For example, when Yulan goes to music lessons after school in her role as music student, she reported that she rides the bus to the teacher's home after getting a quick snack at a street vendor near her school. And once she arrives at her teacher's studio, she practices for two hours on a *zheng* (Chinese zither) provided by the teacher who bought it at a music instrument store, one recommended by the teacher to Yulan's parents as a place to buy musical instruments. At the end of the two hours of listening to the teacher, practicing on the zheng, having tea with the teacher, and using the restroom in the apartment, she pays the teacher 40 Yuan ($5), catches the bus home, and arrives just in time for dinner. In this brief description of Yulan's music student role, it is difficult to separate those parts of it that *are not* consumer behavior. The plain fact of the matter is that beginning at birth and for the rest of her life Yulan will perform in the consumer role 24/7/360. Precisely all those activities that we normally call consumer behavior—CB—are performed by Yulan and millions of other children every hour of every day in virtually every aspect of life. Thus, from the standpoint of time alone, CB is easily the most important role in people's lives, at least in the lives of people in market-driven nations such as the United States and increasingly in China, the largest population of young consumers. While most reports of children's consumer behavior found in books and journals examine *being* a consumer, in this book the focus is primarily on *becoming* a consumer as depicted in the childhood of Yulan Wang. We will explain in detail the life of an infant consumer who must rely on her parents for choosing foods for her, for example, and how she becomes a toddler consumer who is able to express her preferences for certain food items to her parents who buy them for her, and then only a short while later becomes an independent consumer who makes her own choices and purchases whatever snacks she likes.

Photos 1-1, 1-2, and 1-3 exemplify this path of consumer development. In Photo 1-1, a Chinese grandmother takes her 16-month-old grandson for

PHOTO 1-1   A Chinese grandmother takes her 16-month-old grandson for a morning walk near a pond while his mother and father work. The child snacks on a cookie selected by his grandmother since he is still too young to make his own food choices.

PHOTO 1-2   A five-year-old Chinese girl pulls on her mother and asks her to buy a wood-carved toy from a street merchant. The girl still lacks the skills to buy it on her own, particularly in China, where the consumer must bargain for each item.

PHOTO 1-3 This eight-year-old Xiamen girl is capable of purchasing a meal on her own at a fast-food restaurant. She also knows it is good manners to spread out the fries and ketchup on the tray and wait for her working mother to join her for a snack and conversation.

a morning walk near a pond while his mother and father are at work. The grandmother chooses a cookie for the child to snack on during the walk since the child is still too young to make his own food choices. However, by nearly age five, the little girl in Photo 1-2 is capable of deciding what she wants—in this case a wood-carved toy she spied at a street marketer's offering—and she holds on to her mother while making repeated requests to buy it for her. The Beijing merchant gives the girl a bit of a sales talk in order to encourage her to ask her mother for the item. By elementary school age, children usually are able to make their own purchases, as demonstrated by the eight-year-old girl in Photo 1-3, who went to a Xiamen, China, McDonald's after school and purchased a meal on her own with her own money. It is clear that she has undertaken this consumer behavior pattern before as demonstrated by her confidence—and she told researchers she goes there about every day and waits for her working mother to meet her. Notice how she lays out the fries, the ketchup on the fries' bag, and her Chicken McNuggets in its box. (Interestingly, this is about the same meal as that preferred by Yulan Wang of Beijing.) The girl said she did not order a drink for herself because her mother told her drinks were fattening, but that she carried a bottle of water in her backpack.

CURRENT ISSUES IN CONSUMER DEVELOPMENT (#1)

Children's Consumer Behavior in China: A Blend of Eastern and Western Cultures

As part of a worldwide research program, we went to China in 1995 to study and document empirically for the first time the consumer behavior of Chinese children. We had some experience with the Chinese culture through study of children's consumer behavior in Hong Kong, Macau, and Taiwan, but we were not prepared for the cultural conflicts that we found in Mainland China. We later referred to this melee as *2X4 China*—it was Eastern versus Western, old versus new culture. Consequently, the research program chugged to a stall while we obtained our bearings, then restarted at a snail's pace to produce some of the most interesting information in our worldwide search.

China has the largest population in the world—1.3 billion people—and therefore the largest population of children—300 million under age 15. Two-thirds of it is rural, where, in the eyes of a Westerner, there is very little consumer behavior. The country is mainly production-oriented rather than market-oriented—its people choose to make rather than buy. Just 800 million people living what one Chinese professor termed "the simple life"—very little gas, electricity and running water; very little education and medical help; and perhaps enough income to eek out an existence, and, of course, buy cigarettes. Consequently, our initial research program ignored most of China and focused on urban China—the new China where the old is rapidly being set aside.

In urban China—mainly the 16 large eastern cities—with slightly over 100 million children under 15, there is a rambunctious economy that even the most skilled social anthropologist has trouble describing. Wide open, early 1900s capitalism—what official China calls a socialist market economy—prevails, and if a Westerner in Beijing closes his eyes—as he often has to do—he may feel he is on a busy, noisy, dirty street in New York City. Here East is gulping up West. Children in their Nike sports clothing gather at a McDonald's or KFC after school to fatten up on French fries and Cokes or Pepsis and talk about their teachers, and, of course, their classmates. Each child eagerly spends a relatively large sum of money obtained by request or demand from his or her dual-working parents—80 percent of moms work. The children's only obligation is to get a good education in order to later take care of the family in its old age. And they can have anything they want that will help accomplish this. Thus, it is the era of the "spoiled brat," where the child decides 68 percent of routine household spending—compared to less than 50 percent in the United States. Moreover, each child's spending and marketplace visits grow at a faster pace than those of any Western country.

Our research program among China's children continues today, and in 2002 we replicated the 1995 study in order to get a measure of any changes in consumer behavior patterns of new China's kids. Some of the key findings from the two studies of children ages 7–11 are shown side by side in Table A as follows.

The robustness of Chinese children's performance in the consumer role is undeniable as shown in these comparative figures. Their incomes, which are mainly from handouts on demand from parents and grandparents, doubled in the seven-year period from 1995 to 2002, and their spending almost tripled. Their independent store visits per week grew from 2.28 to 3.0 or almost a third, and the number of different kinds of stores shopped independently almost doubled.

Our research program has recently been extended to China's rural population, which is being awakened by the possibility that it can have what its urban counterpart has. And many of the 200 million rural children are beginning to take on an unmistakable Western aura. Thus, East and West have melded through the consumer behavior of the children who choose to be members of a common consumer culture.

TABLE A

Finding	1995	2002
Income (Yuan/week)	11.6	24
Savings Rate (%)	60	36
Amount Spent (Yuan/week)	5.6	15.4
Store Visits with Parents (week)	2.18	2.68
Store Visits Alone (week)	2.28	3.0
Stores Shopped Alone	1.6	2.9

****
Sources: James U. McNeal and Chyon-Hwa Yeh (1997); James U. McNeal and Chyon-Hwa Yeh (2003).

WHAT IS CONSUMER BEHAVIOR AND WHO IS A CONSUMER?

Before we dig into the development aspects of consumers, it seems appropriate to examine and explain a couple of basic terms in order to head off the What-about-this and What-do-you-mean-by-that questions that might interrupt the flow of the reading. Let me resort to one of my own consumer behavior books (McNeal, 1982) that contains a glossary of definitions for students and teachers. Its descriptions are probably representative of those found in most consumer behavior texts.

Consumer behavior is defined simply as *prepurchase, purchase, and postpurchase actions toward a commercial object.* While the focus is on the purchase act in these terms, there is an apparent time order of occurrence in this short definition that puts the purchase in perspective. That is, the *prepurchase* activities come first such as planning to purchase—talking it over with others; writing a list; seeking out sellers; searching for objects to purchase; checking packages at home for exact brands, sizes, contents; going through catalogs, websites—also going to the marketplace—driving to the mall, riding a bus to the marketplace, sitting down in front of the computer and finding a website such as Amazon.com—and confirming means of payment in advance of any purchases. Of course, there may be little prepurchase activity in the case of buying another bottle of milk, although there is almost always some, but there will be lots of planning and searching in the case of buying a relatively expensive item such as a computer, carpet, or car. There is less complexity, probably, about the actual *purchase.* In marketing jargon we are talking about the exchange—money for goods and services—between consumer and marketer—an act of commerce that likely takes place at a store, maybe a street market, although increasingly it happens at home on the Internet. Finally, *postpurchase* behavior refers to what a person does with the product (or service) after it is bought—its use. For example, it is unwrapped or removed from its package if there is any; then it is used by the purchaser or others, used up, added to, or mixed with other products that are utilized together, and any remainder is disposed of, recycled, thrown away, given away, or stored away. This last step, using the products, is the end purpose of the previous two steps and therefore the most important, because in addition to being the purpose of the purchase and preparation for the purpose, it will determine future purchases of the same or similar products. It is also in this last phase that children perform thousands of consumer acts compared to a much smaller number in the first two.

All of these activities, behaviors, actions, whatever term is appropriate to describe them, are performed by a person we call a *consumer.* Specifically, then, a *consumer is any person who performs any of the prepurchase, purchase, or postpurchase activities,* and not just those few listed in the preceding paragraph. Many terms refer to the parts of consumer behavior that we have just described, and we will invoke them at the appropriate time. And a number of terms can be used instead of the term *consumer.* However, interestingly, there is not really any one term that refers to the *act* of consumer behavior, probably because CB pervades virtually all other roles performed by people, and it therefore is referred to by the words used for the particular role. For example, rather than calling it consumer behavior, we call it sleeping or eating or going to school. Later I will coin a term to describe a unit of consumer behavior. I must note here, however, that the term *consumerism* is *not* a term that should be used to refer to the acts or general practice of being a consumer although some journalists use it this way. Consumerism refers specifically to the acts, people, and organizations involved with the *protection* of the consumer, shows concern for the *welfare* of the consumer, and is somewhat of a public policy term. For example, in any principles of marketing textbook, one can find the terms *consumerism* and *consumerism movement*, the latter referring to time periods of concern for particular consumer problems and the initiation of solutions to the problems. For instance, in the early 1900s, consumers were being sold so many unreliable medicines and bad foods that books were written about the problem, and legislation was enacted to deal with it. From that era of consumerism came the Pure Food and Drug Act that established the Food and Drug Administration (FDA) to administer it.

INDEPENDENT AND DEPENDENT CONSUMER BEHAVIOR

Some qualification of the preceding definitions of consumer behavior and consumer are in order. There is a tendency in the literature to describe consumer behavior as an *independent* act, which often is simply not the case. Therefore, we should address this misconception now. Most consumer behavior is *dependent* on others to some extent and often to a great extent. That is, people must rely on others for some help in much of their consumer behavior. This is most apparent in the case of children who prior to elementary school time are almost totally reliant on parents (or other caretakers) for providing them satisfaction of their needs including food, clothing, shelter, and play items. This is certainly true when they are infants, such as the 16-month-old in Photo 1-1 who must depend on his grandmother to provide him with a cookie or other snack. Later, as children become motorized—can walk or ride—they depend on parental assistance for transportation—bicycle, car, shopping cart—in addition to providing most products. Children must also rely on the consumer competence of adults and older children for guidance in new consumer behavior patterns. Always, children depend on parents for money, although in the United States many children start earning some money outside the home by the time they reach the fourth or fifth grade and certainly by middle school. But even then, most of their work-for-money income is a result of work in their households, and the amount is not nearly adequate to purchase all they need (McNeal, 1992). For instance, the little girl in Photo 1-2 who begged her mother to buy her a toy from a street merchant expects her mother to pay for it. And the eight-year-old girl in Photo 1-3 who bought her own fast-food meal depends on her parents for money to pay for the meal. Today, in the United States, many children grow up and remain at home until they are married; thus, they depend to some extent on parents for help with purchases even as young adults. Therefore, when we speak of children's consumer behavior, we usually are talking about some degree of dependent consumer behavior even though we will describe in detail the children's development into autonomous consumers.

Children do start operating with a reasonable degree of independence at around age eight or nine—100 months, on average, according to my research (McNeal, 1992, 1999). That is, they tend to make decisions about what they want without consulting parents much, although they may consult peers. They also may go to the marketplace without parents at this age. For example, they may hang out at the mall or a convenience store after school. From this point on, independence, or what the psychologist calls autonomy and autonomous behavior, increases. But again, there usually is some dependence on parents. Moreover, what may be forgotten in this kind of discussion is the 24-hour-a-day dependence of the children on parents for major consumer goods such as the home, car, furnishings, utilities, and recreational equipment. As they grow away from their parents as tweenagers and teenagers, they place more reliance on peers for guidance in consumer decision making. So, actually there is little completely independent consumer behavior among children. This is very apparent in China, a population of relatively new consumers—but the largest population of consumers in the world—that we will describe in visual and verbal forms throughout the book.

Very important, also, as children grow up, they will shift much dependence on parents and peers to marketers. That is, at some juncture in early life, children discover that all those wonderful, satisfying things that mom and dad have been providing are available in the marketplace from marketers. In fact, moms identify many of these commercial providers for their children during infancy. Soon after, the youngsters start looking to marketers for satisfaction of their needs and wants, although this initially takes the form of requests from the kids to the parents for the satisfying objects. Thus, the child moves toward marketers' product information and presentation, and parents tend to encourage this action, even push it. Thus, with parents pushing and marketers pulling, children form relations with marketers, often long-term relations and often through the medium of brands.

WHY DWELL ON DEVELOPMENT OF CONSUMER BEHAVIOR PATTERNS IN CHILDHOOD?

There ought to be very good reasons for devoting an entire book to the topic of becoming consumers. There are. Besides the fact that it has not been done and should be useful to consumer behavior students, theorists, and practitioners, and to those in several other fields of thinking, the most important reasons are described in the following sections.

1. Most Behavior of People Is Consumer Behavior

If there were some way to total all the acts of people in an industrialized society such as the United States or Japan for a typical day, *most* of them would be consumer behavior (CB). An act may be called going to school, going to work, sleeping, eating, bathing, driving, playing, but every one of them is mostly CB. Moreover, this is true for infants, children, teens, thirty-somethings, and seniors—humans of all ages—in the sense that all people continually think about commercial objects, ask others for commercial objects, select commercial objects, buy commercial objects, and use commercial objects in practically all of their daily activities. Of course, the stereotypical activities of going to the store, buying fresh vegetables, and fixing dinner are all CB, too, but what we are calling consumer behavior goes far beyond shopping and buying. It pervades our lives. *Precisely that behavior we term human behavior in our society is characterized primarily by its expression in the consumer role.*

2. Consumer Behavior Is 24/7/360

In the introduction, we noted that from the standpoint of *time* alone, consumer behavior is the most important role in people's lives. Let me explain. I once attempted to count the units of consumer behavior, what I call *tekrams*,[1] that are performed by a 10-year-old kid in one day in order to make the point of CB's dominance in people's lives. I tried to add up all the *commercial objects* in what I thought was a typical child's room, multiplied that figure by five as an average number of times daily (24 hours) they are used—consumed. For example, the rug might be used 20 times; the TV, 3; the bed, 2; the lamp, 1. Then I added to that all the items in the remainder of a typical three-bedroom, one-bath house or apartment regularly used by a kid—carpet, sofa, cereal bowl, bathtub, refrigerator—and multiplied that number by two. While both of these home usage rates are estimates, I considered them conservative. Then I attempted to factor in the personal items of the child, including clothing, toys, books, foods and beverages, and toiletries. After obtaining a measure of tekrams in daily home life, I next attempted to count the school-related items that are consumed (used) in a school day by the kid, for example, desks, chalk, paper and pencil, crayons, backpacks, and school lunches. I already knew through research that the typical kid goes to a retail outlet of some sort at least once a day on average (with and without parents), so I estimated the store visits, the purchases, the point-of-purchase promotions and advertisements experienced, the exami-

---

[1] I got the idea for a unit of consumer behavior when I was in graduate school at The University of Texas. I borrowed it from Frank B. Gilbreth, whom I read about and talked about in one of my industrial management classes (Lansburgh and Spriegel, 1946). Gilbreth studied time and motion of workers and measured the units of movement that he thought were common to all types of work. He called them *therbligs*, his construction of his family name spelled backward (roughly). I realized in my consumer behavior studies that we had many terms for various consumer behaviors but no general term for all of them, or any one of them. I figured that each act resulted in a potential market for business, so I coined the term *tekram* for *market* spelled backward.

nations of units of merchandise, and the store clerks with whom the child interacted. This gave me the tekrams for a typical visit to a shopping mall, for instance, where 10-year-olds often congregate. I added to this some tekram estimates for once-a-week visits to church and two units of after-school classes such as karate, piano, or athletics. Then I tried to factor in tekrams for a once-a-year vacation, a once-a-year visit to a relative, and a twice-a-year job-related trip with parents. Finally, I added the number of ads the child observes in print and broadcast media, one tekram for each. While I was making these estimates, two research assistants agreed to also make the same estimates after we brainstormed this effort as a possible idea for an undergraduate consumer behavior class. At the end of one week we met, compared notes, agreed and disagreed, and reached what we believed were conservative estimates—conservative mainly because we did *not* include any numbers for the planning, contemplating, searching, and talking to others about purchases—also all acts of consumers. The net results, after adjusting for a nine-month, five-day-a-week school year, were over *10,000 units of consumer behavior a day*, 3,650,000 a year—for one child. That comes to well over a billion tekrams (consumer acts) a year just for the approximately 4 million 10-year-olds just in the United States. Multiply this number by the approximately 4 million kids in each age group in the United States, and it is little wonder that there are producers and sellers that specialize, for example, in serving only children, or specialize in serving only tweens, the group of children who are ages 8–12, or even more specialized, in serving only tween girls.

From another perspective, we might ask when is human behavior *not* consumer behavior? Starting in infanthood, we enter the consumer role before we even emerge from the birthing center and before we grow beyond reflex behavior (described in detail later). Virtually all of our subsequent behavior from birth could be classified as consumer behavior. It is 360 degrees. It is in everything we do, in every dimension of our life. Consider some examples. We sleep (use) for at least 15 hours a day in a crib bought by the folks, and when we are not sleeping, we play (use) with a jillion commercial objects called toys (also provided by the folks). Then we go to school for around 15 years, schools that are bought and paid for with taxes and fees; use commercial textbooks, paper, and pencils; carry them in a brand-name backpack on a Detroit-produced bus, a mountain bike, or SUV that we bought. We make love wearing attractive clothing (under and outer), use name-brand protection, kiss with name-brand lipstick, buy a wedding ring online, pay a preacher to marry us, and then rent a little apartment and begin a family—when we can afford such consumer behavior. Along the way, we get our health care from the heaviest advertisers, bring suit against them for malpractice using lawyers that advertise in the Yellow Pages. We go to a church that advertises for members and is paid for by the members it attracts, and who also own at least one Bible purchased at a religious-oriented bookstore. At church we are taught by a pastor whom we pay after advertising for him or her. We sleep in a bed we bought, in bed-clothes we bought, in a rented apartment, and use sleeping pills we bought at a drugstore. (The sleeping pills are to help us sleep because we worry so much about paying for all of these tekrams—finances are people's number one worry.) I could go on and on with many more examples, but I hope I made the point that our lives are primarily commercial lives—they consist primarily of tekrams that we call life.

Remember the old movie *It's a Wonderful Life*, with James Stewart? It and most movies revolve around consumer behavior—tekrams—including love stories, adventures, and comedies. CB is usually their focal point, as it is of much literature because most of life is spent performing in the consumer role—most crime, most schooling, and most work.

Related to the consumer behavior that is practiced 24–7 is the fact that it fosters more consumer behavior. We want more of what we have, we want better than what we have, so we buy or ask for new items. Of course, many of the products we buy are used up, worn out, take on a bad appearance, and so we buy replacements. Some replacements are frequent, such as a loaf of bread, whereas some are rare but predictable, such as a new condominium. But consumer behavior almost always begets more consumer behavior through product and brand preferences and usage habits. Also, the consumer behavior of others often creates new consumer behavior patterns in our lives in the sense that what they have we want once we have seen it, or we may simply want it to keep up with them. In any case there is no breaking the chain of consumer behavior even if we burn our credit cards; it keeps growing longer and more complex. Thus, we are interacting with commercial objects all the time, from cradle to grave.

Notice the term *commercial object* that is frequently used here as evidence of our consumer behavior. It refers to a product that normally is business-provided rather than nature-provided, although most products of nature are commercialized such as pets, water, and plants. Actually, it may not be a product, per se, but a *service* such as dry cleaning or lawn maintenance or a coin-operated video game. But in marketing parlance these are also called *products*. It may not even be a product or a service but an *idea*, what might be termed a *commercialized concept* in the sense that someone has attempted to sell an idea to us. For example, political candidates, charities, and organized religions are often commercialized and marketed. In any case, we buy them in the sense we spend money on them as requested by the seller.

As a side note, none of what is being said is intended to sound pejorative or critical any more than the term *materialism* should be construed as a negative term. For instance, what is called *materialistic behavior* often is consumer behavior that is intended to own more of a good thing or replace something that is used up or worn out. In an industrialized society such as ours, in which we have chosen to buy our goods rather than make them, we have opted for the consumer life. There are still plenty of societies around the world in which their members produce practically everything for their needs and barter some of their production for that of others. In those cases we would say that their lives are characterized by production and self-sufficiency, and they teach these principles to their children as soon as possible. And there are plenty of philosophers and academicians who are ready to argue for one life or the other, but that is not our purpose here.

3. Consumer Behavior Provides for Others

What is suggested so far is that consumer behavior is everybody's job all the time in an economy such as that of the United States. It is necessary in order for people to have what they need to be happy, satisfied, contented, successful, safe, and healthy. But not all consumer behavior is intended to satisfy the needs of the one who performs it. Much CB of an individual may be for the benefit of others. In fact, the CB that is for others could easily be viewed as a CB of a higher order. What we are referring to are such activities as

A. Consuming on behalf of children. If mom or some other caretaker did not plan and purchase for all the needs of her babies, they would not survive. This process begins with paying the hospital bills and then providing the nursery, the formula, the cleaning products, the toys, and so on. So, while mom might be classified as the primary consumer in this case and baby the secondary consumer, both are important consumers to each other and to the marketplace. Approximately 4 million children are born each year in the United States—really 4 million consumers—and somebody must take care of them until they reach the age when they can vocalize their wants and needs and begin taking care of themselves. Most marketers target moms as providers in order to reach the infants, although some also target their infants directly in various ways. Just as consumer behavior commences at birth, so does market targeting.

B. Consuming on behalf of the family. In addition to being a consumer for the children, someone also assumes the responsibility for planning and buying products and services for the household. The household may not have any children in it, or they may be grown, but one member whom we usually describe as the homemaker tends to take care of the other members of the household. The term *taking care of* usually means planning and buying for the needs of the other people in the household. In China, for instance, there may be three generations living in one household that must be taken care of. Of course, this includes buying food, clothing, and shelter, but doing much more. It also includes providing education, health care, and travel. There may or may not be pleasure for the homemakers from all this consumer behavior, but it is necessary. In this case marketers may focus their efforts on the homemakers, on the household in general, or on specific individuals in the household.

C. Consuming on behalf of coworkers. A lot of consumer behavior is intended for the satisfaction of coworkers at an organization, an office, or at a factory. For example, in departments at universities where I have worked for many years, people are assigned to shop for and purchase products and services for the members such as coffee, refrigerators, copiers, and computers. The list of products and services provided is endless, and the persons who perform this CB are applying their skills that they use in other CB efforts such as purchasing for their households. Such efforts may account for millions of dollars of purchases and attract many business-to-business marketers who want to win some of the business.

D. Consuming on behalf of impaired people. Many consumers must devote or want to devote much time, energy, and money to buying for those individuals who are unable to get to the marketplace on their own due to impairments. This may mean buying for impaired family members or friends, for those in hospitals and nursing homes, and for those who can barely function independently but have their own household. The Internet has become a lifeline for some of these people, allowing them to shop and buy on their own and get the products delivered directly to them.

4. Consumer Behavior Is for Self-Image

How people see themselves may have a major impact on their consumer behavior. That is, the self-image that they develop very early in childhood may determine where they shop—stores, malls, online—what they buy—products and brands—and how much they pay for these items. Often kids ask for and buy clothing items that have brands on them as one way of saying, "This is who I am." This becomes noticeable about the time kids are developing their sports-related motor skills around age seven. In fact, it is probably rare that any of us buy a product such as a sandwich just to feed ourselves. Sure, that product is intended to satisfy our hunger as a rule, but additionally it is probably intended to match with our self-image—the sandwich we buy and the place where we buy it. Products, and particularly their brands, are often imbued with images or personalities that communicate to others for whom they are intended. A Burger King Whopper, for instance, is probably not the hamburger for modest, quiet, dainty eaters, but fits best with those who have a big appetite, who are big or see themselves as big, and who are a big influence on other people. People wear brand names on their T-shirts, glue them to their car bumpers, tack them on the walls of their rooms, and put them in many other conspicuous places not by accident but by intention. They may carry traveling items in shopping bags with certain store names on them to let fellow travelers know who they are. Elementary school boys love to wear clothing and shoes with athletic names on them, girls too, but the girls seem to migrate toward brand names that suggest their gender such as Barbie or Britney. Of course, such clothing items cost more, often much more, than the same clothing without a signature. But apparently they are worth the extra cost to express one's self-image. In order for it to work, however, that is, for purchased items to enhance one's self-image, others have to be acquainted with the symbols used to represent the self—and they usually are. Otherwise, when a brand name is displayed on a child's apparel, for instance, as a representation of that child's self-image and other children do not recognize it, these are not the results sought by the displayer. This behavior of using brands to symbolize the self may start as early as age two and continue for the rest of a person's life.

5. Consumer Behavior Is Part of the Imagination

Perhaps closely related to the self-image are the imagination and fantasies of people and children, particularly, that direct some of their consumer behavior. More will be said about this later in the book when it is noted that children learn much consumer behavior through pretending or imagined acts. But the point being made here is that children's imagination both directs consumer behavior and creates consumer behavior. Children particularly like to imagine themselves as grown-ups; therefore, buying and using grown-up things underpin this pretension. We know, for instance, that eight- and nine-year-olds may try smoking just to be adult-like. Ditto for alcoholic beverages. And they like to visit video game parlors and play grown-up games such as those that focus on racing, athletics, and lots of violence. Children also pretend to be certain grown-ups (role models) such as professional athletes and buy products used by them—for instance, clothing items and chewing tobacco. Kids also buy products to make them taller, bigger, and faster. Again, their imagination has produced these ideas, and it directs them to buy or ask parents to buy certain products to fulfill their creative thinking. They may simply imagine using certain products as part of their dreams and aspirations. Thus, some consumer behavior acts are not physical acts per se; they may be solely mental acts. But they may still produce much satisfaction—and additional consumer behavior patterns.

6. Consumer Behavior Facilitates Cognitive and Physical Development

Beyond genetics, the growth of the mind and that of the body are largely a result of consumer behavior, of perceiving and consuming commercial objects. Impoverish a child's environment by taking away all commercial objects, and the child is unlikely to become a normal functioning human being. Cognitive development theory such as Jean Piaget's theory that will be frequently noted in this book is in great part based on the child's interactions with objects in his environment (Flavell, 1963). These interactions are, as noted earlier, primarily consumer behavior although we may call them something else. ("Look at how she squeezes and sleeps with her new bunny," mom might say to an ethnographer about her infant's response to a new plush toy.) Even before infants know that objects exist separately (at around 8–10 months old), they are practicing consumer behavior toward them that contributes to their intellectual development—Piaget's primary concern. Consuming bottled milk causes preferences for the bottle—versus another container—and preferences for the milk—versus another beverage—to be printed in the infants' minds. This same statement could be made for many other environmental elements such as the bed, a rattle, a mobile, even a certain sound such as that of a noise toy or a talking plush animal. Books and articles on cognitive development like to discuss, for instance, children's learning of their self-images—attitudes toward the self—through looking at themselves in a mirror. Using the mirror is, of course, consumer behavior, although this is rarely, if ever, noted by the psychologists who study this behavior. So, the development of neural networks, memory, and perceptions are directly related to consumer behavior. This point is so important that we will devote an entire chapter to it.

Likewise, the physical development of youngsters is facilitated by consumer acts. The growth of the body and the development of its motor skills often are tied to a variety of consumer acts (Gallahue, 1982). Learning to move the head and eyes to follow a mobile placed above the child's bed is one important example of CB facilitating physical development. Reaching for the milk bottle helps children learn neck movement and grasping. Babies may learn that simply shaking their body will move the overhead mobile, a prelude to learning to roll over. Of course, once children begin crawling and walking, the role of furniture, shoes, and toys in these actions cannot be overstated. As we point out in a later chapter, motor actions are responsible for much cognitive development, and these motor actions are usually aimed toward some commercial object. So, if we could measure the tekrams of a one-year-old—as we attempted to do earlier for a 10-year-old—we might also derive some measurements of the child's cognitive and physical developments and their intertwining. These motor actions toward objects also produce speech, such as naming the objects including their brands. As children get beyond walking age, more complex objects such as tricycles, pedal cars, and construction toys facilitate the development of both gross and fine motor skills. Eventually, the children will learn to ride in a shopping cart and then steer it, as this consumer act produces more motor skills. Later, we will devote several chapters to children's learning through the consumption of commercial objects and note that the consumer behavior that is learned may be greater than that learned from parents. In sum, the development of consumer behavior patterns is responsible for much of the development of cognitive and motor behavior patterns.

7. Consumer Behavior Is the Most Gratifying of All Activities

Perhaps one of the most basic reasons to study the development of consumer behavior patterns is the fact that it is the most pleasing, gratifying, rewarding activity there is among our behavioral repertoire. When one steps back and looks at the major roles assumed by people, such as worker, student, and family member, none of them produces the total satisfaction of the consumer role. In fact, to a great extent, most other efforts are to make consumer behavior possible—our working, our schooling. Likewise, as has already been pointed out, CB makes other roles possible (e.g., musician, athlete, teacher). Country-and-western music stars like to talk about, even write about, getting their first guitar "before they could even play a note." And scientists like to talk about their first science project in school in which they assembled a number of items, mostly commercial items, to produce an amazing new result. Thus, planning, buying, and using goods and services produce most of our life satisfactions.

Sure, there are many unpleasant consumer tasks—going to the dentist, paying taxes, providing funeral services for those passing on. And there is much unhappiness among people living in poverty due to their inability to perform many consumer tasks. But each of the 10,000 or so consumer acts a day we perform produces some satisfaction and, in total, a great deal. This reason alone makes study of the development of CB patterns essential to understanding and improving the lives of all people.

8. Consumer Behavior Is the Essence of a Developed Society

The preceding comments about consumer satisfaction refer mainly to a developed society such as the United Kingdom or the United States. Specifically, if we divide all nations into undeveloped, developing, and developed, we find that consumer behavior is integrated into virtually all human activities in the *developed* ones. Therefore, CB is the dominant role and at the heart of all role behavior in a developed society. Thus, whatever the focal activities of a person are in a developed society—working, worshipping, schooling, housekeeping, playing—consumer behavior usually is a dominant part of it; that is, using commercial objects produces much of the satisfaction in the activity. For example, satisfying results from working are usually due to utilizing commercial objects such as office and factory fixtures and tools such as computers, furniture, and vehicles. Likewise, satisfaction from schooling is due in great part to utilizing such commercial objects as desks, computers, laboratory equipment, books, paper, and writing instruments.

In an *undeveloped* society, the dominant role is that of producer; that is, the main activity at this level of development is making the necessities of life—food, clothing, housing, tools. Further, in an undeveloped society, the tools used in making the necessities are likely also produced by the people by utilizing objects from nature such as plants, wildlife, and minerals rather than buying them. Thus, the role of producer is linked to all other roles and greatly determines their character. Schooling, for example, in an undeveloped society probably focuses mainly on training younger members of the society in the use of tools so that they may become producers. Most likely, the consumer role is present in undeveloped societies but is unimportant; perhaps its activities are seen as ostentatious, such as was the case in the early 1800s in the United States.

In a *developing* nation, the dominant role is that of *worker*, in which the focus is on the job of the head of household, and it, in turn, directs the activities in all the other roles. Going to school, for instance, is expected to improve the knowledge and skills of young people so that they can obtain worker positions in which they can succeed in earning attractive wages. There is a good chance that the worker in the developing society might say that his or her motive for getting a job and devoting so much energy to it is to "make good money," "get ahead," "have a good life," and "have all those things that my parents didn't have." These explanations are often heard in urban China, for instance. Thus, the worker's frequent focus is on performance in the consumer role, and success as a worker is often measured by the satisfaction received from consumer behavior.

9. Consumer Behavior Is a Directive to Marketers

Finally, a good understanding of consumer development is a necessity for successful marketing, meaning satisfying consumers and satisfying the goals of the marketing organization. (The marketing organization may be for-profit such as a toy maker/seller or not-for-profit such as government units and charities.) The only way that marketers in the business area can accomplish their goals is to take guidance from consumers through study of their consumer behavior patterns that develop. By observing children's consumer behavior patterns on a regular basis, marketers can see what products and services satisfy them and provide them more and better ones—new and improved as the marketers would say. Thus, current consumer behavior patterns of children, or anyone, are, in effect, a directive for astute marketers. *If* they correctly take the cues, the children will be satisfied at least as much as before—one hopes more. In turn, the businesses will succeed in their goals and support themselves, the economy, and the government.

There is a flip side to this thinking regarding satisfying children as consumers. Many marketing theorists and practitioners believe that the consumer behavior patterns that are developed in childhood will follow the youngsters into their adult life. In fact, it is believed that many of the consumer behavior patterns that children learn are put in storage, so to speak, until they can use them as adults (e.g., consumption of autos, alcoholic beverages, tobacco, guns, and sexual objects including their sources, brands, and prices). The result is that many marketers put in place a strategy of "growing customers," the notion of getting customers in childhood and marketing to them all the way to their senior years—also called "cradle to grave" marketing (McNeal, 1999). We will devote an entire chapter to marketers' responses to consumer development after we describe it in detail in several chapters.

WHAT IS MEANT BY CONSUMER DEVELOPMENT?

American kids, ages 4–12, spent an estimated $42 billion of their own money on products and services in 2005, and those ages 2–14 influenced directly and indirectly over $700 billion of parents' spending, according to my analyses. Thus, as primary consumers spending their own money on whatever they want, kids buy snacks, play items, and clothing to the tune of over $100 million a day. As influence consumers, they decide their household purchases of well over $1.5 billion a day. The latter are purchases that many of the kids would prefer to make themselves if they had the money and the consumer skills. But, as they have been taught by mom and dad, they ask for the items, even demand them if necessary. Incidentally, add to these consumption figures the spending and influence on household spending of teens (14–18), and children's total buying power comes to almost $1 trillion.

But these kids were not born consumers; they developed into the role beginning the day they were born. It is this development that is under focus in these pages. Virtually all studies of children developing into consumers have been done under the banner of something called consumer *socialization*, a term introduced by Scott Ward (1974, p. 2) in the 1970s to describe the "processes by which young people acquire skills, knowledge, and attitudes relevant to their functioning as consumers in the marketplace." This definition was simply a modification of earlier definitions of the general concept of socialization, such as that of Brim (1966). But Ward utilized the concept to produce his seminal study of children's consumer behavior (Ward, Wackman, and Wartella, 1977) that became the guiding light for most subsequent studies of childhood consumer behavior.

This choice of terms by Ward and those who opted for it as a description of their research, including this researcher on several occasions, probably was an unfortunate one for several reasons. The notion of socialization began as a child-rearing theory. As Irvin Child (1954, p. 655) so aptly put it: "Socialization refers to a problem which is old and pervasive in human life—the problem of how to rear children so that they will become adequate adult members of the society to which they belong." So researchers and reporters of kids' consumer behavior have tended to cast their thinking in this vein, that is, to focus on the processes by which children learn consumer behavior chiefly from their family life (e.g., Carlson and Grossbart, 1988). Ward (1974) noted up front in his initial article on the subject that ". . . child development and socialization researchers have virtually ignored consumer learning and behavior among children, focusing instead on the acquisition of fundamental orientations relevant to a wide range of behavior such as sex-role learning and moral development" (p. 1). Of course, these researchers focused on "fundamental orientations" taught by parents; that is what child-rearing thinking was about in the 1950s and 1960s when socialization was a hot topic. It was the age of Benjamin Spock (1946) and his work in permissive child training. Also, even Ward and his colleagues surely knew that psychologists, who are the principal students of child development and socialization, never want to appear to support or align with marketers who are the principal students of consumer behavior. Quite the contrary, most psychologists try to distance themselves from anything marketing, at least in the public eye.

Continuing on this line of thinking about what came to be called consumer socialization, perhaps most damaging to a strong research stream in it was the *social* in the term *consumer socialization*. It no doubt caused many consumer researchers to focus on people, mainly parents, as the primary source of change in children's consumer behavior patterns. There is no question that children learn much CB from others, particularly their parents, but learning on their own—*teaching themselves*—has been practically ignored, as has been learning from *objects*, a very basic way for children to assume any role and one that we will give much consideration to later. Writing further in his now-classic article in the *Journal of Consumer Research* (1974, p. 4), Ward emphatically noted that, "The point of view in this paper is that children's consumer behavior is best studied as a *developmental* phenomenon. . . ." (the emphasis is mine). But it never really came to be. The consumer socialization die was cast, not consumer development, and it behooved researchers to somehow join the two conceptualizations. Perhaps Ward and his followers simply subsumed development under socialization or considered them to be pretty much the same—just different angles for getting at the same thing. Two pages before Ward stated that his seminal paper's point of view was developmental, he said (p. 2), "The central purpose of this paper is to propose conceptual notions for research in the area of 'consumer socialization.'" That was over 30 years ago, and hundreds of studies have followed, studies of children's consumer socialization that are also sometimes referred to as developmental.

Actually, Ward's work always had a development tone to it, but it was primarily limited to *cognitive* development, that is, the changes in the minds of children that took place with age. In fact, the notion of cognitive development, which apparently fascinated Ward, became the secondary banner under which children's consumer behavior was studied by him and his followers such as George Moschis (1977). Specifically, Ward adapted Jean Piaget's theory of cognitive development as a basic framework for studying children's consumer behavior, particularly Piaget's development-in-stages idea. And as Ward went, so went most other researchers of the topic. Piaget's thinking was having a rebirth in the 1960s in the psychological literature, and no doubt had a tremendous influence on Ward and others who did their graduate work in the 1960s and 1970s. Thus, the consumer research among children narrowed to mainly their thinking with virtual disregard for their behavior.

Then one more diversion occurred that took most children's consumer behavior research out of the realm of behavior and centered it principally on their thinking. Ward and his colleagues had devoted quite a bit of study to mass media's influence on children as consumers, mass media at that time being a code word for television and television advertising. Although not very social, as in socialization, they were motivated by the government's interest (and funding) in *television advertising's* effects on children's minds, particularly those under age eight. So public policy drove many studies of television advertising's influence on the minds of children. And usually these studies were under the rubric of consumer socialization—television viewing was part of family life—and were guided, at least implicitly, by Piaget's cognitive development theory. The net result was that advertising's effects became mainstream consumer socialization research and over-shadowed a lesser number of studies of people's effects on children's socialization. In simple terms, virtually all of the studies of advertising influence on children's consumer socialization were really studies of advertising effects on children's thinking, not their behavior. As one of the leading researchers on children's cognitive development/socialization explained in one of her early research reports in *JCR*, ". . . consumer socialization can be thought of as resulting in the development of memory structures that organize children's information about consumer subjects" (John and Whitney, 1986, p. 407). In fact, when John (1999) recently summarized the many consumer socialization studies over a 25-year period—since Ward's seminal study in 1974—she ended up using a modified Piaget stage theory to report mainly advertising's effects on children's minds with very little devoted to behavior patterns. That is how narrow consumer development research, as Ward proposed, has become. It is developmental in the sense that researchers examine changes in cognitive structures of kids in an age range of 7–12 usually, but almost never in the very important developmental ages of preschoolers, toddlers, and infants. In this book we will examine children's *behavioral* development as well as their *thinking* development—as Ward would have had it—and we will look at the development phenomenon in the important early years of childhood—when a month of development is worth a year of results.

Let us now consider the notion of *consumer development* more critically, introduce it more formally, and briefly explain it since it is the gist of the following chapters. A broad, useful definition of consumer development is as follows: *Consumer development consists of the changes in an individual's level of functioning in the consumer role that result from the enduring changes in thinking and behavior.* (The enduring changes may or may not result from socialization.) Subsumed under the terms *thinking* and *behavior* are social relations, the sensory system, memory, language, speech, physical growth, and motor activities. Thus, in our examination of consumer development, we will give in-depth consideration to cognitive development, social development, sensory development, physical development, motor development, language development, and speech development. In fact, as noted earlier, consumer development is so intertwined with the development of these other human dimensions that it is difficult to separate them. A change in one produces change in the others.

All of these developmental relations are created through normal human behavior as characterized by this basic model:

$$B = f(E, P)$$

That is, behavior (B) toward the environment (E) produces mental traces in the person (P) that direct later behavior. This formulation is symbolically identical to that of the German-born psychologist Kurt Lewin (1953) and varies little in its interpretation from his, although he usually referred to the person and the environment together as "life space." This formulation also summarizes the essential views found, for example, in the cognitive development theory of Piaget (1963) and Erikson (1950), the motor development theory of Gallahue (1976), and the social development theory of Grusec and Lytton (1988), probably most theories of brain development (Eliot, 1999), and those of language and speech development (Kail, 1979). The reason why this formulation is the basis of most development theories is it is the most fundamental characterization of all human behavior whether it be that of the brain or the body, both of which are always participants in consumer behavior.

However, when one reads some reports of children's consumer behavior in the journals, as noted, they usually describe this behavior from the cognitive perspective of the person (P) with little regard for the person's motor behavior or the environment (E) in which it occurs. Thus, their reporting is often incomplete, or worse, half-right. This is simply researcher error, for cognitive development rarely takes place without some behavior (experience) in the physical environment. That is, in fact, the essence of Piagetian theory—environmental experience produces cognitive change—but somehow even in the interpretations of Piaget's findings, the physical aspects usually receive little attention. Consider, for example, the many reports of children's TV viewing in order to describe TV advertising's effect on their cognitive development, and vice versa. These reports—journal articles, books, monographs—constantly use terms such as *liking*, *perceiving*, *understanding*, *believing*, and *deciding* to refer to the cognitive domain but say little about the physical nature of the kids such as their height and weight, or their actual physical activities of TV viewing—sitting, standing, talking, and snacking—and virtually nothing of the physical environment such as the TV set, the chairs, and the lights. Yet, the results that they report are dependent on E as well as P and dependent on P's body behavior as well as P's mental behavior.

Another basic characteristic of consumer development is its occurrence in steps, phases, or stages. It appears that virtually all developmental theorists utilize the concept of *stage* to describe as precisely as possible the development on which they are focusing. Piaget's stages of cognitive development are probably the best-known stage system—or better said, Piaget is best known for his utilization of stages to describe children's cognitive development. But it is likely that he borrowed the stage idea from Sigmund Freud (Singer and Revenson, 1996), who found it useful to describe children's psychosexual development. Then others borrowed the idea from Piaget, such as Erikson (1950), who theorized about the eight stages of man, as well as most of those who write about the development and socialization of consumer behavior. Using stages to describe development of anything is a way of saying that this is the line the development follows—these are the steps the development takes. As for stages of consumer development, there has been little work. Valkenburg and Cantor (2001) proposed a phase theory of consumer development among children based on what appears to be a basic decision-making model: wants, search, choice, and evaluation. However, it is questionable to call these the four phases of consumer development when they do not constitute an invariant sequence. For example, choice (phase three) actually may occur in phases one and two as well as three. Seriously missing from their phases is the consumption act itself, that is, the use of the chosen product. Also, using a decision-making paradigm to frame a theory of consumer development tends to ignore those critics such as Olshavsky and Grandbois (1979) who say that consumers may not go through a decision-making process to obtain all goods and services. Piaget's cognitive development theory and his stages of cognitive development have been attacked and criticized many times in all the related journals. But the stages have survived, while other parts of his theory have tended to fade somewhat under the burden of too many questions. Piaget intended his stages to be *invariant*, which seems to bother some psychologists—that any description of human behavior could be so perfect, so in place—but they are logically in order and the order cannot be changed. The stages used here to describe consumer development feel invariant to me, but I will leave that to others to debate if they want.

The stages of consumer development that will be utilized throughout these pages have been tinkered with for at least 15 years, although I did not report them out until I briefly noted them in my 1992 book as "stages of consumer development." Along with Dr. Chyon-Hwa Yeh, I then gave some details to them at a 1993 American Statistical Association meeting and in its proceedings under the title of "Stages of Consumer Socialization in Childhood" (McNeal and Yeh, 1994). In that paper we emphasized the notion of *becoming* a consumer in contrast to *being* a consumer, but we couched it in terms of socialization more than development in order to give it some appeal among the academic public. I later devoted a full chapter to these stages in my 1999 book and have noted them in several other publications. I have not borrowed the stages from another consumer developmentalist or another consumer behavior theorist; they are my own. I have given names to the stages, changing them several times while striving for as much description yet brevity as possible. Probably they ought to simply be called Stage One, Stage Two . . . to indicate an order, what I believe is an invariant order, and not to confuse the user of them with terminology as Piaget did (and Erikson and Freud and others). Then each child consumer could be referred to as a Stage One (S1), Stage Two (S2) . . . child depending on that child's consumer behavior. Further, the stages are based at least as much on what the children teach themselves about consumption as what they learn from others. Here, very briefly are the stages of consumer development that will be expanded upon in great detail in the rest of the book. They are identified with one or two descriptors to refer to the basic new behavior that occurs in them.

Stage One: Observation (0–6 Months)

Stage One is the first stage of life and therefore the beginning of consumer behavior. It consists of two substages:

Random Observation (0–2 months). While the consumer behavior of infants depends on movement, of using their body to discover objects in their environment that will satisfy them, all movements at this point are reflexes. The babies' sensory system is, for the most part, unfolding, but until it does, they cannot observe except through random movements, movements that come with the wiring. Rapidly, though, the senses of smelling, hearing, tasting, feeling, seeing, and balancing emerge, and through them the random movements are replaced by voluntary movements toward foods, people, comfort objects, and play objects that satisfy. Mom's breasts get the most attention, being the most important consumption objects up to now.

Voluntary Observational (2–6 months). At this point most noticeable reflex movements are replaced by voluntary movements as more than one sense modality at a time now directs movements toward consumption objects that are increasingly becoming commercial objects. Habits appear as a result of repeating some movements that were random but produced satisfying results. Thus begins a memory, what might be termed a *motor memory* at this point, of what is good and what is not good as a result of such sensory/physical acts as tasting and touching. For instance, a baby finds that rocking movements will activate the mobile above the crib that mother bought for her, and turning her head will discover the rattle, the noise toy that gives her delight. Assimilation of such pleasure-giving experiences and recognition of the environmental objects that provide it produce memory units in increasing numbers.

Some of a baby's movements that result in pleasures are provided by parents. When he is around age two or three months, mom often takes him to the marketplace for the first time. Given that his senses are now well developed—about as good as an adult's— he can see, smell, hear, feel, even taste the attributes of the marketplace. These observations are his first in a commercial environment. For example, mom may give him a little taste of soft ice cream she buys with her coffee at the Dairy Queen in the mall after an hour or two of shopping and toting her new baby— like Mrs. Wang did for Yulan. A few of these "sweet stop" experiences will begin an association in baby's mind that will eventually make the marketplace as important of a provider of good things as mom. For now, this first experience with a commercial source of satisfiers is mainly credited to mom.

Stage Two: Requesting/Seeking (6–24 Months)

As in Stage One, there are two substages to Stage Two:

Pre-Language/Pre-Legs (6–14 months): During the first substage infants have not yet developed talking or walking abilities. At around five or six months, there is a surging growth in the baby's body including brain, neck muscles, and arms. Experiences with commercial objects in the home are virtually 24/7 with the new body power. The child starts sitting up by six months, thus opening a panorama of things to reach for, touch, grasp, put in the mouth, and make noises (utterances) about. There is no shortage of these things sought, as they are provided almost daily by mom, dad, older siblings, and grandparents. Trips to the marketplace continue, and some of the pleasure-giving items are provided by mom in this commercial setting, thus bonding baby with the buying place. But in spite of trying to seek the many commercial objects that promise satisfaction, the babies' motor skills limit their actions. Perhaps worse, when they cannot obtain an object on their own, they are limited in their ability to vocalize their wants.

Post-Language/Post-Legs (15–24 months): Starting around 12–14 months, infants begin to walk and talk—not just like that, but over a 4-month period they become walking-talking toddlers thanks in great part to some of their consumer behavior patterns. The objects of these new motor/vocal gestures are given labels by mom, and they are remembered and soon will be sounded out by baby, such as *baba* (bottle), *bird* (Big Bird), and *baree* (Barney). The next step logically follows when baby sees these items during marketplace visits and asks for them at around 18–24 months. And since baby is the center of the universe—in her mind—she expects and gets those things requested. Parents and grandparents delight in how she can now walk to the objects—in a store, at daycare—pick them up, and take them uttering, "Mine" or "My bunny." This particularly happens a lot at the nearby Toys 'R Us store when Grandpa takes her there. These in-store requests in the presence of the products begin to take place at home more as baby discovers the same products pictured in books and on the TV that mom has placed in her room. Mom has now invited the marketplace into the baby's home in addition to taking her there at least once a week, thus completing the furnishing of the room as another commercial center. And baby is grateful.

Stage Three: Selecting/Taking (24–48 Months)

Highly developed motor skills, muscles, and memory now encourage the child to take what is his but also to take what is not his by reaching, grabbing, taking—from others, from the refrigerator and pantry, from store shelves—and requesting and demanding from parents. Parents have repeatedly told him if he wants anything, just ask for it; don't take it. He does both, with his request rate at the store at about 12–15 per visit—a level that mom is beginning to rebel against with an increasing number of no's. With these negatives comes more taking, often through a combination of asking and then taking. For example, his new muscles and overwhelming memory at 36 months may prompt him upon entering the supermarket to ask mom if he can go get his own cereal. His social skills and means-ends knowledge are beginning to show, too, and he can read mom's voice tones and facial gestures and knows when he should bargain and plead. He is also noticing what his classmates at daycare own and may take those things, too and is increasingly telling mom about the items and his need for them. His articulation of brand names, store names, and TV programs built around brand names such as Barney and TeleTubbies makes his marketplace knowledge apparent to mom—who begins to blame marketers for it.

Stage Four: Co-Purchase (48–72 Months)

The child's means-ends memory is building fast as she figures out that it takes money or mom or both to get what she wants at the store. She has constructed in her mind a repertoire of stores and their offerings including vending machines and their offerings, and the locations of those offerings in each store, and the names (brands) of those offerings, and is prepared at a moment's notice to put in requests for them. So, when mom says that she is going grocery shopping after work, requests flow in, including, of course, "I want to go. I need a book." Another action is likely to occur at around 60–66 months that accompanies these requests. The child will go to her bedroom and get some money. This is one of the means-ends links that is being put in place at around this time. The child now senses that all those commercial objects in her room came from commercial sources and that they require money—"You can't take them, you have to buy them," mom often says. So another set of objects that has been gradually represented in the child's mind are coins and bills and their denominations. Now, it's purchase time.

On the next store visit the child asks to buy it "with my money," which impresses mom enough to test it. The child has stored in mind the procedure for doing this: (1) Go to the store; (2) find and select the product; (3) take it to the cashier; (4) pay for it; (5) unwrap it and use (consume) it, often in the store. She has even acted this out many times when alone. With mom's help, the child makes a purchase in spite of the complications at the checkout counter. And the book is taken home where it is immediately read and placed with the many others on a shelf in her room.

Stage Five: Independent Purchase (72–100 Months)

Over the next year or so, the child makes a number of co-purchases with mom and dad—at the toy store, at the fast-food restaurant, at the mass merchandiser, and from many vending machines—and by the time he gets into the second grade, he is asking to do it on his own. He has figured out that all those good things that have come from mom and dad ultimately came from a store, and that it took money to obtain them. So, as part of his quest for independence—a drive that seems to kick into high gear by the time the kid enters kindergarten—he also seeks permission to buy on his own. And he does it, having tested it out with mom's help (in the previous stage). It may be a quick snack purchase after school at the convenience store near school, or it may be a purchase of a beverage at McDonald's while mom is at the mall, but it is a completion of the means-ends chain that consists of literally thousands of tekrams stored away in that beautiful mind. The child no longer needs parents, he may think, but he will keep them around, mainly for the money to fund his newfound habit—being a consumer.

IN THE REST OF THE BOOK

I have tried to overview the importance of consumer behavior here and justify an extensive examination of its development. Let me emphasize again that consumer development is so intricately intertwined with the development of the child's mind and body and with the child's physical and social environments that no one of these can be talked about without invoking, the developing consumer behavior patterns. This means that readers need to be prepared for some redundancy as they proceed through the following pages. But I hope this is interesting enough that some of the repetition can be absorbed without disruption. So, we will take the preceding, very brief description of the development of the consumer and expand it as we examine the total development of the child consumer from 0–100 months.

We will begin in Part II by looking first at E—at the *environment* in which and toward which development takes place. Thus, the next chapter will examine the physical environment, and that will be followed by a chapter on the social environment. Both will be related to the development of consumer behavior patterns.

Next in Part III we will look at *personal development*—the physical/motor and cognitive changes that occur with time. It is the advancements in the body that allow adaptation to the environment. This is followed by a description and analysis of the other half of the child, cognitive development. While this is where most consumer socialization descriptions begin, they often also end there. We will follow Piaget as much as possible but also broaden the explanation with some psychiatry, neurology, and physiology.

What will then follow in Part IV will be a five-chapter, in-depth examination of each of the *stages of consumer behavior*, naturally repeating some material that has been stated in the preceding chapters.

We will close in Part V with a discussion of the role of *parenting* and *marketing* in consumer development. Of course, these two subjects could be a separate book, but we will "hit the high points," as one of my favorite professors used to tell his students.

REFERENCES

Brim, O. (1966). Socialization through the life cycle. In O. Brim and S. Wheeler (eds.), *Socialization after Childhood* (pp. 1–49). New York: John Wiley & Sons, Inc.

Carlson, L., and S. Grossbart. (1988, June). Parental style and parenting behavior. *Journal of Consumer Research*, *15*, 77–92.

Child, I. L. (1954). Socialization. In G. Lindzey (ed.), *Handbook of Social Psychology* (Vol. 2, pp. 655–692). Reading, MA: Addison-Wesley Publishing Company, Inc.

Eliot, L. (1999). *What's Going On in There?: How the Brain and Mind Develop in the First Five Years of Life.* New York: Bantam Books.

Erikson, E. H. (1950). *Childhood and Society.* New York: W. W. Norton & Company.

Flavell, J. H. (1963). *The Developmental Psychology of Jean Piaget.* New York: D. Van Nostrand Company.

Gallahue, D. L. (1976). *Motor Development and Movement Experiences for Young Children (3–7).* New York: John Wiley & Sons, Inc.

Gallahue, D. L. (1982). *Understanding Motor Development in Children.* New York: John Wiley & Sons, Inc.

Grusec, J. E., and H. Lytton. (1988). *Social Development: History, Theory, and Research.* New York: Springer.

John, D. R. (1999). Consumer socialization of children: A retrospective look at twenty-five years of research. *Journal of Consumer Research*, *26* (December), 183–213.

John, D. R., and J. C. Whitney. (1986). The development of consumer knowledge in children: A cognitive structure approach. *Journal of Consumer Research*, *12*(4), 406–417.

Kail, R. (1979). *The Development of Memory in Children.* San Francisco: W. H. Freeman and Company.

Lansburgh, R. H., and W. R. Spriegel. (1946). *Industrial Management* (3rd ed.). New York: John Wiley and Sons, Inc.

Lewin, K. (1953). Studies in group decision. In D. Cartwright and A. Zander (eds.), *Group Dynamics: Research and Theory* (pp. 287–301). New York: Harper and Row.

McNeal, J. U. (1982). *Consumer Behavior: An Integrative Approach.* Boston: Little, Brown and Company.

McNeal, J. U. (1992). *Kids as Customers: A Handbook of Marketing to Children.* New York: Lexington Books.

McNeal, J. U. (1999). *The Kids Market: Myth and Realities.* Ithaca, NY: Paramount Market Publishers.

McNeal, J. U., and C. H. Yeh. (1994). Stages of consumer socialization in childhood. In *1993 Proceedings of the Social Statistics Section* (pp. 856–860). Alexandria, VA: American Statistical Association.

McNeal, J. U., and C. H. Yeh. (1997). Development of consumer behavior patterns among Chinese children. *Journal of Consumer Marketing*, *14*(1), 45–59.

McNeal, J. U., and C. H. Yeh. (2003). Consumer behavior of Chinese children: 1995–2002. *Journal of Consumer Marketing*, *20*(6), 542–554.

Moschis, G. P. (1977). *Consumer socialization.* Lexington, MA: D. C. Heath.

Olshavsky, R. W., and D. H. Grandbois (1979). Consumer decision making—fact or fiction. *Journal of Consumer Research*, *6* (September), 93–100.

Piaget, J. (1963). *The Origins of Intelligence in Children.* New York: W. W. Norton & Company.

Singer, D. G., and T. A. Revenson. (1996). *A Piaget Primer: How a Child Thinks* (rev. ed.). New York: Plume.

Spock, B. (1946). *Baby and Child Care.* New York: Pocket Books.

Valkenburg, P. M., and J. Cantor. (2001). The development of a child into a consumer. *Journal of Applied Developmental Psychology*, *22*, 61–72.

Ward, S. (1974). Consumer socialization. *Journal of Consumer Research*, *1* (September), 1–13.

Ward, S., D. B. Wackman, and E. Wartella. (1977). *How Children Learn to Buy.* Beverly Hills, CA: Sage Publications, Inc.

PART II

ENVIRONMENTS IN WHICH CONSUMER BEHAVIOR PATTERNS DEVELOP

Behavior is a function of the environment (E) and the person (P). In the following two chapters, the two halves of the child's environment—the physical (Chapter 2) and the social (Chapter 3) domains—will be examined from the perspective of the development of consumer behavior patterns.

This watercolor of children playing hide-and-seek among the furniture in old China was done by the artist Chen XueMei of Chengdu, China. In this time period of several hundred years ago, many children ordinarily populated the home. This particular consumer behavior pattern—social play of hide-and-seek among physical objects in the house—has been handed down for many generations. Today, in new China there are no families with several children— the parents would be severely punished—but preschool children at kindergarten playgrounds and at play areas of some fast-food restaurants still play hide-and-seek.

2

THE PHYSICAL ENVIRONMENT AND ITS INFLUENCE ON THE DEVELOPMENT OF CONSUMER BEHAVIOR PATTERNS

Tony's Photo of His Favorite Place and Favorite Things

Third-graders were given a disposable camera, printed instructions, and money to pay for development of the pictures requested. The children were asked to take pictures of their favorite place, food, friend, and play item; develop the pictures; and return them to class for one-on-one discussions with researchers. An overweight boy named Tony who was "nearly ten" and described his grades as "OK" gave us a picture (along with others) that he said contained all the favorites requested. As described by him, it was a photo of his bedroom (favorite place), in which there was a bag of Cheetos and a can of Pepsi-Cola (favorite food) on the night stand, a Game Boy video game (favorite play item) on the full-size bed, and a photo of him and his pal, Paul (favorite friend), on a bulletin board on a wall. Also on the walls were posters of Emmet Smith, a running back for the Dallas Cowboys, Michael Jordan, the professional basketball player, and one of the Six Flags Over Texas theme park. There was a book shelf with many books, but on the top shelf was a row of plastic drink cups with comic book characters portrayed on them. He told us that the cups were free with the purchase of a fountain drink at a nearby convenience store. There was a TV set near the foot of the bed on a desk that he was quick to identify as a Sony brand, also a radio beside the bed on a table, and on the bed was a Dallas Cowboys bedspread. He referred to the room as his "room" and sometimes his "bedroom." The interviewer dubbed it his "brandroom."

Here is some of the dialogue between the interviewer and the boy:

Interviewer: Why is your bedroom your favorite place?

Tony: I can do what I want to there. No one comes in unless I want them to. I play [video] games, watch TV, sleep a lot. All my things are there.

Interviewer: Do you study there?

Tony: Yes.

Interviewer: Do you study every night?

Tony: Not every night. Just sometimes.

Interviewer: When do you come home from school?

Tony: When I get out at three. I ride my bike home.

Interviewer: Who is at home when you get home?

Tony: No one. I've got the house all to myself. I like that.

Interviewer: Do your parents respect your privacy?

Tony: They never come in much. My father isn't here much and my mother works at the dry cleaners. So she's always tired from being on her feet all day [perhaps quoting his mother]. She comes home around seven usually and goes to her bedroom mostly.

Interviewer: What do you normally eat for supper?

Tony: My mother brings a pizza home a lot of times. I eat that. Maybe a bowl of cereal. And for sure some Cheetos.

Interviewer: You show Cheetos and Pepsi-Cola as your favorite foods. Why are they your favorite?

Tony: I like their taste. They're gooder than good [apparently a characterization used by his age group]. I could eat 'em all time.

Interviewer: You show a nice TV in your picture. How often do you watch TV?

Tony: Just about every day when I come home from school. I like to just kick back and watch TV, eat, and sometimes snooze. And I watch it at night quite a bit.

Interviewer: Does your mother watch it with you?

Tony: Sometimes, but she usually watches it in her room.

Interviewer: Tell me about your favorite friend, Paul.

Tony: Paul's cool. He's in the fourth grade. His dad has a Harley [motorcycle]. He [Paul] sometimes helps me with my homework.

Interviewer: Do you do things together?

Tony: Sure. All the time. He sometimes comes home with me from school. We have fun watching movies on TV, talking.

Interviewer: Do you visit at Paul's home too?

Tony: I have, but his dad I don't think wants me to.

Interviewer: Why is that?

Tony: I just don't think he does. You know. But we have good times together at my house. He's funny. He makes me laugh a lot.

THE TWO ENVIRONMENTS: PHYSICAL VERSUS SOCIAL

All human behavior including consumer behavior (CB) is a function of the *environment* (E) and the *person* (P). The environment consists of two domains, *physical* and *social,* which usually cannot be separated completely except for purposes of exposition. A consumer experience may result primarily from one or the other although actual consumer behavior always occurs in a physical environment. (Now that I have used the term *always* I am reminded that much consumer behavior occurs in the imagination. This will be discussed later.) For example, a child riding his tricycle in the driveway of his home is an expression primarily of consumer behavior in a physical environment. His mother who is watching from the window of the house might say that he is playing "outside." Two children sitting in the floor playing patty-cake with their hands is primarily consumer behavior in a social environment. Often a consumer situation is difficult to describe as either physical or social. For instance, a father and his daughter driving bumper cars at the amusement park is consumer behavior in both a physical and a social environment, although either may be isolated for discussion. Children learn consumer behavior from both the social and physical domains. In the case of the physical domain, the learning is a result of interaction with *physical objects*, usually just called *objects*, whereas in the social domain, learning is a result of interaction with *social objects*—usually called *people.* (Later, we will talk about exceptions in which physical objects are treated as people.) Precisely the thinking and behavior patterns that characterize children as consumers may be learned from a host of inanimate objects that populate their physical environment—home, school, neighborhood, city, and, of course, the marketplace.

We stereotypically think that children learn CB only from others—mainly from parents and peers and teachers and marketers—that they must have a social experience in order to learn—to learn anything. We too often ignore the fact that children learn CB essentially in three ways, two of which are on their own and may not directly involve people: (1) through trial and error, or what might be termed *participation*—extracting information on their own through experiencing events and activities that involve objects and their attributes; (2) through *imitation,* that is, by the children rehearsing activities of others performing in a physical environment, such as shopping, and providing their own interpretations; and (3) through *training* (teaching) by others (McNeal, 1987). Only the latter is learning primarily through a social experience in the pure sense of the word, while the first two efforts are children learning (teaching themselves) through interacting with and/or manipulating environmental factors. Even in the case in which a child chooses to copy the consumer behavior of another person, for example, an 8-year-old copies the smoking behavior of a 12-year-old— what we often call *modeling*—it seems to be a learning effort much more than a teaching effort even though we might speak of the bad influence of the 12-year-old. Thus, in pounds and ounces, children probably learn a majority of their CB on their own and learn at least half of it from the physical environment—a practice that begins at day one.

As observed in Chapter 1, we in the academic world also tend to think that children have to have a social experience in order to learn a behavior pattern simply because the terms *socialization* and *consumer socialization* contain the prefix *social*, referring, of course, to people—people teaching people. Actually, the *social* prefix refers at least as much to the result as the cause—the child learning to fit into society and its defined roles including the consumer role. Moreover, as noted in the first chapter, researchers and writers marching forth under the banner of consumer socialization—a topic that pervades our consumer behavior journals—may have unintentionally misled thinkers and researchers about the origins of consumer behavior patterns. There is no denying the importance of others in transferring cultural concepts to newborns including consumer behavior patterns. The titles of this part of the book and this chapter reflect that fact. Moreover, we acknowledge that many of the physical environment influences on children's development are also mediated by social environmental parameters such as the case just mentioned of the father and daughter learning to drive bumper cars together. In fact, there are those theorists who would say that the only influence the physical environment has on behavior is that mediated by someone from the social environment (e.g., Clarke-Stewart, 1973). Where appropriate, we will show that while it is difficult to separate the two domains and their individual influences, there are numerous instances in which objects cause change in consumer behavior without social intervention. As a special case, we will show also that from a child's perspective social objects may be transformed into physical objects and, alternatively, that physical objects may be transformed into social objects. Therefore, calling one only a physical environment influence and another only a social influence would be theoretically incorrect, at least from the children's standpoint. So the two domains—physical and social—are often intertwined, but in this chapter on the physical domain and the next on the social domain, we will try to keep them separated for sake of discussion.

THE CONTENTS OF THE PHYSICAL ENVIRONMENT: OBJECTS, OBJECTS, OBJECTS

Before we look at the nature of the physical environment and its influence on consumer development, we probably ought to put it in perspective by commenting about its *contents*—all the physical *objects* it contains. Children might call them things or stuff, such as in "These are my things" and "Look at all my stuff," but most are probably unaware of how much their behavior is influenced by objects. (Tony called them "All my things," with an emphasis on "my" perhaps indicating that he is still somewhat egocentric.) I think that sometimes we slight the influence of the physical domain on consumer development research because it surrounds us, it engulfs us, it is with us everywhere at all times. We are always within it, never without it. That is somewhat less true of the social environment, which is on a more selective basis—we choose it to a great extent—and therefore its influence on consumer behavior may seem more apparent. For instance, Tony chose to come home from school with his friend, Paul. We probably ought to have a comparable word for the physical environment's influence as we do for people's influence (socialization), for example, *objectilization* since it is the objects in it that do most of the influencing—the attracting, instructing, and producing change in the child. Perhaps we already have a useful word— *behavior*—because when we use the term *behavior*, we usually refer to actions toward an object or event and actions involving an object. However, the term *behavior*, as typically used, also embraces social objects as well. Thus, it is a bit broad, and that is probably why we usually substitute other terms for behavior such as reading, playing, talking, or having fun. Another term that is basic to describing the impact of objects on development is *experience*. This is the term used most by the developmental psychologist Jean Piaget to describe the production of intelligence in children (e.g., Piaget, 1963). It is through experiencing objects that the child learns their good and bad attributes, and by recording the experiences (in the mind) can decide if they will be repeated. Again, though, the child may experience physical objects and social objects. Thus, the term *experience* is broad, also. To demonstrate why a term such as *objectilization* makes sense, consider just one classic example—building blocks or construction blocks—to show the great influence of just one ordinary object on a toddler's consumer behavior and how it instructs and gives meaning to her:

> *A building block will not let the child lay it on any of its 12 edges—only on its six sides, thus teaching several physical/geometric principles. It will not let the child put it in her mouth because of its size, nor will it let her see all sides at once because it is a solid, thus confirming a couple of other physical/geometric principles. It also will play a role in*

*teaching the letters, colors, and other symbols to the child. It
will participate in the child's uses of her hands such as lifting,
grasping, and aligning, as well as the concepts of work and
play. It often is one of the child's earliest teachers of the
concepts of size, shape, and weight, and of specific concepts
such as square, cube, angle, and buoyancy (in her bath water).*

And that's just one building block! Think about the additional learning from a set of blocks as infants learn to stack them, build with them, and
spell with them. No wonder that most kids like them and will play with them
for hours. Multiply the influence of the building block by the hundreds or
thousands of objects in the child's physical environment—or subtract some
for a child who lives in an impoverished environment—and one begins to
get an idea of the powerful role of the physical environment in consumer
development during early childhood. Hence, the ubiquity of the physical
environment makes it fundamental in all development, not just consumer
development, and therefore begs to at least be counted in some major way,
with some kind of distinguishing nomenclature.

As noted, the contents of the physical environment are objects, each
with a name and each with special attributes. How many there are at a point
in time is difficult to measure. In Chapter 1 we roughly estimated that a
typical 10-year-old performs 10,000 consumer acts—*tekrams*—a day. Most
of these tekrams involve physical objects, thus giving a hint about the
number of physical objects in a 10-year-old child's environment. For sure,
a list of objects from which children may learn consumer behavior is much
longer than the list of people from whom they may learn. Beginning with
marketing objects, the list includes all the print media—newspapers, magazines, catalogs, phone books—and all the electronic media—radio, TV, video
games, and the Internet—and outdoor billboards and movies—both a combination of print and electronic—and the editorial contents of magazines
and the programming contents of radio and television. Even more important, the list includes products and stores. And common to both products
and stores are the packages that hold the products, display them in the store
(and at home), and beckon the consumer in the self-service environment—
all having the purposes of informing and persuading the consumer to buy
and use. As compared to mom, for example, who may teach a lot of CB to
her children unintentionally, these marketing objects teach a lot of CB
intentionally. A door knob, for instance, teaches a lot of CB intentionally.

Inside the stores the child's array of physical objects continues—shopping carts and baskets, shelves, fixtures, point-of-purchase promotion materials (hanging, standing, even embedded in the floor tiles), the product in
sample form, the cash register receipt, tray liners (at fast-food restaurants),
and shopping bags. Outside the store are other objects—the stores' exterior appointments that include doors, parking areas, building features,
window messages, and signs—all with a teaching goal. For example, the

color scheme of the exterior may be intended to substitute for the name of the store. This is particularly important in the case of youngsters since they do much visual learning as compared to verbal learning—they usually recognize the Golden Arches before they can say the name, McDonald's—in the United States and in China.

Then there is the product proper, the object of affection for the marketer who wants it to be that to consumers also. Each product has its own physical qualities and functions, its brands, and as noted, its package. The package separately contains brand messages, product messages such as contents and directions for use, and promotion messages and materials for the product inside as well as others, and there are often play materials, in and on the package, in the case of products for kids. One should bear in mind that these zillions of products and packages that we are talking about are transported by parents (and other caretakers) to other physical environments of the children, mainly the home and school, where they have even more impact on the children's consumer development—more impact because they are in more credible, more personal parts of the children's environment.

At school, which is really just another kind of retailer, although a very basic environment to kids, objects include many marketing communications materials—posters on bulletin boards, ads on school buses, scoreboards, and in the locker rooms. Also, some objects are actually designed as consumer education materials, even those in toy form or play form, such as games, and those in books and in teaching materials. In the case of most of these items, teachers and administrators, rather than parents, provide them. Naturally, the school domain includes the standard paper and pencils, crayons and glue, books, backpacks, and special clothing—all commercial objects sold in the marketplace (and perhaps also by the school). Oh yes, the school also contains many edible products—even though it is a school. As noted, it is also a retailer of foods—such as soft drinks, hamburgers, pizzas, and all kinds of candies and chips—perhaps the Pepsi-Cola and Cheetos that Tony loves so much. Again, these are provided mostly by the school, not for education but for other purposes such as making money. (While not for education, per se, they are intended by their makers and marketers to teach consumer behavior patterns.)

As the children walk home from school, they find many other marketing institutions in addition to the ever-present convenience stores—and tobacco stores in China—that offer products and services. They include hospitals, law offices, doctors' offices, and tax preparation offices that we might not think of as objects that socialize but are intended to influence and produce consumer behavior patterns, patterns that usually are intended to last the consumer a lifetime. Some of these service retailers market at the schools, too, for example, by putting their names on the children's athletic uniforms—like they did in the movie *Bad News Bears*. That is their way of maintaining a relationship with the children and their parents—and using the kids as an advertising medium. And that is just a few of the objects that are primarily exterior to the child's home and with which the child may interact daily. I say a "few" because we should remember that the typical Wal-Mart superstore, for example, probably houses 200,000 products for sale in addition to the building and furnishings mentioned previously.

In the child's home area—the neighborhood, the yard, the garage, and the house proper—literally thousands more objects teach consumer behavior. In fact, practically all the objects at home—yard furniture, boat, car, furnishings, furniture, appliances, clothing, and edibles—are intended to teach consumer behavior patterns. That is why I sometimes call the home the commercial center of children. It is often difficult to tell if parents are in charge of it or if marketers are. (As will be noted later, parents are in charge at first but soon cede the authority to the children and marketers.) Going back to Tony's bedroom, as suggested, it might more correctly be called a "brandroom" than a bedroom. There are commercial objects everywhere in it, and most have a brand name. While it is the parents who bring most of these items home from the marketplace for the use of all members of the family, particularly for the kids, it is the marketers who usually suggest them—through store displays, packaging, publicity, and advertising. By the way, as a reminder, all of these "teachers" have names that are intended to identify them—company names (General Motors), brand names (Cheerios), and consumer-contrived names (e.g., Chevy for the Chevrolet in the garage, Tony for Kellogg's Frosted Flakes in the pantry)—and the children are taught these names right along with the names of nature's objects and social objects. Thus, again, children are never separate from objects as they might be in the case of people. All those things—all that stuff that children ask for, wish for, want, and demand—are mostly objects in the physical environment. Children would not know about them and therefore would not seek them if they had not interacted with them or with an image of them such as that they may see in television programming and advertising. For instance, they would not know about Happy Meals if good ol' mom, the real super marketer, did not bring them home from the marketplace or buy them for the kids at the restaurant and insist that they eat them—and play with the "free" action figure that comes with them.

While we have spoken of the children's environments as consisting of various places such as home, school, and marketplace, they are rarely separated; they overlap, conflict with each other, and complement each other. Some examples are home and school where children take objects from home to school such as food, clothing, books, and money. And they bring objects home from school such as books, papers, and, of course, homework. Between home and school the children may stop at a marketing environment and buy something for school or for the home. In middle childhood—starting around the time children enter the fourth grade—boys and girls may work after school doing various cleaning tasks in stores and offices,

PHOTO 2-1   A 12-year-old Chinese girl sits amid vegetables that she helps her family sell while finding time to play with her dolls.

thus combining in various degrees home and school environments with a new environment of work. Consequently, the commercial objects in their daily life are increased in number substantially—including products, money, and structures. In addition, their social environment—discussed in the next chapter—expands also by adding the people the children work with, including customers in some cases. Photo 2-1 shows an example of this combination of home, marketplace, and work environments. A 12-year-old girl works with her parents at a street market selling fruits and vegetables in rural Mentougou District of Beijing, China. She helps clean and display the fresh produce and runs errands for her parents. And as shown in the photo, when she gets a break, she plays with her Barbie-like dolls she brought from home; at the same time, her little brother, who also helps out with the family business, watches nearby while having a snack.

THE NATURE OF THE PHYSICAL ENVIRONMENT

In addition to the ubiquity of the physical environment, several other basic characteristics are responsible for its fundamental role in consumer development. On a negative note first: If it were possible to describe a physical environment without these characteristics, we would quickly say the opposite. That is, an impoverished physical environment does not assist development of any kind; it hinders it. In a few cases reported in the literature, children have been born or placed in an extremely impoverished environment, and in short, they did not develop to their potential. They did not display most normal behavior patterns. The children were more vegetable than animal, more animal than human. So, in this discussion of the physical environment, we are talking, in general, about one that may be found in Japan and the United States, or perhaps in the urban parts of a developing country such as China and India. (My personal observations indicate that the poorer and lesser educated people are, the more impoverished the children's physical environment—a shameful phenomenon found in all countries including the United States, although China's rural areas ring the bell in impoverished environment, at home, and at school.)

The Physical Environment Develops with the Child

At birth the physical environment is minimal, and in the mind of the infant, it does not exist separately from him or her. To the extent that the physical domain of an infant might be described by an ethnologist, it consists of the normal things that might be found in a child's nursery: a room of some sort, a bed of some sort, some clothing, light, normal temperature, and probably several play items in and about the bed, particularly some kind of entertainment mobile above the crib. None of these things, however, exists and has meaning to the infant as the parents come to realize in spite of a lot of money spent on them. Only mom's breast has meaning, and even then, for at least the first several weeks, it is an extension of the baby, not of mom. But as the child grows physically and mentally, so does the physical environment. During the first month or so, the infant sleeps 15–16 hours a day. Thus, only a few items in the physical domain are noticeable, and most of them are responded to through reflexes. For example, sudden bright lights and noises will elicit a startled reflex, a flinging out of the arms and then returning them to her chest. (Reflexes are discussed in some detail in a later chapter on physical/motor development.)

But the infant's *sensory system* develops fast and with it the rapid discovery of the physical world. The chemical senses of smell and taste quickly identify mom's breast first and then many other odors and flavors. In fact, newborns are capable of discriminating nearly as many different odors (of objects) as adults, including concentration differences of a single odor as well as localized odors in space (Eliot, 1999). Moreover, they rapidly demonstrate preferences for pleasant tastes (for objects) and dislike for unpleasant tastes. The taste of *sweets*—of sweet objects—seems to be innately pleasurable, according to Lis Eliot (1999), a neurologist, and from birth onward the child responds positively to sugar. It is apparently a brain thing, but if given a choice early in life, baby will choose table sugar (sucrose) over sweet fruits (fructose), and sweet fruits over mom's sweet milk (lactose), a pattern of choice, incidentally to be monitored for fear of contributing to obesity and other health problems. (Note to the reader: Childhood obesity became an epidemic in the 1990s, and today it is a killer among us—of children and adults—second only to tobacco. So, I will pause where appropriate and discuss how it became an epidemic, for it is a consumer behavior matter. For now, this mention about babies distinguishing and loving sweets ought to cue the reader to think about it.)

Vision develops a bit later, seeing *movement* of objects first, then bright *colors*. In fact, the bright, bold colors are as fascinating to the eyes as sugar is to the mouth, and the infant will devote much time studying them as soon as she can focus. And some of those color schemes help her focus her vision. Hearing is functioning at birth, even before birth apparently, and mom quickly learns that her baby loves *music*. Touch also has been active since birth, and it gives the infant directions to mom's breast as much as smell and taste do. In fact, much of baby's feeling is done with the lips that are highly sensitive; hands are second in sensitivity.

Putting these findings altogether, one can imagine how a two-month-old baby might respond to his introduction to McDonald's that includes his first taste of ice cream provided by mom in a brightly colored McDonald's that is also playing rock music over the wired music system and venting the smell of French fries into the air. (Another red flag related to obesity: fat-fried foods always smell good to children.) No wonder, then, that we might expect that the marketplace visits have great impact on an infant. And all of these stimulants in one place at one time are sure to be a double or triple whammy. While the memory system of the baby is crude at this time—more of a motor memory, or what Piaget (1954) would call sensorimotor memory—it nevertheless is at work cataloging the good things in life.

So, as the senses develop, the objects grow in number as they are discovered and liked or disliked, and these links are filed away in the baby's mind in the form of *schema*, as Piaget would call them. Thus, the formula is pretty simple: If an object gives baby pleasure, it is liked; if it does not, it is not liked—both becoming part of memory and both contributing to the child's well-being and to her cognitive development. Mom figures this out in short order and provides more of the pleasure-giving objects—sweets, brightly colored mobiles, and lots of noise toys such as rattles and music makers, and fewer of those that are not pleasurable. (Another obesity flag: mom developing a pattern in infanthood of providing what's pleasurable.) Interestingly, as we can see from stepping back, the physical environment is also contributing to mom's cognitive development, as she tends to ignore grandpa's constant reminder that "You're spoiling that child," and provides her child more of the same. One might ponder some mathematical formula that states that the physical environment of the baby expands exponentially with the number of times the baby expresses pleasure. As a side note, some of baby's pleasure-giving items provided at home by mom are used to calm or quiet her baby. A few years later, mom may purchase some of these pleasure-giving items for her child while shopping at the marketplace, and for the same purpose—to quiet her child. Retailers sometimes call these items "shut-ups" and place a variety of them at the checkout.

Then, the child's *motor* development, which is detailed in a later chapter, takes front and center and expands the physical environment even more than that of the sensory system. And the combination—the sensori-motor system—brings the whole physical world into focus and gives it meaning. It is through movement that the baby is able to truly interact with the elements of the physical environment. At around 2–3 months—about the time that mom is likely to take her baby to the marketplace for the first time—lifting the head, looking around, reaching, and shaking the legs produce much information about the physical environment—and more motor memory. Objects such as rattles and mobiles are brought into obser-vation by such movements, and by 3–4 months the baby is sitting with support, turning his body back and forth, and trying to grasp objects. Mom also provides some motoring of sorts by carrying and carting her baby, par-ticularly at around 6 months when the infant can sit on her own. Now the world of objects becomes her world. The wallpaper, the carpet, the furni-ture, and many other objects in the home all become interesting. And the many objects in the marketplace where mom takes her baby more fre-quently assume astonishing importance, too, all of which are tested when baby begins to walk at around 12 months and lend new meaning to the term *motor behavior.*

Around a year later real *language* begins, which permits the baby to utilize another motor skill—speaking. She already comprehends many words, but now production sets in. She will begin *naming* objects—her first effort at *classification*—and never seems to let up—ball, doll, diaper, bottle, which may at first sound like baw, daw, dyer, and bobble—but is final proof that now she is aware of the physical environment separate from herself. This is a major milestone that we will analyze later. Many objects will have a brand name that mom and dad have been using since baby could hear, such as Barney, Cheerios, Kleenex, and Nick (for Nickelodeon). Baby's vocal classification and branding of some objects may also be a gift from the TV, in addition to parents, but gives parents much pleasure—as the baby can now discern by reading their faces.

Learning to talk about objects and learning to give them names—dis-cerning specific objects for specific consumption purposes—will soon turn into requests and demands, even screams for them when in their presence, often to mom's displeasure. But this give and take between mom and the baby regarding objects reinforces their existence while providing a medium through which mother and child may bond. Thus, the physical environment grows as the baby grows, and it keeps going, beyond his room to the kitchen pantry, beyond the house to the yard, and beyond the neighborhood to the school and the mall. The thousands of daily tekrams—units of CB that were described in Chapter 1—become standard operating procedure by age two and on. The physical environment of Tony's bedroom is a result of his becoming older and more knowing of objects—it did not look like this at age three, for instance. It changes as he—or mom—adds newly discovered objects to it and removes some undesirable objects.

The Physical Environment Participates in the Child's Development

While the child must develop physically and mentally in order to interact with the many objects in his physical environment, those objects, in turn, facilitate his development. As Wachs (1985, p. 33) stated, "Unique patterns of relationship have been found to occur between the physical environment and a wide variety of developmental parameters, including cognitive development, exploratory behavior, language development and social interactions." Objects, in effect, permit infants to test and hone their sensory skills, their motor skills, and most important, their cognitive skills, as they develop an inventory of the objects in their minds as well as in their physical space. Using a "map in the mind," Tony is able to describe his bedroom in great detail while he is in his classroom.

Toys, as a special case of objects, contribute a great deal to infants' development and exemplify how objects in general participate in human development. As Wachs (1985) suggested, the right toy for a specific child of a specific age can facilitate all aspects of her development. Rattles and mobiles stimulate watching, reaching, grasping, and locating through listening—observing—so that the child identifies her space and its contents and thus defines her home, her secure space. Several years later mom is likely to say about video games what she says at this time about mobiles, that is, "They help develop hand-eye coordination." This is probably true of both types of toys plus many others. Recognizing this is all the feedback that mom needs to prompt her to buy more in order to teach her child basic hand-eye behaviors.

While the child wants toys for their fun value—to be entertained by them—moms prefer those that have educational value such as those that teach hand-eye coordination. The marketplace has heard her and responded by providing both benefits. Often called "edutainment" and "edutainers," many toys are designed to teach sensorimotor skills as well as school subjects such as language and math while kids have fun playing with them. Practically all toys, in fact, have some inherent educational value such as jump ropes that teach some fine motor skills, jacks that teach some hand-eye coordination, and board games that teach arithmetic and social skills, but the toy makers are usually careful to emphasize their fun value since it is the children who normally make the purchase decisions that bring them home. During the past decade many more play items for children have been introduced that encourage children to be sedentary, to sit rather than stand, to lie down rather than move around. Parents just recently have begun to realize that such items as video games—those in systems, on computers, and the hand-held ones—board games, and many educational toys foster sedentary behavior and contribute to childhood obesity. Ironically, parents purchased these toys for the children to keep them home safe from street dangers and give them pleasure as well as education. Some video games marketers are now introducing games that encourage movement, standing, stepping, even dancing.

While all objects potentially may teach consumer behavior patterns of some sort, another special class of toys or play items is designed to teach specific consumer behavior. I identified these types of play items in some research in the late 1980s and reported them in detail in *Children as Consumers* (McNeal, 1987). Briefly, they consist of four categories as follows:

1. Toys that teach how to shop or buy. This group includes such items as pretend credit cards; miniature shopping carts and baskets; board games about buying; and books about business types such as bakeries, grocery stores, and barber shops.
2. Toys that teach awareness of brands and company names. This group includes toy cars that are replicas of well-known brands, riding toys that are branded with manufacturers' names of the real thing, books for children about a brand of products, and board games with company names and brands.
3. Toys that teach consumption of complementary products. In this group there are toys that suggest the purchase of a specific product or brand to go with a cookout or a party; toy baking sets from well-known brands of cooking needs; and others that teach how to serve a meal, tea, and what items should be included.
4. Toys that teach business operations. Some examples in this group are toy sets that contain items for operating a store, a manufacturing plant, a bank, a cash register, an auto service center, and a fast-food restaurant.

A word of caution seems appropriate about using the term *toys* to refer to all the items that have play value for children. Actually, at a point in time there is play value in practically all objects in children's physical environment—in the pots and pans that they find when they begin to crawl; in the cardboard boxes in which gifts are given to them; and, of course, in nature's provision of mud, sand, dirt, and trees. Play is a very basic need to children just as it is to puppies and kittens, and often seems more important than food and sleep, both of which kids may often postpone when involved with play. Elsewhere I have noted that beyond food and rest, children's four or five most important needs probably are play (fun for fun's sake), sentience (need for sensory experiences), affiliation (need for relationships), achievement (need to accomplish something difficult), and autonomy (need for independent action; McNeal, 1992). If given the chance, children will try to satisfy all of these in their play, and given the chance, marketers will help them. For example, candy makers provide kids with whistles made of tasty wax on which tunes can be played, and then the whistle can be eaten. But inferred in what has been said is the reminder that parents need not buy some toys but simply permit their children to explore the household and yard and they will find (create) some.

While toys have been a focus here, physical objects of all sorts are involved in every dimension of children's development:

- Cognitive development: Objects participate in development of the memory, attitudes, and knowledge by being the focus of most mental activity.
- Motor development: Objects play a basic role in children's learning to crawl, walk, run, grip and release, climb, skip, and in virtually all sports.
- Physical development: Objects are responsible for much of the muscle development in children since they are participants in their playing, eating, and sleeping.
- Social development: Objects often provide the medium through which children interact with mom and dad, schoolteacher, and other children such as playmates and classmates.
- Language development: Most of the words that children learn in early childhood are names of objects, actions of objects, and responses of objects.

The Physical Environment Is Inanimate but Can Seem Animate to Children

The very nature of the physical environment is its inanimateness. The psychologist Wachs (1985, p. 32) said, "The primary dimension differentiating the physical and social environments involves the distinction between *animate* versus *inanimate* features of the environment." Thus, a rock is one of nature's inanimate objects, whereas the baby's crib mobile is one of nurture's inanimate objects—the latter provided by mom and most likely via a marketer. But almost collusive like, marketers and moms often tend to give life to some inanimate objects, transforming them, at least theoretically, into social objects (beings) for children. How does this occur? Can it be reversed? That is, can moms and marketers also convert animate objects into inanimate objects? Let's consider these questions and some possible answers as they pertain to objects in the children's environment.

There is a tendency for developmental research to show that the social environment is supreme to the physical environment in determining children's behavior patterns. Perhaps it achieves this status, in part, through its ability to turn physical objects into social objects. Maybe we can get to the answers to the preceding questions by posing one more question and a bit more complexity: Is Ronald McDonald a social object or a physical object?

The answer to this question seems to be "Both," in the sense that the child sees him talking and moving in TV ads while also seeing him as a non-moving, nontalking object in McDonald's restaurants. Certainly, then, a kid may sense Ronald—or Santa or Barney—as both physical and social, inanimate and animate. Actually, from a kid's perspective, depending on the child's age, any inanimate object may be perceived as alive. The 4-year-old Beijing girl in Photo 2-2 seems to be in awe of the over-towering Ronald McDonald figure and probably sees him as more alive—as more human—than sculpture. Piaget (1963) gave this phenomenon the term *animism*, referring to children's attribution of life to inanimate objects. Marketers also practice animism by giving life to cartoon characters such as Teletubbies, to brand characters, or what (or whom) might be termed spokescharacters, such as the Nesquik rabbit (from Nestlé) or Tony the Tiger (from Kellogg's). Marketers intend these characters to have influence like a person, so they imbue them with human qualities—movement, speech. Mom may reinforce the child's belief that Ronald is alive by either talking to him at the opening of a McDonald's restaurant, letting the child hear him

PHOTO 2-2   This 4-year-old Beijing girl seems to be awed by the bigger-than-life Ronald McDonald figure outside a McDonald's restaurant. At her age she probably sees him as more animate than inanimate.

talk in a television commercial, or maybe buying a talking Ronald at a toy store (if there is such a thing).

Figure 2-1 shows a continuum that ranges from animate to inanimate objects and gives some examples of perceived degrees of aliveness, or animation. Notice that at one end are the live (real) persons such as mom, playmate, teacher, and salesperson, and next to them are people known by children but not personally such as celebrities and professional football players who talk to the children via TV programming and advertisements and perhaps through visits to their schools. Then, next to them are live animals such as pets, zoo animals, and farm animals with which children may have little social relationship but that may act or "talk," even sing. At the other end of the continuum are objects that ordinarily are seen by children or adults as inanimate, such as nature's rocks, trees, and lakes, and those nonliving objects in the home such as the carpet, refrigerator, and piano. So to speak, we might term this group *nonpeople*, at least from the children's perspective. In the middle of the continuum are objects that are given life by marketers and parents, through the eager imagination of the children, and include cartoon characters, brand spokescharacters, and some of nature's objects such as the man-in-the-moon (first introduced by mom and dad). We could term these *near-people*, from the children's perspective.

ANIMATE------------------------------------|------------------------------------INANIMATE
(Alive)   (May Be Made Alive)   (Not Alive)

Parents	Celebrities	Pets	Cartoon Characters	Toys	Rocks
Playmates	Policemen	Zoo Animals	Brand Characters	Family Car	Trees
Teachers	Presidents	Farm Animals	Transitionals	Photo	Table

FIGURE 2-1   *Children's perceptions of objects' aliveness.*

Also in the near-people part of the continuum is a special class of objects that are called *transitional* objects. Transitional objects play an important role in infants' attempts to make the transition from total dependence on mom, called *symbiosis*, to some degree of independence, called *differentiation*. A transitional object enables infants to begin to soothe themselves by transferring functions previously performed by the mother or other caretaker in the environment to an inanimate object, often a blanket or other soft object. Through these transitionals infants create an illusion of self-sufficiency while at the same time creating gradual increments in self-soothing as they use the transitional objects. Perhaps a shining illustration of this kind of transitional object is Hobbes, the best "friend" of Calvin in Bill Watterson's comic strip, *Calvin and Hobbes*. While Hobbes is nothing more than a stuffed animal, a tiger, he is the constant companion of Calvin and a companion to whom Calvin tells his troubles and seeks advice. It could as well be a Raggedy Ann doll or some soft object such as a pillow or blanket (a Linus blanket as found in the *Peanuts* comic strip by Charles Schulz). These objects are given life by marketers, mothers, and the children themselves.

And from them, children learn much even though they are inanimate. For example, there may be concerns among parents about little girls learning from Barbie dolls that slim is loved or from Barney dolls that fat is loved. Turkel (1998), a psychiatrist, wrote in detail in the *Journal of the American Academy of Psychoanalysis* about all the negative values supposedly taught by Barbie and other dolls that may serve as transitionals.

Another dimension of inanimate objects that is relatively new is their *interactive* and *robotic* abilities—human qualities wired into inanimate objects. Today, dolls may talk, talk back, and give advice out loud to little children who themselves may be able to speak little but can comprehend language. Some play dolls may even dance with a child as in the case of "Let's Dance Barbie," a Barbie doll that can respond to dance movements of the child (Best Stuff.com, 2006) and thus be a "good friend." In addition to such dolls, the interactive nature of most video games, board games, and computers gives them a life of their own even though they are inanimate objects. Now, a real person such as Britney Spears, a spokeswoman for the "bubble-gum set," as the tween girls are called who worship her, can be transformed by marketers into an inanimate object, a doll, but a talking doll who may teach much consumer behavior to children just as, for example, Winnie the Pooh does who is an inanimate object given life by marketers.

In sum, physical objects may be humanized by marketers, parents, and the children themselves to the point that they become social objects in the eyes of children, thus complicating the standard classification of physical and social domains. Even if we say it is children's imagination, if asked, children of age two or three may say that certain objects are real; they are real persons. By the time children are age three or four, studies by Wellman, Hickling, and Schult (1997) suggest that children begin to reason that people but not dolls can think, remember, and feel happy. However, what these researchers did not take into account is the fact that children may still *pretend* that their dolls or any other humanized, inanimate objects can think, talk, and therefore be companions. We probably need not worry that all this may confuse children; they have amazing memories that catalog the objects in the right place at the right time. But as Turkel (1998) warned, parents ought to be concerned with what specifically the inanimate objects are teaching when in a social role.

The Physical Environment Is Mostly Commercial

By now it should be apparent to the reader that virtually all the objects in the physical environment of children at all ages are *commercial objects*. Even rocks, trees, water, fish, and many other *objects of nature* may be—often are—commercial objects—or maybe *commercialized objects* might be a better term for some of them. The term *commercial objects* denotes that items are results of production and marketing efforts of business organizations. From the baby's food formula, body powders, and paper diapers that were given to her at the hospital where she was born as a greeting by the likes of Procter & Gamble and Johnson & Johnson; from the bottle that holds the milk or formula; to the crib that holds the infant, from the mobile above it, to the carpet below, from the lighting to the air conditioning; and with all the toys, clothing, baby powder, and baby lotion, the baby's immediate world—her room, her home—is essentially a *commercial center* where potentially all marketers of children's products may be represented, or at least those chosen by mom and dad. When babies are able to sit up, they will see more commercial presentations—mom's clothing, the book shelves, curtains, furniture, and furnishings—the list is endless. It is the use of these products—tekrams—that makes babies prime consumers—and markets—and it is their use that teaches children to consume more, thus meeting marketing expectations and predictions. So, while all these physical objects participate directly in baby's physical and mental development, they are commercial objects, and their use is termed consumer behavior. And using them produces consumer behavior patterns. Thus, consumer behavior toward objects may contribute much to a child's total development, to her becoming a person, and definitely to her becoming a consumer of them.

It should be noted that just as children may combine two or more environments such as home and school, they may also combine nature's objects and commercial objects to make one or the other more valuable to them—and more complex. For example, a commercial pail and shovel are more valuable to children when there is nature's sand in which to use them such as at the beach. And likewise, the water at the beach makes a fishing pole much more useful. A memorable example for children is going outside to play where they may climb trees, ride bicycles, and roll in the grass. In Photo 2-3 a child displays a simple example of combining nature and commercial sources of play—a stick from one of nature's trees with a commercial string tied to it. This child's parents operate a magazine and newspaper kiosk on a Beijing street, and to give her something to play with while they work, they tied a string to the stick. Then her imagination and her strong need for play gives the stick-string combination a variety of play scenarios.

The Physical Environment Has Its Dangerous Side

The physical domain contains many dangerous objects although the child is usually unaware of them. Most of these dangers originate in the marketplace, and most of them are provided by adults. I am not referring to such products as bicycles and skateboards that may be dangerous to children if they are not taught how to use the products properly. In fact, accidents from objects are probably the biggest cause of fatalities in childhood. What I am referring to here are objects that are inherently danger-

PHOTO 2-3   A Chinese child plays on the streets of Beijing using a string tied to a stick for a toy. Nature provided the stick; commerce provided the string.

ous when in the possession of children as well as those that are overused. This category would include firearms, tobacco, illicit drugs, alcoholic beverages, and toxic chemicals such as some of those found in cleaning compounds. As I warned many years ago, "... all the products that are not advertised to children because rules of good taste forbid it, all the products assessed as being of poor quality by rating services such as Consumer Union, and all the products that are forbidden by parents, are offered for sale in retail stores" (McNeal, 1987). As noted, most of these objects are provided by adults, mainly parents, and constitute part of the physical environment of children. Any object may be attractive to children and viewed as a play object, an ingestible, or just something curious, but many can harm children who cannot protect themselves.

Bear in mind that all objects can teach consumer behavior patterns, particularly when parents use them. One of the basic ways that children learn, as was pointed out earlier, is to imitate adults who have been observed using a particular product, including overusing a product. Parents want and expect their children to copy them, but many seem to expect unconceptualizing children to know when not to. Of course, this is not the case, and in fact, parents know that not only do children copy their behavior but revere it. So, overeating of fattening foods, smoking, drinking, all look pleasurable to children if they seem pleasurable to parents. For instance, Chinese men use tobacco as almost a religious experience. Cigarettes are given to one another as tokens of friendship. Smoking a cigarette often appears to be special ritual. So, what are children to think when their father reveres tobacco? A five-year-old cannot think abstractly, think ahead, and understand, for example, that overeating will produce overweightness or that smoking will kill the smoker and the people with the smoker. So, dangerous objects may be just about anything when in the hands of a parent. Much of Tony's home setting seems to be detrimental to his health and has caused him to be overweight—his snacking on fattening foods; eating heavily salted, fattening foods for meals; watching TV a lot in bed; playing video games; and probably most important, apparently receiving little parenting. He and millions of other children are pretty much on their own afloat in an environment of commercial objects they choose and following the lead of marketers and friends.

ORIGINS OF THE PHYSICAL ENVIRONMENT

If an outer space character entered the home of a typical five-year-old in middle class America or any other industrialized country, and asked, "Where did all this stuff come from?" what would be the answer? Who could or should provide the answer. Or what if the character asked, "Why is it all here?" what would be the answer? None of it just happened by accident or by miracle. In theory, no unit of it is necessary. Yet, there are thousands of objects in a home such as this. And most homes contain similar objects. What are their origins?

We have already noted that virtually all of the objects in the physical environment of the child come from the *marketplace*. They are commercial objects offered and sold by marketers as discussed previously. This is one answer to the initial question. But how do those objects get from the marketplace to home? Of course, *parents* primarily provide them as we have also noted. Virtually all the objects that the child will interact with, learn from, want, and consume come from parents, and probably some from grandparents, particularly in the case of collective societies such as China. What determines what objects the caretakers provide? There's not one simple answer to this question. The objects purchased specifically for the children by the parents are intended, we can assume, to help the children develop, reach their potential, be happy and healthy—sort of a fulfillment of parental responsibilities. What about basic items such as furniture, auto, house, or apartment? These would also be part of the responsibilities of the parents to make a house a home—for the children and for them—for the family. Or they might say that all of it is "for the good life." As mentioned in Chapter 1 and will be discussed as a separate chapter later, children have a lot to say about what objects are in their homes and what objects are purchased for them. But again, it is assumed that caretakers act responsibly—or should act responsibly—in responding to children's requests and are the major determinant of what the children receive.

The parents, of course, are the main source of commercial objects in the possession of children. The marketplace is the primary source of the commercial objects for the parents. Consequently, the parents are the gatekeepers for what objects the children consume. Photo 2-4 illustrates this

PHOTO 2-4 A mother shops for cucumbers after buying her five-year-old daughter an ice cream treat at a marketplace in Mentougou, China, a rural suburb of Beijing. The mother reported buying her daughter most treats that she requests including fattening ones such as this.

channel of distribution to children. A little five-year-old girl enjoys an ice cream treat while her mother shops the spiny cucumbers in a marketplace in Mentougou, China. The girl asked for the treat, and her mother bought it for her without hesitation, perhaps as a "shut-up" but most likely a motherly gesture. Moms tend to buy just about everything their children request. This is one of the ways that children get fat—regularly requesting and receiving fattening products from parents.

Most developmental psychologists such as Piaget, Erikson, and Vygotsky would note that the objects that are in the child's physical environment are a function of the *culture* or the society in which they are found. Erikson (1968, p. 92) said it this way: "At birth the baby leaves the chemical exchange of the womb for the social exchange system of his society, where his gradually increasing capacities meet the opportunities and limitations of his culture." That is, conceptually, objects are passed along from generation to generation, although classes of objects such as toys and snacks are pretty much universal. But specific toys or specific snacks may be culture-specific. Thus, many harmful products noted previously are "standard equipment" for the child's household—guns in the United States, tobacco in China—and the children are expected to adapt to them and survive them. Vygotsky (1978, p. 30) described a line along which both good and bad objects reach the child: "The path from object to child and from child to object passes through another person." That person may be a parent or a marketer, usually a combination of the two. That is, someone makes sure children receive what they need as well as what they do not need. Additionally, many parents may overdo it by forcing their children into additional physical environments such as after-school tutoring programs, sports programs, and summer camps that are stocked with special objects presumably to improve the lot of children but may be to serve the parents. In the "advanced" societies such as Europe and America, the children have a say in what parents furnish to their children as soon as the children can speak. Reams are written about the power of children over their parents, and we will write more in later chapters about it, but once children reach some mastery of the language, they request and require many objects from parents. Thus, all the healthy and unhealthy objects, useful and harmful objects, necessary and unnecessary objects, in a variety of settings originate mainly from the two *M*s—Moms and Marketers—as the culture dictates or allows. Tony and his parents are probably good examples of the flow of commercial objects from marketers to working parents to children via a cultural conduit.

CURRENT ISSUES IN CONSUMER DEVELOPMENT (#2)

Childhood Burnout: Experiencing Stress in Today's Families

Parents are organizing their children's lives around an array of schooling, athletics, special training, and play that consumes every minute of many children's time and allows none for just being kids. For example, one four-year-old complained to her mother that she wanted a break from her hectic schedule. Starting at 18 months, the little girl was placed in gymnastics, then later in music and dance classes, and then in organized play groups. It's understandable when she and other children say they just want to stay home—normally the one comfortable environment for them.

This pattern of family behavior has paralleled the growth of two-career families that blossomed in the mid-1980s and has become a major concern of pediatricians and child-rearing experts. Studies by Nickelodeon show that two-thirds of working moms report being so time-stressed that they are forced to take shortcuts such as buying fast foods and other take-out meals—to take home and to other environments such as the soccer field. And they complain about not having enough time with their family members or themselves. Surely, this hustle-bustle household atmosphere adds additional stress to the all-day scheduling of their children. Childhood burnout, a relatively new phenomenon, is the result all too often of stress stacked on top of stress. David Elkind, author of *The Hurried Child*, says that the overprogramming of children's lives is producing many health problems such as depression, drug use, injuries to yet developing bones and tendons, even peptic ulcers.

What is the explanation for parents taking away their children's freedom to develop as they may and forcing their development down a variety of avenues? It is due to a complex of reasons, some good, some logical, and some bad.

- Most parents need someone to take care of their children for around 12 hours a day. Placing children in the hands of responsible people such as teachers and coaches accomplishes this, at least in part, while justifying it as improving the children's knowledge, skills, and abilities in preparation for life's competitive culture.
- Many parents reason that their children must be good at something in order to be successful in life. It's just a matter of discovering what that something is. So, at one time or the other the children are placed in various special training classes before school years, during and after school, and in summer camps. One mom who started her daughter in soccer at age six said that she wanted her to learn it well so that she could make the team when she reached adolescence.
- In some cases parents are just "keeping up with the Joneses" by placing their children in special training classes like their friends are doing with their children. In many cases the parents seek out classes that are known to be expensive, or more expensive than those of their friends' children. Children have been termed the BMWs of many parents, so parents feel it is necessary to show them off through their special skills such as that in foreign languages, music instruments, and athletics.

Many marketers are cheering this behavior of parents and encouraging more. Of course, all the manufacturers of sporting goods equipment and musical instruments and their trade associations just love it. So do the managers of the 12,000 or so summer camps. And particularly excited are all the teachers and coaches whose success with these children results in more parents who want more training for their kids. And last but not least, the medical industry is having a boom in treating sports injuries and psychological disorders of these hurried, no-comfort-zone children.

When soccer moms get together at the playing field, in a fast-food restaurant, or in one of their homes, the main topic of conversation is how they—the moms—are stressed out dealing with juggling their job, their family obligations, and their children's activities. And they may complain that they have little personal time. Interestingly, that is also a complaint of many of their children.

****
Sources: Elkind, 1998; Kantrowitz and Wingert, 2001; Kantrowitz and Witherspoon, 2006; Richardson, 2006; Sabino, 2002.

Because of my years of researching children's consumer behavior in the United States and in China—and in several other countries—I am often asked about the differences between Chinese and American children. There certainly are many observable differences between the two cultures and therefore some differences between the children. For some detailed comparative descriptions, see Chan and McNeal (2004), McNeal and Zhang (2000), and McNeal and Yeh (1997). In sum, it is mainly China's governmental policies that make its children's consumer behavior both different and the same as that of American children. Its limitation of one child per family is a major factor in Chinese children's consumer behavior not found in other populous countries. With only one child in the family, that child is given as much as possible in order to assure success in life. This means that each child grows up in a relatively luxurious life—compared to that child's parents—without earning it in any way and generally expecting it. For instance, I estimate that children in the United States determine around 45–50 percent of routine household purchases, whereas Chinese children determine around 68 percent. And a much greater share of household income is spent on the Chinese children's education as compared to that of U.S. children. Since Chinese children are pampered much more than Western children, they may have just about anything they want. Through mass media, they learn to want what American children have—the same products, the same brands. The result is an amazing similarity in consumer behavior patterns among children of both cultures.

Today, in the United States around a quarter of children are members of two or more households due to divorce, separation, abandonment, and having children as a hobby. The net result is even more objects are available to the children—more good ones and more bad ones. Some of these are what I call *DWI objects*. These are commercial objects given by separated and divorced fathers and mothers to their children as a way for the children to "**d**eal **with it**"—with a broken home and multiple parents. In the United States, parents often show their affection and kindness to children with commercial objects. They even compete—mothers and stepmothers, fathers and stepfathers—on the basis of the items given to the children. The outcome for these 10–15 million children is a cluttered commercial environment consisting of two or more of many of the same items. We are beginning to see similar results in urban China where divorce is becoming more common.

DISCUSSION

To say that Behavior is a function of the Person and the Environment is not profound; it is simply basic thinking that should underlie all human behavior research. Yet, for some reason it seems that the Environment, and particularly the physical dimension of the environment, gets shortchanged in most consumer research—probably in most human research. For example, harking back again to the studies of infants discovering their self-image in a mirror, I do not think that I have ever read one of the reports that described in any detail the nature of the mirror, or even a note that described the minimum attributes of the mirror for the experiment. Developmental psychologists are so absorbed with the Person in the study, the developing Person, that they ignore at least one-half of the determinants of what baby sees or thinks. I understand this singular focus of the psychologist; after all, it is the human that is under the microscope; not the objects in the experimental setting. But I also understand the room for error in this kind of thinking. I suggest that much of the consumer development research—and the consumer socialization research—makes this same error. As some confirmation of my concerns, I refer to a relatively recent study by Moore and Lutz (2000) reported in the *Journal of Consumer Research*. Their study is the umpteenth on the topic of the influence of advertising on children's thinking, but their work takes it a step further and gives some slight consideration to the environment and its physical contents. In the introduction (p. 2) the researchers refer to the many studies of advertising's effects on children, but then add: "However . . . the potential role played by *actual product experience* in interacting with advertising *has simply not been studied* with children" (the emphasis mine). Imagine finding this kind of statement in the year 2000, particularly in this very prestigious consumer research journal. And as one might imagine, also, the investigators found that experience with products—with key objects in the physical environment—had much influence on the thinking of the children, in fact, maybe more than advertising in the case of younger children. Interestingly, also, the reporters acknowledged that the many studies of product advertising's influence on children's cognitive development have ignored the influence of the products themselves. When both marketing theorists and consumer behavior theorists first read this report, several questions surely arose in their minds. For example, is it possible that all those studies of advertising's influence on children's consumer behavior have overstated its influence? Are the reported results of advertising's influence really mostly the results of product influence? Or, are the results of advertising's influence only half, or less, of the marketing influence on children's consumer behavior? These questions are posed here but not answered here, although I hope that they are at least partially answered by a reading of this book.

What has been suggested in this chapter on the role of the physical environment in the development of consumers is that while we usually give most credit to the social environment for shaping children's consumer behavior, the physical domain actually has at least as much influence—sort of like products have at least as much influence as their advertising—on children's development. The greater presence of the physical environment (objects) in children's lives compared to that of the social environment (people) ought to alert us to this possibility. That, in fact, is the main purpose of this chapter—to focus the reader's thinking on this possibility. It is not to focus thinking on research errors, but to note researcher bias. The investigator always inserts self-interest into the experiment—can't keep from it—and as noted, the infant's thinking about herself is always of more interest than the mirror that produced it. And virtually all developmental students are more interested in the influence of parents on child development than the influence of the things provided the child by the parents.

This chapter spends a lot of time and words trying to make it apparent that the physical environment has characteristics that give it a very important role in consumer development. The ubiquity of objects, mostly commercial objects, surely accounts for its powerful influence on the overall general development of children and specifically on their consumer development. Today, in the developed and developing world three-quarters of children's moms and dads work, so the few hours a day moms get and the few minutes a day dads get with their kids do not compare with the 24 hours a day that objects get. We will say more about working moms in the next chapter on social environment, but the fact is that they have pretty much turned over the rearing of their kids to the various physical environments and consequently indirectly to marketers. So, commercial objects surround the kids all the time. There is no escaping them, there is no isolation from them except in some special case of a highly impoverished environment. So, they have their way with the children from birth on and greatly determine their cognitive and motor development.

It was Piaget who noted that children's intelligence is mainly a result of their interactions with objects in their environment, causing one developmentalist to summarize Piaget's theory of cognitive development as: Action = Knowledge (Feldman, 2000, p. 150). Or said another way, "Children learn by doing." That is, by interacting with objects in the environment they enrich their minds. Diamond (1982) reminded us that tots spend so much time and effort exploring and conceptualizing their environment because practically all of it is unfamiliar as compared to the adult world that is largely familiar. So, there is a lot to learn for the new humans, and they spend as much of their time and effort as they can feeling, sucking on, watching, and listening to all elements of the environment, social and physical. But it is the physical that presides most of the time.

The intense interest of children in the physical environment is attested to by the fact that they assign life to some of its objects. Adults ordinarily do not do this. This practice of animism is something that children do as a way of assigning some objects special significance. This seems comparable to the two-month-old infant who will stare for lengthy periods of time at one object such as her finger or a thread on a toy (as compared to the whole toy). Two- and three-year-olds often play alone—they seem to prefer it that way—and they talk to their play objects as if they were people. Children's singling out objects for special consideration—for conversation—demonstrates their importance to them. When children first begin to speak, some of their first words are the possessives, *My* and *Mine*, as they attempt to classify some of the objects in their surroundings, thus giving them even more clout in their lives. This has been noticeable in the case of commercial objects such as food and clothing. Children may refer to their cereal as "My Cheerios," and their shoes as "My Nikes," and when interacting with another child may emphatically state, "That's mine."

In this chapter I did not do a good job of classifying the objects in the child's environment—probably not as good of a job as the child does. But as some kind of fundamental classification, I did suggest that if the objects were not from nature, they were from a commercial source although usually provided by parents. And the commercial objects were divided into those that were purchased from commercial sources for the satisfaction of the children and those that were provided by a commercial source whose primary purpose was to persuade the children (and parents) to want and buy more of certain products from specific commercial sources. However, I should have given greater emphasis to the fact that often commercial objects have both goals—to satisfy the consumer and to sell more products. That is certainly the case of packaging, sometimes called the "silent salesman." Some of my research has shown that the packages that accompany the use of the product, such as the cereal box or the toothpaste tube, have great impact on children's cognitive development and their motor development. I will say more about this later, but for now I will just note that cereal packages particularly enter children's memory almost in their entirety. When I have asked children to draw a cereal package, they often produce one that is almost the exact likeness of the original, including shape, color schemes, branding, wording, and even the nutritional contents in some cases (McNeal and Ji, 2003). So, objects printed with pictures and words, such as the cereal packages or children's story books, and used repeatedly, seem to have teaching power that equals or exceeds that of humans.

Mentioning the children's story books reminds me that I said practically nothing about the influence of objects on children's reading ability. But both packages and books, with moms' assist, appear to contribute substantially to children learning to read, learning vocabulary, and learning the naming of objects. Parents often help their children read the cereal box at breakfast and their books at bedtime. This includes learning some "hard words," some brand names such as Chef Boyardee, and always some new words that the children seem to want. Of course, the marketers of these objects as well as their spokescharacters deserve some of the credit. I can't tell you how many kids wrote on their drawings of Kellogg's Frosted Flakes packages, "It's Grrrreat," referring, of course, to the words of Tony the Tiger, the cereal's spokescharacter.

I mentioned that packages as objects often contribute to children's motor skills. Toothpaste tubes and cereal boxes both teach through their use of certain fine motor skills that are required in their opening and closing. Naturally, some urging from mom about these tasks helps too. Probably all objects in children's physical environments do some teaching of motor skills (which we will also talk a lot about later). I tend to think that children would learn to walk, for example, later in life if it were not for some items on rollers (such as strollers) that allow the children to push them with their feet, and some items with pedals (such as pedal cars) that encourage the early use of their feet. Many toys have a way of assisting children with their gross motor skills that include balancing, walking, hopping, and jumping. This is equally true for some of their fine motor skills—gripping, releasing, writing, drawing—that get help from pencils, crayons, and paper, for instance.

But what is being said here about toys could in some way be said for most of the objects in a child's physical environment. I could mention the slats of his crib, the design of the wallpaper in his room, the shape and color of the lamp beside his bed; all these normal objects participate in the youngster's cognitive and motor development just as do his fingers and toes that, incidentally, are not viewed as his or as part of his person until several months later but are treated much like other objects in the physical environment. However, a few years later those fingers and toes that got their training in his bedroom will grip handlebars and pedals, respectively, of a tricycle, then a bicycle with training wheels, and finally one without them. While mom may have mediated many times—bought him the vehicles, showed him how to ride them—it was the objects that contributed most to the child's motor and cognitive skills, even to his social skills as he shows off for his friends. Eventually, he may be able to con mom and dad into buying him a motorized miniature automobile just like they drive, and just like the one he has been practicing on in his imagination for some time. Ask any five-year-old. Life's an objects world.

REFERENCES

BestStuff.com. (2006). Mattel and Fisher-Price launch tech-friendly line at toy fair 2006. Retrieved from http://www.beststuff.com/search/node/Mattel+and+Fisher-Price+launch+tech-friendly+line+at+toy+fair

Chan, K., and J. U. McNeal. (2004). *Advertising to Children in China.* Hong Kong: The Chinese University Press.

Clarke-Stewart, A. (1973). Interactions between mothers and their young children: Characteristics and consequences. *Monographs of the Society of Research in Child Development, 38,* 6–7.

Diamond, N. (1982). Cognitive theory. In B. B. Wolman (ed.), *Handbook of Developmental Psychology* (pp. 3–22). Englewood Cliffs, NJ: Prentice-Hall, Inc.

Eliot, L. (1999). *What's Going On in There?: How the Brain and Mind Develop in the First Five Years of Life.* New York: Bantam Books.

Elkind, D. (1988). *The Hurried Child.* Cambridge, MA: Perseus Publishing.

Erikson, E. H. (1968). *Identity: Youth and Crisis.* New York: W. W. Norton & Company.

Feldman, R. S. (2000). *Development Across the Life Span* (2nd ed.). Upper Saddle River, NJ: Prentice-Hall.

Kantrowitz, B., and P. Wingert. (2001, January 29). The parent trap. *Newsweek,* 49–53.

Kantrowitz, B., and D. Witherspoon. (1986, March 3). Penciling in playtime. *Newsweek,* 57.

McNeal, J. U. (1987). *Children as Consumers: Insights and Implications.* Lexington, MA: D. C. Heath and Company.

McNeal, J. U. (1992). *Kids as Customers: A Handbook of Marketing to Children.* New York: Lexington Books.

McNeal, J. U., and M. F. Ji (2003). Children's visual memory of packaging. *Journal of Consumer Marketing, 20*(5), 400–427.

McNeal, J. U., and C. H. Yeh. (1997). Development of consumer behavior patterns among Chinese children. *Journal of Consumer Marketing, 14*(1), 45–59.

McNeal, J. U., and H. Zhang. (2000, March–April). Chinese children as consumers: A review. *The International Journal of Advertising & Marketing to Children,* 32–37.

Moore, E. S., and R. J. Lutz. (2000, June). Children, advertising, and product experiences: A multi-method inquiry. *Journal of Consumer Research, 27,* 31–48.

Piaget, J. (1954). *The construction of reality in the child.* New York: Basic Books.

Piaget, J. (1963). *The origins of intelligence in children.* New York: W. W. Norton & Company.

Richardson, V. (2006, April 12). *More bang for a bunk: Picking a summer camp.* Accessed August 28, 2006, from www.msnbc.msn.com/id/12286975/print/1/displaymode/1098

Sabino, D. (2002, October–December). Changing families, changing kids. *International Journal of Advertising & Marketing to Children,* 9–12.

Turkel, A. R. (1998). All about Barbie: Distortions of transitional object. *Journal of the American Academy of Psychoanalysis, 26*(1), 165–177.

Vygotsky, L. S. (1978). *Mind in society: The development of higher psychological processes.* Cambridge, MA: Harvard University Press.

Wachs, T. D. (1985). Toys as an aspect of the physical environment: Constraints and nature of relationship to development. *Topics in Early Childhood Special Education, 5*(3), 31–46.

Wellman, H. M., A. K., Hickling, and C. A. Schult. (1997). Young children's psychological, physical, and biological explanations. In H. M. Wellman and K. Inagaki (eds.), *The Emergence of Core Domains of Thought; Children's Reasoning about Physical, Psychological, and Biological Phenomena,* pp. 7–25, San Francisco: Jossey-Bass/Pfeiffer.

3

THE SOCIAL ENVIRONMENT: CONTRIBUTIONS OF SOCIAL OBJECTS TO THE DEVELOPMENT OF CONSUMERS

Two-Year-Old Howie Finds His Favorite Brand at Daycare

In an interview with a North Houston working mother of two children, the topic of brands of products for children came up. Her son, Howie (Howard), age two, and her daughter, Cindy (Cynthia), age four, both were brand conscious, she related, and often asked for things by brand name—usually treating the brand as a noun. Some examples she offered were Howie's awareness of brands of cereals and soft drinks and Cindy's awareness of brands of cereal, cars, and candy. She added, "Neither my husband nor I are very wrapped up with brands, so I don't think they get it from us. We try to buy everything by its value, not its name. I buy a good many things at Wal-Mart in their brands because to me they represent good value. And another thing," she noted, "Cindy and Howie don't watch much TV, so I don't think they learn a lot of brand stuff there. They are not allowed to watch TV except with me, maybe their daddy. I usually sit down with them and watch some Disney stuff and that's about all the TV they see." (Later in the interview she did note that both kids sometimes watch TV together on Saturday mornings while she works in the house and also occasionally with parents in the early evening.)

When asked if the children talk about or ask for any Disney brands, she answered, "No, I don't guess they even know there is a Disney brand. Of course," she added, "They both have a Mickey Mouse in their room and some Mickey Mouse books."

Then she volunteered, "But when we go shopping like at Wal-Mart, Howie sees that Spiderman stuff and he starts shouting, 'Spiderman, barummm, Spiderman, barummm.' Then he starts in with I want this and I want that," she said. "Even when we're on

our way home," She added, "He will still talk about Spiderman
things. It drives me crazy. I asked him where he learned about it
and he said at daycare." She explained that both kids go to a
daycare center that is sponsored by her church. "I guess he picks it
up from the other kids there; in fact, now I'm pretty sure he does."
Then she added, "Can you believe a child who just turned two
learning such stuff like that from other kids that age? You just
never know what to expect when kids get together."

CHILDREN'S TWO ENVIRONMENTS: SOCIAL AND PHYSICAL

In the preceding chapter we examined the physical environment and its
substantial influence on the development of children and their consumer
behavior patterns, and we noted that it was one-half of their total environment, with the social domain being the other half. Here, we will consider
that other half, the *social domain*, the one from which Howie probably
learned about Spiderman, according to his mother. We will discuss its
nature, contents, and its role in the development of children and their consumer behavior patterns from birth to around 100 months. Of course, in
actuality the two domains, physical and social, are inseparable except in an
analysis such as this. The reader should bear in mind that the determinants
of consumer behavior patterns are multifaceted even though we treat them
singularly. There is probably not one tekram of consumer behavior that is
due solely to one domain or the other.

While we intuitively expect children to learn everything they know
from others, we might not expect two-year-olds to learn about Spiderman
and other marketing objects from other two-year-olds—at least Howie's
mom did not. That probably sounds a little young to most of us. But we
have already indicated in the preceding two chapters that children are not
passive learners, but active learners, and extract much information from the
environment on their own beginning shortly after birth. Chances are Howie
learned about this commercial character by simply observing it on the possessions of others such as clothing, backpacks, and toys. Perhaps, too, visits
to the marketplace, such as the one his mother mentioned to Wal-Mart, may
have introduced the character and character-based items to him through
signs and displays. Finally, while Howie's mother indicated that she did not
believe that Howie learned about Spiderman from TV, that is certainly a
possibility, perhaps from TV at daycare as well as TV at home that his older
sister watches (although presumably with mom), or TV when he visits a
neighbor's kids. Thus, children learn consumer behavior from the physical
classroom formed by many inanimate objects (discussed in the preceding
chapter) and from the social setting containing many animate objects,
the people with whom they interact. We did try to demonstrate earlier
how much consumer learning results from the physical environment—we

think at least half of it, perhaps more among today's children—but we also observed that the social environment may mediate some of the influence of the physical environment as well as operate pretty much alone as an influencer on the child consumer. This mediating influence and direct influence of the social environment are the main topics of this chapter as we move toward an understanding of the development of consumer behavior patterns in childhood. However, be prepared to hear about the physical environment again because of the constant intermingling of the two domains. Also, as children develop socially, they also develop into individuals who express their inner self—their self-image—through the consumer role. We will spell out this process that was noted in Chapter 1. After all, it explains much of the consumer behavior of children (as well as adults).

CONTENTS OF THE CHILD'S SOCIAL ENVIRONMENT: PEOPLE AND NEAR-PEOPLE

Naturally, the content of the social environment consists of people, but it also contains *near-people* (as they were called in Chapter 2 on physical environment), artificially created beings with whom developing children have some kind of relationship. The social environment does not contain everybody or everybody with whom a child might have contact. It is a here-and-now thing and refers to only one child's social setting, one child's social contacts such as family or school classroom. All together these social contacts form a major part of the context of children's consumer behavior. Imagine a funnel, if you will, that expands in depth and width over time, and you have a model of children's social relationships. At first the infant has no one except the *self* to relate to and that is his sole focus—the narrowest end of the funnel. It remains pretty much that way for a relatively long time, during which the infant thinks of his survival only, his views only, his body only. Call it egocentric or self-centered, but it is really a natural outcome of being born immaturely (not prematurely) and having to fend for oneself as best one can with only a few reflexes that came as standard equipment. The famous motivation psychologist Abraham Maslow (1943) once described the behavior of a hungry man in great detail in one of his writings, and if one steps back and only skims the article, it sounds very much like he is talking about a newborn. He stated:

> It is fair to characterize the whole organism by saying simply that it is hungry, for consciousness is almost preempted by hunger. All capacities are put into the service of hunger-satisfaction, and the organization of these capacities is almost entirely determined by the one purpose of satisfying hunger. The receptors and effectors, the intelligence, memory, habits, all may now be defined simply as hunger-gratifying tools. Capacities that are not useful for this purpose lie dormant, or are pushed into the background. (p. 373)

Thus, for the first couple of weeks of life, the newborn is characterized by eating and sleeping—she sleeps around 15 hours a day. That is how *mom* gets into the picture (into the funnel); she is initially the only source of food for the baby, probably the only provider of hunger satisfaction. However, within a few weeks mom also becomes the only source of warmth, love, and fun, thus expanding her role in the life of the baby who, once fed and rested, is looking for other pleasures. Soon *dad* enters the picture (expanding the funnel) as a caregiver also, and along with him comes big *sister* and/or big *brother*. Still, at this point in the baby's life, these significant others are not seen as real others, per se, but as extensions of self just as physical objects are. It is not until around 8–10 months or so according to most developmentalists such as Piaget (Crane, 1992) that the self and others become separate entities, along with the physical objects in the self's environment. Thus, the stage at which the child regularly experiences object permanence (including social objects)—at about the same time that she begins to sit up, crawl, and try to take a step—is the point in life that social relations really begin, or at least become defined in the mind of the child. Motor abilities such as reaching, crawling, and walking not only permit interacting with social objects but also attract social objects, thus expanding the width and depth of the funnel.

Once the self separates and the child begins to seek differentiation, to seek individuality, to seek to become a person distinct from others—a practice that psychologists often call *individuation* (Damon, 1983)—others are permitted (by the child) to enter the child's life (the funnel). Thus, the toddler becomes a self in society, an I and a Me, as the pioneering psychologist William James (1950) would call her, a person among persons, a knower and a known, a subject and an object. Now begins a sometimes complementary, sometimes contradictory period in the child's life when she seeks connectedness and separateness at the same time, a paradox for sure that forms the stuff that psychoanalysts thrive on (Damon, 1983). The social relations in the home expand (and expand the funnel) to include *grandparents,* other *relatives,* and perhaps the *child's parents' friends*. Most of these people find paths into the child's life through commercial objects (gifts) of play items and food goods. Some of these commercial objects that the child receives such as *stuffed animals* also become friends of sorts as they are given life by the child through her communications—*near-people* as we might call them. They are near-people from the perspective of a child in the sense that the child tries to interact with them through talking, touching, holding, and hugging. Additionally, pets enter the social environment of the child and provide pleasures through interactions. For example, the child and her pet dog may share food and play. (In early childhood a child's life revolves around food and play, in that order, during the first year; then starting around the second year, the order is reversed with play first and remaining first until the tween years.)

As children venture outside their homes, their social world rapidly grows complex (as does the funnel). They meet and play with *peers* at daycare, such as Howie did, then kindergarten, then elementary school, and they also connect with and learn from a growing number of *teachers* and *caretakers* at these organizations, some of which function as parent substitutes. These new kids and new adults bring with them new thinking and behavior from which the growing children learn just as Howie likely learned about Spiderman. With the number of social objects increasing, the number of interactions is bound to increase. For example, classmates and teachers may be seen and visited with not only at school but perhaps in shopping settings, in church-related activities, in recreational settings, and in after-school activities. This broadening of the social environment also produces many more tekrams, units of consumer behavior, as children learn consumer behavior patterns from the growing number of people in their lives—as demonstrated by Howie asking for Spiderman "stuff" when he goes shopping with his mom. The number of people that become members of a child's social world will continue to grow even as some leave. Very important, the self, a very real person, is constructed by the child through feedback from this increasing number of significant others. So, while the social domain grows and changes, the personal domain does too—as Howie's mom noticed.

In addition to these direct associations with such people as parents, siblings, relatives, and teachers, children may have indirect associations with others that are remote to their social environment but nevertheless members of it from the perspective of the children. These associations include near-people that have been given life, so to speak, by children, perhaps also by their parents or by marketers. As described in Chapter 2, these are inanimate objects such as stuffed animals or cartoon characters or product (brand) spokescharacters; they may be any combination of these such as a Barney doll that is also seen on TV programming and on products. Although these near-people are not human beings, per se, children may give them special names, talk to them, share with them, and take comfort and guidance from them. We termed some of these near-people *transitional objects* in Chapter 2 since they help the children transition from dependence on parents to independence. For some, these near-people often are substitutes for real people with whom children do not or cannot interact. The children may insist on not going anywhere without carrying these near-people with them even if they are nothing more (to adults) than a pillow ("pibbie") or blanket ("blankie"). Some of these transitionals come to life in TV programs and commercials, video games, and movies and may have such a presence in children's worlds that they may influence what they like in food or clothing, for instance. Others, such as Santa Claus, Ronald McDonald, and Geoffrey (the Toys 'R Us giraffe), come to life—through the actions of parents and/or marketers—when the children visit the marketplace. In just about every sense of the word, children can have an interpersonal relationship with these near-people. For instance, a child may talk to her Bunny—her stuffed rabbit—and imagine that Bunny is talking back to her, saying things she wants to hear from her parents.

Children, particularly those of school-age, often respond to real people whom they do not know personally but respect and would like to be like—would like to practice their consumer behavior. These individuals may be termed *reference groups* and/or *role models* (Kemper, 1968). They are reference groups in the sense that children refer to them for guidance when making a decision about undertaking an activity such as buying and/or using a product. They might be movie stars, professional athletes, or simply older children at school. They are role models in the sense that they occupy a position in society that children revere and would like to hold also, for instance, a Broadway actor they saw on a visit to New York City, a racecar driver they saw at the Daytona 500, maybe a revered teacher at school, or an impressive fourth-grader (to a second-grader). Children may pretend to talk to these people and thus demonstrate an interpersonal relationship with them. Children might display pictures and posters of some of these people in their bedroom, as Tony did in Chapter 2, and even talk to them there.

Older children are often a reference group for younger children—children regardless of age usually want to be older. For example, my research and that of others shows that some preschoolers and first-graders look up to tweens (those 8–12 years-old) for guidance in clothing styles (McNeal, 1999). Likewise, tweens look up to teens for guidance in much of their consumer behavior. These are mostly indirect relationships, but younger children often do try to talk to older children or at least see them close up. In their own ways—often in imaginary ways—they have developed relationships with these people. Perhaps the sculpture in Photo 3-1 has captured this concept of "looking up" by children. The sculpture is located in the front of the Tong Sheng He shoe store on Wangfujing Avenue in Beijing. It shows a child trying to fit into the shoes of an older person while friends look on in admiration.

The fact that children take guidance from reference groups and role models may result in degrees of tragedy for them. Sometimes children select a reference group or role model that is socially undesirable, such as some celebrities who commit socially undesirable acts such as smoking. Children imitate these people and their actions as a way to have some kind of relationship with them—and often to be viewed by friends as being like those imitated. Often younger children copy the socially undesirable behavior of older children believing that it is a grown-up thing to do. One tragic result, for instance, is that children become new customers for the tobacco companies. It should be noted that there is a move by an organization—Smoke Free Movies—currently to reduce the amount of smoking in movies that children see. (You can see a full-page ad for this organization on page A5 of the November 18, 2005, *New York Times*.) This organization has "com-

PHOTO 3-1   A sculpture located on Wangfujing Avenue in Beijing conveying the notion that children try to fit into the shoes of older people, often to impress peers.

pelling evidence" showing that smoking by movie stars may encourage children to take up the dangerous habit. Of course, the tobacco companies also have similar research results, so they try to buy their way into movies through what is called product placement.

NATURE OF THE SOCIAL ENVIRONMENT

It is more difficult to characterize the social environment than the physical environment of children; people are more difficult to describe than wallpaper or cereal. Just as children are born into a physical world, they are born into a social world, and of course, at the time of this event the two are not really separate as explained in the preceding chapter on the physical environment. Perhaps Willard Hartup (1979) has in some ways done the best job of characterizing children's social environment by theorizing that there are two social worlds of childhood. One is the *adult-child* social world; the other is the *peer-child* social world. Each expands with and plays a distinct role in the social development of children—and in their consumer development. The adult-child world appears first to children but is linked to the other set of social relationships by preparation given the children for participating in the peer-child world. Notably missing from Hartup's two-part social world of children are those social objects we have termed *near-people*. Perhaps he would not see these as social beings—capable of relationships—as the children may since he is coming from the perspective of the psychologist and not that of the sociologist.

The adult-child domain is initially made up primarily of parents followed by all the other adults that the parents bring into this setting, including grandparents and other relatives, doctors, teachers, baby-sitters, daycare administrators, and marketers. According to Hartup (1979) the identifying features of the adult-child world are its *protection* (security) and *constraint* (control). Both form the foundation of child rearing, or socialization, as it also was termed in Chapter 1, and both are necessary in order for children to become functioning members of the society in which they are born. It is through adults that the *culture* is first passed on to the child in the forms of acceptable objects, behavior patterns, and relationships.

Protection comes first as newborn infants are unable to take care of themselves. Feeding, clothing, and bedding the babies are basics of protection, but comforting, communicating, and humoring are also very important. All of these protective activities that ordinarily are provided by the parents also include intentional and incidental teaching of consumer behavior patterns such as eating, sleeping, and playing that permit and encourage the infant to become a functioning human being. These three general activities become the infants' first tekrams—units of consumer behavior—initially taught by the parents and performed by the infants. Sleeping, for example, is a wired-in bodily activity, but how and where sleeping takes place are tekrams taught by parents and are often culture based. Use of food objects and play objects are also passed on through parents' concerns for infant welfare, and again, often are a function of the culture. For instance, both American and Chinese toddlers usually begin their eating skills with a spoon because that specific tekram is usually taught first by parents. Later, after more fine motor skills develop, culture takes over and Chinese children are taught by parents to use chopsticks (*kwai-dz*), whereas American children are taught by parents to use a fork. The result is that there are "cultural differences" in eating utensils between Chinese and American children. When they talk about these differences, Chinese children see a fork (sort of four chopsticks) as hard to use and not too practical; American children see chopsticks (two sticks) similarly. In Photo 3-2 a three-year-old Chinese girl is eating charcoal-grilled mutton on a skewer stick (sort of one chopstick), which she learns to do very early in childhood, and according to her mother, she has not yet mastered two sticks—chopsticks. Again, eating with a stick is viewed by Chinese children and their parents who taught them as very practical—and very inexpensive compared to metal utensils.

In order for protection to be accomplished fully, the parents also introduce many other adults into the social setting of the infant, including grandparents (particularly in Asian societies), teachers (e.g., when the children are taken to preschools), marketers (e.g., when the children are taken to a shopping setting), and neighbors (e.g., when the children are taken to visit neighbors' kids). All of these adults may offer children protection in some

PHOTO 3-2 A three-year-old Chinese girl eating charcoal-grilled mutton from a skewer stick, thus mastering one stick before she masters chopsticks.

form. Thus, while children are going through the process of physical and mental development, they are also going through the processes of socialization and enculturation at the hands of adults.

The second dimension of the adult-child world is constraint, or if you might, the introduction of society-approved behaviors, rules, or what might be termed *social forces* (McNeal, 1982). Thus, more enculturation is performed by adults. Under the banner of constraint, the parents and other adults introduce the values and value-based actions that are necessary for a good and proper life in a particular society—teaching right and wrong and rules, lots of rules. In fact, one of them often is called The Golden Rule. The list is endless but includes language (e.g., the right words), motor behavior (e.g., the right posture and gait), dress (e.g., the right clothing), nutrition (e.g., the right foods), and manners (e.g., the right way to relate to others). It is in this arena, particularly, that we witness the authoritarian adults directing the behavior of children in order to pass on the cultural standards. Socialization is not a one-way street, however. Parents expect their children to copy their behaviors, although there are a lot of inconsistencies through the "Don't do as I do, do as I say" teaching style. One smoking father told me this rather confusing set of rules for his 12-year-old, "I'd rather that he didn't smoke. But if he's going to, I'd rather that he did it at home and not sneak around about it." One working mom who sat at her breakfast table along side her 7-year-old daughter smoking with one hand and holding either a pack of cigarettes or a lighter in the other said this to me: "I told her a number of times I don't want her smoking. No siree." Actually, much research shows that children want to copy their parents' behavior patterns as a means of winning their love and approval (e.g., Ainsworth, 1989). So, as long as the parents consider themselves proper role models, the two are a winning team at fitting the children into society. As a side note, when we talk about the constraints that parents introduce to their children, these need not be harsh and threatening, for as noted, children want to please their parents and in many ways seek out their guidance. The harshness, even violence, that some parents impose on their children in order to get them to behave according to society's rules usually originates from the inside of the unpracticed parents, not from the inside of the unpracticed children.

The *peer-child* (child-child) social world is in great part the responsibility of the parents to initiate but involves only children of various ages and is characterized by its *mutuality* and *cooperation* (Hartup, 1979). We have already noted that parent-child relations possess some degree of mutuality and cooperation, but they exist for different motivations than those in peer-child relations. There are almost always socialization goals in the parent-child relationship; the parents want to lead the children to the acceptable ways of doing things, and the children want to do the right thing in order to have parents' approval. In the peer-child relationship, there is more symmetry and equality in the interactions, with neither trying to gain in the ordinary sense of the word but just trying to enjoy each other.

Children may interact with one another for many reasons—to watch TV together, to study together, to take baths together, to eat a meal together, to name a few. Count on it, most peer-child interactions take place through the medium of tekrams. Thus, social relations development is a basic outcome of consumer behavior in early childhood (and throughout life). Photo 3-3 shows three children, each around five years old, interacting while seriously involved with their favorite activity—playing. In this case they are playing on the swings and slide at kindergarten while laughing and talking, although some of it is bound to be parallel play at this age. Lots of tekrams may be learned from such social/play sessions as these that may occur several times a day in China and America.

A special case of peer-child influence is in the home in the form of *siblings*. Where there is only one child in the family, such as is normally the case in China, these first-borns take their cues from parents. However, where there is a second-born, first-borns often take much guidance from

PHOTO 3-3 Children play together on swings and slide at kindergarten. Through this social play, they learn many tekrams.

them—as long as there is not much age difference. Where a child has a brother or sister who is one to five years older, the child is likely to see the older children as peers—playmates, pals—and look to the older children for cues regarding what to say, eat, wear, watch on TV, and respond to other peers. A recent study reported in *Time* magazine (Kluger, 2006) summed it up this way:

> From the time they are born, our brothers and sisters are our collabora-tors and co-conspirators, our role models and cautionary tales. They are our scolds, protectors, goads, tormentors, playmates, counselors, sources of envy, objects of pride. (p. 47)

The best and probably most recognizable example of the peer-child social world, however, is *play*—the most important activity of children start-ing between 12 and 24 months and one that probably accounts for the most tekrams experienced by them. *Play*, as the term is used here, refers to play for play's sake, for bodily and mental pleasure, or as the child would prob-ably say, for fun. Some developmentalists see fun and play as one in the same (e.g., Poris, 2005). Actually, play is always fun—enjoyable, pleasur-able—to children, but activities that are termed *fun* by children may not be play for play's sake. Children with their limited vocabularies often describe activities as fun when they mean they are enjoyable. For instance, eight-year-olds often explain that they like to be with their friends because being with them is fun but it may not always be play.

Social psychologists might term play *social play* (Damon, 1983) when it is in the company of another; much play by very young children does take place alone. In the realm of play, young children usually cast aside the three *R*s—reality, rules, and rudeness—and create their own reality and their own rules, and if there is any rudeness intended, it is usually directed toward an inanimate object such as a toy. (Children often talk to inanimate objects and without the embarrassment experienced by adults who are seen doing it.) Very young children may participate in what is often termed *parallel play*, in which none of the children communicate meaningfully with another but still play side by side. At this point, at two or three years old, the children have not really learned to play together in the sense of taking each other's views into consideration. Both are in the egocentric stage of their lives and simply cannot yet anticipate the reactions of another child. But they are sharing at best they can the space they occupy, the play items, and of course, their own views on life although usually in monologue form. Mutuality and cooperation are present, but neither in a mature kind of way. In fact, these children might be compared with the millions of adults working in the cubicles of many large offices—working together in the same space; having different conversations on their phones; and generally ignoring one another's feelings, needs, views, and activities.

But soon, particularly by first grade, the kids will play together, touch each other, talk the same topic with each other, take turns at some step in a game, and in general, cooperate and have fun. The children do learn rules of fairness from their play—interestingly, what is often termed *fair play*—which is what adults want them to do. But the learning is mainly under the conditions set by the children and therefore is more palatable. And there may be attempts at control, mainly based on the egocentric nature of one or both that still hangs on from toddlerhood, but it is done with less authority than in the adult-child social world. At some point, probably near adolescence, peer-child relations begin to look much like adult-adult relations as the children try to appear to be grown-ups at the repeated commands of teachers and employers.

STAGES OF SOCIAL DEVELOPMENT

There are change-with-age aspects to children's development of social relations, social self, and the social activities that have been delineated in research, but they appear not to be formalized stages that characterize motor or cognitive development as described in the next two chapters. That is, when one looks at the development of the social dimensions of children, one can see some sequencing, sometimes invariant sequencing, in all of them. Some of this sequencing in children's social development has been theoretically and empirically examined by social psychologists and sociologists for many years and will be discussed here briefly.

Becoming a Relational Person

First, there is much research documenting the change in children from egocentrism to altruism—from self-interest to other-interest—what I would call the change from an "I" to a "We" orientation. It is not one step, but a series of day-to-day events. This change gradually occurs from birth to somewhere in the middle elementary school years, or approximately during the period of 0–100 months, the age-range focus of this book. If one has studied infants, one is keenly aware that there is little reason to expect them to take others into consideration. Yet, within a few weeks a newborn can be detected looking hard at mom, then later others, at least appearing to take an interest in them. This is the earliest sign of altruism—if we can call it that—in the self-centered newborn. It seems that other people gradually become of interest, also, if for no other reason than the fact that they can provide some satisfiers for the infant. By toddler time and into the preschool years, when the child is walking and talking, more consideration is given to others, but again, mainly because they can provide something for the child. It is not that the affiliation need—the need for cooperative relations with others—is absent and therefore the child is not driven to seek relations with others; only that it plays a minor role in day-to-day functioning in very early childhood. However, when the child is around age three or four, a sense of *sharing,* a sense that provisions can be exchanged, appears. Children discover, for instance, that they can take turns in some play and it is more fun, that they can give each other gifts that brings them together in an enjoyable and satisfying manner, that they can give one another more time, such as watching TV together, and it makes life feel better for both. Finally, by the time children reach the third grade, approximately, they can sense and usually understand the feelings and viewpoints of playmates and respond to them.

Relations between infants and their mothers is the first of a growing number that occur in the first few months of life. *Attachment,* a term used by psychologists to refer to a social-based relationship with mom (as compared to a biological relationship often termed *bonding*), comes through actions of both moms and their newborns. Bowlby (1969) many years ago identified seven behaviors (reflexes initially) of infants that connect them with their mothers: crying, cooing, babbling, smiling, clinging, non-nutritional sucking, and following. All help bring the two people into closer contact. Particularly the first four actions bring moms closer to their babies, and the last three bring the infants closer to moms. As the process of providing satisfiers for the baby expands, more attachment to the giver occurs; some would say that the attachment grows as the baby gets mom trained Pavlovian style: When the infant cries, Mom comes running.

Thus, through observations of children in the age range of 0–100 months, one can witness the change in the child from *individuation* to *integration,* from "forging of a special place for oneself within the social order" to "maintaining satisfying and productive relations with others and with society-at-large" (Damon, 1983, p. 2). Steps or stages are not so apparent in this process of becoming a relational person, but the change can be observed and documented as a gradual event that occurs over the first eight to nine years of life. Notice that the foundation of becoming a member of relationships is often consumer behavior—giving, receiving, sharing of commercial objects.

Becoming a Boy or Girl

It may seem strange to talk about becoming a girl or a boy. After all, we all know that one is born either a boy or girl. But the infant does not know that and will not realize it for at least two years. Physically, a newborn probably does not look like a girl or a boy to most adults, which is evidenced by the question new moms often get while holding and tending their babies: "Boy or girl?"

It is not until around 24 months that children can distinguish between male and female in others, and it is likely several more months before they can distinguish their own gender. At the point at which children have stable gender identity, they spontaneously develop sex-appropriate values and standards (Kohlberg, 1984). From day one, however, mom and dad have been responding to their new baby as a girl or as a boy, and it is in fact these many social responses that start the baby on the road to genderhood. Pink and blue (for girls and boys, respectively) are introduced even before birth in the forms of baby clothing, bedding, and room furnishings. And after birth, even more of one or the other color is forthcoming, along with many "girl things" or "boy things" to signify or confirm to others the newborn's gender status.

At around 12 months when the baby is beginning to walk and talk, he or she receives more gender grooming in the form of clothing, shoes, toys, and, of course, hair styling. By 24 months the toddler has been firmly cast in a gender role by adults through a wide range of symbols including verbal ones such as naming and referencing—"What a lovely little girl"; "What a handsome little boy." At this point being a boy or a girl is a function of society at least as much as biology. The psychologist William Damon (1983) said it this way:

> Well before the age of three, the young child has been exposed to so much gender-related social feedback that any biologically "pure" behavioral sex differences—if ever they existed—have long since been elaborated, shaped, discouraged, encouraged, or otherwise modified by environmental influences. It is a simple fact, well documented in the psychological

literature, that people respond to boys and girls differently from birth onward. (p. 214)

Two gender-distinguishing activities become noticeable at around age three onward that seem to be more congenital than social in origin: *aggression* among boys; *nurturance* among girls. One might want to call these two characteristics *instincts* or some other term that would indicate that they come with the wiring. Maccoby (1980) confirmed that these features of boys and girls transcend culture and can be witnessed in early childhood play around the world. In any case little boys play in a more "rough-and-tumble" fashion, whereas little girls show a greater propensity to nurture others, particularly those who are younger. These gender characteristics are so expected by parents that, when they appear, they almost act as confirmation, justifying all those boy things and girl things that have been provided the children in their infancy. Once aggression and nurturance are apparent in boys and girls, respectively, much more consumer behavior is determined by these traits with boys asking for and receiving, for example, more sporting goods and girls asking for and receiving more dolls. Notice, again, that consumer behavior on the part of the parents first, then the children, plays a major role in fostering and signifying the children's gender—now and forever.

Identity Formation

Another sequence that can be observed in early childhood, and one that has been given in-depth treatment in the psychoanalytical theories of Erik Erikson (1968) and Margaret Mahler (1968), is the search for *identity*. According to Damon (1983, p. 84), Mahler saw the newborn infant "as akin to a bird's egg within its shell . . . shut off from the external world by his exclusive focus on his own needs and feelings" (which seems like a bit of an exaggeration since a closed system could not change). She called this first level of identity-seeking that occurs during approximately the first month of life *normal autism*, definitely an extreme choice of terms, also. During this time period, infants are so intensely focused on their satisfaction that they cannot separate themselves from the origins of the satisfaction. Thus, on a scale of taker to giver, they are almost 100 percent taker. But in the next level that occurs during the infant's second and third months that Mahler called *separation-individuation*, there is recognition of mother as caretaker even though the boundaries between the two are confusing to the infant for several more months. But in a subsequent stage late in the first year, the infant begins to construct her own body image as one and the body image of mother as another. (Note: If mother—the second most important person in the world—is overweight, this may be the beginning of the child's acceptance of fat, of pairing fat with love, which today might be a very important thought in the search for answers to childhood obesity.) Hence, in separation the baby becomes a person who relates to mother and other caretakers through many acts such as smiling, crying, touching, cooing, and even laughing. This separation from mother into a person is a very slow process; the child vacillates between mother's security and care and the autonomy that the child seems to be seeking. I have documented this pulling-to and pulling-away-from among toddlers who go shopping at the supermarket with their moms. They can be seen racing to the cereal aisle, for example, examining the boxes of cereal, then rushing back to mom and the shopping cart, touching each, then rushing back to the cereal display again (McNeal, 1992, 1999).

Erikson's theory of identity formation is more detailed and more structured than Mahler's and covers the entire life cycle from birth to death in what Erikson called the "eight ages of man" (1950, p. 247). He also referred to these eight ages as psychosocial stages, thus taking a page from his mentor, Sigmund Freud. His first four stages occur before adolescence and are of most interest to our analyses; he usually called them *stages* rather than *phases* or *levels* or *states*. Each stage is based on turning points in the child's psychosocial life, or what Erikson would call *crises*. Each stage also is based on consumer behavior, according to my analysis, and will be pointed out as we briefly consider each stage.

Stage one, which begins at around 12 months of age, is labeled *trust vs. mistrust*. In this stage, infants move from autistic isolation—the inability to relate normally to others—toward recognition of the separateness of the self and others. In order for this change to take place, babies must trust others, mainly mom, to deliver satisfaction to their needs at the right time in the right amount. At this age infants learn that they are distinct individuals who are in a trusting relationship with other individuals. According to Erikson, if mom does not regularly deliver the satisfiers desired by the baby, the baby will continue to live in a somewhat autistic world. Fundamental and apparent in this event is the consumer role of mother in providing the child with what she wants under the proper circumstances. Thus, the foundation of the relationship in which caretaker as giver and child as taker is firmly established will lend confidence to the child that she can want something and expect to receive it from parents. This is a natural beginning of the child's direct influence on parental purchase behavior.

In stage two that transpires at around two to three years old, the toddler takes his separateness to a new level when he begins to express his autonomous free will—take more control of his life. Erikson called this stage *autonomy vs. shame and doubt*. At this time the children begin to assert control—a time that parents often call the "terrible twos"—but face growing controls and regimen from the parents. Both cannot win, so the parents sense that they must relinquish some control to the children, and if they do, and if they do it in the right amount, children will sense that they can stand on their own two feet, that they have a life that they can determine. However, this is another crisis time, according to Erikson, and if the children fail, they experience much doubt about their abilities to do things on their own, to choose and guide their own future. At this time the "gimmes," as parents would call them, are occurring at a rapid pace concurrent with the children's development of language—the children are making what seems like constant requests (demands) for things. Both children and parents are trying to outlast the other in getting their views out front with one-word declarations ("No" and "Yes"). For example, when mom and child go shopping together, research shows the child of this age is apt to make at least a dozen requests while in the food or toy store. Erikson's psychoanalytical theory would suggest that if relatively few of the child's requests are met, the child will wallow in a sense of self-doubt and not advance in identity formation. On the other hand, if mom and child usually have a meeting of the minds on these matters and the resolution provides the child with a feeling of being in charge of her will to be herself, then she gradually advances to the next stage that begins at around age four.

Stage three, the *initiative vs. guilt* stage, normally takes place at approximately ages four and five, or around the time the child enters kindergarten. At this time the child has the power of language and locomotion in place and uses them to perform in the roles of other people—pretending to be a race car driver, a teacher, a parent. By trying out new possibilities for himself, he has an opportunity to advance his identity, to learn that he can be more than he is now. In effect, the child begins anticipating performing in the roles of older children, even adults; of accomplishing more as a person than he does now; of being more of an influential, more powerful person, if you might. Chances are at this time the child is asking for things at the store that support these new images of self, for example, a Spiderman uniform or a grown-up video game. If these role performances are not supported, if they are inhibited, then according to Erikson, a sense of guilt will accompany these mental ventures and the child will gradually draw back. My research shows that most parents understand this experimenting at role behavior of their children, and while parents may ponder its benefits to them, they usually respond positively to the children's requests for such items as a Barbie doll or a set of army uniforms for her.

The final childhood stage, although not the final stage in Erikson's model, is the *industry vs. inferiority* stage that begins at around age five or six and continues through elementary school. Thus, it if often referred to as the *school-age stage*. During this period children acquire skills and knowledge that permit them to achieve some significant accomplishments—they do not have to imagine them; they can do them. Children may discover an ability to run fast or ride a bicycle fast. Or rather than special motor abilities they may achieve various academic skills such as reading, math operations, or an understanding of science. Children at this time are exposed to many instructions from teachers and parents that may reveal special talents. For example, the little girl at the beginning of Chapter 1 who took *zheng* lessons after school did so because she and her parents had discovered some raw musical talent in her repertoire of abilities during kindergarten. And she was quick to brag about this to the researcher who interviewed her and her parents. During this period the child is not putting away play, which is so important to the preschooler, but often subordinating it to "work." Thus, the child becomes more than just an individual—for example, she becomes a fourth-grade girl—and feels and represents herself as a musician ("I play the *zheng*") or an athlete ("I'm on the volleyball team"). On the other hand, if children are not permitted to fulfill these roles they are assuming, or if they are not successful, they may be made to feel inferior, particularly at a time when they regularly compare themselves with others in their grade and/or gender. Fulfilling these actual roles requires many commercial objects that most likely the children may select and buy with their own money, money provided mostly by parents. Likewise, and regrettably, the inferior feelings that may result from failure to succeed in this stage may generate many consumer purchases, too, but their purpose will often be to temporarily bolster the inferior child with such treats as cookies and ice cream or possibly weapons to make them feel equal to or more superior to socially successful cohorts.

Cognitions of Self

While Erikson's stages outline the normal parts of identity development, they do not embrace a number of other significant variations in identity development. These variations merit consideration for their implications for consumer behavior. One important aspect of identity development is *knowledge of self* that arises simultaneously with knowledge of others. In order for a child to socialize with others, the child must be an individual who is known to the child. While this sounds awkward, the plain fact of the matter is that children are not really people in a social sense until they can see themselves as people, as specific, describable persons. Only then can they relate to others who must also be defined in order for the relationships to develop. Having an image of oneself means that the child is aware of characteristics of the self and can describe them and relate to them. In turn, by having an identifiable self, a child can relate to others.

Self-identity that grows in stages in childhood, as shown in Erikson's theory, is normally a result of interactions with others and often uses input from others. But the construction is the individual's. Early and late childhood research by John Broughton (1978) in which he asked children about the self, the mind, and the body produced a development sequence of sorts of the self. Broughton found that in early childhood, specifically in preschool years, children perceive the self as strictly made up of physical characteristics. At this age children believe the *self is the body*. So, they distinguish themselves from other children on the basis of their physical features and the commercial objects they own that are related to the body. For example, a four-year-old might see himself different from a playmate because he has blond hair or he is tall or he wears running shoes. By around 100 months, the children begin to separate the self from the body and its parts and see it as part of the mind. This separation is not complete until the beginning of teen years. As a mental concept—covert rather than overt—the children say the self is made up of feelings about themselves that are different from those held by others.

Another very important characteristic of self not really covered by the model of Erikson is its evaluation, what is often called *self-esteem*. It is a combined result of the *direction* of feelings about self—positive or negative—and *degree* of feelings—high or low. Thus, children's attitudes toward their self can be measured—there seem to be many instruments for this—and placed on a scale of some sort indicating high to low self-esteem. (See, for instance, Kail, 1979.) The existence of self-esteem apparently accompanies the development of the self and therefore changes over time. Self-esteem as a concept is given much importance by psychologists because it is associated with so many other thoughts and behaviors. For example, it manifests itself in a child's posture and speech, and it is related to success in school, to life satisfaction, mental health, work performance, and social relationships. Its causes are many, also, according to years of research and include body stature, health, and particularly parents' rearing styles. It is a major influence on children's consumer behavior through which products are sought that fit with either low or high self-esteem. For instance, children with high self-esteem may emphasize it by wearing fashionable and brightly colored clothing, while those with low self-esteem may overindulge themselves with food and drink—and get fat—which ironically usually lowers self-esteem even more.

Cognitions of Others

Cognition is not a social act, per se, but *thinking about what others are thinking* is. How children react to others is in great part due to what they think is going on in the minds of others. Recalling the dichotomy of egocentrism-altruism, we are reminded that at an early point in the life of children, others are not thought of at all, and certainly not others' mindsets. But that changes and the thoughts and views of others gradually come under consideration by children. In fact, it is the responses of others to a child that help the child to construct the self, what is sometimes called the *reflected self* or *looking-glass self*, terms that originated with Charles Cooley more than a century ago (1902).

Social cognitions—thoughts about others and their mental activities—among children begin once they reach the stage of object permanence somewhere between 8 and 12 months in what Piaget (1954) called the *sensorimotor period.* Object permanence occurs when children are able to realize that physical and social objects exist on their own and apart from any action of the children. Only when there is an awareness of independent others—social objects—can children develop attitudes and knowledge about them. But this does not happen quickly. The egocentrism of children lasts at least until they enter elementary school—although it ebbs in preschool—and at around the first grade they can begin to understand the views of others and take those views into consideration.

This set of mental activities that we are calling social cognitions was termed *role-taking* by Selman (1976) in the sense that children put themselves in the shoes of others in order to understand the thinking of others. Selman configured this ability into a set of five stages, zero to four. The first stage, stage zero (3–6 years), is presumably called this (zero) to reflect the fact that children cannot perceive the thoughts of others even though they are aware that others exist. They can even name some of the feelings of others such as when they ask a playmate if an injury hurts. However, in stage one (6–8 years) a child becomes aware that others can have interpretations of an event that are different from his. He may, for example, see a TV actor as funny while a playmate does not. But the child does not have the cognitive abilities to see the relationships of the two feelings or to analyze the feelings of the other.

Starting in Selman's stage two (8–10 years)—at around 100 months—the child begins to see the perspective of another. She, for example, can see that a playmate has a viewpoint different from hers and she can see that the playmate can see her viewpoint. But the child is usually not yet able to coordinate or reconcile these two different views; they simply exist in a sequence. However, in stage three (10–12 years) the child is able to consider simultaneously the two viewpoints of himself and another child and can begin to see the two viewpoints from that of a third person. Thus, he may say that he can see how his playmate and he disagree about a matter but friends sometimes disagree. This is truly consideration and understanding of the feelings of others. Selman adds one more stage, stage four (12–15 years), to reflect differences in thinking that are due to the social system. The child can see the differences, understand them, and explain them in terms of the other's background or social setting. For example, the child might see that her classmate expresses a different view because she is from another culture.

If one compares children's gift-giving in stage one with that in stage three or four, one can see some of the effects of this development of perspective taking. For example, an 8-year-old might give his pal a birthday gift of a video game that he likes and "knows," therefore, that his friend will like it. But at age 12 he is more likely to give his friend a video game that he knows his friend will like because he knows his friend's tastes in video games.

CURRENT ISSUES IN CONSUMER DEVELOPMENT (#3)

Peer Power and Its Role in Consumer Development among Preschool Children

Would a mother want her child under the influence of other children twice his age who have little moral structure, possess a poor sense of values, are self-absorbed and not at all concerned about her child's welfare? That is precisely the situation daily for millions of infants and toddlers who are placed in daycare centers where more influence may come from one-on-one interactions with other children than from the spread-thin caretakers who are responsible for maintaining order among growing numbers of children.

The influence of peers on children's behavior patterns has been a topic of research and discussions among developmentalists since the 1960s. But what's new is the increased potency of this influence and its movement down the age ladder into preschool environments such as daycare centers that house over 12 million children under age five. Taking cues from contemporaries is a natural behavior of humans. Among adults it may be called "keeping up with the Joneses" when referring to consumer behavior patterns. Moreover, it is expected of teens who flee from parents to the comfort of cohorts, and maybe of tweens who often use teens as models. But parents and social scientists are surprised by this behavior among one- to three-year-olds who normally pay little attention to others. According to famous child development theorists such as Sigmund Freud and Erik Erikson, children at this age ordinarily take most of their behavioral cues from their parents.

In order to understand the interpersonal influences on consumer behavior of today's children, we must factor in a major change in social structure and social dynamics—pass-along parenting. With most millennium moms working and working longer hours, they increasingly pass along their children at a very early age to others, such as daycare centers. Thus, the children have much less time or opportunity to learn parents' behavior patterns and values than the children who grew up, say, in Freud's or Erikson's time. Never mind the quality-time argument; quantity of time matters for toddlers whose learning equipment is still in development along with the rest of their bodies. Thus, as the children look around at the behavior of others to find out what's appropriate for a kid, they see other kids much more and parents much less than was once the case.

Social learning theory that appeared in the 1960s, such as that of Albert Bandura, says that much of human behavior is acquired through the observation of others, and further, children often copy minute details of the behavior patterns of parents, including voice inflections and posture. And they do. But increasingly we hear parents say about some of their toddlers' undesirable behavior patterns that they must have learned it at daycare. The reason is that some millions of moms are placing their kids in out-of-home environments such as nursery schools and daycare centers—in the care of others—where the kids observe and copy minute details of whomever they're around—and that's mostly kids five and under. So, whereas much of their day used to be spent with parents until they went to primary school, kids now are in the company of other kids starting as infants and toddlers.

Not all of what young children learn at daycare is undesirable. One New York City mom who placed her two-year-old in a daycare center reported that she was awed by how quickly he became toilet trained in the new environment. Her explanation was that he saw others his age wearing big-boy pants—character-branded big-boy pants—and he did not want to be humiliated by being seen in his baby diapers. So, through observing and imitating his peers, he achieved in a month what usually takes moms many months. In this case relinquishing some of the parenting function to others—to other children—relieved a mom of a difficult and frustrating task.

Positive peer pressure at preschool may accomplish what parents cannot. Take the case of speaking the language properly. Foreign-born moms often report that their little children learn properly spoken English at daycare—from other children, more than from caretakers. In fact, the parents may learn appropriate language from their toddlers who learned it from other toddlers.

But all too often the payoff is not so positive. The consumer behavior patterns of those children at daycare who are imitated may not meet the approval of parents. Older kids may own more expensive things than some parents can afford, such as hand-held video games, or they simply have things that parents don't want their kids to have such as message tee shirts. Yet, when toddlers see desirable possessions of others, they naturally follow with requests for them to parents. Also, older kids may be experimenting with dangerous products such as skateboards or fattening products such as colas and unknowingly pass on these undesirable behaviors to younger ones.

Older kids may also use coarse language that they have learned from still-older kids, and it is copied by the younger ones. For example, two-year-olds may copy four-year-olds who learned some of their behavior from still-older children. This cascade of bad habits may even have had its start among elementary-schoolers who, for example, can be observed from the daycare's playground. What the little children learn is, of course, filtered through what they have learned from their parents. However, it is increasingly likely that they are put out of the house so early that they have not really received a foundation of right and wrong. Two- and three-year-old children do not possess a moral structure to help them defend against ideas from other children. That is why watching television without parents is risky. Toddlers also may copy behavior of older children in television programs—television programs chosen by parents or daycare personnel as "baby-sitters."

Older children at daycare may be the source of another socially undesirable behavior: violence. Kids who go through the "terrible twos," as they may be termed—the fits and moodiness that often characterize two- and three-year-olds—begin to act more aggressively toward parents. Some children's antics at daycare reinforce this behavior, making it more logical to the egocentric child who cannot yet reason in terms of the perspective of others. One mom who controls what her preschooler watches on TV realized that her efforts were fruitless since other children at daycare were permitted to watch those forbidden programs and passed on the bad features of it to her kid.

In sum, good and bad behavior patterns exogenous to a child's family may be entering the household through preschool experiences with peers. This is not what busy working parents who are shelling out somewhere between $3,803 and $13,480 a year for daycare need or expect. They may blame the preschools and go through musical chairs of changing them or asking for changes in their personnel. But the plain fact of the matter is that once parents turn over their parenting responsibilities to others—even for just a half-day—they have relinquished their right to decide what their children will learn and from whom they will learn it.

****
Sources: Armour, 2006; Harris, 1999; Holcomb, 1999.

DISCUSSION

The prepurchase, purchase, and postpurchase activities of children that in total constitute their consumer behavior almost always occur in a social setting. Thus, children's consumer behavior is dependent to some extent on others by being learned from others, aided by others, directed by others, performed by others and with others. In effect, the extent and nature of becoming a consumer are a result of the environment in which one is born and grows—the environment being made up of two domains: the physical and the social. In this chapter we have described the social domain of the children's environment and have indicated its role in consumer development.

The opposite is also the case. Consumer behavior of children and significant others influences their social environment. As newborns become social beings, they also becomes consumers; as newborns become consumers, they become social beings. *Consumer behavior is thus the medium of social development and its resulting social relations.* What children become is in great part determined by consumer behavior of the children and those in their social setting. Consider Howie, again, the child who discovered Spiderman at his daycare center. Apparently, Howie saw Spiderman on the belongings of another child who attended his daycare. The social setting of the daycare center and the children there contributed to Howie's becoming a social being—and a consumer. By interacting with the peer who displayed Spiderman—a consumer behavior act of that peer—Howie formed a social relationship with the peer. The two children connected. Howie's attention to the Spiderman symbol displayed by the peer was a consumer act—a tekram—and it was followed by another: Howie's asking his mom for Spiderman items in the store—to which he gave his attention. While this is a relatively simple formation of a social relationship, it is also the formation of some consumer behavior patterns. It is not easy to separate the social and the commercial in this case, just as the two are so often intertwined.

If we knew more about the display of the Spiderman symbol at daycare, we could produce more social and commercial analyses from this one event. For example, assume that the Spiderman symbol was displayed on the shirt of a little boy Howie's age. Chances are the boy was trying to say something about himself through his Spiderman shirt—maybe just that he likes Spiderman or maybe that he saw the Spiderman movie. One click back, it may be that his parents bought him the shirt as a way of saying something about him, for example, to express his boyness. Another possibility is that the little boy, like Howie, saw the shirt in a store and asked for it, and his mother bought it for him as a bonding gesture. Note the possibility of several tekrams underlying the social connections between Howie and his classmate: the boy asking his mom for the shirt while in a store; his mother buying the shirt for personal reasons; his wearing of the shirt at daycare; and Howie's seeing it, wanting it, and asking for it. Note also the social acts intertwined with the consumer acts—between the classmate and his mother, between the classmate and Howie, and between Howie and his mother.

Now, if we can transpose this social/commercial scenario to a child's birth and development, we can begin to appreciate the close association of social behavior and consumer behavior. Consider mom giving a bottle of formula to her newborn. This is the beginning of their getting acquainted, of becoming family. In this case the social relationship does not yet exist; it is anticipated by the mother. Within a few weeks it will become a conditioned relationship. The baby will cry, and mom will respond with a bottle. Concurrent with feeding, mom is also providing warmth through clothing and comfort through bedding. Again, the child does not yet know all this is being provided by mom since she does not yet separate others and other things from self. But the conditioned relationship grows as the two communicate through sounds and touch, primarily. This *conditioned relationship*, as I am terming it, is based almost totally on consumer behavior of the infant and mom. For example, when the infant cries (communicates need), mom gives her a bottle, after which, the infant coos (communicates satisfaction), and mom smiles and cuddles with her. This CB pattern will continue to the point that the infant can use words to express her needs and need satisfaction, and mom will also use words to confirm their relationship. As noted, in addition to mom providing food, she also provides clothing, bedding, and play items—all acts of consumer behavior by both her and her baby. Thus, this adult-child relationship between mother and child has a consumer behavior foundation.

If we examine the motives for each person entering the relationship, we can be sure that in the case of the infant, the motives are biology based, whereas for adults it could likely be described as psychologically based. The baby is trying to survive, while mom is trying to help him survive, to be comfortable and happy, and to form a mother-child relationship that she needs. She is trying to please her infant; later the child will do things to try to please mom—a habit pattern gleaned from mom's behavior. This kind of relationship, this adult-child relationship, will eventually be extended by mom and the child to other adults such as grandmother, and to other children such as playmates. When one steps back and takes a hard look at all this mutual behavior, it is difficult to call it social behavior or consumer behavior. It is both. The social and commercial are one.

As the child becomes a person—a social being—and her social setting expands to include playmates and classmates, she begins initiating more social interactions. In order to introduce herself to others, she utilizes consumer behavior to tell them who she is. The self has developed, and it is the self that does the interacting, so through CB the child can express to others who she is. Of course, she can and does use words now that she has some command of the language: "I am the best speller in the second grade" and "I take violin lessons." But some of these words plus other symbols are expressed through such CB as placing brands on her shirt, shoes, and coat and displaying brands on her bicycle, musical instrument, and school supplies. Thus, brands may be used as another means of conveying to others who children are. By the time the children reach 100 months or so, shopping malls are often used as a means to create and cement social relationships. "Hanging out" at the mall supposedly says a lot about tween boys and girls—something about their tastes, their income, their maturity.

Another important point to be made about the child's social relationships is that they provide the medium through which *culture* is passed on to the child. In fact, much of the consumer behavior that occurs in adult-child and peer-child relationships is culture inspired. The foods that the child eats, the clothing the child wears, the toys with which the child plays, all are probably culture based. They are consumer behavior, but they are culturally determined and passed on to children through their social relationships—who will pass them on to their children 20 years later with a few modifications.

Just which set of social relationships—those with adults or those with other children—is most important in determining consumer behavior patterns is not easy to nail down. Certainly, the basic patterns of consumer behavior learned the first year of life—eating, sleeping, wearing clothes, using soap in the bath—all are taught by parents and other caretakers. But it would be easy to say that they are all modified by peers later on, and that would be equally correct. Plenty of theorists out there would say that the influence of parents has now become subordinated to that of peers (e.g., Harris, 1999). If one looks at it from the perspective of the millennium child, such theorists are probably on firm ground. Given that there are so many reasons for the parents to be separated from their children—work, social obligations, personal time, schooling of parents and children—the time spent with children today is generally much less than that spent by the children with others, particularly if one includes such media as TV, Internet, and cell phone. But while the parents would say that it is not the quantity of time but the quality of time that matters, such semantics probably no longer hold much water. Interestingly, the parents also say that their tween children spend too much time with their friends, particularly certain friends. So, the time element must be very important in social relations, whether according to the research talk of theorists or the double-talk of parents. Access of one to the other surely determines the amounts and kinds of influence parents and peers have in developing children. As parents find more reasons to be away from their children, the children are placed in proximity to other children—at daycare, kindergarten, school, organized athletics. Thus, access to today's children is growing for peers, declining for parents.

REFERENCES

Ainsworth, M. D. S. (1989). Attachments beyond infancy. *American Psychologist, 44*, 709–716.

Armour, S. (2006, April 18). High costs of child care can lead to lifestyle changes, adjustments, *USA Today*, pp. B1, B2.

Bowlby, J. (1969). *Attachment and Loss.* New York: Basic Books.

Broughton, J. (1978). Development of concepts of self, mind, reality, and knowledge. *New Directions for Child Development, 1,* 75–100.

Cooley, C. H. (1902). *Human Nature and the Social Order.* New York: Charles Scribners.

Crane, W. (1992). *Theories of Development: Concepts and Applications.* Englewood Cliffs, NJ: Prentice-Hall, Inc.

Damon, W. (1983). *Social and Personality Development: Infancy through Adolescence.* New York: W. W. Norton & Company.

Erikson, E. H. (1950). *Childhood and Society.* New York: W. W. Norton & Company.

Erikson, E. H. (1968). *Identity: Youth and Crisis.* New York: W. W. Norton & Company.

Harris, J. R. (1999). *The Nurture Assumption: Why Children Turn Out the Way They Do.* New York: Touchstone.

Hartup, W. (1979). The social worlds of childhood. *American Psychologist, 34,* 944–950.

Holcomb, B. (1999, August). The power of peers. *Parenting,* 110–119.

James, W. (1950). *The Principles of Psychology.* New York: Dover.

Kail, R. (1979). *The Development of Memory in Children.* San Francisco: W. H. Freeman and Company.

Kemper, T. D. (1968, February). Reference groups, socialization and achievement. *American Sociological Review,* 30–39.

Kluger, J. (2006, July 10). The new science of siblings, *Time,* 47–55.

Kohlberg, L. (1984). *The Psychology of Moral Development: Essays on Moral Development* (V. 2), San Francisco: Harper & Row.

McNeal, J. U. (1982). *Consumer Behavior: An Integrative Approach.* Boston: Little, Brown and Company.

McNeal, J. U. (1992). *Kids as Customers: A Handbook of Marketing to Children.* New York: Lexington Books.

McNeal, J. U. (1999). *The Kids Market: Myth and Realities.* Ithaca, NY: Paramount Market Publishers.

Maccoby, E. (1980). *Social Development: Psychological Growth and the Parent-Child Relationship.* New York: Harcourt Brace Jovanovich.

Mahler, M. S. (1968). *On Human Symbiosis and the Vicissitudes of Individuation: Infantile Psychosis* (vol. 1). New York: International Universities Press.

Maslow, A. H. (1943, July). A theory of human motivation. *Psychological Review, 50,* 370–396.

Piaget, J. (1954). *The Construction of Reality in the Child.* New York: Basic Books.

Poris, M. (2005). Understanding what fun means to today's kids. *Young Consumers, 7* (Quarter 4), 14–24.

Selman, R. L. (1976). Social-cognitive understanding: A guide to educational and clinical practice. In T. Lickona (ed.), *Moral Development and Behavior: Theory, Research, and Social Issues.* New York: Holt, Rinehart & Winston.

PART III

THE RELATIONSHIP BETWEEN CONSUMER DEVELOPMENT AND THE DEVELOPMENT OF THE PERSON

Behavior is a function of the person (P) and the environment (E). In this part of the book, consumer development from two perspectives of the person is examined. Chapter 4 will treat the development of the physical person, including the body and motor skills. Chapter 5 will delve into the development of the mental person, including cognitive skills and language.

This watercolor of children playing outside—note the birds and grass—was done by artist Chen XueMei of Chengdu, China. She was trying to capture the children in old China playing a game called Eagle Catches Chicks, one of many games played by children of low-income families that do not require any commercial products except shoes and clothing. The idea of the game is for the chicks to hide behind the mother hen—the girl extending her arms to protect her chicks—so that the Eagle—the little boy who is trying to reach and tag the chicks—cannot get them. Games such as this contribute much to children's physical and mental development.

4

PHYSICAL/MOTOR DEVELOPMENT AND ITS RELATIONSHIP TO CONSUMER DEVELOPMENT

Wei Shen's Fast-Food Purchase

Management of the KFC (Kentucky Fried Chicken) restaurant on the square at Chengdu, China, decided to target children as consumers more effectively by installing a stairway at its counter. This was an unusual effort to facilitate purchases by children, and one not seen in any other fast-food restaurant anywhere in a large city in China. The idea was to accommodate those toddlers who were unable to reach the counter and therefore place their order and give their money to the cashier. Management of the restaurant became aware of the rapidly growing purchase potential of children ages 4–12 from an article written in a Chinese marketing magazine. The article reported, for instance, that Chinese mothers were increasingly permitting and encouraging their children— usually one child per family, by government policy—to learn to make purchases on their own at an early age. Further, the article stated that some four- and five-year-olds were actually making purchases or co-purchases with a parent at McDonald's, the restaurant's chief competitor, although it was difficult for them to make a purchase due to the height of the counter. The article went on to say that often parents held their children in their arms or sat them on the counter while the children made purchases, or what might be more correctly described as co-purchases.

Once constructed, the meter-wide wood stairway consisted of three steps and a hand rail on each side. When children stood on the top step, their waist was about even with the top of the counter—comparable to adults standing at the counter. The unpainted stairway looked a bit out of place with the colorful fixtures in the restaurant, and it had no signs on it to suggest its use. But little kids immediately figured it out and started using the stairway, and showed in various ways that they loved the idea—the special treatment. Parents seemed generally responsive to it, also.

One recorded example of the use of the stairway by a young consumer is as follows. A father and mother gave money to their five-year-old son and urged him to go to the counter and make a purchase at the KFC restaurant while they waited at a table. They also told him to use the stairs. (Later in conversation it was discovered that an additional reason for suggesting he use the stairs was so that he would not have to stand in the long lines common at fast-food restaurants in China.) The child used the stairway while mom shouted instructions in a somewhat showy manner from the back of the restaurant. This approach worked, and he was applauded by his parents when he returned with several items on a tray and the correct change. The parents agreed to talk to a Chinese interviewer about this event. When asked if that was the child's first independent purchase in the restaurant, they said it was. When asked if making the purchase was the child's idea or theirs, the mother and father responded at the same time saying it was the child's idea and that he had made co-purchases with them at a convenience store near their apartment. The father said that he had pushed the child to make the purchase. Usually, he noted, the child sat at a table while one of the parents went to the counter, stood in line, and made the purchase. He added that the child was still learning the use of money and did not want to be embarrassed by making a mistake.

Both parents indicated they were pleased with the outcome and that the child would be encouraged to do it more. "He has to learn to buy things that his father or I never had when we were children," the mother said in her language. Then she added, "I think I made my first purchase when I was around 10-years-old—of some cucumbers and cabbage at the (street) market after school. I did it to help my parents who both worked on a farm all day." During this interview their little boy, whose name was Wei Shen, listened attentively, smiled each time his name was mentioned, and alternatively ate among chicken wings, French fries, and ice cream while occasionally sipping a Pepsi-Cola through a straw. In this case the parents did not have the child buy anything for them. They nibbled on the wings that Wei Shen had eaten and one or two fries. This is a common practice in China due to the relatively high cost of fast food there and the fact that many adults do not like much of it. When the interviewer asked if it was difficult for him to make the food purchase, Wei Shen

*responded with a simple, "No." The smile on his face while
looking at the food on his tray revealed how proud he felt. When
asked if he liked the idea of the stairs being placed at the counter
to assist children, he answered, "It makes it easier to see
everything"—reminding us of the child's perspective in an adult
world.*

INTRODUCTION

Before children can develop into functioning consumers, they have to
develop physically. Their bodies have to grow, and their motor abilities have
to mature. For example, they have to be tall enough to reach the counter
at a convenience store or fast-food restaurant—as in the case of Wei Shen.
Also, children have to have enough motor skills to climb the stairs while
holding on to the rail and the appropriate motor skills to walk down the
stairs with a tray of food and beverages in both hands. Sounds easy for us
adults, but it can be monumental for a four- or five-year-old. In fact, very
few tekrams—units of consumer behavior—can be performed by children
without substantial physical and motor development. These are the topics
of this chapter, and while physical and motor development occurs simultaneously, we will give them somewhat separate treatment in order to highlight the relevance of each to consumer behavior development. Another
point that should be repeated here is that body development is also intertwined with mind development, the topic of the next chapter. Therefore, we
will allude to the mind when talking about the body. We must, for it is
through body actions that infants fill their minds with knowledge and
understanding of the components of their new world. The plain fact of the
matter is that body development is tied not only to mind development but
also to sensory development, social development, speech development, and
again, consumer development. This is apparent in what adults tell their children, such as, "When you get as big as your sister, you will go to school like
her"; "In another year you will be big enough to ride a bicycle"; "You have
to wait until you get big before you can ride in the back seat"; "You are
getting big enough to stay by yourself"; "When you are bigger, you can help
me in the kitchen."

The essential relationships between motor behavior and consumer
behavior are these: (1) All motor activity facilitates consumer behavior; (2)
most motor activity develops as a result of consumer behavior; and (3) most
motor behavior is consumer behavior. The plain fact of the matter is that
any and all motor actions may be classified as tekrams—as consumer acts—
thus demonstrating the fact that at least in industrial societies most visible
human behavior is consumer behavior. Consider these randomly selected
motor activities.

Walking—To a store, through a store, to the refrigerator

Standing—At the counter of a fast-food restaurant, in the
    shower, waiting for a bus

Reaching—For a displayed item, for food on the pantry shelf, for
    a book on the shelf

Looking—Moving eyes side to side watching a tennis game, a
    video game, a movie

Gripping—A toy, milk bottle, buttons on clothing

Bending over—To smell a cake on display, to pick up a ball, to
    play hopscotch

Pushing/pulling—Toys, handles on vending machines, the
    refrigerator door

Kicking—A football, soccer ball, a door

Manipulating—Chop sticks, fork and knife, hand-held video game

Thus, behavior of the body is intertwined with consumer behavior and rarely can be separated as we will do here for examination and description.

PHYSICAL GROWTH

When American babies are born, they weigh an average of slightly over seven pounds (7.5 for boys, 7.1 for girls). Their *weight* typically doubles within five months, and by their first birthday it usually has tripled. By two years old, children's average weight is four times their birth weight, and before they enter elementary school, they will put on nearly five pounds a year. As for their length—we usually call it *height* after they can walk—they start out at around 20 inches, by the end of the first year they are at 30 inches, and by their second birthday they average three feet tall. (Once children reach age two, we normally speak of their height in feet rather than inches.) From then until they reach the first grade, they will grow almost 3 inches a year. "When you get big, you can go to the store by yourself," one first-grader told me, reminding us that in addition to know-how it takes physical stature to perform many consumer behavior acts. By the time this child completes the first grade, chances are he will have walked through supermarkets hundreds of times with his parents, selected a couple of thousand products and placed them in a shopping cart that he once sat in, including several hundred boxes of cereal, and may even have bicycled alone to a nearby convenience store for a snack. Of course, all this growth requires increasing amounts of food including cereal and snacks, but also clothing, shoes, bedding, and school supplies, which are many more reasons for parents and children to do even more shopping.

Growth is not at the same rate or same time for all body parts (Payne and Isaacs, 1999). The head starts out disproportionately larger, consisting of one-quarter of the total body, then one-fifth at age two, and one-sixth at age six. In order to raise her relatively large head, the infant will first have to develop some neck and shoulder muscles. The lower regions of the body quickly catch up with the head, reflecting what is called the *cephalocaudal principle* of growth. From Greek and Latin roots referring to head-to-tail, this principle dictates that body growth follows a pattern that begins with the head and proceeds down to the rest of the body. For instance, the organs in the head develop before the trunk that develops before the legs and feet—a child can see and hear long before she can sit up and walk. Another growth principle, the *proximodistal principle,* dictates the development of the body from the center outward. In this case, the trunk grows before the arms and the arms before the hands and fingers. Of course, the hands and fingers have to develop in order to hold food and toys, and the feet and toes have to develop before baby can walk or run through the toy section of a store. That is, there must be body development before there can be much motor development, and there must be both before there can be much development of consumer behavior patterns.

While the rate of growth from age two decelerates compared with infancy, between two and four the toddler doubles her birth length and adds at least five pounds per year while at the same time decreasing her fatty tissue. Thus, the child adds a lot of muscle between two and four, mainly as a result of walking, running, and playing during every waking hour. There is a noticeable change in body proportions between two and four. The chest becomes larger than the stomach and the stomach gradually protrudes less than it did at age two. Between ages two and four, the toddler becomes less chubby and roundish. By the time the child reaches kindergarten, she has body proportions closely resembling those of the first-grader. No longer are the head and abdomen out of proportion, and the arms and legs look like they belong to that body.

Body mass index (BMI) is a measure of the relationship between weight and height and is directly related to fatness. It is also related to a wide range of diseases including diabetes, hypertension, and cardiovascular diseases. The mean BMI for children at age 2 is 16.1 for girls and 16.3 for boys. It tends to decline during the preschool years and then starts increasing gradually around the first grade to 16.4 for girls and 16.6 for boys at age 8. But then it really takes off and reaches a mean of 19.6 for boys and 20.1 for girls at age 13. However, around 20–25 percent of elementary school children are overweight, and about 15 percent are obese—with a BMI of 26–28. Consumer behavior, according to the authorities on the topic, is the culprit, specifically, consuming of fat-laden and sedentary products—eating chips and watching TV, for instance. We will say more about this later, much more, because it is a very serious matter due to its production of deadly diseases—in children and adults.

Concurrent with the apparent changes in the body are some less apparent but major changes in the *nervous system* that is composed of the brain and the nerves that flow throughout the body and makes motor development possible. Neurologists say that infants are born with between 100 and 200 billion neurons, the basic nerve cells of the nervous system, and no more develop after birth (Eliot, 1999). In fact, during the first few years of life, there is a pruning of these neurons apparently involving those that are not needed. (Nobody knows for sure why some neurons are not needed after birth except that they were needed for dealing with womb-life.) There is growth in the size of the neurons that remain as they become coated with *myelin*, a fatty substance that helps to insulate them and speed the transmission of nerve impulses. Myelination is absolutely necessary before the child's motor system can function properly. Thus, the infant's brain rapidly puts on weight; on average, it triples its weight in the first 24 months, reaching 75 percent of adult weight. As input is made to the brain by the child, the neurons increase their networks and quickly become amazingly complex. These networks at this point are in large part the results of motor behavior (discussed in the next section). As the nervous system fires up the child's muscles, the muscles, along with the sensory system, send information back to the brain that is stored and modified frequently. At some point soon the brain will accumulate patterns of information—called *schema* in the next chapter—that direct the muscles in crawling, walking, and riding a tricycle, to note only a few of the motor feats during the first two years.

By the time children are 100 months old—the age at which they are first considered bona fide consumers—they are around 50 inches tall and weigh somewhere around 60 pounds—girls normally around 10 percent less than boys. They can reach the average one-meter high counter at any fast-food restaurant and mass merchandising store, but probably not the 1.3-meter cosmetic counter at most department stores that was designed strictly for adults. In the latter case, it appears that in the eyes of some retailers the size of the customer is a measure of her economic value. Maybe in another decade or two—if they have not completely disappeared—department stores will install steps at their cosmetic counters—as was done at the KFC mentioned in the beginning of this chapter—or lower a portion of the counter in order to attract some of those millions of dollars spent by tweens (8–12-year-olds) on cosmetics at other stores.

MOTOR DEVELOPMENT

Motor development is not a separate aspect of physical development, per se, but is treated that way here in order to dwell on some details. Motor development, in simple terms, refers to learning to *move* the body, or parts of the body, with control and efficiency through space (Gallahue, 1976). Movement is necessary in order to *adjust* to one's environment, *control* it, *understand* it, and *communicate* within it (Gallahue, Werner, and Luedke,

1975). According to most theories of cognitive development (discussed in the next chapter), it is through direct motor behavior that infants develop much of their knowledge and intelligence (Phillips, 1969). The title of a recent book by Carol Hannaford (2005) confirms this—*Smart Moves: Why Learning Is Not All in Your Head.* She stated in its first chapter:

> [L]earning, thought, creativity, and intelligence are not processes of the brain alone but of the whole body. Sensations, movements, emotions and brain integrative functions are grounded in the body. (p. 15)

Certainly, motor skills are necessary for children (and adults) to fulfill the consumer role. In fact, motor development leads virtually all consumer development.

Three basic categories of human movement develop in infancy: (1) stability; (2) locomotion; and (3) manipulation. Within these categories the specific bodily movements that develop are usually divided into two forms called gross and fine movements (Payne and Isaacs, 1999). *Gross movements* are those performed by the large muscles of the trunk and limbs for stability and locomotion. *Fine movements* are those performed by the smaller muscles of the body, such as those in the arms and hands, and basically are required for manipulation. In most cases a movement skill is a function of both large and small muscle systems. For instance, in order for children to learn to write, they must control their large shoulder muscles to position their arms before the small muscles of the hands can perform the writing. Basic physical skills such as writing and reading are also basic tekrams that adults take for granted but that cannot take place until much body development transpires over a period of several years.

Stability "refers to the ability to maintain one's balance in relationship to the force of gravity even though the nature of the application of the force may be altered or parts of the body may be placed in unusual positions" (Gallahue, Werner, and Luedke, 1975, p. 11). Actually stability underlies the other two basic categories of human movement, locomotion and manipulation, since neither is effective without a child maintaining her balance. Stability could be viewed also as nonmovement of sorts since it refers to the ability of the child to keep her trunk in one place while she "twists and turns" in the seat of a shopping cart, for example. This is often termed *static balance* when the body is stationary and termed *dynamic balance* when the body is moving but maintaining a certain posture. In regard to the infant, one immediately thinks of her learning enough stability to first sit up alone, turn her head, and survey her new environment (her crib, for instance) and all of its objects—primarily commercial objects—for the first time. In China, where the most widespread transportation mode is the bicycle, one often sees little children riding on the back of the bicycle while mom is "in the driver's seat." But it takes at least a year for a child to learn this stability skill.

The term *locomotion* sounds like movement, and it is. It refers to "changes in the location of the body relative to fixed points on the ground" (Gallahue, Werner, and Luedke, 1975, p. 12). Again, in the case of the infant, it is easy for most parents to recall the excitement of their baby's first steps. But before he takes his first step, he must creep and crawl for probably a year. Thus, locomotion means such gross motor activities as creeping, crawling, walking, skipping, running, jumping, and leaping. For the infant it means more than that. It is escaping the confines of his crib, his room, his home, and going outside and playing with, for example, toy vehicles.

When we think of the term *manipulation,* we can imagine a baby grasping an object with her hand and bringing it to her mouth, or lifting an object and putting it down, such as she might do with her bottle. Manipulation means "giving force to objects and absorbing force from objects by use of the hands and feet" (Gallahue, Werner, and Luedke, 1975, p. 12). Thus, it also includes throwing and catching, kicking and striking, all basic dimensions of most sports and most of the fun activities of children. Some fine motor skills (and tekrams) of buttoning, tying, drawing, and cutting would also be included. One of the first manipulation actions parents witness is the baby playing in bed with her hands and feet and then with her rattle.

PHASES OF MOTOR DEVELOPMENT

Theory and research demonstrate that motor development occurs in stages somewhat like cognitive development does, as discussed in detail in the next chapter. However, in the case of motor development, there are fewer restrictions, fewer limitations in the stages; they do not seem invariant to the extent that cognitive development stages are as proposed and tested by Jean Piaget, the noted Swiss psychologist. Therefore, rather than call them *stages*, those who study them tend to call them *phases*. Lis Eliot (1999, p. 261), a neurologist, said, however, that "the most striking thing about motor development is its predictability" suggesting that the phases are to a great extent *invariant*. She explains, "Virtually every baby from virtually every culture acquires the same fine and gross motor skills in the same consistent sequence." Sequenced motor development among children appears to be the perspective of most parents. For instance, they usually start off their children in four-wheel vehicles such as pedal-cars, then go to three-wheel types such as the standard tricycle, then to a two-wheel bicycle with training wheels, and finally to a bicycle without training wheels. We will describe motor development in accordance to the phases (sequence) prescribed by Gallahue and his colleagues (Gallahue, 1976; Gallahue, Werner, and Luedke, 1975). In all phases of motor development presented here, the three categories of movement—stability, locomotion, manipulation—described previously are examined and will be used as a format.

Reflexive Behavior Phase (–5–12 Months)

Motor behavior actually begins well before birth—just ask any mother—in the form of reflexes that continue into the first year. For example, arm movements probably begin even earlier than what is suggested by this age range (e.g., Eliot, 1999), but there is no indication that these neonatal movements make the arms any more advanced at birth than say the legs or that they produce arm-related consumer behavior very early in life. So, we will mention this fact only in passing since our concern is with motor development as it pertains to consumer behavior after birth and on. *Reflexes* are built-in involuntary movements apparently for survival value and last usually a few weeks or a few months for most of them although a couple continue with us for life such as knee jerks and eye blinks. They are the genetic bases for our movements, and while there is some debate about their role in formal movements, it does appear that they are internalized and used when attempting similar voluntary movements, including the beginning of some consumer behavior patterns. Thus, the first movements of the newborn human are what might be termed *automatic*, not controlled by him or her, and appear to be precursors of purposeful movements.

Table 4-1 is a composite of several developmental researchers that describe briefly the common reflexes. It seems apparent, at least to a layman, that most if not all of them are wired in to aid in the infant's survival after birth. Also, it seems apparent that they are the beginnings of overt consumer behavior patterns. The rooting and sucking reflexes, for instance, surely are intended to provide the newborn with nourishment, whereas such reflexes as stepping, swimming, and eye-blinking are intended to protect. Some theorists argue that some of the reflexes, such as the Moro reflex, are a hand-me-down from nonhuman ancestors (e.g., Prechtl, 1982). Again, there is little value in entering into such debates for the sake of explaining the development of consumer behavior patterns.

TABLE 4-1   Reflex Movements at Birth That Precede Some Consumer Behavior Development

Babinski	Baby's toes fan out, then curl, when bottom of feet is tickled.
Crawl	Baby moves arms and legs in concert when placed on stomach and pressure is applied to feet.
Grasp	Baby closes hand when an object is pressed against palm.
Moro	Baby throws arms outward, then inward when startled by a loud noise.
Rooting	Baby turns head and opens mouth when cheek is touched.
Stepping	Baby attempts walking action when held upright and moved forward.
Sucking	Baby commences sucking action when object is placed on lips.
Swimming	Baby appears to try to swim when held in a body of water.

Sources: Cole, Cole, and Lightfoot, 2005; Feldman, 2000; Kail, 1998.

There are less simple explanations for why most of the reflex movements disappear and are replaced by *voluntary movements*. In fact, some even disappear before their voluntary counterparts appear. But the best explanations are probably by neurologists who say that voluntary motor movements require a lot of wiring up of motor circuits and that takes time. These are normally two-way circuits—from hand to brain and then back to muscles in the hand, for example—as compared to the one-way circuits of the sensory system such as from eyes to brain. Therefore, their construction is much more complex and much slower than those for the sensory system. At the same time that the two-way motor circuits are being formed, the three motor areas of the cerebral cortex gradually are firing up, thus adding more time to motor development. When one realizes how complex all of this is, it is remarkable that so many motor behaviors are learned during the first year or so. We will look at these behaviors in the next phase.

Rudimentary Movement Abilities Phase (0–24 Months)

Notice that the Rudimentary Movement Abilities phase of motor development begins during the first phase, Reflexive Behavior, reflecting the replacement of some reflexes with voluntary movements. Thus, learning to move begins at birth (just as does consumer behavior although it may be random at first). There is a debate here, also, about the role of heredity versus the role of the environment in the development of movement abilities. The hereditarians say that movement is a result of maturation and is unaffected by the environment, whereas environmentalists say essentially the opposite—that movement is a result of experience with the environment. (See Gallahue, Werner, and Luedke, 1975, for a discussion of this debate.) Again, we will avoid such debates since they add little to our goal of exposing the development of consumer behavior patterns. However, we do know that the many tekrams—units of consumer behavior—that children display by age two are mainly a result of experience with physical and social objects in their environment, as we pointed out in the preceding chapters. In fact, it is difficult to refer to consumer behavior *patterns*—the focal point of this book—until children interact with commercial objects enough to form networks of them and their use in their minds.

Rudimentary movements include stability movements such as gaining control over the head and neck, then the trunk, and then the legs in accordance with the cephalocaudal principle of development. Specifically, then, the infant proceeds from a lying position to a sitting position to a standing position. At birth the infant has no control over his oversized head and undersized neck. At the end of approximately one month, however, he can hold his head erect when supported at the base of the neck, and he can lift his chin off his mattress when lying in a prone position. Since his eyes are already working well, he gets a better look at his surroundings with this achievement. He, for example, sees the stuffed animals, perhaps for the first time, that populate his crib. This is not an insignificant event—tekram. The movement of the head and neck producing the discovery of "critters" in the crib probably marks the beginning of some form of interpersonal relations with one or more of them.

During the second month of life, the infant gains some control over the trunk muscles, and by the end of the second month should be lifting her chest and even trying to draw her knees up toward her chest. This movement will eventually lead to locomotion such as scooting backward and forward. By the third or fourth month, she has learned to roll over from her tummy to her back, and by the sixth month, to roll back to her tummy. This stability movement permits a much better view of the objects in her environment and gradually puts some of them within reach.

Sitting does not come easily since it requires complete control over the trunk. At three to four months, the infant gains control over the upper trunk and can sit with some support. By six months the infant usually can sit unassisted after going through many hours of sitting with his head leaning over his chest until he gains greater control over the lower region of the trunk. At this point the job is half-done, so to speak; the infant controls the upper half of his body. Now he has a lot more control over his environment, also, being able to see all the commercial objects that surround him thanks to loving parents and grandparents. Hence, as the baby develops, the environment grows, including the number of physical objects, most of which are commercial objects.

Standing represents the ultimate in stability movements and develops in about the same amount of time as it took to sit. First there is the step of pulling to stand up, which usually comes concurrently with crawling at around 8 or 9 months. Then with mom's hands under her arms to help her with her balance, the infant extends her legs, tenses her leg muscles, and stands on her own two feet for the first time. This act seems to motivate the infant to seek more standing by crawling to and pulling up while holding onto furniture. These acts strengthen the back muscles and soon, at around 11 or 12 months, infants are standing alone without the assistance of objects or others. At this point mom is likely to get very concerned about her baby's shoes—major commercial objects—and the support they offer to that 20-pound body.

Standing develops only after the child has conquered the stability task and learned to grip and let go. First comes creeping after gains in control of the head, neck, and back. Arms usually are first used to move forward while in a prone position; then the legs are recruited for help, with all of this taking place at around six or seven months. Crawling comes a couple of months later in the hand-and-knee position, and it takes some doing, some struggling and frustration to accomplish it—one leg at a time, one arm at a time. Finally, the baby is able to synchronize her arms and legs and really motor. Mom may wonder if her baby will ever walk since she enjoys crawling so much. By the way, it does appear that babies who are restrained

PHOTO 4-1   A 13-month-old boy in Wuhan, China, teaches himself to walk by holding on to the handle of his vehicle and following the vehicle as it rolls and tends to pull him along.

in body cradles for long hours each day take longer to learn locomotor behaviors, but when freed tend to catch up with the others very quickly. It does suggest that placing the baby in a greater space than her bed, such as on the floor, promotes locomotor efforts. In effect, the baby can learn locomotion on her own when provided the opportunity.

But at around 12–14 months after learning to stand, the infant takes his first step, maybe two. This solo act is probably preceded by some steps taken while mom is leading. The act of independent *walking* has some developmental features to it also. At first the feet are turned out and the knees are bent and steps are irregular. Far from being a little soldier, reciprocal arm movements are yet to be put in place until some more neurological wiring. Around 14 months, though, the infant will likely walk maturely side by side with mom throughout the mall—as long as mom walks slowly. The 13-month-old in Photo 4-1 is teaching himself to walk by holding on to his vehicle and pushing it. The rolling motion tends to pull him along and aids in his walking. He probably is replicating his earlier efforts of pulling himself up on furniture.

To play with most toys, for example, a baby's *manipulation* movements must develop. Manipulation movements are mainly a function of the arms and hands as compared with locomotion, which is mainly a function of the legs and feet. Manipulation involves principally three abilities: reaching, grasping, and releasing. Each of these skills has been studied in depth. Ages ago, for instance, Halverson (1931), through intensive research of grasping (prehension), was able to show that this skill develops through 13 stages. In another work, Newell, Scully, Tenenbaum, and Hardiman (1989) were able to identify over 1,000 combinations of finger-thumb grips. We will not go into that detail here, but those who study fine-motor–based consumer behavior such as toy manufacturers may wish to consider such analyses.

Reaching requires the upper and lower arms and the hands. During the first two to three months, the baby seems to be reaching out to objects—more than just reflexes—but while the baby is able to use the upper arms, the lower arms and hands need more development (the proximodistal principle at work). By the fourth month, however, reaching is accomplished after the baby goes through many days of globular reaching in which encircling motions are made with the lower arms and hands and intended contact is made. Of course, a lot of hand-eye coordination is necessary for this accomplishment. In fact, if you watch closely, you can see the baby eyeing his hand, then the object he is reaching for, and then back to his hand, then to the object until finally achieving success. That wobbly reach shows that the wrist and fingers need more work. But by the end of the fifth month, he is able to reach out and touch and grasp an object with ease—rattlers, stuffed animals, and, of course, his pet dog's tail, which always seems to be a target of early reaching.

Grasping (gripping) may take some doing, although the baby has been trying it since about two or three months and has managed to do it clumsily by three or four months, for example, when she is handed her favorite rattle. But the reaching and grasping combination is another story. Reaching out and trying to touch mommy's nose, for example, can be frustrating, but supposedly according to Freudian theorists, the frustration is a motivator. First, the baby needs to locate mom's nose visually, which can be done with mommy's help—"Where's my nose?" Then the infant needs the hand-eye coordination to get the wobbling hand and arm out to the nose. This means the upper arms need some practice first, then the lower arms, then the wrist and hands and fingers. Subsequently, the infant needs to be able to wrap her hand around the nose—mommy would prefer just touching it. Probably all of this will not happen in the proper order until age four or five months and will not be done with confidence until the sixth month. But it will happen by the time she is sitting up alone. It will be another couple of months for most infants until they can reach and grasp an object between the thumb and forefinger, what is called the *pincer grasp*. At that time mom has to be on guard constantly because whatever baby picks up between those two fingers goes straight to the mouth—button, ball, or bug.

There is still a bit of skill left to master in manipulation movements. Whatever the baby picks up, she has to put down, has to *release* (let go).

That is not as easy as it seems to you and me. In fact, we often see a baby happily reach out and grasp a toy, and only a few minutes later begin crying with it in her hand. Most likely, she is crying not because she is unhappy with grabbing the toy; she is unhappy because she cannot let go of it. The reversal of gripping is ungripping, and it is not a simple movement to the 6-month-old who has mastered the gripping. In fact, it may be a year for some kids before they can routinely let go. For a good example of this, watch a one-year-old trying to stack two or three building blocks. It will probably take 2 months of frustrating effort before she can do it. Same thing with turning the pages in her books. She watches mom do it when mom is reading to her. Mom may even suggest to her to turn the page, but chances are several pages will be torn before that act is accomplished. It is a fine motor skill that really takes a lot of honing. But by 18 months, baby can sit in her highchair and repeatedly pick up those little round pieces of cereal with thumb and forefinger and drop them to the floor, where her pet dog appreciatively laps them up. At this time the reaching, grasping, and releasing are used for many purposes rather than just to have and hold something attractive. It is a set of motor skills that baby uses to learn about the object environment she now rules. She will repeatedly put covers on pots and pans and take them off again, and pull apart or take apart just about anything complex that can be found in the house. This includes cardboard packages such as those of cereal and chips that to the child are particularly complex and may require some ripping and tearing—which explains why "child-proof" containers were invented. Photo 4-2 shows a 24-month-old child trying to turn the pages of a book while pretending to read it. But making the hands and fingers do what mom's do—at age two—is no easy task and will take much practice—and many books.

Speech is another fine motor skill that is developed during this rudimental movement phase. While the activity seems not to fit neatly into these categories defined by motor specialists, it is definitely an important motor skill that develops somewhere between 10 and 14 months. Eliot (1999, p. 170), a neurologist, said that talking "is actually an intricate motor task requiring the rapid coordination of dozens of muscles controlling the lips, tongue, palate, and larynx." It basically starts at around 2 months with babbling—making sounds—which is the first form of practicing sounds that the infants hear. Then for the next year the infant adds cooing, oohing, and aahing, sounds that seem to be common to all languages. Then these easier-to-say sounds are followed by some consonants such as *b*, *m*, and *j*. When the child reaches 10 months, vowels and a few consonants are put together to produce *mama* and *dada*, although the parents on hearing this often are not sure of their meaning—they may think it is more babbling. *Understanding* words (discussed in Chapter 5, the cognitive development chapter) comes well before speaking them—comprehension before production. At 12 months, according to Eliot (1999), the child likely understands 70 words

PHOTO 4-2 A two-year-old Chinese boy learns with difficulty to turn the pages of his book while pretending to read it like mom does.

and speaks around 6. During the following 12 months, the child's vocabulary explodes, and by 18–20 months the child most likely can speak a median of around 170 words while some may speak 500 words. My best guess, based on requesting behavior of toddlers in the shopping setting, is that 10 percent or more of the spoken words are brand names and another 40 percent or more are words for commercial objects such as ice cream and books. (Noncommercial words might be *dog*, *cat*, *tree*, and *water*, although all of these may also be commercial objects, as noted in Chapter 2.)

By 24 months, the toddler is sleeping much less than he did a year ago and seems to have only one thing in mind: play, play, play. Perhaps it is because he finally has all the necessary motor skills to play and feels compelled to apply them. Actually play for play's sake is more important than sleeping or eating to a child, it seems, and finally at night he drops into bed after hours of resisting eating his dinner, getting a bath, and going to bed. *Active* is the best descriptor of the child at this point, and in fact, parents may worry that he or she is overactive—perhaps due in part to the many advertisements of drug companies that mention it. Since both parents probably work, they are often exhausted at the end of the day and may not be so impressed with their constantly wound-up child.

Also at this point in life, the child is going through a phase that some parents call the "terrible twos" in which she has developed enough motor skills—and cognitive skills—along with a ton of curiosity to want and seek independence from parents. But on the other hand, the child really is not yet equipped emotionally to succeed in this endeavor and often experiences separation anxiety. So, she must vacillate between dependence and independence while coping with her ever-changing environment. Add to this push-and-pull such major matters as cutting teeth and toilet training, and busy parents really have their hands full. One of the common answers to all this conflict is to turn the children over to marketers—buy the children everything they ask for, keep the TV going, and take them shopping frequently. And these are the conditions under which most children enter the next stage of motor development.

Fundamental Movement Abilities Phase (24–84 Months)

By their second birthday, potentially all infants have mastered the rudimentary movement abilities described in the previous phase. This accomplishment provides them a base from which they can practice *fundamental movement abilities* that develop from age two to the time they are comfortably in elementary school at age seven. The fundamental movement phase "is a time for discovering how to perform a variety of locomotor, stability, and manipulative movements, first in isolation and then in combination with one another," according to Gallahue (1982, p. 45), who divides this phase into three stages. In the *initial* stage, the child is making his first goal-oriented attempts to perform fundamental movements. The second stage, the *elementary* stage, involves greater control and coordination of fundamental movements. Finally, in the third stage, the *mature* stage, the child efficiently performs coordinated movement patterns. In effect, starting at age 24 months approximately, the child is involved in refining fundamental movements to the point that he develops acceptable levels of proficiency in them. This is accomplished through *control* and *knowledge* of the body and its actions. The awkwardness, clumsiness, error-proneness of the two-year-old gradually disappear in this phase of movement to the point that we can overhear both boys and girls in the first grade often boasting about their motor skills, particularly those related directly to commercial objects. For instance, children may boast about how fast they can bicycle or skate, how high they can fly a kite, and how accurately they throw or hit a ball. It seems that commercial objects not only make the children knowledgeable of their body and its abilities but encourages and aids its development. The West China two-year-old in Photo 4-3 is learning and improving many motor skills from his combination stroller and tricycle. He learns to manipulate the pedals with his feet and learns to manipulate the items on the console with his hands.

PHOTO 4-3   This West China two-year-old is improving a number of his motor skills while riding in a combination stroller-tricycle. His feet learn to manipulate the pedals while his hands learn to manipulate the knobs and buttons on the console of the vehicle.

   Improvement in stability is apparent when one observes a two-year-old child in the seat of a shopping cart bending forward, sideward, and even backward in his efforts to co-shop with his mother. In addition, he twists his body to the right and then to the left in order to see the products displayed on the shelves of the store. Maintaining balance is what it is all about. While sitting or standing, toddlers learn to maintain a point of origin for the explorations they make in space. Using what are called *axial movements* (Gallahue, Werner, and Luedke, 1975), the child remains in a static position while turning the trunk and/or limbs. When he was 12 months old, he would literally fall over when he performed this movement. Now he twists and squirms in mom's arms, in his car seat, and in his highchair. Also, while sitting in the highchair, the child can lean forward and lean sideward to watch the food drop to the floor. He can also perform these feats while standing, although maintenance of his center of gravity requires skill development over time. Otherwise, when he leans over to pick up the food on the floor from a standing position, he may often fall over until he is three. Perhaps through these accidents he learns to perform somersaults at around this age.

   Now that the child has learned to walk it is only a matter of time until she learns how to run, jump, hop, skip, and climb—all exaggerated forms of walking. These locomotor experiences are fundamental movement abilities that come slowly and with many falls. Parents are astounded by their children's abilities to run, fall, and get up and do it again. But by the time they are four, they seem to live by the rule "why walk when you can run." A lot of coordination of arms and legs is required to learn how to walk fast or to run. But coordination of legs, trunk, even neck and mouth is necessary to jump, hop, and skip. Many children have bitten their tongues during these actions. So, along with the motor activities the child must gain knowledge of her body and her body parts in order to have control over the locomotion.

Walking and its exaggerated forms of running and jumping have been studied in detail. Consider running. It has been examined according to stride distance, run distance, speed, and coordination of legs and other body parts, and these and other aspects of running have been analyzed according to age, gender, and culture. A number of investigators have described stages of running just as others have identified stages of walking, jumping, and skipping. Six- to seven-year-old children also do some analyses of their own running skills and use the results to form part of their self-concept (Grusec and Lytton, 1988). Of course, all these running activities and their assessments have been utilized by running shoe manufacturers in order to produce and promote their products—to the point that many children believe they could not perform as well without certain shoes.

Manipulation of objects can be divided into gross manipulation and fine manipulation. The former, for example, includes throwing and catching a ball, whereas the latter includes drawing, writing, and tying shoelaces. Gross manipulation skills are apparent when the child is able to reach for a box of cereal at the supermarket shelf, lift it off, put her arms around it, and carry it to the shopping cart. The same set of skills is used in picking up a beach ball, carrying it to the water, and throwing it in. Such skills do not come easily or quickly. For example, when lifting the ball to throw it, the child may drop it behind her, hit herself in the face with it, or throw it without releasing it. Releasing a big object such a box of cereal into a shopping cart is a manipulative skill that takes lots of practice. Picking it up is actually easier than putting it down. Eventually, the children will combine fine and gross motor skills that will permit them to play various ball games as well as play with a variety of toys.

Fine manipulation tends to follow gross manipulation in accomplishment. Consider the act of writing with a pencil, which is usually attempted sometime after the second birthday. The child must learn to hold the pencil, and tends to go through a series of stages from holding it with the entire hand, then finally at around age five or six, gripping it with thumb and forefinger and cradling it between the two (Rosenbloom and Horton, 1971). The toddler usually holds the pencil at first far away from the tip until she discovers that control is better holding it nearer the tip. Holding it near the eraser and moving the shoulders to draw shows that her gross motor skills are in control. Later, she will use her elbow to move the pencil, and most likely at this time her hand will slide down to the tip of the pencil, relying on fine manipulation skills.

Chances are that any writing, or drawing, first occurs by accident at around 20–24 months, but the primitive results seem to motivate the child to try again and again. Usually, the child attempts to draw before she attempts to write with a pencil, perhaps due simply to environmental influences—children are usually given drawing instruments and equipment (crayons and coloring books) before they are given writing instruments (pencils). Drawing is an analytical tool of clinical psychologists and psychiatrists, so it has been studied a great deal. Kellogg (1969) was able to identify four stages in the development of drawing skills. It starts with the scribbling stage and then moves to the combined stage in which the child produces various geometric figures. In stage three, the aggregate stage, the child creates more complex drawings by putting together several geometric figures. Finally, the child enters the pictorial stage in which the product is an identifiable object such as a person or house. Drawing usually entails use of colors, a dimension that both pleases and frustrates the child. Starting in early infancy, the child responds to colors, particularly to bold colors. But she needs to develop knowledge of the various colors in order to produce a drawing. This is a reminder that the body never works correctly without the mind, the cognitive skills. It is also a reminder that most fine motor skills require gross motor skills for there to be the proper outcome. For example, in the case of drawing, the child must utilize the fine manipulative skills of holding the crayon, moving it, and lifting it off the paper. But all this is done well only when the trunk of the body is held erect, the head is bent over at a slight angle, and the feet and legs are supporting the trunk. Amazingly, however, all this combination of motor skills is developed and refined by the time the child reaches elementary school. There is a good chance too that she can combine even more of these gross and fine motor skills to be able to dress herself and ride her bike to school on the first day.

Sports-Related Movement Phase (7–14 Years and Up)

Finally, all the fundamental movements that have been learned between ages two and seven years are applied to a wide range of sports. This phase "is a period when basic locomotor, manipulation, and stability skills are progressively refined, combined, and elaborated upon in order that they may be used in increasingly demanding activities" (Gallahue, 1982, pp. 46–47). Gallahue (1982) also divided this phase into three stages. The first stage is termed the *general* or *transitional* stage in which seven- and eight-year-olds begin to combine and apply fundamental movement skills to the performance of sports-related skills. Thus, "fundamental movement skills that were developed and refined for their own sake are now applied to play and game situations" (p. 47). Usually, training from parents and teachers is introduced at this stage and will continue throughout it. Formalized sports also are introduced by the school and community during this period. The children are becoming consumers of a wide range of sports equipment, usually with cooperative parents who foot the bills and schoolteachers who offer a list of suggested products usually by brand name.

Stage two is the *specific movement skill* stage that is the focus of the middle-school years. Here, "increased cognitive sophistication and a broadened experience base enable the individual child to make numerous learning and participation decisions based on a variety of factors" (Gallahue, 1982, p. 48). For instance, the youngster at this age may make a decision to participate more in team sports such as baseball or in individual sports such as track or tennis, depending on such factors as body size, motor skills, and, of course, family and school inputs. Then more emphasis is given to honing certain skills such as throwing, running, and swimming.

In the *specialized movement skill* stage, the third stage that begins around age 14, the kid tends to make a commitment to participate in a limited number of movement activities. Some of the motor skills that have been developed and honed throughout elementary school and middle school receive more focus while some receive less. Thus, a ninth-grader may decide to follow in the footsteps of Mia Hamm and devote her time, energy, and talents to soccer—for fun and for competition. Such a decision may be made on the basis of recognizing one's own special talents, but probably it is mostly a function of parents and teachers recognizing such talents and pushing the kid to emphasize them. Today, there is a trend of handpicking children in elementary school and pushing them into specialized skill sports so that they can be ready for professional sports upon graduation from high school or college. In such a case, the child takes on a specialized consumer life, also, in which hundreds of tekrams constantly result from the specialized motor effort.

It should be noted here that the development of fundamental movement abilities that start at age two and sports-related movement abilities that occur in elementary school and middle school are fostered not only by parents and schools but also by marketers. Movies, television, and video games all promote movement abilities to children as a way of selling a wide range of products to them and their parents. For instance, cartoon characters such as Spiderman, Ninja Turtles, and Superman are created around their special motor skills that often become the envy—and the models—of children who watch their TV programs and movies and buy their videos and video games—and, of course, all kinds of toys and clothing. Additionally, the marketing departments of every major sport such as football and baseball is cranking out advertising, programming, and promotion materials 24–7 that target kids. And it should not go unnoticed that many other products pair themselves with all these activities—alcoholic beverages are always paired with professional sports—in order to get a piece of the pie.

CURRENT ISSUES IN CONSUMER DEVELOPMENT (#4)

Exercise: The Other Half of the Formula for Healthier, Happier, and Smarter Kids

We have been hearing for years that the root cause of children's bad health, poor performance in school, and their overall outlook on life is their diet—what they eat, what they don't eat, and how much they eat. When the childhood obesity alarm starting going off during the 1990s, even more attention was given to children's diets. But now scientists who study children's development realize that nutrition must be teamed with exercise for it to produce its good results.

Perhaps those watching out for children assumed they were getting adequate exercise but not always adequate diets since kids and activity tend to be assumed together in the minds of adults. In fact, overactivity among many children has been a concern of those in education and health. Thus, they apparently didn't notice that parents were not letting their children play as much as they used to, and schools weren't either. Almost concurrently but for different reasons over the past two decades, parents and schools phased out outdoor exercise, opting for more schooling and safe keeping. Working parents fearing for their children's safety put them into the care of baby-sitters and after-school special training classes rather than permit them to come home and play outdoors. If they do come home after school, they are required by parents to stay inside and play with their video games, watch TV, and study. Schools taking heat from parents for not teaching kids enough gradually cut out physical education (PE) and added more class time for academic subjects.

Now there is the realization—again—that all school work and no play make Jack a dull, fat boy. For years we have known that the actions of the body play an integral part in all of a child's intellectual processes. Motor activities not only express knowledge and facilitate greater cognitive functioning, but they actually grow the brain as they increase in complexity. But when we are behind in the space race or in math scores and SAT scores compared to the rest of the world, we logically resort to pounding the brain more and the body less. We should do both, of course, since we have known for ages that physical education produces healthier minds (higher academic scores) as well as healthier bodies.

According to a recent article in *USA Today*, the American Academy of Pediatrics (AAP) has made some new recommendations to deal with the lack of activity in children's lives:

(1) The AAP is asking children's doctors to monitor how active their young patients are as well as their parents. Apparently, this is something that pediatricians have not been doing, perhaps because many have been getting fat off children's fat.

(2) Also, the AAP adds that pediatricians should monitor children's sedentary activities such as TV viewing and playing video games, although they have known for years that sedentary activities are favored by both children and parents.

(3) The AAP is recommending that schools reinstate mandatory daily physical education from kindergarten through high school. All states have dropped this requirement except one—Illinois—due to the complaints of parents and their (fat) kids. And lawmakers are reluctant to pass a law requiring it again because it would place an undue burden on the schools.

(4) The AAP suggests also that preschoolers should undertake more unorganized outdoor activities—code for go out and play after school, which most parents don't allow. And the entire family should pursue an active lifestyle.

Their recommendations fall short of telling the children, their parents, and educators that physical activity not only improves the body, but it also improves cognitive activity—learning, memory, thinking—turning Jack into a bright, handsome lad. But maybe another space race or math race or increased competition from international students for seats in our good universities will remind them of this. And, perhaps they should be reminded that good health does not have to be bought from the medical industry; it is virtually free in the kids' backyards and neighborhood playgrounds.

****

Sources: Daily PE Class a Remnant of the Past? 2006; Hannaford, 2005; Pediatricians Urged to Track Kids' Exercise, 2006.

DISCUSSION

In this chapter we have tried briefly to explain the physical and motor development of the child from birth through tweenhood. We have also given some hints of the many relationships between consumer development and body development. A basic point in all this is that the body and its actions are the overt person to all others such as parents, teachers, and friends. If we ask a mom to describe her child, she is likely to refer to physical features and in fact may reply, "He looks just like his father." If we ask an elementary school child to describe himself or a classmate, chances are he will reference such characteristics as "run fast," "good at catching a ball," and "very tall." Physical features probably define a person, particularly a child, more than do the mental features such as thinking ability and personality.

A very important point that was probably slighted to some extent is the close relation between mind and body. This chapter did not emphasize this point enough probably because it will be a focus in the next chapter on cognitive development. But there is stereotypical thinking that pervades most sciences that being smart, intelligent, and creative are functions of the mind, when, as pointed out by Hannaford (2005) and a few others, it is experience with objects by the body that produces the "smarts" in the mind. As will be repeatedly noted in the upcoming chapter on cognitive development, sensorimotor input from the body is the way we become intelligent. Thus, all the thousands of tekrams a day performed by children with their body and motor skills produce cognitive abilities. In fact, the body produces more mind elements than the mind produces for itself through creative thinking. So, the intertwining of body and mind through consumer behavior results in what we call an intelligent being.

Another point is that consumer behavior is almost always social behavior in some way. As noted in Chapters 1 and 3, consumer behavior is dependent to some extent on others—learned from others, aided by others, directed by others, performed by others and with others. So little of it can take place without the involvement, directly or indirectly, of others. But these social dimensions of prepurchase, purchase, and postpurchase CB assume a minimum level of physical and motor development on the part of the actor. Infants are expected to be born with a sucking ability, 6-month-olds are expected to be able to sit and nurse, 18-month-olds are expected to walk rather than be carried in the store, 3-year-olds are expected to play in the sandbox with their peers, 6-year-olds are expected to strap on their own seatbelt when they drive to the shopping center with mom, 8-year-olds are expected to ride their bicycles to school with their peers, and so on. One of the common ways that children learn CB is to observe others and imitate their behavior. For example, preschool children may be seen using their fine motor skills pretending to "light up" as a result of copying their parents' smoking behavior. Social learning theorists such as Bandura (1977) tell us that children learn not only the basic behaviors such as smoking or drinking, but the subtle voice inflections and gestures that go with these behaviors. So, imitating parents as models depends on physical and motor abilities as much as cognitive abilities.

Many marketers also tend to define children by their body more than by their mind. All the clothing merchandised to and for children is sold in body sizes even if they are only small, medium, and large. In addition, there is a multitude of sporting goods that target kids' body sizes such as baseball mitts and baseball bats for certain hand sizes, swim fins for children's feet sizes, and football helmets for children's head sizes. Of course, all of this specialized marketing makes senses since these items are intended to fit the children, suit the children, and satisfy the children. Additionally, retailers who depend on children as customers assume minimum height (to reach an item on a shelf), strength (to lift that item), speaking ability (to ask for an item), and such minimum motor skills as walking (to where the item is displayed), reaching (to grasp the item on the shelf), lifting (to take the item from the shelf), pushing (the shopping cart), pulling (mom's hand to the item), and sitting (in the shopping cart).

Back to the children and their physical and motor development, not only do their physical and motor behaviors define them as consumers, but they also cause them to be consumers. For instance, as children grow in body stature, they need more of this and less of that—foods, clothing, bedding, toys. As they learn to move, they become aware of and seek more of the objects in their environment that are put there by their parents. Lying down reveals commercial objects such as mobiles, sitting up reveals a set of commercial objects such as rattles, standing reveals yet another group of commercial objects such as furniture, and walking reveals a whole house full of commercial objects such as refrigerator and pantry. Likewise, learning to grasp an object with her hand makes many objects suddenly desirable to a child, while learning to write and draw with that hand makes many more objects desirable. Fine motor skills of speaking language permit children to obtain commercial products from parents and marketers. And when we examine those spoken words stored in the mind, we find that many, perhaps most, are related to consumer behavior patterns. Gross motor skills such as running, skipping, and jumping create demand for even more commercial objects.

Another important point about body development is that it is absolutely necessary in order to fulfill the consumer role. In addition to the changes in physical stature and motor behavior that cause use of many products and services, those changes are also necessary in order for the child to be able to go to the retail setting, shop, select products, and buy them. So, body changes cause as well as permit consumer behavior. In sum, if we count the daily or annual tekrams of a 10-year-old as we demonstrated in Chapter 1, most of them will be related to physical and motor development. So, consumer development and physical/motor development are inseparably intertwined. This is equally true for social development and cognitive development, which are discussed in more detail in the next chapter.

REFERENCES

Bandura, A. (1977). *Social Learning Theory.* Upper Saddle River, NJ: Prentice Hall, Inc.

Cole, M., S. R. Cole, and C. Lightfoot. (2005). *The Development of Children* (5th ed.). New York: Worth Publishers.

Daily PE class a remnant of the past? (2006, April 10). MSNBC.com. Retrieved from http://www.msnbc.msn.com/id/12255239/

Eliot, L. (1999). *What's Going On in There?: How the Brain and Mind Develop in the First Five Years of Life.* New York: Bantam Books.

Feldman, R. S. (2000). *Development Across the Life Span* (2nd ed.). Upper Saddle River, NJ: Prentice Hall.

Gallahue, D. L. (1976). *Motor Development and Movement Experiences for Young Children (3–7).* New York: John Wiley & Sons, Inc.

Gallahue, D. L. (1982). *Understanding Motor Development in Children*. New York: John Wiley & Sons, Inc.

Gallahue, D. L., P. H. Werner, and G. C. Luedke. (1975). *A Conceptual Approach to Moving and Learning*. New York: John Wiley & Sons, Inc.

Grusec, J. E., and H. Lytton. (1988). *Social Development: History, Theory, and Research*. New York: Springer.

Halverson, H. M. (1931). An environmental study of prehension in infants by means of systematic cinema records. *Genetic Psychology Monographs, 10*, 107–186.

Hannaford, C. (2005). *Smart Moves: Why Learning Is Not All in Your Head*. Salt Lake City, UT: Great River Books.

Kail, R. V. (1998). *Children and Their Development*. Upper Saddle River, NJ: Prentice Hall, Inc.

Kellogg, R. (1969). *Analyzing Children's Art*. Palo Alto, CA: Mayfield.

Newell, K. M., D. M. Scully, F. Tenenbaum, and S. Hardiman. (1989). Body scale and the development of prehension. *Developmental Psychobiology, 22*(1), 1–13.

Payne, V. G., and L. D. Isaacs. (1999). *Human Motor Development: A Lifespan Approach* (4th ed.). Mountain View, CA: Mayfield Publishing Company.

Pediatricians urged to track kids' exercise. (2006, April 30). USATODAY.com. Retrieved from http://www.usatoday.com/news/health/2006-04-30-kids-exercise_x.htm

Phillips Jr., J. L. (1969). *The Origins of Intellect: Piaget's Theory*. San Francisco, CA: W. H. Freeman and Company.

Prechtl, H. F. R. (1982). Regressions and transformations during neurological development. In T. G. Bever (ed.), *Regressions in Mental Development* (pp. 103–118). Hillsdale, NJ: Erlbaum.

Rosenbloom, L., and M. E. Horton. (1971). The maturation of fine prehension in young children. *Developmental Medicine and Child Neurology, 13*, 38.

5

COGNITIVE DEVELOPMENT AND ITS RELATIONSHIP TO CONSUMER DEVELOPMENT

Shandra, the Eight-Year-Old Housekeeper

An interview was held one evening with an eight-year-old second-grader in her home, a duplex in a public housing area. Her mother, who works in the janitorial service at a nearby university, agreed to let her daughter, Shandra, be interviewed for one hour for payment of $25 and the stipulation that she—the mother—be present during the interview. What follows are some excerpts from that interview held at their breakfast table:

Interviewer: *[Upon learning that the second-grader did much of the housework] Tell me about the ways you help your mother in the house.*

Shandra: *[Looking at her mother first for approval] I do the dishes every night, I mop and sweep, I take the garbage out, and I take the washing and do it.*

Mother: *[Sitting on the sofa interrupting with shouting] You don't tell that man a lie. You haven't done the washing but two or three times since we've been at this place. You know I don't want you at that wash house.*

Interviewer: *Any other household chores you do?*

Shandra: *[To her mother] I just said I do it; I didn't say how many times. I bet I've done it 10 times.*

Mother: *[Shouting] That's a damn lie and you know it. You ain't done 10 washings in your life, child.*

Interviewer: *Let's talk about other things you do in your home, Shandra. Do you do any of the shopping?*

Shandra: Sure. Sometimes. There's an Easy-Shop just down the street, and I go there sometimes and get things in the afternoon after school before Momma gets home. I sometimes have supper fixed and set the table before Momma gets here.

Mother: Sure you do; frozen enchiladas. That's supper.

Interviewer: What are some of the things you buy when you go to the store?

Shandra: I get bread, sometimes a gallon of milk, which is really heavy, ice cream, Froot-Loops, big Dr. Pepper, and I sometimes get things for Momma [implying that these items bought are for her mother's personal consumption, which she confirmed later].

Interviewer: [To the mother] Is it all right if she tells me about the things she buys for you?

Mother: Sure. I agreed you could talk to her and ask her anything. It ain't much for sure. As long as she don't lie.

Shandra: I get Momma's pads and sometimes her cigarettes.

Mother: [Shouting] Shandra Sue, you know you ain't supposed to tell him about getting my smokes. That's against the law. But sometimes when I'm down she does get them. But only when I'm sick. The one guy there knows me and her real well and he lets her buy them for me 'cause he knows I'm sick sometimes.

Interviewer: Where do you get the money to pay for the items you buy on your shopping trips to the store?

Shandra: Momma usually leaves me money to pay for it, but I sometimes do for like candy and drinks.

Interviewer: When you pay for it with your money, where do you get that money?

Shandra: Momma gives me $5 a week, although sometimes she misses, and I sometimes baby-sit for the people next door and make money.

Interviewer: I understand you are in the second grade. Do you like school?

Shandra: I love it, especially reading and music. I have trouble with numbers, but the teacher teaches me the best she can. She's good.

Interviewer: When do you do your school homework?

Shandra: I don't have much usually. Sometimes I do it after school. And I sometimes do some when I baby-sit.

Interviewer: What do you plan to do when you grow up?

Shandra: I'm gonna go to music school. I like to sing. My daddy said he'd pay for it if I make good grades in school.

Mother: Your daddy ain't gonna pay stick and you know it. [Then adding] She sure can sing good too already. But she'll end up married with babies before she gets out of school like I did. It's in her blood.

INTRODUCTION

In this chapter we will examine the development of the mind much as we did the development of the body in the preceding chapter. But we have to remember that while we may examine separately the development of each, they occur inseparably. The mind is never far from the body. Moreover, as we look at each of these two dimensions of human development and relate them to the development of consumer behavior patterns, the same caveat is in order: They occur concurrently and inseparably. That is, consumer behavior is the result of mind and body development, while most mind and body development is the result of consumer behavior. This is a premise established in earlier chapters and will be demonstrated in this chapter also.

WHAT IS MEANT BY COGNITIVE DEVELOPMENT?

In simplest terms, *cognitive development* refers to changes in knowledge and in the use of knowledge that occur as a human ages. Some psychologists might say that cognitive development is *cognition* development or the production of processes by which "sensory input is transformed, reduced, elaborated, stored, recovered and used" (Neisser, 1967, p. 4). Other terms arise—*brain, mind, memory, attitudes, intelligence, thought, creative thinking, reasoning, perception(s), schemes*—when we use the terms *cognition, knowledge,* and *sensory input.* All of these terms are closely related, often interchangeable, and we will use them all to talk about the child's discovery of reality. *Reality* is constructed by cognitive processes using information extracted from the environment by the sensory system that is facilitated by physical and motor development. Thus, what the child *experiences,* including particular commercial objects and the marketplace, is determined by cognitive development, but at the same time, cognitive development is shaped by the child's experiences, including those related to commercial objects and the marketplace. Each experience of a child leaves traces in the mind that influence its structure and the child's subsequent thinking and behavior. That is the essence of cognition. When a baby is born, there are few traces of experience—what we could call memory—in the mind to guide new experiences. Thus, much of behavior at first is random. Also, the form in which traces are stored in memory and recalled is different for newborns than for two-year-olds. Thus, knowledge of one's environment and therefore the ability to function in it varies by age—by the quality and quantity of the child's cognitive world. Shandra's experience as a child in a single-parent household has given her knowledge perhaps beyond that of an ordinary eight-year-old. She has had to learn how to do housekeeping in order to be a partner with her mother, who demands help from Shandra. So, circumstances—the physical and social environments—can have a great impact on the cognitive development of a child. Notice, for example, that while Shandra possesses some skills of an adult, she has difficulty learning mathematics ("numbers") probably because it is not needed as badly as other concepts such as the cognitive and motor skills of cooking and cleaning. Apparently, however, she knows enough about "numbers" to be able to use money, since she routinely makes purchases at a nearby convenience store.

Gaining intellectual abilities is a topic dear to the hearts of psychologists, and particularly developmental psychologists. To describe the child's cognitive development, as noted, we will utilize mainly the work and writings of Jean Piaget, who was a psychologist by trade, not by training, but famous as the master of cognitive development from the 1930s to today. His doctorate was actually in biology, but his first two positions were in developmental psychology in which he learned the psychoanalytical thinking of Sigmund Freud, including his clinical interviewing techniques. Along with some more study in psychology and other topics at the Sorbonne in Paris, he used his work experience to get a job at the Alfred Binet Laboratory in Paris standardizing the French version of the Binet intelligence test. It was there that Piaget became intrigued with children's thinking and intelligence and started writing about the topic, producing five books in five years, the first being *The Language and Thought of the Child* in 1923 that was translated into English in 1926. (For a good biographical sketch of Jean Piaget, see Patricia Miller, 1993.) What follows here, then, is mostly his theory of cognitive development from his writings and from interpretations by several psychologists (Crain, 1992; Diamond, 1982; Flavell, 1963; Miller, 1993; Phillips, 1969; Singer and Revenson, 1996) and a few consumer behavior theorists (John, 1999; Ward, 1974), including this author.

STAGES OF COGNITIVE DEVELOPMENT

The idea that the mind develops in *stages* is associated with Piaget more than any other aspect of his theory and more than with any other developmentalist. But the idea that human growth, development, and maturation all happen in an orderly fashion is logical and not novel to Piaget. It is likely, in fact, that he appropriated the idea from Sigmund Freud, who wrote much about the psychosexual stages through which children pass in order to reach maturity in thinking and behavior (e.g., Freud, 1920/1965). In any case Piaget's stages are considered *invariant* stages: Their order cannot be changed; one always comes before the next. And while it is logical that a child at any moment in time might be functioning in two of the stages—moving into another stage, digressing to a former stage—this is a temporary matter and does not discredit the stage concept. However, it does remind us that cognitive development is not a stair step but a slope. In Piaget's theory, movement from one stage to the next occurs when a child reaches an appropriate level of physical maturation (talked about in depth in the preceding chapter) and achieves relevant types of experience with the environment. Thus, the intertwining of mind and body development (that has been emphasized in earlier chapters), along with the changing (developing) environment, was acknowledged by Piaget in several of his writings (e.g., Piaget, 1954).

Another characteristic of Piagetian theory is that the mind of the child is made of mental structures called *schemata* or *schemes*. I would refer to them as *tekrams* when, as often is the case, they are consumer behavior patterns. *Schemes*, as a general term, are stored patterns of actions that are formed as a result of *experiences with the environment*—with its objects and events—and are used to *interpret* more encountered (sensed) objects and events (Singer and Revenson, 1996). There probably are many terms for what Piaget called schemes, such as traces in the mind, associations in the mind, and patterns of thinking, but the idea is that experiences of any sort produce a residual image in the mind of the action and its results. In turn, these images or schemes are integrated and used to interpret subsequent experiences with environmental elements—physical and social objects. Thus, cognitive development is cumulative; interpretation of a new experience grows out of what was learned during previous experiences.

Gradually, a child learns to adapt to the environment by learning from it and adjusting to it. Piaget believed that *adaptation* consists of two complementary processes he called *assimilation* and *accommodation* (Phillips, 1969). Assimilation refers to bringing into the mind new information and fitting it in with existing information about the objects and events, or related objects and events, in the environment. In simple terms it is the understanding of an action on an object—sucking a bottle, shaking a rattle, stacking building blocks, eating an ice cream bar, riding a bicycle. *Accommodation,* according to Piaget, means changing existing mental structures—existing ways of thinking—to fit the new information about an action on an object. As the environment places new demands on the child, the child restructures his activities and thus his stored information about them—and he will keep doing this forever many times a day in order to survive and grow in his environment. He may also be told to do this, and how to do it, by socialization agents such as parents and marketers. For instance, broken homes such as Shandra's require a great deal of adaptation by a child, and Shandra's mother apparently reminds her of this frequently. Adaptation—adjusting one's behavior to a changing environment—can be witnessed among newborns. If the baby sucks on her thumb and does not get milk from it, she files away this new information about thumbs and food in her primitive memory—sucking thumbs feels great but does not fill the tummy. Thus, one can observe the development aspects to the baby's life: She responds to the environment, makes a record of the results, uses this record to respond again in the same or in a more effective way, and if necessary, changes the way she responds, and files this new information away in a modified mental structure, and on and on and on for life. Piaget and others would say that the resulting mental structures and their applications constitute *intelligence*. In a distillation of Piaget's theory, Diamond (1982, p. 12) stated, "[I]ntelligence is a process of continuous active psychological adaptation to a complex physical and social world." And further, "Action, whether direct or executed on the representational plane, is thus the essence of intelligence" (p. 12). Piaget would go on to say that actions of a child cannot be understood in isolation nor be explained by an examination of the objects acted on, but must be defined by the mental structures that underlie the actions. For example, explaining why a five-year-old prefers sweetened cereal more than unsweetened cereal requires examining earlier experiences with cereals that have been recorded as schemes.

The action of the four-year-old in Photo 5-1 is testament to his existing mental structures. He leans against an ATM and attempts to push buttons on its keyboard. Clearly, he is replicating an action previously performed by one or both of his parents. Thus, he possesses many images in his mind related to this one tekram: of his mother and/or father punching the keyboard, using a finger as a tool, on this device and receiving a response, of the appearance and detail of the machine, perhaps of others using the machine, and of the physical environment in which the ATM is situated. This additional experience with the ATM is guided by these previously formed schemes, but those schemes will likely be modified by this current action of the child. He is a picture of cognitive development in action.

Constructing one's cognitive skills as well as the motor skills that likely produced them initially takes time. We would expect, for example, the consumer knowledge and thinking of a six-year-old to be much different—more elaborate, more complex—from that of a two-year-old. Thus, Piaget's stages are age-graded; the age range of each stage is estimated based on many observations of children's behavior. But while we utilize the stages here according to Piaget, we should bear in mind that they are only esti-

PHOTO 5-1 A four-year-old lad in Xiamen, China, attempts to use the keyboard on an ATM even though he cannot see it. It's apparent that he has an image in his mind of its motor use by parents and others, and he is able to partially replicate that image in his own actions.

mates based on observations of children in a particular culture at a particular time. For instance, Piaget found that the age range for each stage varied between urban and rural children of Switzerland, where much of his research was conducted. I have found such differences also in rural and urban China, but none of significance in rural and urban America. (See, for example, Chan and McNeal, 2006.) If there is one major factor that explains these differences—and there rarely is—I believe it is parenting style, which, of course, is likely a reflection of the culture in which the parenting takes place. On the other hand, I would remind anyone interested in this variance to remember that positive and negative values should not be assigned to them. For example, the fact that children in rural China display some specific intelligence earlier or later than those in urban China does not mean smarter children or better parenting or the opposite.

Sensorimotor Stage: Composed of Six Substages (0–24 Months)

The most important stage, in the eyes of Piaget and those that think like him, is the first stage, called the *sensorimotor stage*, which occurs from birth to around 24 months.[1] Unlike later stages, Piaget (1963) divided this stage into six substages because there is so much happening, so much being learned, including much basic consumer behavior (which was not referenced directly by Piaget or other developmental psychologists). Terms for the stages and substages are essentially those of Piaget, and sometimes their meanings are not apparent and beg for some explanation that is provided.

Random and Reflex Actions Substage (0–1 Month)

In this first substage, prenatal *reflexes* (wired-in sensorimotor mechanisms) of the newborn continue in a new environment, making spontaneous repetitions in response to internal and external stimulation. The baby emits orienting responses to touch, light, and sound, thus interacting with his new world and getting acquainted with it. Most movements are random, disorganized, uncoordinated. However, rhythm is soon established through practice, and some *habits* are formed, replacing the reflexes and emerging as voluntary movements. These form the beginnings of intellectual development. For example, the rooting reflex is gradually replaced by a systematic pattern of sucking movements around the breast that are figured out by the baby and held in his mind as some primitive scheme. Thus, the manner in which the baby consumes mother's milk is soon applied, although awkwardly, to a bottle of milk or formula with a nursing nipple and constitutes some of the first tekrams performed by the infant.

Orienting responses are made possible and guided by a sensory system that is already intact although inexperienced. Vision (20/200–20/600 at birth) permits sensing of mother's form and some wired-in color preferences, senses of smell and taste provide identification of mother's breast right away, auditory abilities soon recognize her voice, and tactile senses around the mouth particularly guarantee that the rooting reflex will find a source of food. The baby's being able to move her neck and lift her head slightly helps also. It may be that the application of reflexes stimulates parts of the brain responsible for similar but more complex behaviors. For example, some researchers argue that exercise of the stepping reflex helps the brain's context later develop the ability to walk.

The subcortical levels of the brain, which regulate such fundamental activities as breathing and heart rate, are the most fully developed at birth. As time passes, however, the cells in the cerebral cortex, which are respon-

---

[1] I usually use months as measures of time and age, rather than years, even though 24 months, for example, is normally referred to as two years by adults. My justification for this is simply that in the first few years of life, a month is a long time during which a lot happens, developmentally. As a case in point, when a 6-month-old reaches 9 months, she has increased in age 50 percent. Moreover, during that time she has learned to sit up, crawl, maybe even taken her first step and concurrently added thousands of schemes to her mental structure, at least half of which are likely to be tekrams—units of consumer behavior.

sible for higher-order processes such as thinking and reasoning, become more developed and interconnected. The infants' sensory experiences toward objects and events affect both the size of individual neurons and the structure of their interconnections. Consequently, compared with those brought up in more enriched environments (containing more social and physical objects), infants reared in severely restricted settings (containing minimal social and physical objects)—impoverished environments— are likely to show differences in brain structure and weight (Kolb, 1995; Rosenweig and Bennett, 1976). Thus, seemingly a very important finding, commercial objects appear to contribute to the most fundamental development of children beginning during their first month of life.

During this first month of life, then, infants might already be considered consumers of commercial goods by their caretakers and marketers, although they are unable to express preferences for objects. They may drink formula in addition to or instead of mother's milk. They are also heavy users of diapers, clothing, blankets, moisturizers, beds and bedding, and probably some medications. It is also likely that parents are providing entertainment objects such as mobiles, rattles, and music. And, again, and very important, infants' developing consumer behavior patterns participate substantially in their mental, physical, and social development. (We will say a lot more about this consumer behavior in subsequent chapters.)

Primary Circular Reactions Substage (1–4 Months)

In this second substage, virtually all of the baby's reflexive movements are replaced by voluntary movements, which means there is some kind of memory system developing, also. (We usually call it a primitive memory system, since apparently none of it will be available for recall, say, once the child enters elementary school.) At this time, at around two or three months, the infant begins to use more than one sensory modality at a time— seeing and hearing, seeing and reaching, for example—permitting coordination of what were separate actions into single, integrated actions. Now, she *repeats* interesting actions such as shaking her hand just for the enjoyment of it—an example of a primary circular reaction—and this in turn produces more cognitive schemes, memory, or what might be better termed *motor memory*. She is beginning to discriminate and show preferences among shapes and forms; she now fully recognizes the silhouettes of mom and dad. In fact, at three months she may surprise mom by reaching for her with both arms when she comes into vision. Accidentally acquired responses, such as making the mobile above her crib move by rocking her body back and forth, become new sensorimotor habits—repeats of movements. Images that come into focus are examined with intensity; the baby will watch the mobile for 30 minutes and stare intensely at mom or dad for that length of time. Assimilation of a pleasure-giving experience, such as moving the rattle, and recognition of the stimulus that triggers the reaction (circular reaction) occur in increasing number. Habits are forming rapidly as schemes are formed and recalled. Now, at three to four months, baby can distinguish consonant sounds of *b* and *l*, vowel word sounds, forming foundations for speaking first words, a feat that is only a few months away. She finds great pleasure from certain items such as her fat teddy bear but still does not know to look for it when it is out of her sight—out of sight is out of mind. Caretakers still have to "find" it for her. She also is excited by any toy that makes sounds, although parents probably have to manipulate them for the effect. The crib is now a miniature commercial center full of toys, extra diapers, a couple of bottles, and perhaps even an intercom to hear her when she cries, and she is performing more tekrams a day than one can accurately count.

Secondary Circular Reactions Substage (4–8 Months)

Mental structures become more complex in this substage as a result of acting more on events in the environment (secondary) rather than on the self (primary). Reactions are the amalgamation of schemes developed earlier and are repetitive and self-reinforcing (circular). At this time the baby tries to make events last that bring pleasure and tries to make events occur as they are discovered by chance. It becomes clear that the baby's life is one of seeking pleasure/avoiding discomfort—sounding very much like a confirmed consumer. By five months, he is able to sit with support, sit in mom's lap, and at the same time grasp an object offered to him. So, all these new physical abilities and their concurrent interactions with environmental objects (usually commercial objects) are filling his mind with many new schemes (and tekrams).

More vocalization (babble) appears as the infant notices that self-made sounds generate responses from others, thus leading to language in a later stage. She also tries to imitate the sounds of others. This prelinguistic communication period includes sounds, facial expressions, gestures, and a growing amount of imitation. The most obvious manifestation of prelinguistic communication is babbling—speechlike but meaningless sounds that start at around three or four months. They seem to please the baby and produce a similar response in parents, so they grow in number and variations.

The baby seems much more sensitive to new objects beyond self. Two or more sensorimotor experiences are now related to one experience sequence (scheme). A multisensory approach to all stimuli is taken as senses are sharpened. The baby shows signs of anticipating events, indicating that some serious thinking is going on in his mind. He demonstrates development of more motor meaning—actions give meaning to events—for instance, kicking and shaking cause mom to respond, but the baby's means-end schemes are not organized well enough to be termed thought-out.

It is in this stage, at around six months, when the baby is able to control the movement of her too-heavy head and sit up alone—and at the same time she crudely uses both hands simultaneously. Consequently, she is exposed to the outside world as she never knew it. It seems that "things" are attractive because of their novelty, and they stimulate head turning and reaching even more. Of course, now that she can use two or more senses at one time, synchronized listening, looking, and reaching become normal. Hence, all those commercial objects that have been ignored, or not seen or heard, are now in her line-of-sight and become very important. Where once her crib was the commercial center of her world, it is now her room or the floor of her room. A new consumer is arising or at least sitting up.

Coordination of Secondary Schemes Substage (8–12 Months)

At this point in the baby's development, she can apply secondary schemes to new situations, thus showing an ability to distinguish means from ends. Now begins what might be called *intentional behavior*, showing determination to possess an object and trying for ways to accomplish it—certainly an essential aspect of consumer behavior. What we see is the infant producing the same results more than one way by using previous achievements—schemes—as a basis for adding new ones. She kicks her crib slats to move the mobile above, and then she hits the crib slats with her hand to accomplish the same thing. Thus, there is increased experimenting that differentiates means from ends. The baby can experience actions by thinking about them while observing a new object. A very important milestone in this substage is *object permanency*—the realizations that people and objects exist even though they are not seen. The baby knows, for example, that the mobile is above her bed and moves when she shakes the bed even though she is lying on her tummy and cannot see it. If she awakes and cannot find her teddy bear, she looks around her crib for it. Another important and related milestone in this stage is that the concept of space emerges and is refined in the child's intellectual repertoire. A game of peek-a-boo, for example, confirms mother's going and coming by proving that when she is gone, she still exists in another space, is permanent, and will return. Knowing that mother exists even though she is not in the room—not in this space but in that space—provides the child security and permits her to expand *motor attention* to other objects without worry. At this point she also begins to sense *causality* and seeks desired results in others; she can get attention from others including the pet dog. Intentions of the infant are more apparent particularly in reaching and grasping activities. There is growing *motor language* such as pointing her hands and fingers and turning her head toward objects. She can now figure out that the reflection in a mirror is herself or a doll; thus, elements of a *self-image* are emerging since she can now separate objects including the self. At 12 months, she can put her finger to mommy's nose when asked, where mommy's nose is, and very soon put a finger to her own nose when asked where her nose is.

Conversational-like babble is heard constantly, and then finally baby's first word—which may be *mama* or *dada*, but may be *bibir* for Big Bird, or *bar* for Barney—thus, this is also the beginning of speaking brand names (although usually not too clearly). Objects spoken can be identified in more than one context, also, such as her personal doll and a similar one on TV or even on a package. We also hear some single words from baby intended for complete sentences (or commands) such as *cookie*, meaning she wants a cookie. And her self-centered attitude assumes she will get it. Thus, asking for products begins and grows in frequency. At this point, comprehension of language far exceeds production of language. For instance, during this period comprehension of words expands at a rate of 22 words a month, whereas production of words increases at a rate of about 9 new words a month (Benedict, 1979). Cooing, crying, gurgling, murmuring, and various types of other noises may not be meaningful in and of themselves but play an important role in linguistic development, thus paving the way for true language (Bloom, 1993).

Baby starts crawling at around 9 or 10 months and by 11 to 12 months can pull to standing by gripping furniture, and she can climb stairs. These motor actions, combined with object permanency and understanding of space, have now changed her commercial center to include the entire room, perhaps several rooms.

Tertiary Circular Reactions Substage (12–18 Months)

The child's understanding of causality learned in the previous substage now produces deliberate elaboration of new means including tools and others—such as using his pillow in his hands to cover his face in peek-a-boo. There is more internal representation of objects, their *space*, and *time* using mainly visual codes and some verbal codes as language comprehension increases. Toward the end of this period, the child enters the world of *symbolic thinking* by grasping that words are labels for objects, that a picture stands for something real, that mom's voice from another room means she will soon arrive. Now the child can speak a number of one-word and double-syllable (e.g., ba-ba) "sentences," thus giving more power to his memory.

Curiosity and novelty-seeking develop fast. *Reasoning* comes into play and develops, too. The child now practices more complex imitation beyond just facial expressions. She copies the play patterns of older children or her parent. For instance, at the end of this substage, she may fake reading, thus copying mom or dad. Play becomes very important at this time because it allows her not only to repeat the action (secondary circular reaction), but deliberately vary it (tertiary circular reaction). The child explores more, takes things apart, touches everything. She is the infant scientist at work. Complex toys and complex foods have more interest, and the supermarket is fast becoming her new commercial center where mom takes her at least once a week.

The child's increasing awareness that objects exist apart from his perception of and action on them causes him to want to know more about them—where are they, why are they in a certain state. We hear more "What's dat (that)?" and "Why?" Interest goes beyond action on objects to the results—grasping and letting go of an object to see what happens to it; the child will now drop his food from his highchair more times than mom is willing to pick it up or clean it up. At 18 months he also says "no" a lot as he repeats the word he hears more often from mom, but uses it to show he is a separate being. Confirming a sense of self is becoming important, along with a desire for independence.

Invention of New Means via Mental Combination Substage (18–24 Months)

Rather than applying familiar schemes (earlier stage) or modifying familiar schemes (recent stage), the child now regularly invents means—what might be termed *true thinking*. Thus, he confirms that he has the ability of symbolic representation—the ability to represent objects and events in the mind (visually mostly as compared to verbally) when they are not present; this includes many items in the supermarket. Also, he begins to think about an action before taking it; he can now picture it and the results in his mind. He demonstrates a more sophisticated view of causality; not only can he infer cause from effect, but he can foresee the effect of a cause. Thus, somewhat contrary to Piaget's theory, the child now seems to be able to see into the near future at this early age. More of the child's thinking and deliberation can be seen and heard as gestures and words. He devotes more of his time to his covert world, and some of that mind time is spent on imagining himself to be another person, such as mom or dad, performing some grown-up tasks. He can now think of something he played with yesterday that was enjoyable and perhaps want it (gesture for it or babble for it). At this point the child can picture the cereal display, for example, in the supermarket and see himself reaching for a particular package when mom wheels the shopping cart into that aisle. An evoked set exists inside that active mind, one that contains a record of all liked products—and their brands in most cases—and it can be used to give directions to parents regarding purchases for the child.

Now the child begins to speak 2-word sentences, for example, "Dog bite" and "Want juice," suggesting the storage of more actions in the mind along with related objects. She now has a vocabulary of at least 50 words to work with, including several 2-word sentences. She copies actions of others, including nonhuman objects such as Donald Duck, and modifies them. Now, play and imitation become fused such as "playing house" and "playing cowboy," including *deferred imitation* in which a person who is no longer present is imitated, thus proving complex mental representations. She will reflect on the benefits of objects in the environment and choose them based on their anticipated benefits. Thus, a ranking skill is becoming a part of the mental operations, although making a choice between two desirable objects is difficult. Through more reflection there is less trial and error, and performance becomes efficient. The child often thinks and talks of objects—people, things, pets—that are not present, thus indicating good understanding of object permanence. Differentiation between self and objects initiates identification, and objects and brands of objects (running shoes, Nike running shoes) are beginning to be used for identity. Amazingly, she knows exactly what store sells them in the mall—another commercial center that is part of the consumer mind.

It seems significant at this point to pause and note that infants have been *learning on their own* during these six substages. The schemes and tekrams that develop in their minds were put there through their experiences with their environment that occurred as a result of their curiosity, need for new experience, whatever the intrinsic motive might be called. I mention this because there is a tendency for us to think that since the newborns know nothing, what they learn is taught to them by adults. But the plain fact of the matter is that much of the behavior and thinking, including their consumer behavior, is a result of their efforts far more than those of parents: Feeling the animal is a better teacher than parents describing the animal. The parents' contribution to their infants' learning (besides genetics) increasingly is that of being models whose behavior their babies imitate. It seems also worthy to note at this time that if parents are absent a lot, then the children may not learn from them what the parents would like and, in fact, may learn from others such as those at daycare and those on TV. So, an impoverished environment—short on social and physical objects—can have a major negative impact on a child's development.

Preoperational Thought Stage (24–84 Months)

In the previous stage, the sensorimotor stage, we witnessed the development of the human from an instinctive organism to a thinking organism through six substages; this development was made possible by concurrent sensory, physical, and motor development. Through sensing and movement, the infant was able to discover his world and interpret it—including the commercial domain. In substage six we saw the first signs of true thinking develop, which is an indication that the child is moving into this next stage Piaget called the *preoperational stage*. What is changing is the way that the child thinks about environmental objects and events. In the sensorimotor stage the child understood things based on actions and sensory inputs— walking on it, feeling it, gripping it, tasting it, and so on. Thus, what were recorded in the child's mind about these actions were mainly images of these interactions—what might be called *motor memories*. But starting in substage six, the child began to think about an object, to wonder about it, to try to make sense out of it with only her mental skills—while the objects and the actions on them are absent. So, now in this new stage the child has moved from making sense of her world using *action schemes* to using *symbolic representations*. This is an almost complete change in mental operations, and it takes time. Piaget termed it *pre*operational in the sense that the child has not yet internalized actual organized operations (found in the next stage) such as logical thinking or abstract thinking, but nevertheless is increasingly using the mind to reflect on the world. But because organized operations have not become a part of thinking, the child does not always figure things out the way they really are; we might describe much of the child's thinking, in fact, as illogical. It seems that Piaget often described the child in this stage in negative terms—what the child cannot do, cannot think of, cannot reason correctly, the mistakes she makes. We will do some of that, too, but try to dwell mainly on the accomplishments, for they are many.

Piaget divided this stage into two substages: a preconceptual substage that ranges from 24–48 months and the intuitive substage that covers the period from 48–84 months. It is not really clear to me the purpose of the two substages except to underline the change in true thinking that takes place during this rather lengthy period in the child's life. We will treat it as one long stage during which many cognitive developmental features transpire.

The child's constant exploration of the environment undertaken in the previous substage six continues, but information about objects encountered is now given more image representation in the mind; social and physical objects are actually thought about, evaluated, and classified whether in their presence or not. However, the thinking that takes place during the majority of this stage is plagued with flaws. According to Miller (1993), the thinking in this stage is characterized by egocentrism, rigidity of thought, semilogical reasoning, and limited social cognition.

Egocentrism refers to "(a) the incomplete differentiation of the self and the world, including other people, and (b) the tendency to perceive, understand, and interpret the world in terms of the self" (Miller, 1993, p. 53). Several psychologists who have examined Piaget's theory are quick to point out that he did not use the term *egocentrism* derogatorily; he did not refer to the child's selfishness but simply to his self-perspective. The child has difficulty seeing things as others see them, of taking the perspective of others. What the little girl sees in the pages of a book when she sits beside her mother who is reading to her is to her what her father sees who is sitting across the room. When two three-year-olds sit side by side and play and talk, they may not really be talking to each other or at each other but just talking with little regard for what the other is saying—the listener is the person speaking. Piaget called this *egocentric speech*. The children's egocentrism does mellow as they have more social interactions with other children and less with adults, such as at the daycare center, a condition that requires that they listen to others in order to get along. Also, at around 60 months, the child begins to understand the idea of *property,* that it always belongs to someone and must be asked for, borrowed, or purchased. Because things—commercial things particularly—are so important to the child at this time, playing with other children who have them and shopping at stores that sell them reinforce the notion of property—and the importance of others who are the possessors. But even at the end of this stage, when the children are entering elementary school, they may still think that the moon and clouds follow them around. Reality is as they perceive it.

Rigidity of thought is tied closely to egocentric thought; both limit the child's ability to see things as others see them. The key to rigidity of thought is what Piaget called *centration,* or the tendency to focus on one feature of an object while ignoring all others. And the one feature focused on is one chosen by the child and may actually provide little information about a physical or social object. For example, a four-year-old tends to see height as the key physical feature of adults rather than other dimensions such as leg length, weight, or waistline. Even though mother might be fatter than father or fatter than the woman next door, she is probably simply seen as tall like both of them.

Some of this rigid thinking is carried into later years such as believing that strawberry-flavored drinks are always red and lemon-flavored drinks are always yellow. *Color* is a common salient characteristic of products for kids in this stage, and it often takes precedence over other features such as quantity or size. If a three-year-old is given six marbles, three red and three yellow, he probably sees two sets of marbles of different colors rather than six marbles. If given a Barbie doll, the three-year-old probably identifies it by the color of its hair and mouth rather than by its slender waist and full bosom. These same three-year-olds are unlikely to see that it is dad in the Santa suit but Santa in his red clothing and white beard. Color usually rules at this stage of cognitive development, perhaps because it is the variable that stands out visually.

Another result of rigidity of thought is the tendency to identify with the one person who most satisfies the child's needs. The awe shown of that person is a result of love and fear—fear of losing that person and thus losing love and caring. In most cases this person is the child's mother even though the father or a sibling or a grandparent is equally loving. But the proximity of mother and child is probably the major concern of the child, and often explains why he goes in a panic when he is unable to see or hear his mother. This result is usually described as *separation anxiety,* and it can occur with others besides mother. Because of the child's awe for the mother, he rarely has any concern for any of mother's negative features such as being overweight, smoking, or speaking with harsh language. At this point the child simply cannot think multidimensionally about people, in terms of both good and bad, but tends to see them as either/or.

Semilogical reasoning, rather than logical reasoning, also characterizes the child in this stage. In addition to believing his views are the only ones and the right ones, the child in this stage feels he can explain his views. He does this, for example, by assigning life to inanimate objects such as trees, toys, and the sun. Further, he usually explains the existence of things in nature by saying that they were created by people. The point is that preoperational youngsters subscribe to a logic that adults see as "funny," "childish," and "fairy tales," and simply incorrect, while the children find it comforting. For instance, a child might say that snow was made for kids to play in and to make the ground soft so they won't get hurt.

A major flaw in children's thinking at this time is that it lacks *reversibility*. The child may logically count from one to five but cannot count backward from five to one. The child may be able to climb a tree but not be able to climb down. Seeing the reverse, the way back home, for instance, is not yet a part of her thinking. Children at age four or five usually are unwilling to try to make a purchase at a supermarket but more willing to try it at a convenience store. Part of the problem is the overwhelming interior of the supermarket and the feeling of getting lost—of not knowing the way out. (We adults may not appreciate how tall those fixtures are in a supermarket to a four-foot-tall kid.) Add to this reversibility deficit the rigidity in thought that was noted previously, and one can begin to see how illogical much of children's thinking is.

Limited social cognition means that the children's egocentric, rigid thinking does not permit them to get along with others. They can exist with others but cannot live with others, except the one or two revered persons that were mentioned. Since they cannot take the viewpoint of others, see things as others see them, it is difficult for them to have meaningful relationships at this time. Caretakers at daycare centers and kindergarten teachers have much trouble getting most of the children to play together, to care for one another, and to make friends. However, child development specialists feel that placing children in these social units fosters social relationships through play.

For a period of around five years, then, children are learning how to think and to use their thinking—and their thinker. As noted, the movement from motor memory to image memory is a slow, confusing process. It seems that at around age two or three, children have everything figured out, only to be informed in a variety of ways by the daycare or kindergarten teacher that they do not. They learn that they must think about things, mull things over, and be willing to change their thinking. By first grade, when children are students of other thinkers who are telling them to learn something—some fact, some words, some logic—they begin to force themselves to change their way of thinking. At the same time they are figuring out the

PHOTO 5-2 Four- and five-year-old children play on a Jungle-Jim at a Beijing kindergarten. Such a play task requires both motor memory and symbolic memory—moving and thinking skills—and some social skills, too.

reverse of a lot of situations, for example, the results of saving money instead of spending it. So, while children will always use sensorimotor thinking, the manipulation of symbols in their heads is becoming the most productive way to have a good life. Thus, logical thinking is beginning to replace illogical thinking.

The kindergarten children playing on the Jungle-Jim in Photo 5-2 use their motor memory and their symbolic memory to climb from limb to limb. They must have learned the concepts of space and distance in addition to many movements including stepping, grasping, reaching, and climbing (vertical crawling). To a four-year-old, mastering these bars by climbing horizontally and vertically is probably comparable to learning to ride a bicycle for a six-year-old. Using the slide requires additional motor actions including stability while moving, sitting, and jumping. Thus, the tekrams performed on this playground equipment are numerous and contribute substantially to both cognitive development and physical/motor development—and to development of social skills.

Concrete Operations Stage (84–132 Months)

In the concrete operations stage, the child is able to perform mental *operations*. In the sensorimotor stage, the child was able to create pictures of objects and actions in the mind during the last substage, and this ability continued and improved in the preoperational stage just discussed. Starting at around age seven, the child can *manipulate* these images to figure out more about the objects or events than are pictured. The stage is termed *concrete* because mental operations are applied only to objects that are physically present. By the end of this stage, however, the youngster will be able to perform operations on objects that do not exist, that are abstract, or that are in the future.

The concrete operations stage has some special features. *Reversibility* is one. While reversibility was beginning in the preoperational stage, it is mastered in this stage. Children are able to envision their route from home to school, and also, they are able to see it in reverse, from school to home. In fact, by around age eight, they can actually draw a map of the home/school route although it probably will not be to scale. Concrete operational children also understand the notions of adding and subtracting, that two can be added to three to get five, and that three can be subtracted from five to get two. They can remember their bicycle ride in the neighborhood and back home, and when they are in the house and mother asks if they put their bicycle in the garage, they can think back and answer yes or no. This means, also, that at this time they probably know the route to ride their bicycle to the nearby convenience store and back, but also how to open and close the freezer case where the frozen ice cream bars are stored. Thus, they can use their mind for more than just storing images of objects; they can operate on those objects.

Another important characteristic of this stage is *conservation.* As the child thinks about an object, he is able to think about it in different appearances. For example, he is able to comprehend the idea that certain soft drinks may be in different size bottles but be the same soft drink. Prior to this time, a change in the shape of a package or container would suggest different products to him. This is no less true of his favorite drinking glass. He senses how much there is in it, and if given juice in another glass, he will be able to judge if it is more or less juice than given before. While the child learns to apply this operation to many objects, it is not learned quickly, and maybe conservation of volume is easy to understand, but conservation of weight may take some time. Piaget would see this new mental operation as growth in intelligence; a mother would see it as getting smarter. But the point is that those images in the mind that have been accumulating for a year or two are no longer static or isolated: They are dynamic; they have life. Interestingly, Shandra referred to a "big Dr. Pepper" and a "gallon of milk," indicating that she has a good understanding of volume. Probably this is due to her repeated experience with these objects and their volume—and weight.

In this stage the child is learning more about *classification,* also, in that he can now see that some things go together, that they are related. For instance, he is able to play certain card games now that he understands the idea that cards with certain pictures are alike, that there are four in the deck, and that there are other sets of pictures in it also. Likewise, he can envision the shelves and fixtures in the supermarket where he and his parents shop and know that some shelves hold cereal, some hold milk, and some hold fruit. He also knows that these go together in smaller quantities to form a bowl of breakfast food. The math teacher often uses this concept of grouping to teach concepts, while the social science teacher uses it to teach the concept of culture. Thus, these applications by others confirm the mental practice of the children.

There is a time-space dimension to the classification system that the child is learning. That is, things go together at a certain time at a certain place. The child realizes that she does not go to school on Saturday, that there are no students gathering at the school on Saturday. She learns also that when she goes to school in the morning people such as her mother and father are going to work—to another building for another purpose. She can also envision the reverse, that she will be leaving the school and getting home before her parents will be leaving work and getting home, and that time difference is to be set aside for TV viewing or study. One senses from the interview at the beginning of this chapter that reversibility was not a problem for Shandra. She understood where the convenience store was and how to get there and back, and she knew where the wash house was and how to get there and back. And apparently, she came home from school alone and often stopped at the convenience store. Again, we can probably chalk up this skill to practice, to experience, but also to being taught by her mother and her teachers. Photo 5-3 shows a classroom setting in Zhengzhou, China. Notice the intensity on the faces of these 10-year-olds. You can almost see the learning taking place inside their heads. At this point

PHOTO 5-3 Ten-year-olds at a Zhengzhou, China, elementary school are paying close attention to their teachers. At this point in their cognitive development, they have trained their minds to be discerning and actually enjoy analyzing an interesting topic.

in children's lives, they have learned to formalize their symbolic thinking and actually enjoy analyzing an interesting topic. Of course, from this daily activity the children rapidly improve their intelligence.

In all these cases the child is dealing with concrete objects, either those present or those mentally represented in the mind. Thus, he is working with what he has, what is, and not what might be. However, he gradually learns the latter, which is characteristic of the next stage, formal operations.

Formal Operations Stage (132–180 Months)

Although this book looks at consumer behavior patterns that are formed from birth to around 100 months, we will briefly consider the last stage of cognitive development proposed by Piaget in order to give closure to the theory. According to Piaget, the formal operations stage, which coincides with the onset of adolescence, provides the youth with the remaining necessary mental tools for living life, and no new mental structures emerge after this. Only the contents change.

It is in this stage that the youth learns to use formal operational thought to analyze the future, the abstract, the hypothetical. In the previous stage her thoughts dealt with the present—the here and now. In this stage she takes the results of the concrete operations from the previous stage and "generates hypotheses (propositions, statements) about their logical relations" (Miller, 1993, p. 60). The youth can deal with what-if statements and generate many of her own. By being able to think about the future, she can plan, make things happen, predict life to a great extent. For example, the 12-year-old can develop a savings plan that will permit her to buy a desired product, such as a backpack, within a time frame. For example, she can figure out that if she saves N per week, she can purchase the item by a certain time period, of if she saves NN per week, she can purchase the item at an earlier date. Thus, consumer behavior can be planned at this stage of cognitive life.

As adolescents move through this stage, they are able to use their imagination that has developed throughout their lives to think about having certain jobs, going to college, or joining the armed forces. Their imitation skills that began in infancy have now been honed to a point where they can mentally participate in such future activities with realism and logical expectations. Having these "thoughts about thoughts" allows the youngster to build a repertoire of outcomes of his actions and thinking. His years of experiences with physical and social objects in his ever-expanding environment provide him with scientific thinking. He actually feels that he can deal with the future, that he has a better understanding of it than he actually does, even a better understanding of it than his parents. "The whole of science is nothing more than a refinement of every day thinking," is how Einstein summarized this thinking power (Miller, 1993, p. 61).

Again, we should be reminded that sensorimotor thinking in the first stage of cognitive development, symbolic thinking in the next stages, and abstract thinking in the last stage are not really taught but learned. Teachers often say that they try to teach children to think, and they certainly can play an important role in the children's learning various mental operations. Perhaps, to some extent though, such skills come with maturation, as is suggested by Arnold Gesell and his group at the Yale Clinic of Child Development (Gesell, Ilg, and Ames, 1977), for it appears that for the most part they are learned by the child rather than taught by another. Parents confirm this "self-teaching" by often telling researchers that they expect their children to learn by watching them. Of course, when the children perform some negative behaviors, parents may deny that the children learned them by observing the parents. Children may be classified as late learners or early learners, but they are learners, thinkers, and their learning results from their own efforts, of course, with some assistance from their genes.

CURRENT ISSUES IN CONSUMER DEVELOPMENT (#5)

Children's Violence Often Bought and Paid for by Parents, but Often Long-Lasting

Violence among children is a serious national issue being described as an epidemic by the U.S. Surgeon General. While violence among teens receives much press attention—shootings, beatings, rapes, robberies among high school students—there are increasing recognition and scientific evidence that it begins in early childhood, develops along with cognitive and motor abilities, and may last a lifetime. Psychologists at the University of Michigan looked longitudinally at a large number of children ages 6–10, then reexamined them when they reached their 20s, and found that young viewers of violence in TV programming were found to be "particularly prone to violent and aggressive behavior as adults. . . ." They concluded that "Humans are born with an innate capacity to imitate. So it doesn't seem too surprising that the violence viewed as a child can become encoded in such strength as to influence their behavior 15, 30, or maybe even 40 years down the road" (APA Online Monitor on Psychology, 2003).

In spite of youth violence being at epidemic levels, we actually don't know what percent of violent preschoolers become violent primary school children or violent middle school or high school children because most childhood violence is disguised or hidden. Scientists believe, for instance, that official arrest records among adolescents reflect only 10 percent of their violent acts, and that self-reports of 30 percent of females and 40 percent of males as violent are understated. Most schoolchildren don't report being bullied, most moms don't report the violent acts of their children, and most school officials don't report those acts. Moreover, violence is not always described as violence as long as it is expressed in socially acceptable ways such as on the football field where it may be described with a gentle term such as *unsportsmanlike conduct*. Statements that adults make about violent children attest to violence's phantom nature such as "He always seemed like such a good boy" and "I can't believe she did that. She's so sweet."

We know that children are not born with bad habits; they learn them from interacting with their environment. Children's first display of intentional violence occurs during the "terrible twos" when, at ages two and three, they demonstrate physical and verbal aggression toward both social and physical objects—screaming at and striking parents and pets, spitting on and biting their playmates, hitting, throwing and breaking toys, kicking the floor and furniture.

Given that much of the violent behavior of children begins in earliest childhood and that violence begets violence, the basic question is from whom or what they learn it. This is a key question since theory has it that if the teachers of violence can be identified, intervention can deal with them. That's theory; here's some reality.

It is much easier to identify the culprits that pass on violent behavior patterns to kids at the ripe young age of 2 or 3 than it is at age 12, the age at which, according to a Surgeon General's report, another cycle of violence begins and manifests itself in teenhood. It should be obvious, and research supports the notion, that 2-year-olds learn most of their good and bad behavior from their parents. The second most important source is likely marketers—mainly TV, movies, and children's products such as video games—and a third is peers including siblings.

Considering the easiest first, how can intervention change the bad influence of marketers and peers? We must recognize that at this early age both of these sources are directly or indirectly provided by parents, thus making the parents the sole provider of violence to most toddlers. As for marketers' influence, that should be easy to get rid of since parents brought it into the home. Stop it at the front door. In simple form, parents should not supply violence-related children products—toy guns, knives, and so on—and they should get rid of the real ones while teaching about their dangers. A relatively new source of marketed violence is video games, but it is fast becoming the main source as parents buy them for their children. Imposing a rating system on them—like movies—seems not to have much effect since close to two-thirds of E- (for everyone) rated games contain intentional violence. Even though many studies have shown that violent video games produce aggressiveness in children after playing them, the industry has the posture of the tobacco industry of 20 years ago—you can't prove it beyond a shadow of a doubt.

Actually, the most violence-related product provided in the home by parents is the television set through which marketers—producers of movies, television programs, and advertisements—enter the home environment. Not providing a TV cuts down an enormous amount of violence learning. The TV that some parents say "keeps the kids out of trouble" actually causes a lot of trouble by teaching children how to use violent products and violent actions to solve problems and have fun doing it. Knowing this, however, does not seem to cause parents to get rid of the TV, an action that apparently is as impossible as getting rid of wars. So most experts such as those at the American Academy of Child & Adolescent Psychiatry offer many suggestions for controlling what emanates from the TV—requiring the pushing of many buttons rather than just one, so to speak.

Peer violence usually is a result of older siblings and playmates that are at daycare and in the neighborhood. Clearly, older siblings are the direct responsibility of parents, and their violent ways should be dealt with through normal parenting. Those external to the home are more difficult for parents to control. But for sure parents rather than others should choose playmates wherever possible. This may mean paying more for child care, driving further for it, or eliminating the need for it.

As for parents, specifically, they are both a direct source of violent behavior for their children through their own actions, and they are an indirect source through the provision of violence-soaked marketing and violence-prone peers. Getting rid of most of the marketers and peers who offer violence is relatively easy, as suggested previously. Getting rid of violent parents is not. In fact, it is impossible except through the courts, which are hesitant to take such action. Parents who hit, shove, and curse each other are children's most effective teachers of violence. Parents who show disrespect for each other as well as for their children can expect the same from their children.

The "peace that surpasses all understanding" often does not exist among the members of today's hustle-bustle households. Parents come home from work strung out from job-related conflicts and often vent their frustrations on family members. Or they try to calm themselves through drinking and watching TV—both conducive to violence. So, too often parents are not good models for their children even though children usually say they are.

So, violent parents seem to be a product of today's work-for-consumption society. Both parents work to provide more for themselves and more for their kids. But this process unknowingly and perhaps unavoidably introduces violence into the home—violent thinking, violent products. So far, there appears to be no effective solution to this dilemma although many are offered. Parents associating with and learning from other parents who understand the problem and perhaps have dealt with it seem to be a good idea. Religious organizations can provide these mentoring relationships for parents and for children, but it is necessary for the parents to seek them, and this seldom happens. In the meantime children are being hurt and are hurting others at a rapid rate, and some kind of early intervention to control or break the chain of violence development is required but lacking. Clearly, such a widespread problem should be a major focus of government, but today's government too often is itself a source of violent thinking. Thus, our work-for-consumption society is producing a behemoth in childhood. Parents create violence and pass it on to their children, and they buy violence in the marketplace for their children, for which they are paying a much higher price than they realize.

****

Sources: Academy of Child & Adolescent Psychiatry, 1999, 2001, 2004, 2005; APA Online Monitor on Psychology, 2003; Wolock, 2004; *Youth Violence: A Report of the Surgeon General*, 2001.

DISCUSSION AND ANALYSIS OF PIAGETIAN THEORY OF COGNITIVE DEVELOPMENT

By utilizing Piaget's theory of cognitive development, we have received a glimpse of the minds of children changing, growing, and functioning as they experience the physical and social objects of their environment. The result is a mental structure that guides children in their responding to the demands of their environment or what Piaget would call intelligence. In the beginning the child enters a new environment in which food and sleep are the chief focus. But within days the infant is acting on objects through a rapidly developing sensory system. These objects eventually take on a life of their own as the child figures out that they are a permanent part of his life and exist separate from him. Each object encountered is evaluated as good or bad, desirable or undesirable, and these responses are filed away in a primitive memory. We called this primitive memory a *motor memory* since it seems to be based entirely on what the child can learn from reaching out, touching, kicking, sucking, and turning the body and head, and observing through the senses.

By the end of the first period, the sensorimotor stage, the child is able to represent these objects as images in her mind and manipulate them, think about them. In the subsequent preoperational stage, the child uses these images in an increasingly logical fashion to deal with her world. She can pretend that one object is another, that she controls the objects in different ways, and even act as one of the objects. Thus, she not only has an understanding of her world but of herself, although that understanding is quite limited. By the time the child reaches the concrete operational stage, she can perform a variety of mental operations on objects that give more accurate assessment of them, thus making them more important or less important. For example, she can compare them and classify them, although both operations are usually what adults might call childish. Concurrently, the environment of the child is expanded by her knowledge of space and time to embrace more objects, clusters of objects, including, of course, both social and physical ones. She now realizes that she lives in a room in a house in a neighborhood near school and shopping, and she knows other people who are located in these venues. By the time she enters the last stage of cognitive development, her thinking is no longer limited to concrete objects but also includes ideas, hypotheses, and reasoning about the future.

Piaget gave us a pretty good idea of "what's going on in there" but left us guessing somewhat about "what's going on out there." Behavior is a function of the person and the environment, and no theorist knows that better than Piaget did, but it is clear in his writings that his purpose was not to expose the environmental factors in child development but the person factors. Even then, he showed some disregard for the physical aspects of the person, both the motor and maturation aspects. He agreed that what takes place in the mind of the developing child is produced by interactions with the environment, its physical and social objects. But he was interested mainly in the results that occur in the mind—the structure that is produced.

So, as we wrap up this chapter on cognitive development, we should remind ourselves that understanding the physical/motor developments described in the other chapter in this part of the book is necessary in order to grasp the complete development of the child—and the complete development of the consumer. It is the physical development of the child that permits interactions with the environment—to be able to reach mother's breast, to sit up and see items in his room, to walk to another room and discover more, and to reach the counter of a fast-food restaurant. All the schemes, as Piaget called them, which develop in the child's mind, are a result of the interactions of the physical self of the child made possible by the child's sensory system. To quote Hannaford (2005, p. 15) again, "Thinking and learning are not all in our head. On the contrary, the body plays an integral part in all our intellectual processes. . . ." Thus, the mind and the body are one system that together produces consumer behavior patterns.

Another element of the environment that Piaget pretty much ignored in his cognitive development framework, but we should not, is the culture. All behavior of the child takes place in a culture and is expected to be in tune with it. Grandmothers in China have much more input into their grandchildren's cognitive development, for instance, than they do in the United States, as they perform the baby-sitting functions for many parents who now both work. The culture is expected to be part of the character of the Chinese child's mind, and often is an explanation, for instance, for why children are generally shyer in China than in the United States. As observed, however, parenting styles are a reflection of the culture, but as more American parents avoid child-rearing by passing its responsibility on to others such as daycare centers, coaches, teachers, and many marketers, enculturation becomes a hit-or-miss effort. Thus, specific cultural values and practices that are expected to be a normal part of the child's mental structure may be changed or not entered at all, depending on what parts of the cultural fabric she is wrapped in.

One of the ways we can see cognitive development in children is to examine their *play*—another very important concept not given enough consideration by Piaget. In the sensorimotor stage, children's play seems strictly to be for the purpose of sensation, of pleasing the seeing, tasting, smelling, listening, and feeling senses. An infant may kick her crib over and over to move the mobile above her head. When she begins walking at around 12 months or so, she pulls a noise toy over and over to hear its sounds. There is also an attempt at mastery—just to see if she can repeat the act—in addition to enjoying it.

Starting in the preoperational stage, play continues for its pleasure and mastery and expands to many more objects, mostly commercial objects. But with the ability to think about an object or event, the child begins more symbolic play. An object may be substituted for another object. A box may be substituted for a car or bus, for example, a hand may become an airplane, and the bathtub may become a swimming pool. What might be called symbolic play is now possible and is enjoyable as the child imagines, or creates images in the mind. Play begins to distort reality as a result of the newfound imagination. Now the child can test life, so to speak, by pretending to be another person, such as mom shopping or dad washing the car. Now she can create her own games, egocentric, of course, in this stage, in which she is master of her house or driving her own car at high rates of speed. If there are any rules, they are made up to serve the child who invented the play game. However, toward the end of this stage, when the child enters elementary school, she will learn the rules for playing various games and at first reluctantly play by them.

Another point about play in this stage is that its egocentric nature continues until elementary school, around age six or seven. Until then even though the child may play with another child, chances are it is what Singer and Revenson (1996) would call *parallel play*. In parallel play two children play in the same place at the same activity or game but are not really playing together. There are, so to speak, two games going on at the same time. The children probably talk but mainly with themselves, and one does not enter into the egocentric conversation of the other. Each is producing a monologue. Yet, if one leaves, the one remaining child may show sadness, indicating some need for the other. But by the time the child enters the first grade, it is likely that she has learned to play with others although she may still do a lot of egocentric play on her own.

There is often a lot of imitation involved in children's play, even in infancy. Children imitate parents' gestures such as waving goodbye, and they imitate their sounds such as humming. Later, when they gain motor abilities, they may imitate motor actions such as clapping hands, driving a car, or riding a bicycle. Finally, as they enter the preoperational stage, their imitations become more complex and may include cooking a meal or going to work. The mere fact that they are imitating people probably helps them to move from egocentric play to social play, from their perspective on things to the perspective of others.

In the concrete operational stage, games take on more rules and more people. They also usually require more motor skills. But they produce more information about the world—the rules used, people who excel in games, and new games or modification of games. Football, for example, becomes a "boy's" game, moves from "touch" football to "tackle" football, becomes a way to achieve more than another person, becomes a way to get recognition, and has various clothing requirements and rules. And very important, football and practically all forms of play are essentially commercial activities.

Another factor not examined in any detail by Piaget as he described the development of the cognitive domain is the *brain*. I assume that this lack of description is due mainly to the fact that so little was known about it when he was constructing his theory in the 1920s and 1930s. If the information that is available today about the brain were available then, chances are some of Piaget's explanations/observations about cognitive development would have been tempered with reference to neural development. For instance, in order to test for object permanence, Piaget would hide an object under a blanket in sight of the six- to eight-month-old infant to determine if she knew it still existed when out of sight. If she did not know it, if she did not reach for it under the blanket after it was placed there, Piaget would conclude that she did not yet possess the concept of object permanence. Neurologist Lis Eliot (1999) would probably disagree, saying that the child's frontal lobes are not fully functioning at this age that would permit her to devote that much attention to the act. Another example of Piaget's that would receive a neural explanation today is the child's learning of language. Piaget devoted an entire book to this topic, but little of it took note of the brain's development. Instead, Piaget saw language learning as mostly a function of social interactions. But as Eliot would say, the advances in language "are a product of left-hemisphere maturation, first in the parietal, then in the frontal lobe" that come into action somewhere between 18 and 24 months (p. 411).

Finally, the theory of cognitive development presented here gives little consideration to the emotional dimension of the mind. That is a bit surprising since Piaget was a believer in Freud's thinking. But again, Piaget's interests were focused on the results of person-environment interactions and not on how the person, the infant or child, feels about the interaction. Yet, Erik Erikson (1950) built an entire theory—"the eight ages of man"—on the child's attitudes toward elements of the environment and the resulting conflicts experienced in growing up. Posner (1989, p. 631) said it this way: "The dynamic significance of the cognitive instability in the psychic life of the child is not explained by Piagetian theory and must be understood with traditional psychoanalytic concepts." Emotions are a normal part of the child's expressions, as any mother who has gone through the "terrible twos" with her baby will attest to. Emotions such as frustration, anger, excitement, love, and happiness characterize the two-year-old and drive him to acts such as screaming, grabbing, and laughing. In fact, some of these negative emotions have spawned what merchants call "shut-ups," the things parents buy for their children in the shopping setting to quiet them. The emotions are also responsible for driving the child to try things, to experiment, to learn. So, although Piaget gave little consideration to emotions in his theory of cognitive development, we should keep them in mind as facilitators or deterrents to cognitive workings.

It is important to note in this chapter on cognitive development that the child is building a memory—what we usually call the mind—of some sort from the very beginning of life. And all this seems intentional on the part of the child, thus supporting the notion of intrinsic motivation—that the child is driven from day one to learn about the environment and how to cope with it. A theorist could simply interpret this as survival, and it is certainly survival, but much more. It is an attempt to become part of the new environment in which the child finds himself, to adapt to it, and to enjoy it—to derive pleasure from it. Of course, the marketplace makes all of this possible, at least in a developed society, by permitting the child to embellish his environment for personal benefit—for fun, health, education, and so on. Where the child is not permitted to establish a personal environment—in those conditions we have termed *impoverished*—cognitive or even bodily development never occurs to the extent the child wants and seeks. So, the egotistical ways of the child serve the child as long as the society in which he is born permits. Piaget did not say it, but the cognitive development that he devoted his life to explaining is in great part a result of intrinsic motives. He did note, even emphasize, however, that the child builds his mind pretty much on his own. The child is self-taught to a great extent, including his consumer thinking and behavior patterns. Advertisers, for example, may try to place messages in his mind, such as brand attributes, but it is the child who decides which messages get in and which do not, assuming no trickery or deceit for which advertisers are famous.

The point here is not to disparage Piaget's theory of cognitive development, or to improve it, but to remind the reader that like any theory, it is incomplete due mainly to theorists imposing their interests and goals into it. But this does not make the theory invalid. In fact, if all developmental psychologists put it to a vote, they would surely salute Piaget's theory of cognitive development as the most thorough and most acceptable. That is why we used it as the vehicle for explaining the development of the mind and its relation to the development of consumer behavior patterns.

REFERENCES

Academy of Child & Adolescent Psychiatry. (1999, April). *Children and TV violence.* AACAP Facts for Families. Retrieved from www.aacap.org/publications/factsfam/violence

Academy of Child & Adolescent Psychiatry. (2001, March). *Bullying.* AACAP Facts for Families Retrieved from www.aacap.org/publications/factsfam/violence

Academy of Child & Adolescent Psychiatry. (2004, July). *Children and firearms.* AACAP Facts for Families. Retrieved from www.aacap.org/publications/factsfam/violence

Academy of Child & Adolescent Psychiatry. (2005, February). *Understanding violent behavior in children and adolescents.* Retrieved from www.aacap.org/publications/factsfam./violence

APA Online Monitor on Psychology. (2003, May). *Childhood exposure to televised violence may predict aggressive behavior in adults.* Retrieved from www.apa.org/monitor/may03/childhood.html

Benedict, H. (1979). Early lexical development: Comprehension and production. *Journal of Child Language, 6*, 183–200.

Bloom, L. (1993). *The Transition from Infancy to Language: Acquiring the Power of Expression.* New York: Cambridge University Press.

Chan, K., and J. U. McNeal. (2006). Children and media in China: An urban-rural comparison study. *Journal of Consumer Marketing, 23*(2), 77–86.

Crain, W. (1992). *Theories of Development: Concepts and Applications.* Englewood Cliffs, NJ: Prentice-Hall, Inc.

Diamond, N. (1982). Cognitive theory. In B. B. Wolman (ed.), *Handbook of Developmental Psychology* (pp. 3–22). Englewood Cliffs, NJ: Prentice-Hall, Inc.

Eliot, L. (1999). *What's Going On in There? How the Brain and Mind Develop in the First Five Years of Life.* New York: Bantam Books.

Erikson, E. H. (1950). *Childhood and Society.* New York: W. W. Norton & Company.

Flavell, J. H. (1963). *The Developmental Psychology of Jean Piaget.* New York: D. Van Nostrand Company.

Freud, S. (1965). *A General Introduction to Psychoanalysis* (J. Riviere, Trans.). New York: Washington Square Press (original work published 1920).

Gesell, A. L., F. B. Ilg, and L. B. Ames. (1977). *The Child from Five to Ten* (rev. ed.). New York: Harper and Row, Publishers.

Hannaford, C. (2005). *Smart Moves: Why Learning Is Not All in Your Head.* Salt Lake City, UT: Great River Books.

John, D. R. (1999, December). Consumer socialization of children: A retrospective look at twenty-five years of research. *Journal of Consumer Research, 26*, 183–213.

Kolb, B. (1995). *Brain Plasticity and Behavior.* Mahwah, NJ: Erlbaum.

Miller, P. (1993). *Theories of Developmental Psychology* (3rd ed.). New York: W. H. Freeman and Company.

Neisser, U. (1967). *Cognitive Psychology.* Englewood Cliffs, NJ: Prentice-Hall, Inc.

Phillips Jr., J. L. (1969). *The Origins of Intellect: Piaget's Theory.* San Francisco, CA: W. H. Freeman and Company.

Piaget, J. (1954). *The Construction of Reality in the Child.* New York: Basic Books.

Piaget, J. (1963). *The Origins of Intelligence in Children.* New York: W. W. Norton & Company.

Posner, (1989). A cognitive perspective on object relations, drive development and ego structure in the second and third years of life. *International Journal of Psychoanalysis, 70,* 627–643.

Rosenweig, M. R., and E. L. Bennett. (1976). Enriched environments: Facts, factors, and fantasies. In L. Petrinovich and J. L. McGaugh (eds.), *Knowing, Thinking, and Believing* (pp. 179–213). New York: Plenum.

Singer, D. G., and T. A. Revenson. (1996). *A Piaget Primer: How a Child Thinks* (rev. ed.). New York: Plume.

Ward, S. (1974, September). Consumer socialization. *Journal of Consumer Research, 1,* 1–13.

Wolock, E. (2004, April–June). Violence in video games. *International Journal of Advertising & Marketing to Children,* 53–58.

Youth violence: A report of the surgeon general. (2001, December). Retrieved from www.surgeongeneral.gov/library/youthviolence

PART IV

STAGES OF CONSUMER BEHAVIOR DEVELOPMENT

In this part of the book, each of the five stages of consumer development will be examined in detail, one per chapter. Each stage of consumer development will be treated in a separate chapter as a major event in children's physical and social environment, and each is related to body and mind development that includes motor, physical, cognitive, speech, social, and language development. While children in the United States are the principal focus, we will look at Chinese children's consumer development also as a way of introducing culture as a variable in the process.

In old China children crowd around a street merchant selling toy pinwheels. The pinwheel, which Chinese children call a *fang cher-cher*, spins and makes a noise when the children run with it. Although most parents in old China were poor—as they are today—they saved a few coins to give to the children so that they may purchase a pinwheel during Chinese New Year (usually the end of January), the most important holiday in China.

6

STAGE ONE OF CONSUMER DEVELOPMENT: OBSERVATION (0–6 MONTHS)

Baby Goes Shopping

A mother of two children, ages three months and two years, was interviewed as she and the children exited a mall in the Washington, D.C., area. In the exit interview the mother was asked four questions about her shopping with her children, and after answering these questions, she agreed to a further interview in her home in exchange for a $50 gift certificate from a merchant in the shopping mall. (The gift certificate from a department store was bartered for insertion of two questions in the interviews.) The mother was told that the interview in her home would last about an hour, was intended to discuss her shopping habits in more detail, and would be audiotaped. In the mall interview the mother said she was a team member of a public relations firm that permitted her to work at home four days a week for a period of six months—the first six months of her newborn's life. She said she has been shopping with the new baby "for at least a month, partly to get some exercise as well as buy some things." She characterized her two-year-old girl, Roma, as "smart" and "... willing to help out with the new baby." Zelda, a healthy three-month-old, was described as "doesn't sleep as much as other babies her age" and "... already loves to go shopping." What follows are a few excerpts from the in-home interview that are mainly related to the three-month-old.

Interviewer: In the mall interview you said that you have taken your two girls shopping several times since Zelda was born. Would you tell me more about those shopping trips?

Mother: I have taken Roma shopping since she was around six weeks old, and I started taking Zelda with us [with her and Roma] when she *was just a month old. Like I told Winnie (the mall interviewer), I work at home and go out shopping in the afternoons a couple of times a week—just to get a break. I always take the kids. Zelda is really no trouble. Never has been. I usually take her in her stroller when I go to the mall. When I go to the supermarket, I often carry her in a sling or recently I prop her up in her cradle and put it in the cart. Roma is really the one who can be a pain in the you-know-what. She's 26 months old and can outrun me. If she gets in one of her moods, she's hell to pay. But usually she minds and tries to help me with her little sister.*

Interviewer: *When we met you at the mall, you were shopping for baby things. Is that right?*

Mother: *Well, for things for both girls.*

Interviewer: *What items were you interested in for Roma, your two-year-old, on that trip?*

Mother: *We looked at some little dresses and just looked around.*

Interviewer: *Did you buy anything for her?*

Mother: *No, I couldn't find anything that caught my eye. She certainly needs clothes. She grows an inch a day I think.*

Interviewer: *Tell me what you looked at for the baby, Zelda.*

Mother: *Clothes also. And are they expensive. I can afford it, but I have trouble paying those prices for some things. A cute dress for Zelda costs about the same as one for Roma, and darn near as much as mine.*

Interviewer: *If you think something costs too much for the baby, do you buy it or pass it up?*

Mother: *Usually, I don't buy it unless she just has to have it, and that's rarely the case. I also go to other stores and look for the same thing. That mall has lots of stores for baby things. But they all cost an arm and a leg. And I go online and look too—for both of them. Nowadays you have to do some shopping to get what you want at a decent price.*

Interviewer: *Do you get tired carrying the baby from store to store and sometimes just buy something so you can finish your shopping?*

Mother: *Not really. She likes the stroller and Roma likes to push her and play momma. So she's no problem. And it's a way to keep Roma busy. And if I take her in the sling and get her just right in it, she is really easy to handle. And often she naps, so that helps. And I just love having her in that sling and looking at her. I know what it sounds like when I say it, but she is a pretty, pretty baby. Just like Roma was at that age. They are my two beauties, as Robert Duvall called his children in that movie,* The Apostle.

Interviewer: I agree that she is very pretty and I would find it hard to pass up a pretty dress for her. But what do you think she thinks about it all?

Mother: About the dresses, you mean?

Interviewer: Yes, the dresses and about the shopping trip in general.

Mother: She is beginning to like going out like that. Put her in that stroller, and when those double doors swing open (at the mall), she almost says, "Let's shop." Roma is the same way. Always has been. They both like to go look around at the stores. They're born shoppers. And I admit it is a good break for me from my work. It gives me quality time with them.

Interviewer: How about the supermarket? Do they like that?

Mother: Do they! Roma is my food shopper. She really knows how to look for things we need. I tell her before we get to the store what I am going to buy, and she really pitches in and helps. Zelda seems happy doing it too. Maybe it's because Roma is always talking to her about something to eat.

Interviewer: So, the new baby doesn't make the food shopping difficult?

Mother: Of course, she slows it down some, but I don't mind that. And when we are there, she is looking, looking, looking. You ought to see those beautiful brown eyes moving from side to side. And Roma constantly tries to pick out things for her. That's kind of nice.

Interviewer: What things does Roma pick out for Zelda?

Mother: Whatever. Candy, fruit, fruit juice, cereal, and always some ice cream. Of course, she doesn't get any of them, except maybe a little of the ice cream. And I usually don't buy them. Most of them really are for Roma, and she thinks she can get them if she says they are for Zelda. Cute, huh?

INTRODUCTION

Consumer behavior starts at birth in the sense that the newborn immediately begins using commercial products such as bedding, formula, and clothing. Consumer behavior develops concurrently and mutually with the physical and mental development of the child. It is directly related to and is fostered by the physical and social elements of the newborn's environment. For instance, Zelda's consumer development is due in part to her enriched physical and social environment. Her mother, who spends each day with her—unlike many U.S. mothers—seems to want to expand her physical environment by including aspects of the marketplace. Her sister, Roma, appears to have a positive influence on her consumer development also. She literally is trying to teach Zelda some consumer behavior patterns. Incidentally, such a social situation is uncommon in China, where families are restricted to one child and a new baby does not have an older sibling to mentor him or her.

In this and the subsequent four chapters, we will look specifically at the development of consumer behavior patterns through five stages in childhood that begin at birth. We will use children's *age* (usually in months) as the measure of the time during which consumer behavior develops since age is a standard that normally is used by biological and social scientists to explain most facets of a child's development. However, age as a single index of the changes that occur in human development has some shortcomings. For example, it is focused on the developing person (P) and says little about the social and physical domains of the children's environment (E) that have great influence on their development. The case of Zelda is a good example in that her age is unrelated to the social influences on her consumer development. However, in practice, age communicates probably more information than any other factor about a child—such as having a big sister, or a stay-at-home, working mother—so we will use it while keeping in mind the caveats that come with its use and frequently note other important indicators.

In this chapter the main concern is with the very beginning of consumer behavior patterns, those that appear during the first six months of life. We will give consideration primarily to children in the United States in our analysis, but in order to inject the concept of culture into the development, we will from time to time also examine consumer development in China. China is an Eastern culture that appears to differ substantially from Western culture in virtually all of its societal institutions. Very important, also, China contains the largest population of children in the world.

CONSUMER DEVELOPMENT BRIEFLY

As we talk about the development of consumers and of consumer behavior patterns, we will use a couple of terms that should be explained. In Chapter 1 *consumer development* was defined as the changes in an individual's level of functioning in the consumer role that results from enduring changes in thinking and behavior. Thus, as a child's mental and motor skills develop (change), they permit, support, and cause changes in the development of consumer behavior patterns. For instance, a six-month-old sitting in her crib and shaking a rattle and babbling constitutes several tekrams—units of consumer behavior. But the sitting and shaking and shouting that make up the consumer acts—the tekrams—are a result of physical and mental changes (development) that have recently occurred. For instance, the child learned to sit up alone in her crib perhaps only a few weeks ago. It is essentially, then, this interaction with commercial objects—bedding, clothing, toys, for example—that we are concerned with, and in this chapter specifically with its beginning.

The development of consumer behavior patterns is the development of consumers—people who display consumer behavior patterns, by definition, are consumers. A *consumer,* as we noted in Chapter 1, is anyone who performs any of the prepurchase, purchase, or postpurchase activities that in this book are termed *tekrams.* Thus, tekrams are consumer behavior patterns; one tekram is one act in the consumer role, that is, one unit of consumer behavior. Recall also that the term *tekram* is *market* spelled backward and thus carries an inherent reminder that any consumer act potentially makes the actor a member of one or more markets. As we also observed, most of the consumer behavior patterns of early childhood are *postpurchase* in nature. That is, parents make purchases of products on behalf of their children who use them—eat, drink, wear, sleep in/on, talk about, look at, listen to, play with them. However, many of these postpurchase tekrams performed by the infant in turn produce preferences and habits that are communicated in some manner to the parents and other caretakers and hence become *prepurchase* consumer behavior. That is, the infant's likes are transmitted to the parents who, in turn, buy more of the preferred item, fewer of other items. In the final two stages of consumer behavior development—discussed in Chapters 9 and 10—the children begin to *purchase* some of the preferred products on their own, ultimately performing in all three phases of consumer behavior—functioning as bona fide consumers. Thus, at that point they have developed into minimally effective consumers—at around 100 months—and are performing thousands of tekrams a day but, of course, will continue on this developmental path for the rest of their lives.

Notice the term *bona fide consumers.* It suggests skill in performance in the consumer role. But it is not intended to suggest degree of skill, just the ability to perform in all three phases of consumer behavior—prepurchase, postpurchase, and purchase—at least at a minimum level. Degree of skill in the consumer role could be described with such terms as *slightly skilled* or *highly skilled,* or on a functional level, *shopping skill* or *skill at understanding advertising,* but such use would imply some kind of proven measures. These measures do not exist and, if they did, would probably be product-specific such as skill in selecting nutritional products or skill in understanding food ads. For example, a three-year-old may be highly skilled in selecting a beverage he likes by tasting several and, through the use of the one dimension of sweetness, choosing the sweetest. (Young children tend to utilize one dimension of an object in choosing a food/beverage product they like, and sweetness is an important attribute to them.) On the other hand, that three-year-old is likely unskilled at choosing a nutritional beverage. So, we will use terms such as *bona fide* and *skilled* to suggest that consumers have reached a plateau of performance at which they can perform in all three phases of consumer behavior, but again we are not suggesting a specific degree of skill. Yet, we would probably all agree that Roma has much more skill as a consumer than her baby sister, Zelda.

Another point that should be made here is that the term *consumer behavior* (CB) refers to behavior toward *commercial* objects—products and their packages, services, retail outlets, and marketing communications such as promotion and advertising. So, when we use the term *consumer behavior*, we are mainly referring to activities in a developed economy such as the United States or in a developing economy such as China. In fact, as mentioned, we will talk about consumer development in both the United States and China, where we have conducted a number of studies on the topic. Of course, we could also describe consumer behavior toward nature's (noncommercial) objects that have been commercialized, such as plants, rocks, water, and fish, but we will try to avoid that extension of the meaning of consumer behavior and just stick to the basics. (We, however, probably should store in a corner of our minds the fact that virtually all noncommercial objects become commercial objects once substantial numbers of people indicate a desire for them. Marketers abhor free products.)

In essence, consumer development is the sensorimotor experiencing of commercial objects in one's environment and assimilating the experiences, that is, converting them into mental schemes that then give directions to future similar acts. When the infant accidentally hears the rattle in her crib, she assimilates this experience, and when she hears it again, she may have a better understanding of it through the scheme that resulted from the first event and seek it or avoid it. By the time the infant is six months old—the latest age in this first stage of consumer development—she is performing hundreds of tekrams a day and recording the results in her mind, thus fostering her cognitive development as well as her physical development.

THE CONSUMER ENVIRONMENT

Babies who are born in a developed economy are born into what we might appropriately term a *consumer environment* or, in business terms, a *consumption-oriented environment*. We referred earlier in Chapters 2 and 3 to the child's environment as E and described it as consisting of two parts: the physical and social. We are not changing that conceptualization but simply characterizing the total environment, E, to reflect its nature much as we might characterize the climate as generally hot and humid or cold and dry. Thus, newborns arrive into what we logically might call *consumerdom*, if there were such a term. It is predetermined by the culture in which they are born that they will perform in the consumer role and in fact will be consumers of specific commercial products and services—initially, those commercial products and services that exist in the physical environment into which they are thrust.

The consumer environment into which children are born and reared is already in place when they arrive. It is only just a matter of their utilizing it. That is also why we also have referred to specific parts of their physical environment such as their crib or bedroom as commercial centers. As set out in Chapters 2 and 3, the environment of the child is made up of two fundamental parts: the physical and social. The physical environment consists mainly of commercial objects that have been purchased by the parents in anticipation of a child consumer. It consists of bedding, clothing, play items, edibles, and a room full of furniture and furnishings inside a dwelling filled with durable goods such as a refrigerator and television sets. The newborn immediately starts consuming some of these items and consumes more and more day by day as he observes them—makes sensory contact with them—and learns to use them. Parents may describe their newborn's behavior with such terms as drinking, sleeping, playing, but virtually all of it is consumer behavior.

As for the social side of the environment, the new arrival will be introduced to the elements of the physical environment and shown how to consume them by the occupants of the dwelling—mom, dad, older sister, grandparents (in China)—who are most likely already bona fide consumers performing in the consumer role. Roma and her mother are two of the most important social objects in Zelda's environment, and both will pass on some consumer behavior patterns to her, some of which we can later call good and some bad. Most of the consumer environment is preplanned by the parents, who ordinarily constitute the baby's primary social environment. The baby will sleep in a type of crib constructed so as to provide maximum rest, play with her scientifically designed dangling toys hung above the crib, wear hypoallergenic and fireproof clothing, drink health-giving formula at specific times—all in a room (nursery) that has a predetermined (purchased) temperature, lighting, and audio-visual system. That is commercial with a capital C, but that is only the beginning. As the baby ages, the family members are prepared to introduce more consumer behavior patterns and show him how to perform them, for instance, how to make a noise-making toy make noise. So, in combination the physical and social environments constitute pretty much a consumer environment—a commercial environment—in which to grow and become a person—a person that is defined pretty much by his consumer behavior patterns. Thus, the baby's physical and mental development will be greatly determined by his performance in this commercial environment—his consumer behavior. And if the environment happens to be impoverished—significantly short on elements in the physical and/or social domains—chances are the child will grow up short in either his physical or mental attributes, or both. By the way, an impover-ished environment for a newborn today is not so remote. In the United States, chances are around one in six that a child will be born in one of the millions of households that live below the poverty level, according to a 2005 report from the Census Bureau. Chances are, also, that only a quarter of U.S. newborns will have a full-time mother. And chances are nearly a fifth will not have a father in the household. At what point these physical and social deprivations constitute child abuse is an important subject for con-sideration and debate.

STAGES OF CONSUMER BEHAVIOR

Before we describe the first stage of consumer development, the topic of stages deserves a bit of setup in addition to that in Chapter 1. The stages presented here are based on many years of research, research that is briefly described in an addendum to this chapter. The stages are constructed on the basis of age ranges. And they are just that—age ranges that are approx-imations based on research mainly in the United States and Asia (China, Hong Kong, Macau, Singapore, and Taiwan). One might expect that the age at which a major activity is practiced would vary by culture, particularly between China and the United States, two very different cultures. But one might also expect the ranges to differ for different family backgrounds within a culture such as one-parent versus two-parent households. And it does, as we will note at the appropriate time.

There are five stages in consumer development, not by design, so to speak, but because that seems to be what is repeatedly suggested by the results from the various research. There is nothing magical about the number five; it could have been three or thirteen; it just kept coming up five, with maybe a couple of substages. There is an order to them, and the order does not seem to change as a result of new research. So, in that sense they seem invariant, although maybe readers will have some other views about them. They begin as postpurchase behavior, such as eating something that mom purchased, become prepurchase behavior, such as asking mom to buy something for them, then become purchase behavior. Of course, con-sumer skills and knowledge continue to grow beyond stage five throughout the life of the individual. Much of developed consumer behavior is passed on to kids later as part of enculturation, but we should emphasize that the developing children do a lot of learning of consumer behavior patterns on their own. For example, not much was passed down from parents of the 1980s to their generation of kids regarding consumer behavior via the Internet, but the kids learned a lot of it nevertheless and began in the 1990s to perform in this new "store"—like the two eight-year-olds in the movie *Sleepless in Seattle* who bought an airline ticket online.

The stages presented here, and mentioned elsewhere (McNeal, 1992, 1999; Chan and McNeal, 2004), are given names to differentiate them from one another. But there is not much good that can be said about the names except that they are intended to reflect a major activity first performed by young consumers during a specific time span that might identify each. These descriptors have been modified a number of times, and none seems very useful—much like the names given to cognitive development stages by Piaget or those of Erikson or their role model, Sigmund Freud. As I noted in the introductory chapter, maybe just calling them numbers would suffice, even make them more useful. At least that would suggest a sequence. I will point out that they are not determined primarily by socialization but by development of the child's body and mind—even though parents play a role in each stage just as they play a role in whatever the children do while they are in a dependent mode. Having defined consumer development as the changes in an individual's level of functioning in the consumer role that results from the enduring changes in thinking and behavior, then stages of consumer development must reflect in some way changes in mind and body. They do, as will be demonstrated in the discussion of each stage. Let us consider the first stage of consumer behavior that begins at birth.

First Stage of Consumer Development: Observation (0–6 Months)

Observation is the stage in which discovery begins. In this stage children make contact with the many elements of their environment, particularly the commercial elements, and this activity, once started, will continue for the rest of the child's life (just as the focal activities of the other four stages of consumer development do once they are launched). In that manner there is an accumulation of consumer behavior patterns—skills and knowledge—that eventually reach a level in around 100 months that we describe as a bona fide consumer.

This beginning stage of consumer behavior is divided into two substages to reflect two very different kinds of behavior. The first part is for a period of around two months—usually closer to six weeks—when the child's connecting with the environment is on automatic—when most of the child's behavior consists of *reflexes* such as rooting and stepping that produce random contact with environmental objects. The second part occurs when *voluntary* actions take over to make the connections. The term *observation*, as used here to characterize stage one, then, refers to the child's *sensing* of commercial concepts that are encountered in the physical and social domains of her environment. It might refer to smelling mom through the detergent or perfume on her clothing, tasting of formula given to her by mom, feeling of the bedding material or mom's dress material, hearing the sounds from a stuffed animal in her crib, or staring at the wallpaper pattern in her room. These are all examples of consumer acts that occur through observations. They begin at birth and continue through all stages of consumer development—and throughout life. Another term for observations used by Jean Piaget and other cognitive developmental theorists is *experience*, both terms suggesting there is some contact with objects that leave an imprint in the child's memory and that, in turn, allows the child to think about the objects later without actual contact with them.

Random Observation Substage (0–2 Months)

In the first part of the first stage of consumer development, the random observation substage, the infant operates on the basis of reflexes much like he did during the last couple of months in the womb. This substage also might be termed *pre-observational* because most contact with the environment is through *random* sensorimotor activity rather than controlled use of the body's motor and sensory systems. For the most part, objects of consumer behavior are not chosen by the child but by the caretaker. The developmental psychoanalyst Erik Erikson (1968) would say that the infant has only changed environments and must re-establish means of meeting basic needs in the new one. Fortunately, mother is usually the key member of the newborn's environment and will meet all those needs until he has the abilities to communicate in some manner with mom what is really wanted or not wanted. For now, as noted, the baby's movements are random as he accidentally discovers objects in the physical and social environments and responds to these objects with a simple plus or minus.

This age of random actions continues for at least a month, maybe two, with the baby emitting orienting responses to sound and light stimuli and to touch by objects such as blankets, bottles, and play items accidentally contacted. The baby's rooting and sucking reflexes discover tasty objects and produce food, while also helping the baby to discover odors and textures. All of these experiences are mainly through the lips, which are highly sensitive, and secondarily through the hands. As reflexes have payoffs for the infant, they tend to be repeated—although often in a clumsy fashion—while those that produce little or no benefits are retired. Just how this works, no one is for sure since it is a stretch to suggest that a *memory*, as the term connotes, is functioning. One developmental psychologist, John Phillips (1969), borrowed a page from the methodological behaviorist O. D. Hebb (1949)—who was schooled on Piaget theory—and compares the infant's behavior with a one-cell animal that approaches and avoids positive and negative objects, respectively. Phillips believed that the infant is already constructing schemes at this time, which comes pretty close to saying that she is constructing a memory. (The memory in this case differs substantially from that constructed just two years later in that it must first be prompted by actual contact with a stimulus rather than by a voluntary thought or image.) The sensory system is working adequately at this time although it is mainly controlled by some prewired reflexes. The eyes permit the baby to *see* forms, silhouettes, movements of objects, and bright, pure colors. (The eyes also protect by blinking rapidly when an object suddenly moves toward the infant.) The senses of *taste* and *smell* also are working when the baby is born and improves rapidly the first week or so, thus permitting the location of food, and most important, mom—specifically, mom's breast. Sense of *hearing,* which is also performing well, helps the baby locate mom and maybe a not-too-noisy toy. Thus, within the first month the baby's sensory system is functioning at a B-minus level and surely is able to assimilate (bring in) elements of the new environment and begin to produce some form of a sensorimotor memory of them. As the baby's cerebral cortex develops—until now all of the baby's actions have been pretty much under the control of the subcortical levels of the brain—higher-order processes help improve the infant's memory and thinking.

During the second month of life, reflexes rapidly become habits, preferences, and voluntary movements that explore and record sensorimotor images of the physical environment—really the commercial environment since most of the physical objects were obtained from the marketplace. Thus, in the same way that will be done for the rest of her life, the infant makes a record of how an object such as a stuffed animal feels when it is accidentally discovered in her crib. But due to the still-developing condition of the brain, the actual image of this feeling does not last very long—as it does when it occurs at age three or four, for instance. From a marketing standpoint the infant has become a heavy user of diapers, clothing, milk, bedding, lotions, and air conditioning during the first month even though she sleeps around two-thirds of the 24-hour day. In the second month, the baby's senses consume a lot more of the commercial world, which presently consists mainly of her crib (its wooden barriers and its mattress) and its contents of play items, bedding, and clothing. Gaining slight control at this time over some of the trunk muscles allows the infant to lie in a prone position—on her tummy—and enjoy the touch and sight of her teddy bear, for example. And now her movements sometimes cause the mobiles above her crib to move and in turn give her enjoyment when she is laid on her back. Mom has probably discovered by now that the black-and-white mobile gets more attention, thus baby is expressing her second or third consumer preference—after milk and perhaps after a pacifier—that of contrasted colors. At this time mom may also be trying to sooth her newborn (as well as herself) with some music during part of the day—sort of a joint consumption act by both baby and mom.

As the baby grows and gains weight, he is eating more and by now is experiencing some variation in his diet; for example, he may be given sugared items such as juices and water or even "ice cream on a finger," as one mother called it. You can tell the human system is working when mom explains the baby's growth by the increased amount of food consumed and dad explains the increased amount of food consumed by the baby's rapid growth.

The number of tekrams performed by the six-week-old is many times more than that performed during week three, thus putting the newborn on an exponential CB track. One can also easily see how his consumer behavior is aiding his mind and body development; the mobile above the bed, for instance, helps build eye-neck coordination and encourages body movement (to move the mobile). Likewise, the stuffed animal in the crib gives practice to the baby's eyes and ears (if it makes sounds) and encourages body movement also in order to see it and touch it. Of course, the milk intake is nourishing the growing mind and body, but so are the play items. As Piaget (1954) found, experiences build the mind and the body simultaneously, although he would have never used the term *consumer experiences*, although appropriate. We should emphasize that at this time none of the objects experienced in the baby's environment is actually sensed as separate from the baby—not even mom—but those liked or wanted are attached to the infant—internalized—and become a part of him—just as mother is. In another six or eight months, however, detachment will begin as physical and social objects take on a life of their own, including that stuffed animal in the crib to whom the baby will start babbling (talking) like he has seen and heard mom and dad do.

Voluntary Observation Substage (2–6 Months)

By this point in time—toward the end of the second month of life—making connections with the physical and social elements of the environment is becoming a full-time job since they are now mostly voluntary. In fact I will note here that *voluntary actions* toward objects that become routine at around six weeks *officially mark the beginning of consumer behavior* in the sense that the infant is making *purposeful choices* of objects in her environment—demonstrating preferences, likes, dislikes, wants. Whereas virtually all needs satisfied by consumer behavior in the random observation substage were physiological needs, the infant in this voluntary observation substage now adds psychological (learned) needs to her list of reasons to seek environmental objects. Satisfying the play need is rapidly becoming the baby's work. Noticeable reflexes are pretty much replaced by voluntary movements—except those that remain for life such as eye blinking—and virtually all waking hours are spent exploring the environment as if being driven by some inner powerful force. (At this point I will not call this inner force a *basic need to consume*, or even the *acquisitive need* or the *sentience need*, as Murray [1938] did. Probably I should simply call it *intrinsic motivation* [Young, 1961]. But years from now we will probably be talking about a consumer gene in the wiring of newborns in developed societies. More will be said about this in a later chapter.) Major developments in the baby's body during just the past month or so aid her exploration efforts. The 7-pound, 20-inch baby is now around 10 pounds and 22 inches. While millions of neurons in the brain have been trimmed away, many millions of connections between the neurons have been established as a result of newly learned behavior patterns during the past two months. By the end of the second month, the baby is able to lift her neck and chest and, by the end of the third, is able to roll over on her back. These stability movements permit a much better view of environmental elements and put more within reach. Seeing all these new things encourages the baby's hands to attempt grasping. For example, the infant may accidentally touch a vertical slat in her crib with her hand and, through looking at it and trying to touch it again, attempt to grasp it—a new and stimulating experience. She stares and feels the edges of the slat, pushes against it, then accidentally uses it to pull herself to it, or pull it to her—probably because she could not let go. Letting go has to be learned too and takes lots more time and trials. The baby then attempts to get her mouth to it—her principal sensor at this time. By being able to use two senses—vision and touch, for example—and integrate them to some extent, she is able to bring in more information that produces more schemes in her mind. This is a primary circular reaction according to Piaget and leads to secondary circular reactions in which the child repeats the experience and tries to make it last. It is hard work and often frustrating since wiring up of motor circuits is still going on and will take much more time. In the meantime she may then stare at the crib slat for a long time as if to figure it out. All of these gestures and movements toward this one object are repeated with other objects within reach—a stuffed animal, a blanket, a rattle, or mom's clothing—as schemes are building networks in the mind—for the most part they are tekrams. She then tries to repeat any of these that are interesting, that produce pleasure for her. Thus, a memory of some sort makes note of the pleasure-giving events and motivates the baby to repeat them—just for the pleasure of it. Many years later all this youngster's choice behavior learned in infancy—seeking more pleasure by having more pleasure-giving experiences with additional pleasure-giving products—will result in the purchase of two cars instead of one and will be labeled materialism and condemned by some purist or Marxist.

During this observational stage of consumer development, the child's social environment usually stays stable and includes only one or two caretakers, mainly mom. It is almost strictly an adult-child social setting for the protection and control of the child (Hartup, 1979). But, at this time in the child's life, he should be learning from adults rather than peers, although hopefully not learning the bad behavior patterns of the parents. For example, one 11-year-old smoker told me that as far back in his childhood as he can remember, he always enjoyed the odor of cigarette smoke in his home, apparently due to the smoking of his father, whom he adored very much. Indeed, during this stage the youngster is learning many odors and sounds such as those of mother, father, and older sibling, and maybe the pet

PHOTO 6-1 Babies in the observation stage—the first stage—of consumer development spend much of their time making contact with objects in their environment that are within reach. This two-month-old Chinese baby examines her mother's hat by rubbing the fabric between her fingers—while her mother shops. The baby will repeat this one consumer act many times a day in order to get to know the environment in which she was born.

dog. He is also learning the feel of mom's blouse as he caresses the material between his fingers sometimes for a half hour if permitted, again, maybe because he does not know yet how to let go.

Notice the infant in Photo 6-1 who is too young to walk or talk, but not too young to learn about objects in her environment such as mom's clothing. This mom and her baby were in the marketplace, and while mom examined food goods, baby examined mom's bonnet. Through the combination of seeing and feeling, the baby learns about one more object of interest to her—her mom's clothing. Significantly, we can assume that the baby was not taught to examine cloth but taught herself how to observe some objects by feeling them. Her exploratory efforts illustrate the essence of this first stage of consumer behavior.

In addition to such items as mom's clothing and the slats in the child's crib, the elements in the physical environment increase rapidly in number with the growth of the child's body and mind. For example, the child's being able to lift his head off the bed may multiply the elements of his social and physical environment tenfold, and being able to reach and grasp may likewise do so. In addition to the growth of the physical environment made possible by the baby's body movements, mom and dad usually add to the physical count by purchasing more play items and nursing items that they sense their baby will enjoy. And there is a likelihood that one or more grandparents may multiply the number of commercial objects, too, particularly Chinese grandparents who often live with and care for their grandchildren. Consequently, baby becomes a major player in the household's postpur-

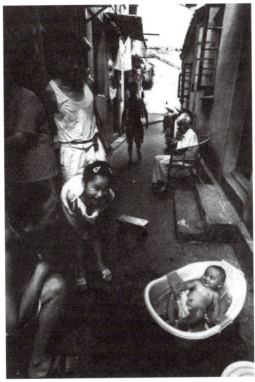

PHOTO 6-2   A baby is given a bath outside her home where it is cool and she can play in the bath water while being tended to by big sister, father, and friends. This Chinese six-month-old is learning many tekrams while enjoying life in the tub.

chase activities, perhaps supplanting the family pet or another child. Some of this is due to the baby's expression of likes and dislikes, for example, through lots of wiggling when he really enjoys something. That is a vivid tekram that makes an impression on most members of his social environment.

Take a look at Photo 6-2 of a stage one infant who has been placed in a plastic tub of water outside her home where it is cooler to play and bathe. Notice the look of joy on her face that is produced by family members and neighbors responding to her wiggling by talking to her, bathing her, and giving her objects to hold while bathing. A number of tekrams are apparent in the photo, but what we cannot appreciate is the language (sounds) that is being developed through this series of consumer behavior, product language such as soap, tub, and towel as well as eehs, oohs, and aahs that will soon beget more consumer behavior.

By five or six months of age, the infant's body and mind have undergone many changes. Body weight has about doubled to 15 pounds, and height has increased a quarter to 25 inches. Now, the infant is able to sit up;

maybe he still has to lean his head on his chest, but he is sitting up according to mom. This body development alone probably multiplies the physical objects in his domain by a hundred times. While her baby is between three and four months, mom has been placing him in some kind of cradle that supports him so that he can sit up and his head not fall to his chest—although this posture gets him a lot of pity, which, in turn, gets him more commercial objects. Then mom places the cradle in various places such as the floor and on her desk, which are in proximity to her while she works. Also, mom may place the baby on the floor inside a playpen so that crawling attempts are possible—among a forest of play items. This event also expands the physical environment tremendously. It is difficult to measure the tekrams—consumer acts—now being learned and performed by the child, but mom is aware of them and how they help the baby develop—and what they cost. In addition to pleasing the baby, these items also keep the baby busy so mom can perform more of her personal and household activities. While the baby is still unaware that all these "things" are not part of him—he still has not reached the stage where he can separate objects from himself—he nevertheless shows his pleasure with them. This pleasure-producing reaction does not escape mom's notice, as she makes a mental note to buy more of some things, fewer of others. Thus, baby is already putting in requests in his own inimitable way for more of everything that is good, thus underscoring his up-and-coming role as a major decision maker in the household. At some point in the not-too-distant future, probably when the child is around age two, four at the latest, his household will be classified by marketing researchers as a *filiarchy* (child in charge) rather than a matriarchy (mom in charge) or a patriarchy (dad in charge).

At four to six months, the baby's mind has become a sponge of sorts, soaking up all the physical features of her environment, all the responses of family members, and the interactions among them all. For example, while she has not yet learned much about space and time, the infant somehow knows that life is better on the floor than in her crib after being fed. And somehow she is able to convey this preference to her caretaker. Actually mom, who is also developing consumer behavior patterns even in adulthood, would tell you that it is not rocket science that the baby is happier in her playpen on the floor—more contented, she would call it. One mom told me that once her little girl is placed on the floor to play, "She's as busy as a bee," suggesting her contentment, and adding, "It is almost like the work whistle goes off." While mom may not be conscious of her measure of this, it probably also includes the additional time it gives her to take care of other matters. Thus, the *floor* becomes the most desired space to the baby, and in some way, then, to mom. This love affair with the floor will continue for a long time, perhaps into tweenhood when the girl gets together with her friends after school to lie in the floor, watch TV, talk, and get pleasures from that venue that was first experienced in infancy. And, of course, none of them will realize that the enjoyment of the floor is due to a neatly-tucked-away scheme that was first constructed before any of them was one year old. By the way, marketers finally figured out children's floor focus a few years ago and started making many more floor-oriented play items for the kids while others started placing advertisements in floor tiles in the various stores patronized regularly by walking children.

Sometime during the child's first stage of consumer development—probably at sitting-up age—many mothers will also figure out that if the floor will give baby pleasure and them more time, then the TV in the floor or near the floor will double this pleasure and time. So, in the interest of both parties, mom introduces children's TV programming to the child's environment. This marks the parent's first formal invitation to marketers to the child's home, and more will follow. At first, it is for a few minutes while the playpen is in the living room or wherever. And like with the floor and its contents, baby shows much interest and pleasure in the TV—perhaps emitting more babble—and mom responds by leaving it on longer. She also reasons that in addition to giving much joy, the TV teaches her baby sounds, colors, and eye focus—another mom in her apartment complex probably told her this. She may even think it teaches her baby the alphabet, vocabulary, and laughter—as indicated by one of the books that her friend gave her. In fact, according to one stay-at-home mom, a dilemma may eventually crop up in which mom must decide whether to watch her programs or her baby's programs. A whole new series of tekrams has suddenly appeared; it's called *television program preferences*. Most likely, the six-month-old baby will decide which programs to watch just as he decides on an increasing number of other household tekrams. This situation, of course, will eventually require two TVs: one for the filiarchy and one for the matriarchy. One mom related to me that she often watches her favorite shows on the TV in her baby's room because the shows "help the baby to fall asleep."

When the baby is around five or six months of age, many moms start experimenting with other beverages and some semisolid foods in addition to breast milk. The beverages include milk formula, juice, and flavored water. Semisolid foods may include baby foods sold in the supermarket as well as some from the home table such as gravy, soup, and ice cream. While there is little reason to introduce at this time such foods and beverages as supplements or substitutes for breast milk, some moms tend to worry about the baby's H and H—health and happiness. In any case, at around the time the baby is able to hold her head up, various ingesta are tried out on her. At about this same time, also, mom will discover that, of all those semisolids, the sweet ones—juice, ice cream, sweetened pureed fruits and vegetables—are most pleasurable to the baby. Mom may be unaware of what is sometimes called the *sucrose reflex* in which the sugar stimulates production of the baby's endorphins and opiates, chemicals that activate the brain's pleasure response system. After experimenting with such *transitional foods* for a month or two, moms settles on a few as supplements to breast milk or other milk. By the time the baby reaches her first birthday, chances are that she is regularly receiving sweets as rewards "because she just loves it," said one mom. Thus, the baby is making decisions about another group of items, and extending her decision-making power to new dimensions.

Also, starting at around two months, the infant tries speaking, perhaps not really speaking from an adult's perspective, but making human sounds. Babbling is what it is usually called during this prelanguage period. It appears that babbling is an attempt to repeat what the baby hears from mom, others, maybe the TV, just as he attempts to repeat other motor actions at this time. By family members responding to the babbling—repeating the sounds, talking baby talk—the infant is encouraged to try more. The infant does not really know that it is he or others repeating the sound at first, only that it is pleasurable—it tickles the senses. After a few months the infant has added more sounds—we usually call them cooing, oohing, and aahing—and following this somewhere between six and eight months a real word may emerge. At least parents think it is a real word. In addition to family members "talking" to the baby, near-people and noise-making toys also do some "talking." Parents also may do some pairing of sounds with objects such as plush toys; that is, they hold the toy and give it a name, for example, hold a stuffed rabbit and repeat the name Bunny a jillion times. While the baby at this time cannot separate objects, he may be cued to make a sound when seeing the object. Likewise, sounds made by characters in kids' TV programs probably stimulate sounds from the baby and produce some pairing of sounds with certain characters, particularly where these are reinforced by mom or dad. For example, in one family we interviewed, the father would often mimic the sounds of Donald Duck to the baby while watching TV, and the baby just loved it. Thus, in this observational stage there is a great deal of influence on the speech of the infant by physical and social objects in his environment. When alone, the four- or five-month-old can be overheard repeating these sounds just for the pleasure of it—over and over and over. It does stimulate talking and probably at an earlier age than in socially and physically impoverished households where it is not done. Thus, consumer behavior fosters the fine motor behavior of speaking.

DEVELOPMENT OF CONSUMER BEHAVIOR PATTERNS OUTSIDE THE HOME

The first environment for children is the womb, and then they are cast into a second environment: the *home* with its social and physical objects. We also referred to this environment as a *consumer environment* because it is usually filled to overflowing with commercial objects to be discovered and consumed. All the consumer behavior patterns that we have mentioned occurred in this home environment. During the first couple of months of life, infants have to assimilate their new home environment, which is much different from their first, the womb. But developmental research shows that they usually approach it with eagerness to know it, learn from it, adapt to it, and make it a part of them. Interacting with the physical and social elements contributes mightily to the infants' physical and mental development as well as their consumer development. During the first two or three months the home environment has expanded at a dazzling pace for a newborn— from the crib to the room in which it is located, to the floor, then to other rooms in the home such as the kitchen and bathroom, each new area being filled with objects with which to interact. That is a lot for an infant to get accustomed to and in just two or three months.

Then, somewhere in this first stage of consumer development, most moms take their babies *outside the home* to the *marketplace* for the first time. This is another upheaval. Imagine being taken from the comfort and pleasure of your home environment, strapped into a baby seat of some sort in a car, then driven to a parking lot of a supermarket, unstrapped from the seat, and carried into the store through a maze of machines with blinking bright lights, bells and whistles, strapped into a shopping cart, and wheeled throughout the market. All the while you are being overwhelmed by a hundred fixtures 10 times taller than you, and hundreds of fluorescent lights glare down at you, and many people pass by and some of them talk to you and say things like, "My, what a pretty baby." It is difficult to imagine what this is like to the infant. We have all seen TV dramas in which medical personnel take an injured person out of an ambulance on a gurney, rapidly wheel him into the emergency ward of a hospital with people shouting at each other and many bright lights glowing overhead as the gurney is rushed down a corridor to a particular emergency room full of machines with flashing lights that make all kinds of strange noises and more people shouting at each other. An infant's trip outside the home might be like that multiplied many times. But this is a milestone in the child's consumer development, since it is the first time that she has had contact with commercial settings where consumer goods are offered, consumer goods that fill her home environment.

We will examine these new consumer development patterns in this new environment mainly from the perspective of American children and their families. But to give our analysis a cultural dimension, we will utilize information from studies conducted in Mainland China. The Chinese culture is definitely different from that of the United States, but just what is culture and what is not are debatable. Is it China's totalitarian government, its limit of one child for each family, its general lack of education, its overall low family income, or its developing status that give its culture its uniqueness? Because on the other side of the ledger, urban Chinese seem bent on copying every detail of Western life and therefore creating clones that would suggest there is little difference between the two. So, we will compare between East and West, while keeping in mind these few details noted here.

In the United States mothers take their infants to a commercial setting at a median age of 2 months, and at least 75 percent take their child there by age 6 months. In urban China these figures are somewhat different with babies of a median age of 10 months going to the marketplace for the first time and 75 percent of them making their first visit by 12 months. Why do Chinese parents wait longer before going shopping with their newborns? The reason appears to be functional, that is, to protect the babies from dirty and germ-filled air that is characteristic of urban China. Chinese parents usually do not own a car and must walk or ride a bus or bicycle that subjects the infants to what many moms perceive as an unhealthy environment.

These first ventures into the marketplace are usually to a supermarket in the case of American infants; usually to a shopping mall, where there is almost always a supermarket, in the case of Chinese. To a lesser extent, babies and moms from both countries (and some grandmas in China) may visit other stores such as toy stores, bookstores, and stores that specialize in infant goods. For both, the first visit is primarily to do some food shopping, although moms from both countries additionally see this as quality time with their babies—as Zelda's and Roma's mother did. It should be added, too, that perhaps half of U.S. and Chinese moms show off their new infants. The babies may be carried in a hand cradle and this in turn placed in a shopping cart, in a stroller that is pushed or also placed in a shopping cart (after some adjustments), and in a specially designed backpack called a *ba-lian* that is very much like a little chair. The Western Chinese grandmother in Photo 6-3 is carrying her grandson in a *ba-lian*. Zelda, the three-month-old described at the beginning of this chapter, was often carried in a sling that placed her in front of her mother so that there was more face-to-face contact than that provided by the Chinese *ba-lian*.

The average time American and Chinese parents and their children actually spend in the shopping setting is about the same, around one hour with a range of a half hour to just under four hours. However, the time spent in reaching the shopping setting is usually substantially more in China due to the necessity of using public transportation, riding a bicycle, or walking, as the grandmother in Photo 6-3 does.

During these first visits virtually all of the mothers report buying something for their babies in addition to household and personal goods. Usually, the purchases consist of at least one food item and at least one nonfood item for the babies. In the case of the food items, there almost always is a semisolid sweet treat included, such as sharing an ice cream or frozen novelty—as is often done at home—and often the treat is a candy sucker that the baby is permitted to suck on for brief periods of time. The first choice of a nonfood item usually includes a play item such as a noise toy

PHOTO 6-3   A Western Chinese grandmother returns from the market carrying her one-year-old grandson on her back in a miniature chair called a *ba-lian*. The child has relative freedom to see in all directions and to feel with his hands and talk to his grandmother.

or a plush toy, and for both moms these toys are expected to be educational in some way. (They will likely say the same thing five years later when they buy their child her first video game.) A number of American mothers said they visited the toy area in a supermarket for the first time as a result of being accompanied by their new baby. Thus, the baby's influence on parents' shopping habits occurs very early in the baby's life. Chinese moms tend to buy a play item that is appropriate for an older child but has a major educational feature to it, such as a book or a talking toy. After the first visit to the marketplace with their babies, moms in both countries report they take their babies shopping with them an average of almost once a week, and usually on the weekend for both.

At this early age of two to six months, the infants have good control of their sensory system and are able to observe a great deal—colors, lights, sounds, odors, even tastes. Combinations of these stimuli appear to leave a positive impression on the babies, according to the mothers and grand-mothers (in China). Perhaps one of the reasons for the infants being impressed by the marketplace in addition to the "bells and whistles" atmos-phere is the purchases made for them, particularly sweets for which infants have a natural craving. Pairing store visits with satisfaction of food and play needs surely gives the visits significance in the minds of the infants in spite of their primitive memories. Also, the marketplace's intense stimulation of the baby's entire sensory system seems important too. The motivational psychologist Henry Murray (1938) noted the predominance of what he termed the *sentience need* among young children, that is, their need to enjoy sensuous impressions. It is almost as if the children are eager to try out their new sensory system and seek stimulation; that is, they have an inherent exploration need, as noted earlier. And the marketplace is the place to test it with what retailers call its ambience.

CURRENT ISSUES IN CONSUMER DEVELOPMENT (#6)

Child Abuse through Neglect: Primarily a Consumer Behavior Matter

We frequently hear of child abuse because it grows more serious with every passing year. Child abuse takes many forms. Figures from the American Academy of Pediatrics show that at least 2.5 million cases of child abuse are reported each year. It is assumed that many more than this are not reported. Of these cases, roughly 35 percent involve physical abuse; 15 percent, sexual abuse; and 50 percent are a result of neglect. Figures from the Department of Health and Human Services show that neglect is responsible for 58.4 percent of the instances of child abuse.

Neglect, in simple terms, is the failure of caretakers to adequately provide for the needs of children. Thus, other terms that are used for neglect include *deprivation* and *omission*. Some state laws define neglect as deprivation of adequate food, clothing, shelter, or medical care. Providing or not providing for the needs of children refers primarily to consumer behavior and consumer decisions mainly on the part of parents rather than the children.

As for the needs of children that are neglected, there is a tendency among child protective agencies to focus on food, clothing, and shelter. For example, where neglect is suspected, agency personnel make home visits and look for such signs as children's being underweight, wearing ill-fitting clothes, and having skin diseases. But several other important needs also should be of concern, including education and medicine. Perhaps one of the most important needs of children, particularly preschool children, and one that is seldom mentioned by child protectors, is play. Play is a mind builder and a body builder just like food and formal education. Thus, lack of play and lack of playthings can endanger a child's health and welfare.

Not providing playthings can result in harm to a child just as not providing educational items can. A jump rope, for instance, can be just as important to a child's development as a book. A child protective services staff member can measure neglect in home visits by inventorying play items as well as inventorying food items. There is a tendency on the part of these people to look at incidents such as an empty refrigerator as a sign of neglect but to disregard an empty toy box.

Child neglect, as might be suspected, is more common in low-income homes than middle-income homes. Many studies have linked poverty to an increased risk of child neglect even though poverty itself does not cause parents to neglect their children. It is the stressors of poverty such as unemployment, single parenthood, and household crowding that produce neglect. In low-income homes there is a tendency for parents to spend a lesser share of household income on their children than in higher-income homes. Often parents in poverty spend a significant share of available monies on bad habits such as tobacco and alcohol, money that could be spent more effectively on the children's health and happiness. In single-parent households—which are almost always low income—there is a tendency for the one parent to focus mainly on food for the children. While this focus may seem logical, it tends to disregard other basic needs such as play and education.

The results of child neglect—of not providing adequately for the needs of children—are many. Research shows them to be low self-esteem, increased dependency, anger, impaired cognitive development and academic achievement, and delinquent behavior. Further, as children grow older, the effects of neglect become more severe.

Solutions to child neglect are constantly sought by those in child protective services. Consumer education seems like a must for parents who are suspected of child neglect or are at risk for child neglect. How to recognize the important needs of children at different ages, how to spend money wisely, and where to spend money that buys the most for children are logical study topics for these parents. For instance, buying at "dollar stores," garage sales, and stores that deal in second-hand items such as clothing and play items is a wise use of money by low-income families. In sum, much child neglect is a result of bad consumer behavior practices by parents on behalf of their children.

****

Sources: American Academy of Pediatrics, 2000; National Clearinghouse on Child Abuse and Neglect Information, 2001; Thomas, 2005.

DISCUSSION: FORMATION OF BASIC CONSUMER BEHAVIOR PATTERNS

What may not be so apparent here in these brief and not so orderly descriptions of children's first stage of consumer development, but profoundly significant nevertheless, is the fact that children are taking their beginning steps down the path to becoming bona fide consumers. Notice the pattern and its sequence:

A. The baby is born into a commercial environment, a ready-made physical environment not unlike the womb from which she came. Much of this environment was planned by the parents to facilitate the child's body and mind development through a variety of consumer acts.

B. In substage one of this observation stage, the baby interacts with appropriately placed commercial objects using mainly inborn reflexes. During this time he learns—assimilates—what is good and moves toward it, and what is not good and moves away from it. Some kind of memory, what might be termed a sensorimotor or motor memory, results. Thus, even in this reflex period, there is some learning of consumer behavior patterns.

C. In substage two, ages two to six months approximately, there is learning of consumer behavior patterns through voluntary actions that replace reflex actions. These movements strengthen the body muscles and concurrently build the mind by contributing schemes to it. Preferences for certain commercial objects such as foods and play items become apparent to mothers who provide more of those preferred, less of those not liked. Such preferences may last a lifetime, such as those for sweets and those for entertaining sounds.

D. Also in substage two, parents take the child to the marketplace—the source of the commercial objects that the child has been consuming in the household—and the source of practically all objects that please. Here, the parents replace those items used by and for the child in the home. The parents also introduce the baby to the marketplace's sights and sounds, features that will be sought for a lifetime and, very important, to its thousands of commercial objects including many new ones—new to the baby. Usually, the child experiences one or more of these objects while in the marketplace, and of course more after returning home. The objects experienced in the marketplace are almost always those preferred by the infant, such as sweets. Just as she has paired movement toward desired objects in the home, the child does the same in the marketplace, thus contributing mental schemes—associations between the marketplace and its attributes—to the baby's cognitive development.

In essence, the child at somewhere between two and six months has participated in the rudiments of consumer behavior—prepurchase (showing preferences for certain products), purchase (by mom of those things preferred by the infant), and postpurchase behavior (using, consuming those preferred things bought in the marketplace, including those that were purchased in preparation for the newborn). How much she learned on her own and how much is taught by parents are impossible to measure, but what is apparent is that the newborn is a developing consumer. What is less apparent but very relevant is the training that parents receive during this first stage of consumer development in satisfying the wants and needs of their new children.

ADDENDUM

Research Thinking and Procedures Used for Measuring and Understanding Consumer Development among Children and Their Households

The studies of children's consumer development that are reported throughout this book and specifically in this chapter and the subsequent four chapters were conducted mainly during the period 1992–2004. In-depth interviews with around 600 mothers of children ranging in age from 3 months to 12 years were supplemented with intensive observation studies of 80 mother-child shopping dyads prior to and following the interviews. However, these specific attempts to assess consumer development were predicated on many earlier studies of consumer behavior patterns among several thousand children and their parents during the previous approximately 15 years.

Be assured that the results that were obtained were biased in some way by all the flaws of consumer research: The results are never objective enough; the researcher always puts himself into the design and implementation of the study as well as the analyses and reporting of the results. While I was constantly conscious of these faults, I confess that early in my research efforts, I naively thought that such subjectivity somehow would be washed out with large random samples and various tests of significance—something I learned from some of my eager-to-publish-eager-to-get-promoted colleagues. But I slowly learned from a few forthright colleagues that this is not the way research works. So I have tried to keep the research procedures and the results presented here as clean as possible. In fact, I would tell you that in my quest for useful, reliable research findings, I have thrown away results that probably could have been converted into another journal article—and another notch in my academic standing that would, in turn, earn me more promotion, pay, and prestige—simply because they did not contain enough quality.

I recognize, too, that some studies funded or partially funded by clients are somehow supposed to come out in favor of the clients—to say what they want to hear, support what they are selling. When I see studies reported on children's health, for example, and some of them quietly note in small print (like many ads on TV) that they were funded by a food or beverage company, I cringe and think the researcher and client both are in the research. Some of the studies mentioned here were in part funded by for-profit organizations, and I can remember some of the pressure to "control" the results, but I did not—at least I consciously tried not to, so I hope none of that is in this book or in any of my writings unless so noted.

There was enough error that crept into these consumer development studies reported here without my adding more through my personal goals. Specifically, when mothers are asked about their developing children as reported here, at least two major problems arise. One, they tend to exaggerate; that is, they sometimes try to make their kids look good like some researchers try to make their findings look good. In both cases it is logical to be proud of one's creations. In some of my writings, I have termed these moms Mrs. McImitys—**M**y **C**hild **I**s **M**ore **I**ntelligent **T**han **Y**ours. If given the chance, many moms will communicate the superior features of their children as compared to other children their age, their grade, in their neighborhood. Consequently, the Mrs. McImitys have to be dealt with in such a way that the *social desirability variable* (Edwards, 1959) is accounted for in the final results.

Probably an even greater source of error was in asking mothers to recall events from several years earlier—from roughly 3 to as long as 10 years earlier. A lot of bad stuff can be forgotten in this time, such as the many tantrums children throw at the frozen novelty case in the supermarket. So, we had to check this in various ways—through additional research among these moms, through asking questions another way, through talking to kids of those moms, and through hundreds of hours of observations. By the way, I do not regret those hundreds of hours of observation work. They produced a lot of truth. Of course, while they keep out the influence of the respondents, they may let in the influence of the field researcher if not properly structured.

I might mention that we—fellow researchers, field workers, and I—did not go to children for information about their consumer behavior that occurred prior to their fifth birthday. Several focus groups of first- and second-graders quickly showed us that either we did not know how to capture this information or, the more likely: The children simply could not recall it. Children usually cannot remember much about when they were two or three or four except for a few critical events. This malfunction, if I can call it that, is what some cognitive developmentalists term *infantile amnesia* (Feldman, 2000) and say that it is due to the early learning methods—storage methods—that children use that make it difficult for them to retrieve much of the internalized knowledge and events from this time period. So, most of the significant results from this phase of their lives are based on reports by moms and a few dads—and many observations.

By the way, we never were able to accomplish much developmental research among dads; they often were uncooperative, even a bit belligerent at times, and really seemed to know little about their kids. In-depth interviews with them were almost impossible because they seemed to possess little in-depth information about their kids. Once in the mid-1990s I was privy to a meeting of fathers where I took advantage of it to do some in-depth interviewing work. In spite of trying hard to keep the interviews on track, I mostly received complaints about their wives and apologies for the lack of time they spent with their kids. As a side note, in recent years more mothers have made similar sounds in interviews with them about child rearing. That is, they regret not spending more time with their kids, and they regret that their husbands have not spent enough time with their kids either.

Specifically, regarding querying mothers about the consumer behavior of their children, we tried to select mothers who had children only a few years older than the behavior we were asking about. Thus, for example, we chose mothers with 2-, 3- and 4-years-olds in daycare or kindergarten to talk to about their kids' consumer behavior (CB) during the previous few years, and we asked mothers of 8-year-olds about their kids' behavior as far back as they could reach, and the same thing for mothers of 10- and 12-year-olds. Researchers were trained to discern when mothers were reaching and when they were inventing information, and they would ask the questions in other ways or ask questions about the information the moms were providing. In this way we were rarely asking moms to recall 10 years or even 5 years, but usually 1–5 years. I should note here that where we could double-check the statements made by moms, they demonstrated remarkable memory whether rich or poor, old or young, educated or uneducated—and all these demographics were included in our research.

Backtracking a bit, in graduate school I began toying with the question of how people become consumers. Among my colleagues and professors, there was more than a passing interest in the topic. One of my psychology professors had a foothold in the whole area of child development and encouraged me to look into the topic—what I called in one of my term papers for him the *consumer embryo*. We tried to theorize about the concept of consumer development, draw all kinds of models of it, and in general describe it as a process. Few substantive results came out of all this effort, but a few seeds were planted that would sprout and grow over the next decade.

When I initiated some measures of children's influence on their parents' consumer behavior in the late 1970s and early 1980s, it became apparent to me that I needed to reach back into infancy to complete the task; I just could not find the beginning with the research tools at my disposal. Moreover, when I conducted studies of children's purchase behavior, it became apparent to me that before actual independent purchases by kids there were attempts with parents. The point is that I had trapped myself in some of my earlier research into studying children *being* consumers rather than children *becoming* consumers—which is the standard practice in studying children's consumer behavior. Finally, the pieces seemed to fall into place without much help from me. I remember one time I was interviewing a first-grader about his first purchase, which he had made at a small-town corner grocery store. Afterward, I sat down at a coffee shop to flesh out the margin notes I had made on the questionnaire guide during the interview. And it suddenly hit me. What about his behavior just before that first purchase? And before that? And before that? The steps or stages or phases, whatever I would call them, seemed to appear before my eyes. And the basic flaw in my thinking—of children being consumers rather than becoming consumers—became apparent. Finally, during the late 1980s and early 1990s, I initiated some testing of the steps in children's consumer development, which I began calling *stages* probably as a result of reading Piaget and his stage theory of cognitive development in graduate school. During the 1990s I continued to tweak the stages of consumer development, mainly with information from case studies.

Once I felt comfortable with the sequence, I tested it more in the United States and then among Chinese populations in Taiwan and Hong Kong and then China. The idea of doing the developmental research in China was to make sure I was not deluding myself, that the researcher was not proving himself rather than the postulates. Also, in China, where research is so difficult for Westerners to do or get done, I could bring the culture factor into my developmental study. The results provide some comparisons between the two cultures—essentially Eastern and Western—which are noted in these pages from time to time. But a reader should view with caution the brief comparisons of consumer development between these two cultures that I have made in these pages for many reasons—mainly the language differences that influenced the conversion of the questionnaire guides, questions, warm-up talks, and perceptions of the field workers.

To be fair to the reader, I should also make another important note here about researching children's consumer development. I have indicated in Chapter 1 and subsequent chapters that there is much intertwinement of consumer development, cognitive development, and physical development, that I am not sure sometimes what I am measuring. For example, when I observe a three-month-old baby in a crib reaching for a rattle, is she performing a tekram of wanting and reaching for a commercial object, is she reaching in order to express her upper arm muscles, is she just randomly choosing this act to satisfy her curiosity need, is she adjusting a mental scheme that she put in place yesterday, or is her behavior really some kind of intermingling of all of these? It is clear to me that consumer behavior facilitates physical and cognitive development, and that physical and cognitive development facilitate consumer development, but discerning one from the others is no small feat for me or for some supposedly sensitive statistical test.

I mentioned large samples of respondents, and I mentioned cases studies among a few respondents. I have learned a lot from both. Studying a few children's consumer behavior over a long period of time somehow gives sanity to all the research I have done. To me, a case study provides all the information about consumer behavior that I could ever want. There is an air of purity about the findings. Likewise, large samples tend to make me feel that I have washed out some serious sampling errors, either those originating with my planning or those introduced by field workers. It is all those other studies my colleagues and I have completed that make me a bit uncomfortable—those of sample size of around 100. That typically is the sample size of most studies reported in our journals, and it seems to me that they have more opportunity for error than a sample of 4 or a sample of 400. So, in the case of sample size, I have tried to stay out of the middle, so to speak.

Now, let me summarize the research procedures that underlie the descriptions of the development of consumer behavior patterns among children ages 0–100+ months that appear in this book. Prior to studying the stages of consumer development, we conducted a couple thousand interviews with mothers and their elementary school children regarding the children's consumer behavior in and outside the household—as being consumers. From these, we derived measures of children's influence on family purchases and the nature and extent of their own purchases in the marketplace. These interviews gave us much information about consumer development among elementary school children. Often before the actual interviews, we held focus group interviews with six or eight kids at a time to get a grip on the language and thinking of the children that then gave us more directions for our in-person interviews.

Hundreds of hours of observation research among American and Chinese mothers and their children—infants, toddlers, preschoolers, and first- to sixth-graders—in the shopping setting provided opportunities to witness children's influence on moms' and dads' consumer behavior patterns. These observations were conducted before and after interviews about the stages of consumer development in order to guide the interviews and to confirm and/or modify information from the interviews, particularly those in China.

Case studies among six children ages 2–10 over an approximately eight-year period (five to eight years depending on the child) provided detailed insights into consumer behavior patterns of kids of all ages. These case studies consisted of reports from mothers and fathers, observations of the children in the household and in the shopping setting, and interviews with the children. These case studies permitted me to see children become consumers at their pace as a natural part of growing up.

Drawing studies were conducted among approximately 2,000 elementary school children in the United States, Canada, Mexico, China, South Korea, Taiwan, and Hong Kong. These drawing studies provided much information about what children know about the marketplace—stores, products, brands, promotion, price—that they could not or would not express in their oral and written interviews. The drawings also helped us to understand some of the learning that takes place in early childhood that is in strictly visual codes.

I should note that qualitative techniques such as drawing studies are always in question because their results are often difficult to quantify. But without their results I doubt if we would know as much as we do about children as consumers. For instance, Coughlin and Wong (2002) fitted children with video cameras built into their hatband in order to see grocery stores as the children see them—through their eyes. In the same vein, children were given cameras to take pictures of specific emotion-loaded objects—favorites, fun items, even disliked items—as a way of describing those objects with pictures in addition to or without words.

Finally, around 600 American and Chinese moms were interviewed in depth about their children's consumer behavior in each of the stages. These children included newborns, those still being held and carried, toddlers, preschoolers, and elementary-school-age kids. The resulting information was converted into averages and ranges and was tested for influence of demographics—income, education, occupation, one-parent households, two-parent households, three-or-more-parents households (such as grandmothers).

As a qualifying note, I recognize that I have used many rounded numbers in this addendum in order to talk about the research that I have done or had done regarding children's consumer development. I did this for two reasons: One, I cannot remember the exact numbers in some cases, and two, I used rounded numbers to accommodate the reader. In all cases, the numbers were intended to be conservative estimates.

REFERENCES

American Academy of Pediatrics. (2000). *Child abuse and neglect.* Retrieved from www.Medem.com

Chan, K., and J. U. McNeal. (2004). *Advertising to Children in China.* Hong Kong: The Chinese University Press.

Coughlin, R., and T. Wong. (2002, October–December). The retail world from a kid's perspective. *International Journal of Advertising & Marketing to Children, 4,* 3–8.

Edwards, A. L. (1959). *Edwards personal preference schedule manual.* New York: The Psychological Corporation.

Erikson, E. H. (1968). *Identity: Youth and Crisis.* New York: W. W. Norton & Company.

Feldman, R. S. (2000). *Development across the Life Span* (2nd ed.). Upper Saddle River, NJ: Prentice Hall.

Hartup, W. (1979). The social worlds of childhood. *American Psychologist, 34,* 944–950.

Hebb, D. O. (1949). *The Organization of Behavior.* New York: John Wiley & Sons, Inc.

McNeal, J. U. (1992). *Kids as Customers: A Handbook of Marketing to Children.* New York: Lexington Books.

McNeal, J. U. (1999). *The Kid's Market: Myth and Realities.* Ithaca, NY: Paramount Market Publishers.

Murray, H. A. (1938). *Explorations in Personality.* New York: Oxford University Press.

National Clearinghouse on Child Abuse and Neglect Information. (2001). *An overview of child neglect.* Retrieved from nccanch.acf.hhs.gov

Phillips Jr., J. L. (1969). *The Origins of Intellect: Piaget's Theory.* San Francisco, CA: W. H. Freeman and Company.

Piaget, J. (1954). *The Construction of Reality in the Child.* New York: Basic Books.

Thomas, G. V. (2005). *CPI: Defining and investigating child abuse.* Baltimore: PublishAmerica.

Young, P. T. (1961). *Motivation and Emotion: A Survey of the Determinants of Human and Animal Activity.* New York: John Wiley & Sons, Inc.

7

STAGE TWO OF CONSUMER DEVELOPMENT: SEEKING/REQUESTING (6–24 MONTHS)

Making a Smart Consumer out of a Two-Year-Old

As part of an investigation to determine what, if any, consumer behavior patterns are intentionally taught to very young children by parents, we asked a 32-year-old mother of a 22-month-old son about this topic in a 30-minute discussion-type interview. Here is some of the dialogue that was recorded.

Lila Beck, a working mom, said she takes her son, Brackett, with her shopping at least once a week, "… usually all day Saturday until he gives out," is how she described their co-shopping. "He isn't two yet but he's smart for his age, so I know he can learn to pick out some things."

When asked about some of the subjects she tries to teach her child, she described some shopping activities as examples. "The main reason I take him with me to the natural foods market is to get him eating healthy," she volunteered. "I figure if he helps pick out the fruits and vegetables he will more likely want to eat them. When we look at fruit, I let him pick out some and I tell him about the vitamins that are in them." She was asked if he was able to understand her. She answered, "I think he can learn that sort of thing at his age if it's done right," meaning, she explained, if the instructions are worded in a way that he can understand. "Like I said, Brackett's smart for his age." Then she added, "My family eats healthy but it wouldn't if I didn't push it."

Asked for other examples of her teaching her child consumer behavior patterns, Mrs. Beck said this. "We also go shopping at the mall together sometimes to look at clothes for him and his daddy. That's another thing I want him to learn is how to shop for clothes and to do it in the men's department when he gets old enough. We look in the children's department now, but we also look in the men's department. Pretty soon he will be trying to buy clothes on his own. He already asked me for a new Dallas Cowboys tee shirt like his Daddy got."

When asked if Brackett ever requests things he sees on TV, she answered, "Heavens yes. Constantly. Kool-Aid, Oreos, you name it, but like I say, I want him to learn to eat healthy." Then she added, "He's reaching that age where he constantly asks for things, but neither me nor his Daddy gives in to him." When asked what she meant when she said that she and her husband do not give in to the child, she answered, "We don't give him everything he asks for; just what we think he should have." She followed with, "We do make some exceptions on special occasions such as when he does well at nursery school, or he is sick, or something like that."

"In sum, then, Brackett can have things he asks for at special times such as when he is sick, and he can have things he asks for if you think they are good for him. Is that correct?" the interviewer asked.

"Yes, unless it is something really expensive like a car," Mrs. Beck laughingly answered. Then she added, "I know what's good for him, and I think he can learn what's good for him, too, if I buy certain things for him that he asks for and not others."

The interviewer tagged on this statement with, "I'm curious. What happens when you tell him no you will not buy an item for him. Does he understand what you are trying to teach him?"

"Oh, sometimes he throws a fit when I won't buy him something, but he has to learn what's right and what's not. He also has to learn that acting up won't get him any more than acting right," she firmly stated.

INTRODUCTION

In the first stage of consumer development—approximately the first six months of life—discussed in Chapter 6, the child is in the beginning process of discovering commercial objects through experiencing the environment in which he is born. It is termed the *observation stage* because a child's consumer behavior consists principally of discovering commercial objects through the sensory system that is facilitated by his motor development. The developmental psychologist Piaget referred to the time period of the first stage of consumer development as the *sensorimotor stage* of cognitive development. This period actually spans the first stage of consumer development and continues through the second stage—seeking/requesting—which is the topic of this chapter.

Before children can seek and/or request commercial objects, however, they must be aware of them. That awareness begins in stage one—in the observation stage. Children's awareness and assimilation of commercial objects ordinarily occur first in the limited environment of their crib or bed. As the children develop physically, they are able to turn and lift their heads and completely scan at least one-half of the crib. By six months—the end of the first stage of consumer development—they can sit up and survey all of their crib and much of the room in which it is located, thus expanding their physical environment manyfold. And they discover that their room, like their crib, is filled with objects to be experienced in the satisfaction of their wants and needs—all put there by their parents and other caretakers for their consuming pleasure. Once the infants are able to sit up, moms place them in different settings such as the floor of their room and other rooms, allowing them to consume with their senses—to observe—many other commercial objects.

Being held in mother's arms is another revealing environment in which the baby may become aware of more commercial objects. Just notice, for example, how an infant holds on to mom's blouse and even feels it with hands and fingers. In addition to mom's clothing, the infant observes other items related to her such as jewelry and fragrances (which babies may use to recognize their moms). By resting in mom's arms, the baby also has a chance to observe more of the nursery and its items, and possibly other rooms such as the parents' bedroom. Sometime between two and six months, moms typically introduce their children to yet another commercial center, the marketplace, that is external to the home and contains many additional commercial objects to observe. Most likely, to get to the marketplace, the children additionally are exposed to other environments, such as those provided by a car, bicycle, or bus. Look again at the infant consumer in Photo 6-1 in the previous chapter. Notice how she is trying to feel her mother's hat while being carried in a back cradle. That is the kind of observation we are describing here, and the kind that leaves impressions—imprints—as a result of such multisensory experiences as seeing and touching. You might also expect the child to explore her mother's other brightly colored clothing since these bold colors usually have an appeal to newborns. And if you will, just imagine how many other commercial objects the child can see, hear, and smell, particularly in the marketplace where this couple was photographed.

Through all these hundreds of observations—seeing, touching, smelling, tasting, and hearing—at home, in the car, at the marketplace—children experience hundreds of objects daily, practically all of them commercial objects, and store these observational results in their mind through a variety of sensorimotor actions. Even though at the very beginning the babies are able to observe with just one sense such as taste, they still file away some awareness of liked objects. And within a month or two, they can integrate two or more senses concurrently with increasing body movements, thus producing a more effective memory. The infants file away these consumer experiences in a memory that is rapidly improving through use, along with a sensory system that by six months is comparable to that of an adult. Thus, at six months or so, children are performing many tekrams a day and storing them in their minds that later will direct more consumer behavior patterns. Hence, consumer development is occurring at a rapid pace in initial infanthood.

It seems significant to repeat again that even in this earliest stage of consumer development children are learning much consumer behavior *on their own*. At parental urging and through modeling, they are learning such tekrams as how to obtain food from a bottle, shake a rattle for entertainment, and squeeze a stuffed animal for companionship. At another level they are also learning consumer behavior patterns definitely not shown or taught by parents but developing them through their own creative thinking. For example, the vertical slats in the babies' cribs are intended to keep them safe and contained in the crib. Moms rely on them to keep the babies from falling out of the crib. But the babies have learned on their own to kick them in order to shake the mobiles over their heads, and to use them as a tool to pull themselves to one side of the crib where they can get a better look at the stuffed animals that populate the crib. In yet another self-taught feat that will occur during the time of the second stage of consumer development, they will curl their toes around the slats to assist them in moving around in their crib, perhaps climbing out of it. So, even during this relatively immobile, somewhat unthinking period in their life, the infants are learning to use—maybe misuse—commercial objects on their own. It should be emphasized, also, that the tekrams performed by the babies are contributing to their physical and cognitive development as well as helping them to hone their senses that transfer information about their environment into their minds. So, while it requires physical and cognitive development to practice consumer behavior patterns, that same consumer behavior is a necessary part of physical and cognitive development, including the development of the central nervous system.

Now, in the *second* stage of consumer development examined in this chapter, the children enter a period in which they intensify their observations of commercial objects—products, packages, stores, displays, advertisements at the point of purchase and on TV—and intensify their attempts to make some of the new commercial objects a part of them through *seeking and requesting*. They bring with them a rapidly improving mental storage system that holds information on desirable items and a rapidly improving motor system that they are learning to use to obtain them. There is a logical progression to it—tasting something they like, for instance, then seeking or asking for more of it. Stage two, like the first one, is divided into two substages to reflect major changes in the children's physical and mental abilities to express consumer behavior patterns. In the first half of this stage, from ages 6 months to roughly 14 months, the children seek and request objects with mainly what might be termed a *motor language*—pointing hands and fingers and nodding their heads. Also, in general, they are utilizing only the upper half of their bodies—sitting up, turning in both directions from a stable center of gravity, and reaching with arms and hands and fingers—to ask for and seek the growing number of environmental objects that are attractive to them—like the child in Photo 6-1 who examines her mother's bonnet. The first substage is labeled *Pre-language/Pre-legs*, since the children do not yet know how to talk or how to walk but are still very active and very determined consumers. The second substage is labeled *Post-language/Post-legs* to reflect the children's consumer behavior after learning how to talk and walk and therefore to be much more effective at asking for and obtaining the many objects, mostly commercial objects, that populate their rapidly expanding environment.

STAGE TWO: SEEKING/REQUESTING (6–24 MONTHS)

Through children's many observations that began in stage one of consumer development and continue and grow in frequency in this stage, they become aware of products that they want and some that they do not want. Thus, a rapidly growing number of preferences are established in their mental structures. For instance, they migrate to products that are attractive because of their bold colors; the pleasant sounds they make; and/or their good taste, smell, and feel. Through the meager means at their disposal, they seek out these particular products. They try to obtain them on their own, but, of course, at this age they cannot do enough on their own to live the life they want, so they need to turn to others, mainly mom, for assistance. This seeking of commercial products is the focus of this second stage of development of consumer behavior patterns, and is divided into two substages as noted previously. The first substage reflects the child's limited language and mobility that characterize children during their first year of life, whereas the second takes into account substantial improvements in both. Of course, the age ranges used here for this stage and the substages are only estimates based on research among children and their families in the United States and China and are not intended to describe any one child.

Substage One: Pre-Language/Pre-Legs (6–14 Months)

In this first substage of stage two of consumer development that begins at six months, children are in the process of developing gross motor actions and first language. Thus, it is termed *Pre-language* and *Pre-legs*.

Pre-Legs

In the first stage of consumer development discussed in the preceding chapter, children go from a *lying* position to a *sitting* position; they gain control of their upper body. Discovery through upper body movements characterized the beginning of stage two of consumer development. In this second stage under consideration here, they go from a sitting position to a *standing* position during the second 6 months of their life—from 6 to around 12 months of age, approximately—and then to *walking* after another month or two. In a standing position they can keep their legs, trunks, and necks in a vertical line and look right and left, thus making it possible to access at least twice as many objects as they could 6 months ago. Of course, before they reach the standing phase, they must *creep* and *crawl*, two locomotive actions that also provide them much opportunity to observe objects new to them. And they seem driven by novelty, to discover new things, to have new experiences. Perhaps they sense what is fact: that movements to access objects help them hone those movements and strengthen their muscles. Most likely, they are seeking *need satisfaction* and have figured out that exploration of the environment leads to it. In any case, whatever the true motives, they are discovering many more things to sample and catalog.

As noted in the preceding chapter, once babies can sit up, mothers have a tendency to put them on the floor, often inside a playpen, where they can enjoy their new vistas as they choose, where they can play, where they can have a life of their own, so to speak. Because they get tired in the sitting position—sitting places a great demand on their trunk, which is still gaining strength—or because they simply fall over from not being able yet to maintain their stability, they begin to attempt some creeping, perhaps to restore their sitting position, perhaps to attempt to reach things found during sitting. Creeping is an arms-and-legs locomotive effort—swimming on the ground, so to speak. First, at around six or seven months come the climbing motions with the arms while the babies are lying on their tummies—upper parts of the body work before lower parts according to the cephalocaudal principle described in Chapter 4. In effect, at first they are dragging their lower halves. But soon the legs are recruited (through new motor-nerve connections), and when placed on the floor, the infants seem motivated to creep around in circles in their playpen while pausing to examine every toy their bodies encounter. And, of course, with their arms and hands, they try to put each one in their mouth. Again, they do not need to be motivated to explore; that seems to come with the wiring. They only need opportunity.

Within another month or two, the babies will push themselves off the floor from a creeping effort and raise themselves up on their hands and arms. From this posture they will crawl while again dragging their lower halves—still hands and arms before legs. But after a month or so, they will also get their legs under them and crawl and crawl and crawl. This new locomotive action is so rewarding in terms of giving them a leap forward in their quest for autonomy that they practically reject sitting and creeping. This newfound freedom gives the children choice in what their sensory system accesses. If freed from their playpens, the children discover many appealing adult items such as furniture, pots and pans, mom's and dad's clothing, trash cans full of playthings, floor lamps, and, regretfully, many dangerous items if parents do not adequately childproof their home. Also, from this crawling position, the babies utilize the pushing power of their legs and arms in this position to begin pushing their toys and any other objects that are not nailed down. They may also run races with the pet dog "on all fours." It is apparent as an outsider watches these crawling actions of the infants that consumer behavior is pushing and pulling them. In fact, the children seem to view these many new tekrams as rewards for the new motor actions of crawling, and if provided the opportunity, they will crawl for a longer time and crawl faster.

Whether because they are obstacles or because they stimulate curiosity, furniture items such as chairs, tables, sofas, and ottomans present opportunities for crawling children to lift themselves to a standing position. And once in this standing position, which requires much leg strength, the children discover yet more objects to examine—anything lying on the chairs, on the end tables, in magazine racks, for instance. They also discover how to squat and to sit down hard from a standing position, since it is such a strain on their trunks and legs. All this, as noted, occurs during the six months following sitting up. Thus, these tekrams involving furniture demonstrate new uses for the items that the children create while concurrently building motor and cognitive skills. A few years later the children may utilize the furniture in games such as hide-and-seek.

It is only a matter of a month or two more until the children try taking their *first step*. Actually, the strain from standing is great, so there is not much motivation to walk—except, again, to discover even more things to enjoy. No pain, no gain, seems to be their banner. So, while some developmental theorists would say that all these motor activities are programmed to occur at a certain time—for example, Arnold Gesell and his colleagues at the Yale Clinic of Child Development (Gesell, Ilg, and Ames, 1977)—it would appear that consumer behavior is another and perhaps more logical explanation. Or it is part of the programming but not acknowledged by Gesell and other maturationists. As one observes infants at play, for example, at daycare centers, it becomes so apparent that in their quest for commercial objects, they push their bodies beyond current capabilities. Toys, particularly, but it could be pots and pans or a box of facial tissue, cause infants to experiment with their bodies, to try new positions, to think about body movements. It would be easy, also, to explain some of their motor behavior with intrinsic motives such as the need for new experiences or rewarding experiences, which then loops us back to consumer behavior patterns made up of children's most desirable experiences.

Locomotion alone is not enough to fulfill the quest to experience novel objects in the child's environment. *Manipulation* is an absolutely necessary partner to locomotion for the development of consumer behavior patterns.

Manipulation involves the use of the arms and hands and fingers in *reaching* for, *grasping*, and *releasing* items. For instance, an 8-month-old may be seen creeping and/or crawling on the floor, stopping, reaching out and grasping a toy with his whole hand, and then sitting up and putting it in his mouth. These combined motor and manipulation actions help the child to experience many objects and determine which of them are worth keeping—experiencing again. When children are able to stand with the aid of furniture and use their manipulative skills, they will experience many more things to like or dislike. They may find it difficult to release objects in their *palmer grip* just as they find it difficult and frustrating to pick up small objects such as a button or paper clip since they have not yet mastered the *pincer grasp*—using their thumbs and forefingers to grip an object. But the hand release and the pincer grasp are likely to be practiced, although not artfully, by the time they can walk at 14 months. And the combination will permit many more consumer behavior patterns—walking to, reaching for, grasping an object, letting it go, and/or placing the object in the mouth.

Pre-Language

This first substage of the seeking/requesting consumer development stage is also a time when *language* is beginning, and consumer behavior plays a major role in its development since it is required for many tekrams. Children six to eight months old cannot yet speak, although in various ways they can ask for things from their mothers who can understand their "motor language." By reaching out their arms, pointing with their hands and fingers, and even turning their upper bodies toward an object, and combining these gestures with utterances such as grunts and uhhs, infants are able to convey their wants to their moms who encourage them, knowingly and unknowingly, to "speak" in this manner. The infants probably do understand some of their moms' often repeated words such as their names and the term *no-no*, since comprehension of symbolic language begins very early in life and precedes its actual use. So, while the infants do rather well on their own seeking out commercial products throughout their homes, their motor language helps them to get more of what they want—and get it quicker.

Starting somewhere around 10 months babies will attempt their first words although such words may be difficult for parents to discern through the babies' constant babble—cooing, aahing, and uhhing—that starts at 2 or 3 months. But after a month or so of new sounds, mom and dad usually do recognize their names—*Mama* and *Dada*—and are very pleased when they hear their newborns speak them. Typically, these first words come with a motor request for a commercial object. Thus, *consumer behavior often stimulates the production of language*. Interestingly, also, you can probably place a safe bet on one or more of a baby's first few words being a *brand name* such as Barney, Winnie the Pooh, or Cheerios, although they are unlikely to be spoken very clearly or with two syllables. Also, according to a number of moms, they are as likely to speak the (brand) name of their favorite stuffed animal or TV character first as they are to speak the name of their parents, although, again, parents may not be able to discern the specific words. And this may hurt a little bit at the adult level. What mom wants her baby's first word to be *Barney* rather than *Mommy*! By age 12 months babies probably can speak a half-dozen words and understand 10 times that many. These words, combined with a lot of motor language, will get the babies a lot of commercial objects from generous parents and grandparents. Thus, the babies' mere act of asking for commercial objects usually is rewarded—they are given what they ask for and often more. Maybe this is one of those "special occasions" that Mrs. Beck spoke about when her child gets whatever he wants.

During this first 6- to 12-month period of the asking/seeking stage of consumer development, visits to the *marketplace* become common for practically all children and usually grow in number. While the first visit for American children is usually at 2 or 3 months, and for Chinese children at 8–10 months, frequency of visits rapidly increases for both once they have been successful. Moms first have to figure out how to manage it all—dressing of the child for a trip outside the home, using transportation such as a seat of some kind for the baby that can be carried in the mom's arms or on the back as well as placed in the car or on the back of a bicycle, and figuring out where to stop and rest the child. But once these logistics are in place, moms with their newborns can be expected to make at least weekly visits to one or more stores. It is a common scene to see an American mom in the supermarket with her nontalking, nonwalking baby sitting atop the shopping cart in a baby seat—either that provided by mom or one provided by the store. Just as likely mom will talk to the baby, the baby will "talk" to her, and mom may give the baby a package of something to hold and to chew in addition to her pacifier during the store visit. Moreover, if mom happens to visit the toy section of the supermarket, she likely will give the baby a toy of some sort to play with and perhaps buy one for her. And there is a chance, also, that her alert observer may recognize one of her toys such as a stuffed animal, and in fact, mom may point it out in order to stimulate a bit of "conversation." Keep in mind that mom is pleased when her baby tries to talk or tries to ask for something, and she knows that favorite consumption objects will stimulate first words or even a string of words.

The likelihood is great that if her baby is sitting up in the seat so that she has a good view of the merchandise, she will ask for something with motor language while in the presence of an object in the store much the same way as at home when the baby asks for something outside her crib. For the baby this tekram in the store is no different from that at home; she is just seeking a commercial object that may give pleasure as confirmed by her *consumer memory*—what is usually termed her *evoked set*. Most mothers will oblige most of the time.

At first none of the objects that the babies seek or ask for are objects in the sense that adults see them. They do not yet exist separately from the infants or have a life of their own, but still they have attractive attributes that cause the babies to want them. Probably the babies want them because they have recorded one or more related tekrams, one or more schemes of touching or tasting an object with those features (color, shape) and received enjoyment from the action. In fact, the babies may demonstrate with motor language—shaking, kicking, smiling—the pleasure they have received from the object before. Yet, the object does not exist "out there" separately from the babies—not until around 10 months or so as a rule. At about this time the babies' cognitive development has reached a point where *object permanence* is occurring; that is, the babies are beginning to see some objects as separate from them. For example, at 6 months if an infant wakes up and sees her favorite stuffed animal in the crib, she may reach for it. If she does not see it, she probably will not remember that it is a member of her crib until around 9 or 10 months—that it is an object that belongs in that space. At that point she will look for it when she awakes, although if it is not in the crib, it may not seem to matter. Soon, however, she will expect the stuffed animal in her field of vision if it is a favorite toy of hers. By the time the child is 12 months old—near the end of the first half of the second stage of consumer development—chances are the baby can remember where some objects are in her room as well as her crib, and quite possibly even in a store frequently visited. Regarding the latter, 12-month-old children can often identify a favorite supermarket and/or their favorite shopping experience by the shopping carts of a certain color that they see when entering the store, according to their mothers. Thus, the shopping carts have taken on separate and positive status not unlike their favorite stuffed critter. But if mom goes into a different store or a different door of the same store, her baby may not recall the previous shopping experience if she is not cued by some recurring stimulus such as color. Mom also knows too that she can skip the toy section and the baby of 10 or 12 months will not notice. But by 15 months, into the second substage, her toddler certainly will notice and may even do some communicating about it with some screams and finger-pointing.

Object permanence/object separation is a critical matter when it comes to the baby's becoming a full-fledged human being and consumer. During the first stage of consumer development, all objects—social and physical—are a part of the infant, and this relationship with the environment continues into the beginning of stage two, the stage under discussion. Babies have no conception of objects existing outside themselves at this time. If a physical object disappears from the known environment, babies' minds easily switch to another object of interest. Out of sight is out of mind. But the process of repeatedly interacting with many physical objects produces some favorites, and at some point the children miss these objects when they are out of sight and seek them. Thus, the preferred objects take on lives of their own; they are separate from the infants. By 10–12 months, the infants often ask for many objects that are not present with special body motions and one-word sentences.

Also around 10 months, the process of the babies themselves gradually becoming separate entities from other social and physical objects begins. Usually termed *separation/individuation*, it mainly marks the second sub-stage of the asking/seeking stage of consumer development. Thus, seeking those things that have given pleasure such as a particular pacifier, food, or toy is logical. Also, seeking new environments where the need for explo-ration can be satisfied makes good sense. It would be just as easy to theo-rize that infants seek out desired objects to keep them as part of themselves, but what is being emphasized here is the beginning of recognition among infants of the separate existence of physical and social objects including themselves. Therefore, there also begins an earnest attempt to have them, to hold onto them, to consume them for the benefit of *self.* And because these infants are unable to use language and legs, this basic task is difficult and frustrating, perhaps prompting both.

Related to separation/individuation, starting at 9 or 10 months, infants can begin to understand that the images they see in a mirror are themselves. At this point in life they are not individuals, per se, in the sense that they do not see themselves as specific persons. But starting at this time they begin to seek separation from mom and to form some perceptions of themselves, what we often call a *self-image.* This is a slow process that really becomes noticeable after more language and more motor skills develop. But it marks the beginning of the *me-my-mine* stage in which mom will start hearing all three terms and hearing them frequently from her little consumer. These terms also mark an outward expression of the egocentrism that is devel-oping in the child—and driving much consumer behavior now and for the next couple of years.

Substage Two: Post-Language and Post-Legs (14–24 Months)

Once children begin to walk and talk around 12–14 months, new, more complex consumer behavior patterns develop at an astronomical rate. These two basic human activities build on the infants' concurrent growing cognitive ability to view objects as separate and permanent. Let's look closer at these two activities, as they provide a foundation for most con-sumer behavior of individuals.

Walking

Learning to walk is the ultimate in balance for the human being and takes a lot of practice following the first effort at standing alone around 10–12 months. While stability is necessary, so are some manipulative movements. Once standing is accomplished by holding onto furniture and/or relying on mom's hand under the arms, then the baby must learn to release his grip on the furniture. Gripping the furniture is easy at 12 months; ungripping, letting go, releasing are not. To an outsider, it may look as though the baby is fearful of letting go of the table he is holding onto, but actually there is no fear, only the lack of manipulative ability. But by 14 months or so, ungripping is learned, and when combined with stepping, it produces walking. Of course, all of this newfound walking ability is applauded by family members, a reward that is probably motivating to the toddler to try more. The baby's first steps are also motivating to parents to buy more—more toys that can be used in walking such as push and pull toys, more foods to build stamina in the hard-working child, and more shoes and socks and other clothing including some padded clothing to facilitate walking and taking some of the shock out of the many falls that will follow.

Once children can walk, they take an increasing number of marketplace visits with their parents. Carrying a 20-pound child is no easy task for a mother, so walking with him and simply holding his hand to prevent him from falling is a reprieve of sorts for her—although a very slow process at first. In fact, mothers of newly walking children probably want to enjoy this new shopping partner and even show him off—brag about him directly or indirectly to other parents. He will still most likely sit in the shopping cart seat, at least until he is 20 months old or more, but he may be permitted to sit and stand in the cart itself. There, however, will be more walking-shopping without a cart such as that available in a shopping mall or department store. Chinese mothers particularly like to walk with their toddlers, in part to foster walking skills. Also, shopping carts that accommodate a child are still uncommon in China.

There is a downside to the children's walking ability for moms. By 15–18 months, the children's walking gives them access to many more products to see and want both at home and in the marketplace. Mothers discover, for instance, that when they check out at the supermarket, their walking children have their hands into all the gum and candies that are put there for that purpose, particularly those that have an attractive aroma. Much of the displayed confections may have little meaning to the children, but their access does; it means more exploration opportunities, and they happen to be exactly at toddler's eye level. Moms quickly attempt to avoid this problem by carrying the toddlers or keeping them in the shopping cart. But the requests that are growing in number accelerate at the checkout (and foster negative reactions among moms toward the merchandisers).

Shopping with children in the street market is still standard fare in China. Rather than the children walking—if they have learned how—they are often pushed in a stroller that is equipped with play items. Not only do the children avoid the dirty street by riding, but it is easier for parents who also may use the vehicle for storage of purchases. Photo 7-1 shows a

PHOTO 7-1 A nine-month-old Chengdu boy sits in his stroller while his grandmother shops for fruits and vegetables nearby. Attached to his stroller is a pretend firecracker that is actually an empty M&M candy package given at lunar New Year's time.

nine-month-old Chengdu boy proudly sitting in his stroller while his grandmother shops nearby for fruits and vegetables. Notice the oversized toy firecracker on the tray that is tied to the stroller for the child to play with. Notice, too, that the firecracker is labeled with the M&M candy brand along with the M&M candy characters. Presumably, the pretend firecracker was purchased with M&M candies inside—fireworks are revered by the Chinese as tools of celebration—and the "package" was retained as a play item. This is about the age when brands first begin to enter the child's world.

American and Chinese moms both report that their children make requests when in the presence of products at a median age of 24 and 18 months, respectively, but their asking becomes significant around 15 months in both cultures. About half the time the request is for a food product among the Chinese children; three-quarters of the requests of American kids is for food, usually foods that parents use as rewards. In both cases the food requests are cued by visits to food markets. If the visits are to toy stores, for instance, most of the requests are for toys. So, what they see is what they want—and usually get. At this point in the children's lives, their asking for things is a bit of novelty for mothers; therefore, it tends not only to be rewarded but encouraged. For example, in Chinese department stores, which usually consist of four to six floors of merchandise, a counter of sweet delicacies primarily for children often is set up at the beginning steps of each floor. Chinese children quickly learn to ask for something at each floor, and moms usually respond positively, seeing it as fun and conversational, and often buy something at least at one of the floors.

It is important to note the impact on the child's psyche of being able to walk without assistance. The quest for *autonomy*, *self-identification*, and *individuation* that is going on at this time started probably the first time the child recognized herself in a mirror held by her mother around 10 months and wanted to be that person in that image. Walking allows the youngster to assert herself, to do more things on her own—get her bottle out of the refrigerator herself—and reinforce an image the child is building of the self. Once object separation occurs on a regular basis, the child begins to see herself as separate from others and from other objects. Now, many consumer behavior patterns—consumer behavior patterns made possible through walking skills—develop that allow children to express their self-image. Walking also allows children to take their moms or dads by the hand and lead them to objects that reflect their self-image. To sum it up, walking introduces a whole new range of tekrams. This is equally true for talking, which is discussed next.

Talking

We have noted often that walking children are beginning to make an increasing number of requests when in the presence of specific goods and services. Of course, it is not the legs that actually make the requests possible but the language. *Speaking* is a fine motor skill requiring coordination of many muscles that control the child's lips, tongue, palate, and larynx and must be learned over a period of several months. Babbling begins in the first 6 months, followed by cooing, oohing, and aahing during the second 6 months, and then words appear around 12–14 months—at about the same time as walking. During the pre-language period, the child spoke with body language, but now he gradually begins to speak a mental language, or what is usually termed *symbolic language*. Words at first symbolize actions. For instance, the word *dog* may mean touching a dog, and the word *cracker* may mean tasting a cracker. That is how infants first learn about their environments: through sensorimotor actions. As such, first words are copies of parents' speech or maybe that of characters on TV or in storybooks that can be related to actions by the children. But somewhere between 15 and 18 months, children enter the world of symbolic language in which they begin to understand that words represent—stand for—physical and social objects as well as actions. This would not happen without the children's mentally experiencing object permanence—and experiencing the objects. Thus, in their minds, children begin to accumulate words and pictures—tekrams and schemes—that are symbolic representations of objects and actions.

While an object prompts its word description, the children need not be in the presence of a box of cookies, for example, in order to think of it and speak of it with "Cookie," meaning "I want a cookie." Through many satisfying experiences with cookies—via mom's assistance—the child has stored actions such as tasting and eating cookies, including certain kinds and/or brands of cookies, and now can think of those actions (tasting, eating) on those objects (cookies) perhaps by just becoming hungry. Once symbolic thinking and speaking begin—and it is a relatively slow process that will advance over the next several years until it is in place at around age five or six—they permit improved seeking. As a child seeks cookies in the home or in the marketplace, he can facilitate the effort with spoken inquiries such as "Where's cookies?"

It seems, moreover, that once symbolic thinking begins, it finds new uses and builds and improves itself. Children continue to use words and thoughts to represent new and familiar social and physical objects and thus develop what we call a *vocabulary*. But they also begin to *think* about others and the actions of others, or what we might call using their *imagination*. Around 20–24 months, they begin to sense the results of their actions on others and the results of the actions of others on them. For example, they imagine what mom will answer when they ask to go shopping with her. Then they play that back in their minds, thus initiating *imitation*. At 20–24 months, they can imitate the actions and words of their parents. Actually, all this started when the children were just a few months old and they would copy their moms' smile or sound. But with symbolic thinking now available to the children, the copying can be done without seeing or hearing mom. Once this process is in place, the children then can pretend to be others such as parents, and imitate their behaviors, including their consumer behavior, through imagination. Also, at this time, imagination and imitation foster *creative thinking*—the rearrangement of existing knowledge. Thus, they may take the words of mom or dad and change them to a more favorable meaning. This is also the crude beginning of storytelling. The objects of their thoughts—parents, pets, foods, play items—do not actually have to be present to be considered. Mental images of them cue the children's thinking and imagination.

A special case of imagining what someone or something will say or do involves *transitional objects*. Beginning about the time of symbolic language development, many children begin to assign life to a doll, stuffed animal, or just a blanket or pillow—but almost always a commercial object—and imagine that it talks, listens, and responds to their talking—a practice called *animism*. If you have ever enjoyed a *Calvin and Hobbes* comic strip (or book), you have seen a transitional object in action. Giving life to an inanimate object is the ultimate in individual consumer behavior and sets the stage for much adult consumer behavior. A child carries her favorite stuffed animal almost everywhere, all the time. It is a companion that substitutes for mom and her niceties now that mom is often separated physically from the child. It ends up being the most valuable item the child owns, a best friend, and yet only a few years later will be discarded. Adults might say that this practice takes a lot of imagination, and they are right. It also could be called creative thinking or creative consumer behavior. For children aged two or three or older, it is not a very big step to assign life to an inanimate object if that object gives them the comfort, security, and friendship of a parent. In fact, they may also expect others to respect the object as a social being. For instance, in the movie *Sleepless in Seattle*, the eight-year-old boy still is very close to his stuffed doll, Howard, as a result of losing his mother. The doll was the main object filling the child's backpack when he packed and took his first airline flight in quest of a new mom. So, to him it was natural when his father kissed him goodnight to request his father to "Kiss Howard."

Somewhere between 18 and 24 months, most American children make their spoken requests to parents for certain objects when in their presence in the shopping setting. The product requested is almost always one that has satisfied them several times, and most likely a food product—and most likely a brand name, although not always pronounced the way the marketer would like. Among the thousands of choices available in a supermarket, the American child's first request is likely to be for a ready-to-eat (RTE) cereal that mom has been using as a *transitional food* (not to be confused with transitional objects). The request most likely occurs because mom wheels the shopping cart to the cereal aisle and looks for more of the cereal that she believes her child likes best. She may be quite surprised and pleased when her child also recognizes the package (a set of colors and shapes) and speaks for it with, for example, "O's" for Cheerios. Moreover, she will probably repeat the brand name and hand the box to the child who is sitting in the shopping cart seat—what we sometimes call the child's *observation post* since it puts him almost at an adult eye level that allows surveillance of practically all that an adult can see. In fact, the child probably sees more than an adult sees since he cannot yet practice selective perception the way that an adult can. At this age this action is probably symbolically recorded in the child's mind and played back at any time the child wants to, particularly at the beginning of the next shopping session when its mention by mom prompts it. In the case of Chinese children, chances are the first request will be for a play item. Even though the children are at this very early age, Chinese mothers are pushing education, and it appears that the children are starved for play items, items that are fun, enjoyable for their play value. Incidentally, as noted in Chapter 1, Chinese parents often take their children to McDonald's, and it appears that the play items in the kids' meal as well as the free balloons—more play items—that often are present at the door to the restaurants make the visits most important to the children. All of these come under the parental heading of rewards usually rather than education, but if McDonald's can figure out a way to make a balloon educational, chances are more moms and their kids will visit the restaurants more frequently.

We do not want to mislead as we talk about the development of symbolic language at this age and stage. Children are learning words rapidly and are becoming verbal rapidly. But most of the information that they take in and store is not in verbal form, but in visual form—not sound, but pictures. That is, most of the information that they use to recognize objects consists of visual symbols that they store in their minds. For instance, the child who recognized her favorite cereal on the shelf at the supermarket most likely recognized the configuration of symbols—colors, package shape, graphics on the package, as well as the brand name—that caused her to say, "I want this one." Remember that children comprehend words and symbols long before they can articulate them. For example, parents often report that while in the car their 12–15-month-olds can recognize the golden arches of McDonald's before they can speak that complex brand name. By the way, young Chinese children learning how to write and speak English often call the golden arches symbol an *M*.

Talking abilities combined with walking abilities are the most likely to expand children's *social environment* in addition to their physical environment. Besides their family members, children now begin to make contact with other children approximately their age. It is about this age—18–24 months—that children are placed in daycare, and there they interact for the first time with other children in large numbers who become a major source of product information. When 18–24-month-old toddlers go to a daycare center—now that they can express themselves somewhat and are somewhat toilet trained—and go to play areas in parks and housing complexes, *peers* naturally become a part of their social domain. Their association with peers prompts more and varied consumer behavior patterns, particularly more tekrams related to play. At this point in their lives, kids love playing more than eating or sleeping, and although they do not yet know how to play with others—they are so egocentric—they love to play in proximity to other children their age and try out their newfound oral skills. This is the beginning of parallel play—sitting side by side in a sand box, for instance, and talking to themselves in monologue form, playing in a fashion like the other kids are playing, and getting a chance to sample the playware (commercial objects) of other kids. It is natural, also, that the toddlers will build desire for some of the play items of their new playmates, desire that will be passed on to parents at the earliest opportunity. Parents tend at this age to be receptive to all the "I want one of those things like Stacy has," because they know that the social interactions, no matter how indirect, foster talking and making friends. And they believe that, in general, these interactions foster cognitive development.

ISSUES IN CONSUMER DEVELOPMENT (#7)

Impact of Today's Child Care on Child Development

With both parents working in most families, the children are placed in the care of a wide range of people and organizations generally referred to as *daycare*. Some of the caretakers are family, such as grandparents, older siblings, and other relatives. But most of the nearly 50 million children under age 12 in the United States are in the hands of nonfamily caretakers sometime during the day—namely, schools (preschools, kindergartens, and elementary schools); daycare facilities operated by individuals, employers, corporations, and governments; and nannies and traditional baby-sitters. Thus, working parents have spawned a whole new industry of child-care specialists, most of whom are strangers to the children they keep, and most are essentially marketers recognizing and providing the need for child-care services.

The daycare industry as well as parents who make this industry possible have attracted many critics—particularly former users of the industry, but also stay-at-home parents and many child-rearing specialists. Criticisms are strongest for caretakers who serve the preschool population of kids from infants through kindergarten—the formative years. Fundamentally, the judgments come down to comparing on three or four dimensions the care the children get at the various daycare facilities with that received from parents:

Education: Most parents today expect daycare for children ages 1–5 to be preparation for kindergarten, just as kindergarten is expected to be preparation for elementary school. Some larger daycare operations advertise that they offer age-graded curricula of academic subjects. But many, if not most, daycare facilities employ hourly employees who often are not qualified to teach such materials to toddlers, according to critics. Also, what children actually learn there may be incorrect and based on the background of the teaching personnel rather than on approved curricula.

Nutrition: Most of the children in daycare centers take one or more of their meals there, in addition to snacks. While most daycare centers say that they provide nutritious foods and beverages as part of balanced meals, some experts question this. For instance, one study of a Head Start facility examined its monthly menus (that are generally handed down by government) with the actual meals served and found of the 269 feedings, only 4 matched the meals described on the menus.

Play/Activities: Parents, child-rearing experts, and daycare center operators know how important play is to children's motor and mental development. Therefore, the individual and group-centered activities provided are the focus of many critics. The main complaint is that many daycare facilities utilize TV programming as a major part of play. While many of the children favor this activity, it contributes little to their development as compared to playing games, singing songs, and enjoying nature's creatures. Another complaint is the lack of a variety of play items, often blamed on the centers' limited budgets. Of course, the greater the variety of play items, the greater the chance the children will exercise their physical and cognitive skills.

Social Relationships/Skills: Two child development experts say that the worst thing about daycare is that it does not meet the children's needs for nurturing, ongoing relationships with significant people—as the parents do. Most daycare centers provide one caretaker for 5 or 6 very young children and maybe one for 10 of the older ones. Critics point out that this ratio cannot compare with parental care, and worse, the turnover of these employees is high, so the children have little chance to form relationships with them. Daycare operators counter with the many social relationships that children build with other children—something that most households cannot provide.

Other complaints by users of daycare include concern for the healthy conditions where toys may not be sanitized and some children may have serious illnesses, cleanliness is not emphasized, and safety features such as sprinkler systems and ample exits may not exist. There are also complaints about the personnel not being well trained or qualified to care properly for children, and worse, their backgrounds too often are not being checked thoroughly. And the rising cost of daycare is receiving commensurate complaints, too, where monthly costs are often in the neighborhood of $1,500.

Critics of parents who use daycare say, in summary, that the parents should not have children and then hand them off to strangers for rearing. Further, they say that parents should not treat their children as being as important as their jobs and then boast or complain about juggling job and family. In sum, critics say there is no substitute for family life as a child-rearing setting. When parents who use daycare are asked what they hope for most for their children at daycare, they answer, over and over, health and happiness. When they are asked if they believe the children receive these, most say no.

****

Sources: Brazelton and Greenspan, 2000; *Dive into Mark*, 2003; Fleischhacker, Cason, and Achterberg, 2006; wikipedia (n.d.).

CONSUMER MEMORY

In previous pages we often referred to the child's memory as playing a vital role in her consumer behavior patterns. We also used the specific term *consumer memory* to hint at some kind of storage of consumer acts of children, or what we have termed *tekrams*. All tekrams are in reference to commercial objects—asking for, interacting with, observing, buying, using, pretending to use, imagining, and talking about commercial objects. As stage two, children begin to practice symbolic representation, that is, to use words and other symbols to stand for objects and actions on those objects, they begin to store this information and use it over and over. This is not to suggest that these children at this age possess some special skills at selecting, labeling, and storing object-related information. It is more of a natural thing they do. As noted earlier, children are born into a commercial world: Their beds are commercial centers, their rooms are commercial centers, their homes are commercial centers, and of course, the marketplace where products are obtained is the ultimate in commercial centers. Many of these commercial objects found in these commercial centers are intended by moms and by marketers to please the children. And both adjust their offerings according to the responses of the children to them. For example, if a product purchased by parents does not please their children, the parents probably will not buy it again, or they will buy another version of the product—another flavor, texture, size, or color. As an example, if a two-year-old does not seem to like a transitional, ready-to-eat cereal, the parents may try a sweetened version, knowing how much their child loves something sweet. Likewise, if a maker of cereals finds (through research) that many young children do not like the taste of one of its cereals very much, and they also know (through research) that kids this age love anything sweet, they may decide to produce a sweetened version. Thus, ever since the child was born, parents and marketers have been trying to satisfy her with a variety of commercial goods. So, these two *ms—moms* and *marketers*—both work hard and often side by side to satisfy the wants and needs of children.

Thus, the results of these efforts produce memories among moms and among marketers. They also produce a memory in the minds of a third m, *me*, the child consumer. What enters the children's memories is motivated almost entirely by pure self-satisfaction. Moms and marketers, on the other hand, are usually motivated by money as well as the responses of their young consumers. In the case of moms, they do not want to buy more of a cereal, for instance, or any other product that does not satisfy their child and have to throw it away. It costs what steak costs—$3–6 a pound—in the United States and more in China. In the case of marketers who buy and/or produce in anticipation of demand, they do not want to have to dump their unpurchased kids' products on the "dollar store" market and lose money. Their stockholders demand higher revenues, not lower revenues, and they concurrently demand more profits. And the marketers' jobs depend on guessing right and producing more of both. (Just what percent of new products marketed to kids are successful is not known for sure, but based on my investigations, it appears to be only around 20 percent.)

Thus, in addition to the memory that results among moms and marketers who try to satisfy children, there is a memory that develops among the kids who consume the products—the *me*'s—or what might be called the consumer memory. Starting at around six weeks, when children begin to intentionally interact with commercial objects, they begin to build some kind of memory of them. At first it is what has been termed a *sensorimotor memory*, in which actions on a product are stored. For example, tasting of bottled milk for the first time is recorded. We do not know much about this sensorimotor memory except that it is children's first memory, that it serves the children adequately at this point in their lives, but not as well as symbolic memory. For example, a child may not recognize the provider of products—mom—if she is dressed differently than usual, demonstrating the failure of some aspect of sensorimotor memory. Gradually, the children's multisensory experiences with commercial objects combined with improved language produce a more efficient memory based on symbols in addition to actions. This symbolic memory that is constructed at about the same rate as learning speech gradually becomes more functional, more permanent, perhaps because it serves better than the old-style memory. So, all the products that children encounter are stored in what we are terming a *consumer memory*, and they appear to be cataloged in some efficient order from most satisfying to least satisfying that makes them easily accessible. In total, the consumer memory constitutes a major share of the total memory of children (and adults) and plays a significant role in children's development.

Hence, around 12–18 months, children begin construction of a product network in their minds that we still know relatively little about (McNeal, McDaniel, and Smart, 1983). Here are a few facts that have been gleaned by researchers over the past couple of decades about the product network. Children record all the products they become aware of in what might be termed a *product awareness set*. As you might imagine, the product awareness set is in a constant growth state, particularly during childhood. Underneath this umbrella the children record specific products usually by symbolic labels such as milk, candy, and shoes. In early childhood these general product labels appear to be stored as sounds and images. At first children learn their labels from parents and other members of the family—a big brother or sister can be very helpful with this—and they use them to cope with the overwhelming but interesting physical environment. So, the thousands of products that you and I encountered when we were kids were recorded in our consumer memories and presumably still exist there. Within each named product awareness set, there is a constantly expanding number of products. At first the products that young children are aware of are few, but as object permanence begins, the number of objects that children know grows at an increasing rate. Thus, the children commence to record in a special subset of the product awareness set certain ones that they dislike and certain ones they like. Of course, likes and dislikes must be identified separately, and they are—usually by name or what we call brand names, trademarks, or simply brands. (For our purposes here, we will use the terms *brand name* and *brand* interchangeably although the latter is usually broader in meaning than the former.) The children probably do not think in terms of brands at first consciousness of products, for they cannot yet conceptualize the notions of brands and products separately. But through parents' and others' use of brand names as objects—as nouns—the children begin to use them in this manner as well. Thus, research shows that children record products they know about and have feelings about by brand name. The group of brands of each product that they like is called the *evoked set* or *consideration set*. The ones they do not like are recorded in what is termed the *inept set*—those that are unsuitable or unfit. It is also believed that there are some brands of a product that children know but do not know enough about and are recorded separately in a group called the *inert set*. These brands are not yet assigned attributes that place them in a liked or disliked class.

As the children grow older, they become aware of more brands of the same product class and tend to order them and rank them. That is, they may like two or three or even four or five brands but normally not equally. So, they put some distance, what is called *psychological distance*, between one brand and the next one in the set. The best liked is ranked first, for instance, the next best is ranked second, and so on. But there are not equal differences among the brands. For instance, between number one and two, there may be lots of distance, indicating a clear winner of the child's heart, but between number two and three, there may be little distance. In effect, the child is saying that he likes number one a whole lot more than number two, and number two slightly more than number three, and so on. At a moment in time, there seems to be a "my favorite cereal" or "my favorite ice cream" for each child where only that brand will do.

Going back to the evoked set in which the favorites are recorded, researchers have ascertained that each time a child thinks about a product (in his product awareness set), for example, thinks about asking mom for it, the set of most favored products in that product class are evoked by name. That is how we generally define the evoked set—the few brands that come to mind when a consumer thinks about buying a product. So, very efficiently, when mom says she is going to the supermarket to get some milk and bread, she may immediately hear from her two-year-old, "I want a Popsicle." We can guess that the brand, Popsicle, is at the top of his list of frozen desserts. Frequent use of the evoked set, and the other sets, gives prominence to brand names in the minds of children. It is a way to describe a

PHOTO 7-2   A little Beijing boy wears the Snoopy brand on his hat, no doubt a choice of his parents. Western brands on Chinese children's clothing are normal in the big cities of China.

product to others. There is a tendency, in fact, among children to become enamored with certain brand names—just like their parents are, just like they learned from their parents, perhaps others—and they often use the brand names as nouns in their ordinary conversations. Additionally, they may wear the brands on their clothing, hang them up in their rooms in the form of posters, and even cover themselves with them in the form of printed bedspreads. Note Photo 7-2. If you look closely, you will see that the little Beijing two-year-old is wearing the Snoopy brand on his hat—in word and picture forms. Obviously, the child did not buy these clothes or unlikely select them at his age. His parents chose them to please the child, perhaps because the child has demonstrated a liking for the brand, Snoopy. Chances are the parents have talked to him about Snoopy, maybe bought him Snoopy action figures, or selected one at McDonald's. And you might guess that he has a Snoopy storybook at home from which his parents read to him—and from which he pretends to read. Referring to the vignette at the beginning of this chapter, remember when Mrs. Beck was asked if her boy,

Brackett, ever asked for things he saw on TV, she responded with the brand names Kool-Aid and Oreos as examples. Surely, Brackett did not dream up those names, but probably heard them spoken on TV, by his parents who bought both for him before, and perhaps spoken by a playmate at daycare. Brands not only are descriptions of favored products, they are a means of communicating these product preferences to others. In the major cities of China, wearing clothing with Western brands such as Snoopy is the norm for children, much as it is in any market-driven economy.

Another important point that should be made here, that was hinted at by Mrs. Beck's remarks, is that most parents hold in their minds their children's evoked sets and inept sets. Moms know what products and brands their kids like and develop mental structures—evoked sets—that hold this information. I have referred to this evoked set in mom's mind as an *evokked set* with the extra *k* denoting their kid's likings—one evokked set for each kid (McNeal, 1999). Of course, mom has her own evoked set filled with her own product and brand preferences, so this means that she carries with her—has on her mind—at least two evoked sets, and uses them to make effective purchases for her family members.

Some other research I have done suggests that these brand names may not be recorded in the minds of children (or adults) as just a list of names (sounds); (McNeal and Ji, 2003). Instead, they appear to be nested in their minds in the form of a network of product attributes, package shapes, colors, symbols, and words that make it easy for the children to recall the products and to recognize them at the marketplace. So, this means, then, that there rapidly develops hundreds, even thousands of product/brand networks in the minds of children by the time they get well into elementary school. These structures grow in complexity as children become aware of many more products and brands and change preferences among them. Who's responsible for constructing these? The three *m*s are and probably in this order—me, moms, marketers. Thus, the development of the mind has been variously characterized as an onion or an artichoke, but probably a more accurate characterization would be a grape vine and its grapes.

Descriptions of products and brands by attributes along with their ranking by preference actually make up only a small part of what we are calling the consumer memory. A first-grader has also formed a detailed image in her mind of the stores that offer the products such as their physical layout, certain aisles, displays, and the checkout areas. Additionally, there are images of people who use certain products and brands of products. Then there are images of advertising and spokespersons and spokescharacters that present these products on TV, along with their slogans and jingles. We should stress, too, that structural images of preferred products and their attributes are not just those that kids consume, but also those consumed by the family, such as automobiles, hotels, boats, yard furniture, and many others. This is why we suggested that the consumer memory constitutes a major share of a child's mental structures.

HOW MUCH/HOW OFTEN DO CHILDREN SEEK/REQUEST THINGS?

Once walking and talking become standard equipment for children, as indicated, they begin seeking and asking for many commercial objects. By the time they reach elementary school, they have perfected their asking so that it is most effective—as described in the next chapter. Asking for products and services thus becomes a normal consumer behavior of children of all ages who are totally dependent on parents for their need satisfaction. For example, when they reach an age where parents begin providing them spending money—usually around the time they enter the first grade—the children will begin to buy some of the things on their own that they normally ask of parents. But, then, as parents will tell you, they start asking for money, more money, more means to buy those things. So, asking, requesting, demanding, suggesting, hinting, conning, cajoling, whatever term is appropriate for the particular verbal and gestural behavior of children who seek commercial objects from parents, becomes a norm for the parent-child relationship in stage two of consumer development. It becomes so routine, in fact, that requests are often not apparent to moms, and perhaps not apparent even to trained researchers who observe the behavior of parent-child dyads.

One of the reasons for not recognizing some of a child's requests for products is the form of the request. Not all requests are direct, such as "I want a __." Many are in negative form, such as "I don't want a __," implying what the child does want. Consider some other forms of requests for commercial objects:

> "I won't eat _____."
> "I won't wear that."
> "I don't want to watch _____."
> "I don't want to go to _____."
> "I won't go to sleep until you give me a _____."
> "I can't read that."
> "I can't reach that."
> "I don't have any _____."
> "I don't like _____."

Thus, children's requests for products come in many forms. When children learn to make more effective requests—by being turned down—they can literally disguise them. For example, children may put the request in the form of a question to the parents such as these:

> "Do you like for me to wear this?"
> "Do you and Daddy want to go to a movie?"
> "Why don't you help me find my red socks?"
> "Would you like for me to go outside and play?

Sometimes children's requests are neither positive nor negative, but in the form of hints such as these:

"Are you going to watch your program on TV?" (I want to watch TV.)
"It's hot in here." (I would like to play in my pool.)
"Is it time for supper?" (I would like to eat.)
"Do you want me to feed Spot?" (I would like to eat.)

Thus, when all the forms of product requests are taken into consideration, the daily number is large, particularly if the day includes a visit to the marketplace. Fortunately, moms try to be sensitive to their children's requests in all forms and tend to respond to them positively—to acknowledge them and honor them. When mothers keep diaries (records) of their children's requests (in all forms) for products, and researchers analyze the diaries with the mothers present, the number of requests is quite large. For example, a typical two-year-old makes around 60–80 product requests a day in some form to caretakers—to moms, dads, grandparents, older siblings, baby-sitters—and if the day includes a visit to the marketplace—supermarket, mall, convenience store—the number approaches 100. This number does vary somewhat with parenting style. Children of permissive parents ask for more; children of authoritarian parents ask for less, particularly as the children get older and can better understand parents' feelings about the requests.

It should be emphasized that children's requests for wanted products are normal. It is their way of communicating their preferences to those who take care of them and provide for them. In fact, as children begin taking products (discussed in detail in the next chapter), parents tell them, "If you want anything, just ask for it; don't take it." So, children try to express their wants by asking parents for them. It is true that as children grow older, their requests increase to the point where parents cannot or will not meet all of them. In such cases there are confrontations between children and parents that may cause parents to view the constant requests negatively—as nagging. Parents may even blame marketers for the large number of requests from children—requests for products that the children see in advertisements and in TV programming, for instance. But requesting itself is a normal act for children. Just notice how Brackett's mother views such requests. When asked if Brackett requests items seen on TV, she calmly answered, "Heavens yes. Constantly."

DISCUSSION

In this chapter we have shown how children go from sitting up to standing up to walking, and from body language to symbolic language, and how these major cognitive and motor changes produce changes in consumer behavior patterns. There is logical progression to it all. For a long time (in the life of a child), commercial objects have been discovered in the home environment through limited sensorimotor efforts. Among these objects, favorites arise and the children seek more of them—more good foods, more fun toys. As the children develop more motor skills—creeping, crawling, standing, walking—they are more able to seek out and obtain many of these pleasure-satisfying objects on their own. Then, as talking abilities develop, the children are able to ask for what they cannot get themselves.

At this time in children's lives—at 6–24 months—they are totally egocentric; they think only of their needs and their satisfaction, and not of those of others. While they are beginning to sense cause and effect, they really do not understand or care about the effects of their actions on others. They live only for themselves. Thus, for all their lives, they have devoted their waking hours to pursuing whatever objects will satisfy their needs. Once they are able to walk and grasp, they can access many more objects for their pleasure. And once they can talk and think symbolically, they can ask for those items that are not in their sight but wanted for their satisfaction. These new abilities actually allow children to be more self-centered since they allow them to be more individual, more a person of their choice with less dependency on parents and other caretakers.

At the end of this stage, these walking, talking 24-month-old consumers are performing hundreds, perhaps thousands, of tekrams a day. At home they are in constant pursuit of commercial objects throughout it. In the shopping setting they are making around 15 requests per visit, mostly by brand name and receiving probably 50 percent of those items. And additionally in the shopping setting, they are physically handling many products by taking them from the shelf and examining them and asking for them. At home from rising to going to bed, they may make many more requests— 60 to 80—in addition to the marketplace requests. They are familiar with two or three kinds of stores and have developed preferences for many products and dislikes for some. According to marketers, the children at this point have become members of the market of influencers since they can request the product names and brand names of the marketers from parents, who make purchases on the children's behalf.

Children's requesting of a wide range of products in this stage of consumer development is possible as a result of reaching a cognitive development level in which objects—social and physical—become separate entities. Moreover, the children themselves become objects along with parents and playmates. All of this is possible because of another cognitive development, that of symbolic thinking. The children are able now to represent in their minds all these physical and social objects, give names to them, and hold attributes of them in their minds that are attached to the names of the objects. So now they have stored networks of commercial objects in their minds, usually by brand names, and include related retail outlets, products, packages, and advertising statements such as claims and jingles.

It is important to note again that from the time they were born, the children have been driven by some intrinsic motives to explore their environments and to discover those objects that satisfy their needs. Development of walking abilities that occurs in this stage allows the children to further their seeking of satisfying objects. Development of speaking abilities allows them to seek the objects through requesting them from their parents and others. Once introduced to the marketplace, the children use these gross and fine motor skills to obtain preferred objects from it.

So, in the first two stages of consumer development, children have followed a logical progression. In the first stage, the observation stage, they utilize their sensory system to discover objects that satisfy their needs. They make some kind of mental records of these and their use—their actions on them. Out of this come picture lists of objects that satisfy while seeking more like them. That is, stage two of consumer development logically consists of seeking and/or requesting those objects that were discovered and continue to be discovered, tried, and found useful and satisfying. Seeking of satisfying objects knows no boundaries—the crib, the nursery, the home, the daycare center, the marketplace. Once the marketplace is discovered as an unlimited source of satisfying objects, children do more seeking there—with the cooperation of parents. And they utilize their newfound language to request those satisfying objects located in the marketplace. Of course, they still have to depend fully on caretakers to provide for them—to stock the refrigerator, to stock the toy box, to stock the drawers with clothing—but they now have the abilities to seek out more items for the stocking efforts and articulate them to their caretakers. Development of language and legs—learning to talk and walk—pays off handsomely for children beginning in this stage of consumer development.

REFERENCES

Brazelton, T. B., and S. Greenspan. (2000). *The Irreducible Needs of Children: What Every Child Must Have to Grow, Learn and Flourish.* Cambridge, MA: Perseus Publishing.

Dive into Mark. (2003, September 19). Retrieved from http://diveintomark.org/archives/2003/09/19/daycare

Fleischhacker, S., K. L. Cason, and C. Achterberg. (2006). "You had peas today?" A pilot study comparing a Head Start child-care center's menu with the actual food served. *Journal of the American Dietary Association, 106*(2), 277–280.

Gesell, A. L., F. L. Ilg, and L. B. Ames (1977). *The Child from Five to Ten* (rev. ed.). New York: Harper and Row, Publishers.

McNeal, J. U. (1999). *The Kid's Market: Myth and Realities.* Ithaca, NY: Paramount Market Publishers.

McNeal, J. U., and M. F. Ji. (2003). Children's visual memory of packaging. *Journal of Consumer Marketing, 20*(5), 400–427.

McNeal, J. U., S. W. McDaniel, and D. Smart. (1983). The brand repertoire: Its contents and organization. In P. Murphy (ed.), *1983 AMA Educators Conference Proceedings* (pp. 92–96). Chicago: American Marketing Association.

Wikipedia. (n.d.). *Day care.* Retrieved from http://en.wikipedia.org/WikiDaycare

8

STAGE THREE OF CONSUMER DEVELOPMENT: SELECTING/TAKING (24–48 MONTHS)

Lawrence: A Terrible-Two Taker

Interviews regarding shopping patterns were conducted with mothers of toddlers at a daycare center in a central Texas city. What follows is some conversation excerpted and recorded from one of the interviews with a working mother of a 30-month-old son. Mrs. Lawson works as a clerk in the sheriff's department, and Mr. Lawson is a rodeo performer.

Interviewer: *Would you please describe for me a typical shopping trip to a supermarket with your son.*

Mrs. Lawson: *Sure, although I don't think there is any typical shopping trip with Lawrence.*

Interviewer: *Why do you say that?*

Mrs. Lawson: *[Laughing] Well, going anywhere with Lawrence is an adventure. I literally have to prepare myself for it.*

Interviewer: *Meaning?*

Mrs. Lawson: *Meaning you don't know what to expect when you go anywhere with him. So before I get him ready to go to, say, Kroger's to get some things, I have a little talk with him about what he must do and not do. He is so strong now that it gets hard to control him. So I tell him what he can get while we're there, that he must stay with me and not wander off, and that he mustn't talk back to me when I'm telling him things. He's really getting a mean mouth on him, and it can get darn embarrassing sometimes. I know all kids his age are like that, but I don't think it's right.*

Interviewer: After you prepare Lawrence for the shopping trip, tell me what usually happens next.

Mrs. Lawson: Well, after we get into the car and I get him strapped in, I start telling him again what not to do. As you know, kids his age have a short memory. But by the time we get there—it's about 10 minutes—he's already asking me for this and that. And I have to remind him that he can only get the one thing we have agreed on.

Interviewer: What is usually that one thing?

Mrs. Lawson: Oh, usually a certain kind of cereal. That boy eats a box of cereal a week himself, so I let him pick out some more. Sometimes it's other things.

Interviewer: Other things?

Mrs. Lawson: You know, like cookies or crackers and things like that—treats of some sort.

Interviewer: Tell me about the shopping itself.

Mrs. Lawson: Well, when we get there I usually go for the fruits and vegetables first. They sort of determine what other things I will buy. Also, Lawrence likes to help me pick out fruits. I've got him on this fruit kick, and so I tell him he can pick out any kinds of fruits. I hate to buy some that are real expensive, but I figure it's all good for us. Lawrence is not interested much in vegetables, so I get those, then we move on to the canned and boxed things.

Interviewer: Does Lawrence sit in the cart or walk beside you?

Mrs. Lawson: I can't get him to sit in the seat anymore. He figures he's too old for it, and actually he is kind of big for it. I'd rather have him in the cart, but he walks along sometimes holding on to the cart and sometimes riding underneath. For a while he would sit in the cart, but not much now. Sometimes he wants to take off and get something, and it can be hard to stop him. I wish he was in the seat still.

Interviewer: You said that Lawrence sometimes takes off and gets something? What do you mean?

Mrs. Lawson: If you don't watch him, he darts off somewhere and I have to go get him. Usually, he heads for the candy, and if I don't get him, he'll grab the biggest bag of candy he can find. Then it's a tug-of-war to get it back on the shelf and not in the shopping cart. [Then, seemingly as a justification, she added] Maybe that's why his daddy calls him "35 pounds of romping, stomping, blue-blazing hell."

Interviewer: I understand. Now continue with the shopping where you said you usually go to the canned and boxed items next.

Mrs. Lawson: Yes, we usually head for the cereal aisle. I try to let him pick out the cereal he likes. Recently, he likes cereals and other things to do with fruit, and I think that's good. So, he goes from one end of the aisle to the other looking at all the cereals, taking out some of them, then putting them back. Finally, he'll settle on one and I let him get that. He puts it in the cart and then we head for the frozen foods. I do have to watch it in the frozen foods. I get some frozen dinners for us and maybe a pizza and some vegetables, then I need to head for the checkout before they thaw. But if I don't watch it, he'll have some ice cream in the cart. That kid can eat his weight in ice cream. [Then she added] Maybe that's why he's chunky like his daddy.

Interviewer: What do you mean he will have some ice cream in the cart?

Mrs. Lawson: Well, he'll just open up a door and grab a pack of bars out of the freezer and toss 'em into the cart in a split second. Then we have to decide whether to get 'em or not, and usually I make him put 'em back. But he'll say no, they're fruit and sometimes they are.

Interviewer: If they are made of fruit, do you let him get those?

Mrs. Lawson: Sometimes. Usually, there's not much time for argument. I've got to get through the checkout with that frozen stuff and get it home.

INTRODUCTION

In the first stage of consumer development, children discover the many commercial objects in their limited environment. In the second stage, they begin to seek and ask for those objects that they have discovered and like—objects they have recorded in their consumer memory in some manner. Now, in stage three, discussed here, they choose objects among many that they want and take them. Concurrently, they continue to discover more objects as their environment expands, and they continue to ask for them from their growing number of caretakers. As they gain improved physical and mental abilities in this third stage, they begin locating those items they want—at home, at daycare, at the marketplace—memorizing their locations and then asking for them at any time. In this third stage, we notice that children continue to ask for things desired, but gradually they begin asking for permission to select and take wanted objects. But if their requests for the items or their requests for permission to take the items are not honored, they tend to take them on their own. These selecting/taking activities are the particular focus of this chapter.

In order to better understand the consumer behavior that develops in this third stage, let us first put it in context by noting significant physical/motor and cognitive developments that occur in its time period of 24–48 months—two to four years. This is an age range (two- and three-year-olds) that includes Lawrence Lawson and around 8 million other U.S. kids and is characterized by a much larger number of tekrams being performed daily than a year ago. Much of physical/motor (body) and cognitive (mind) developments are due to developments in consumer behavior patterns. Likewise, changes in consumer behavior patterns—such as taking rather than or after asking—are mainly a result of changes in physical/motor and cognitive development. Thus, it is difficult to talk about consumer development, particularly in this third stage, without putting it in an appropriate physical and mental context for toddlers this age.

Physical/Motor Skills (24–48 Months)

By two years old the child is no longer an infant or a baby; he is a seasoned toddler and often referred to by mom as a child, and by the next door neighbor as a kid, or even a mean little kid. But he is not too little to be seen and heard, as demonstrated by 30-month-old Lawrence. At two years old children weigh nearly four times their birth weight and are adding around 5 pounds a year over the next couple of years (Payne and Isaacs, 1999). Thus, at 24 months the typical American child weighs around 28–30 pounds, will weigh 33–36 pounds by age three, and reach around 40 pounds at age four, thus showing a substantial growth in skeletal and muscle mass during this consumer development stage. It is a good thing the child can walk by this time; that is far too much weight for mom to tote around. But it goes both ways. Children at 24 months probably would not want to be seen in their mothers' arms since they have entered an age of independence seeking, or at least they tend to act like it as long as they are not separated from their moms for very long. (It should be noted that Lawrence's mother estimated his weight at 35 pounds, and said he was "chunky like his father," a term used in her region of the country to mean muscular or overweight. Depending on the child's height, an observer might call him overweight, as hinted at by his mother who said he "eats his weight in ice cream.")

Children at two are also around three feet tall, which would make them a lot of luggage for their moms. However, this height is good for the children since it gives them the ability to reach high up on the supermarket shelf, retrieve items, and pitch them into the lower end of a typical shopping cart. During ages two and three, they will grow up another three inches each year, so that by the time they reach age four—the end of this consumer development stage—they will average more than 40 inches tall. By then, they will be able to see the top of a fast-food serving counter—they usually are eager to see what the counter personnel are placing on the tray while parents are ordering in order to make sure their requests are met. This new physical ability encourages them to participate in the purchase act although they still do not have the mind for it. But through repetitious purchase behavior of parents on their behalf, children begin to figure out the system, and by the end of this stage, some will be asking to try it.

A noticeable change in body proportions also comes with these weight and height advances. The children's chests become larger while their stomachs gradually protrude less—except for 15 percent of those that seemingly are being groomed by mom and dad to be a "fatty" like one or both of them. There is a reduction in fattiness, in general, or what we sometimes call *baby fat*. Arms and legs seem to fit their body better, and their walking manner appears close to normal. By the end of this stage at around 48 months, most of the children look very much like they have the same body proportions as older kids in kindergarten or first grade.

Some of the increase in body weight, in fact a lot of it, is due to a hidden factor: the increase in weight of the toddler's brain (Eliot, 1999). We tend to forget that body growth is inside as well as outside. Now, at 24 months, the brain's weight is three-quarters of that of an adult. Its rapid increase in size can be explained principally by the developments in the child's muscles that rapidly produce the physical abilities of sitting, crawling, standing, walking, reaching, and grasping. All of this body behavior sends back to the brain millions of messages during the first two years, and these message results—*schemes* as they often are called in cognitive development theory—create an enormous number of networks in the brain. These, along with much more myelinating of nerve fiber, rapidly add weight to the head. But, noticeably, the baby's big head no longer looks big as it did a year ago, because the rest of the body has grown to meet it.

Perhaps more important to consumer development than the body developments are the development in its uses—in the children's motor skills—that have brought the children to age two and will carry them to age four, characteristically running and shouting. By age two, the children have developed the standard rudimental movement abilities and have entered the fundamental movement abilities stage that will take them to around age seven (Gallahue, 1982). During the rudimental movement stage, the children learned to sit up, creep and crawl, stand up, and finally walk. Concurrently, they learned manipulation movements that permitted them to effectively use their arms, hands, and fingers. Now, in this new fundamental movement stage of motor development, the youngsters seek to discover how to perform a variety of locomotion, stability, and manipulative movements by refining them to the point that they develop acceptable levels of proficiency in them. In order for them to accomplish this, they must learn much more about their bodies, in some ways no small order for children who are just beginning to think symbolically. For example, they must figure out how to use their arms to achieve more running speed. (They will devote a lot of attention to television advertisements that show kids running, jumping, and playing games, and, of course, some of the ads will help them figure out how to select the right shoes for these tasks.) But on the other hand, they are so self-centered at this point in their life that they have little trouble focusing on themselves and their bodies—just give them access to a mirror or some photographs of themselves. Thus, they take their standing and walking skills; combine them with their reaching, grasping, and ungrasping skills; and add a lot more balance to become the people that they imagine themselves to be—they do imagine a self-concept at this time. Thus, their awkwardness and error-proneness of 14 months—when they started walking—are gradually replaced with confident movements that are performed with greater speed.

According to Payne and Isaacs (1999), some of the significant accomplishments in motor abilities at this time—in stage three of consumer development—include the following:

- The children achieve big improvements in axial movements so that they can remain in a static position while turning the trunk and/or limbs, such as sitting in a shopping cart and looking at displays on both sides of the aisle. These new abilities also provide preparation for such tekrams as sitting at a desk in kindergarten, in a high chair, or a chair at the kitchen table.
- The new axial movements combined with the stability skills to lean over and return to a standing position allow the children at age two to push and pull toys of both small and large sizes—even learn to walk the pet dog. They can also begin to put on their shoes and try to tie the laces by age four.
- They can use their walking skills and the stability skills of leaning and turning to walk up stairs. This takes some doing because strengthening of some back and leg muscles is necessary, but it happens by age three. This ability not only facilitates living in apartments and condominiums but shopping at old-fashioned department stores.
- By age three, the kids have developed a number of significant new special locomotive skills that feed off walking: They, for example, can pedal a tricycle, kick a ball, hop on one foot, all of which means they need a lot more play items—that most likely are in their driveway or backyard by their third birthday.
- By age four, they have mastered balance to the point that they can stand on tiptoes—to better see the tray on the service counter at a fast-food restaurant—can stand on one leg, and can lean over and walk on hands and feet—like they did at age one but now with little effort and lots more fun. This means they can play hopscotch and jump rope, for instance, and ride on mom's or dad's back. They can run skillfully and, by age three, will adopt the attitude of why

walk when you can run. This means they are going to hear a lot more of "No running"—and they will wonder why—along with a rapidly growing number of *no*'s in general.

- Talking is standard motor equipment now at two, and it gets better on a daily basis—or worse, depending on who has to listen to it, the talker or the talkees (tired parents). By age three, they can talk on the telephone with grandma—this is quickly becoming a standard tekram—and during the phone conversation, they may be heard putting in an order for certain toys—and the following year they will learn to dial the phone. They also talk a lot with their hands—even while talking on the telephone—and will most likely keep this motor language as backup to their symbolic language at least for a long time if not a lifetime.

- Manipulation skills blossom between ages two and four. At age two, children begin, for example, to scribble with a palmer grip with their pencil or crayon. Then by age three, their hands and eyes are coordinated enough to draw with a palmer grip. By age four, they probably can grip the pencil or drawing tool with the standard tripod grasp and begin to produce writing and art, of sorts—and begin a lifetime of drawing/writing tekrams. Chance are, however, that even by age six they will still not be very skilled at either, and their first-grade teacher will have to retrain them, particularly if they are left-handed.

- Starting when children are age two and continuing into elementary school, physical play is their predominant need (McNeal, 1982). It even supercedes eating, sleeping, and being with others, much to the chagrin of many parents. All activities are turned into play, including eating and sleeping, and even though a social setting may have a serious tone, the egocentric two- to four-year-old will play if permitted. Very important, much of the play, which consists mostly of tekrams, contributes to development of muscles and bones as well as to cognitive development. Mom and dad are aware of this. Just notice how many play products are merchandised to assist the development of physical and mental capacities and the large number of these that parents seek and buy. The preschool teacher is also equally aware of the dominant need for play and often integrates play into learning—makes learning fun—and of course utilizes many tekrams in the process—in the classroom and on the playground. One of the more useful, relatively inexpensive products for building motor skills, cognitive skills, and social skills at age two or three is a large soft-rubber ball such as that shown with the child in Photo 8-1. It is lightweight so that it will do little damage to the child or the environment, yet it offers so much play variety. Little kids can sit on it, fall on it, bounce it, throw it, and

PHOTO 8-1   A three-year-old Beijing kindergartener plays with a large rubber ball on her playground. It is a good type of play item that promotes physical and mental development as well as social interaction.

create other play with it. It promotes independent play and play with others. The Beijing kindergarten that this three-year-old in Photo 8-1 attends has several of these balls available on the playground at all times.

Cognitive Skills (24–48 Months)

At age two, children are completing the sensorimotor stage of cognitive development and are changing from understanding environmental objects through *actions* on them to thinking about them by representing them in their minds with symbols, images, and pictures (Phillips, 1969). This is the beginning of real thinking, and children stay very busy undertaking this reorganization of their minds regarding external objects and events— they begin to ask adults a lot of "What's this" questions. This mental exercise will continue throughout this consumer development stage of two to four years and all the way into elementary school. Age two marks the beginning of what Piaget (1963) called the *preoperational thought stage* in which children are reworking their thinking system and therefore cannot yet use it logically. In fact, their thinking at this time is often characterized as illogical or semilogical by those that study children's cognitive development. Perhaps Piaget should have called it *prelogical* rather than *preoperational* since children at this time cannot yet utilize much logic to understand their ever-expanding environment. This also is a time period in cognitive development when Piaget dwelled on what the children cannot do with their minds. In addition to not being able to think logically, the toddlers possess some other shortcomings. Two- to four-year-olds generally cannot take the perspective of others; practically all their thinking revolves around themselves. If they ask their mother to buy a birthday gift for their father, for instance, due to their egocentric thinking they will ask her to buy what they like, not necessarily what their father would like. This my-perspective-only thinking causes kids lots of trouble in their interactions with others. The result is that what may appear to be social interaction to an adult often is not, or on a scale of 1–10 is a 3. For example, as noted in previous chapters, much of children's play with others at this time is parallel play with little concern for one another. Yet, these tekrams of parallel play will gradually, almost begrudgingly, lead to socially interactive play, particularly on the preschool playground. Play at least facilitates the development of friendships at this time, since it is the number one requirement of all kids. Thus, play provides a medium through which virtually all children will seek and accept other children at least to a degree that will promote their play.

Object permanence is in place now so that social and physical objects receive individual categorization in children's minds, thus building many new mental networks. But they may not see the truth about each. For example, this is a time of animism when children assign life to inanimate objects such as the moon or a doll. It is a time when they make judgments—often bad judgments—about objects according to one dimension such as height or color. Object permanence without the ability to see things as others see them is at least a click away from reality, but the children are unaware of it—even when told so by adults.

But life is not all negative in this preoperational stage of cognitive development. Some important cognitive accomplishments occur between ages two and four (Cole, Cole, and Lightfoot, 2005). Some accomplishments that impact substantially on consumer development, making much of it possible, are as follows:

- **Self-image:** At age two, children have begun to think out an image of themselves that initially consists primarily of a physical image— two arms, two legs, a nose, hair color, and so on. They can easily recognize a photo of themselves and would like to repeat this tekram often; they love to hear others talk about them and how they look in pictures and videos. They even like for mom to break out their baby pictures and talk at length about each. And when company comes, they are quick to stand in front of them, perform some act such as jumping up and down, and repeating, "Look what I can do." At three and four, children continue with their physical self-image but add to it their newfound physical capabilities such as running fast and jumping rope "better than anyone." As noted, they are at an egocentric stage and think almost solely of their welfare, the impact of others on them, and how they look to others—they hope they are tall, big, or fast in the eyes of those giving the attention.

- **Gender Discovery:** Related to the discovery of a self during this stage of consumer development is the discovery of gender. Around age two, children begin to see gender differences in others such as playmates and daycare partners and in their parents. Then usually around age three, children begin to transfer this understanding to self and realize that they are a boy or girl. Actually, parents probably start working on the gender thing from the day their child is born, but it takes around two or three years for this information to soak in. So, by 30–36 months, children possess a stable gender identity and thus some gender-appropriate behavior, much to the pleasure of parents. Boys become more aggressive, thus fitting in nicely with the terrible-twos behavior, which will be discussed shortly—and was hinted at by Lawrence's mom. Girls, on the other hand, take on a nurturing character. In both cases their consumer behavior patterns start changing as they start seeking more products befitting their new gender. Boys, for example, seek more outdoor play items such as footballs and running shoes, whereas girls desire more stereotypically feminine things such as dolls and dresses. While most of this behavior is imposed and reinforced by parents, the children begin to fit into their gender roles and tend to demonstrate them outside the home at daycare, at church, and in the marketplace. In somewhat contrary fashion, by the end of this consumer development stage, when dad tucks his little girl in bed one night, to his chagrin he may hear, "I can run faster than boys, Daddy. Can I have some Air Nikes?"

- **Verbal Language:** At the beginning of this consumer stage—at age two—children have a vocabulary of 100–200 words; at three, 300–600 words; and at four, 600–1,200 words. Once children begin the symbolic language process at 18–24 months and understand that words stand for objects—and they have such a strong interest in objects—the two come together in an exploding vocabulary of nouns. By age three, children are building two-, three-, and four-word sentences with some use of "glue" words such as "to" and "of" with the nouns. I estimate that probably half of the nouns consist of commercial objects—book, bike, banana—and probably 10 percent or more of them are brands. So, children's consumer memory is being reorganized for the near future and they will use the image representations of these objects to ask for more of them and to practice imaginary play including imaginary shopping.

- **Visual Language:** Before children entered the verbal language time, they stored information about objects and events in visual form according to their actions on them. This behavior continues and intensifies along with learning of sounds (words). But now that the children have the capability to think symbolically, they begin to think with the images—pictures—of objects and events that are nested in their minds. In fact, it appears that one word, such as *cereal*, evokes many images, such as eating breakfast in the kitchen or in front of the TV with mom, dad, and the dog. Now, children do not have to be in the presence of an object or event in order to consider it. It is believed that at least two-thirds of children's incoming information is stored in visual form. Thus, if a three-year-old has a vocabulary of 300–600 words and these words represent one-third of stored units of information, then the child also stores twice that many visual images, or somewhere between 600–1,200 pictures. In effect, children can recall moving pictures of a shopping mall, a favorite store, their room, and particularly their toy chest. These images make imitation possible by imagining, for example, shopping with mom and buying various products. While we can measure rather accurately the words children store in their memories, it is more difficult to measure the pictures children age two to four store—and one picture is worth a thousand words. Older children, those in the first grade and higher, can produce many of these images on paper through their drawing (McNeal, 1999).
- **Reading:** Speaking and reading are associated. Parents normally read to their children daily, in addition to the children likely viewing TV daily (reading pictures, so to speak). Thus, they are exposed to many new words including a host of new commercial words, characters, and stories. At age two, the children have integrated their visual and motor skills enough to try writing and reading. By 30 months, they are at least pretending to read—imitating tekrams of mom and dad—and they can be seen turning the pages and mumbling to themselves and often speaking the names of a few characters, particularly a couple of television characters that are duplicated in the books that moms buy. So, the combination of print and broadcast media helps the children to learn to read with, of course, assistance from their parents and perhaps some from the caretakers at their daycare center. By age

three, the children are doing lots of pretend reading: They understand that books are read from front to back, recognize the books that they like, and regularly point out the characters in the books that they know and perhaps identify with. By the end of the third year, they are aware that the words tell the story about the pictures as well as the pictures tell the story that is in the words. They also understand some of the actions of some of the characters in the books, and this helps them to understand some of the same characters on TV. Thus, for all those characters on TV that are directly and indirectly recommending their books and videos during programming and in print advertising—it's working. By now, the children can recognize the names of some of the characters in printed (word) form as well as names that are similar to theirs—that contain some of the same letters.[1]

TERRIBLE TWOS: A SPECIAL SITUATION AT THIS TIME

A special situation occurs in the lives of children at around 24 months and lasts for at least a year—approximately the duration of stage three of consumer development; it has substantial impact on consumer development and deserves some separate treatment. This situation has been popularized as the *terrible twos* (TTs), referring to a time period roughly between age two and three when child-rearing principles—and parents' patience—are tested to their limits. One mom in discussing the terrible twos referred to it as the "Too terribles," indicating its severe impact on her household. But, depending on how the TTs are handled by parents and other caretakers, they may continue for a couple of years. This is a time of highly complex emotional development that produces conflict for the children internally and also externally between the children and their caretakers. This period is characterized by moody behavior—sad-happy, shouting-quiet, aggressing-loving, helpful-unhelpful, independent-dependent—and by tantrums—falling down, screaming, crying, kicking, hitting, and holding-the-breath tantrums. It is a normal phase for most children, although some parents in desperation may suspect their child is hyperactive, perhaps due to hearing and seeing the term frequently in abundant advertisements from the medical industry. There has never been a clear explanation for the TTs—there is probably not just one explanation—so we cannot present one

---

[1] These comments about children's reading may give the impression that all parents read to their children—bedtime stores, newspaper comics, whatever. Actually around 20 percent of the U.S. adult population is functionally illiterate and probably cannot read a storybook or the comics. Just what limitations this may place on the children are unknown, but they may be substantial from the standpoint of intelligence development.

here. But we can present some simple thoughts about this very complex situation and, most important, relate it to consumer development since both are intricately intertwined.

When children are around age two, several factors come together that create a substantial amount of turmoil for them. They encounter many obstacles that lie in the way of their conquest of their expanding world. Starting around 12–15 months, children who have been relying on mom for everything begin to obtain some of their preferred objects on their own through newfound motor and cognitive abilities. Through crawling and walking, children are able to make contact with more objects they desire, and with developing manipulation skills, they can begin to reach and take these objects. Concomitant with the acquisition of these basic motor skills, including speaking, comes an increasing understanding of objects existing as units of the environment. The net result is a growing separation of the self from social and physical objects. Children desire this separation that allows them to maintain a needed level of independence. Yet, the separation reveals weaknesses. When children cannot perform a task, they may feel helpless. This condition, in turn, reminds them that they must enlist the help and support of powerful people such as mom who may not be available at that moment. One of the results of this dilemma is what is termed *separation anxiety*—fear of not being able to cope, not being able to obtain desired objects without mom or someone reliable to help. This result manifests itself at this time in the form of crying, screaming, holding the breath, whenever the child loses sight of mom for a length of time.

By the time the child reaches 18–24 months, most environmental objects exist separately, and the child has an image of each in mind. And each one can be evoked—thought about—without being in its presence. Actually, the child may have several images of an object in mind, somewhat like a moving picture. For instance, mom may be represented in different clothing, leaving and coming home, cooking, reading, and playing a game with the child. Gradually, though, these different images of the same object become integrated into a network of attributes with the object at the center. Thus, the child knows what and whom he likes and wants, and recalls them and seeks them at any time—and has the language to articulate the wants. As we have noted, there is a logical sequence to beginning consumer behavior: Mom provides what the child wants (stage one), then he will begin to ask mom (with gestures and words) for the desired objects (stage two), and this is followed by the child seeking them out independently when motor and cognitive skills permit (stage three).

The trouble is that so many obstacles get in the way of obtaining the objects of desire that the child often cannot cope. And when this happens, TTs happen. The child becomes angry, frustrated, and then maybe enters a long crying stage, followed by tantrums if the crying does not gain the objects. As children are able to think more clearly, they begin to analyze their behavior and its impact on others. Consequently, they develop strategies to improve the results of their asking for objects. But still many obstacles stand in their way of getting what they want. Obstacles are numerous. They include body and health matters such as cutting primary teeth and its accompanying distracting pain that goes on until around age three; still developing leg muscles that do not permit easy climbing of stairs, for instance; still developing manipulation skills that thwart attempts to put on shoes and clothing or stack building blocks; and toilet training matters that, as Freud explained, cause much grief for the children and caretakers. Also, even with knowledge of several stores as sources of pleasure-giving items, the children cannot go to the stores alone and obtain them—like adults do. Then there are all the "mean" people who prevent the children's attempts at happiness—in their perceptions. Most important, there is mom, who has provided for every want and need and who now begins to refuse as she reaches her parenting limits—what she will buy, what TV programs she will allow, what foods are served at a meal. And mom also tends to be gone more—she usually goes back to work by this time in the child's life—and this separation from her help and comfort frightens the child. To help the child deal with the separation, mom tries to introduce more reasoning into the parent-child conflict—rules she hopes will prevent conflict. In addition to parents, there are grandparents, baby-sitters, and daycare keepers, who all seem to have a tendency to say no, over and over and over, and who may appear to be less tolerant than mom. Thus, from adults who can and should provide the child with relief and assistance come frequent refusals, frequent disappointments. All these negatives are probably heard more frequently in those many homes with only one parent who also may be frustrated, angry, and count on it, almost always poor. Additionally, in the single-parent homes there is a tendency to try to rush the children to maturity so that they can be more helpful in the household. But, of course, the children do not want to be helpful to others at this time; they want to help themselves in their normal egocentric manner.

At ages two and three, children turn to transitional objects for comfort, for imagined caresses and kindness that an absent mom cannot provide. The transitional objects may become a sounding board through which the toddlers can try to understand parents who seem not to be there or to care enough. Children may talk to these contrived friends about their moms since they can say things to them they could not say to their moms. They can express their anger and disappointment—like Calvin does to Hobbes in the comic strip. Parents may even become frustrated with their children who seem to spend too much time with their transitionals and treat them like another human being. However, parents should keep in mind that their children are trying to cope with obstacles the best they can through the use of the transitionals.

A related behavior that also provides children comfort during these terrible times is fantasy. This cognitive activity, like the use of transitional objects, comforts children, particularly when they are alone. Fantasy also offers self-pity for weaknesses and for being unable to obtain wanted items. And according to Freudian psychology, fantasy may even allow children to punish parents who fail to meet their demands. Fantasy utilizes those many pictures that now exist in the children's minds—some put there by the imaginations of the children, some put there by parents through descriptions of what happens to bad children, and many put there by TV that actually shows what happens to bad children and to bad parents. Fantasy can use these pictures to help children cope with uncooperative adults, for example, by providing them with alternatives to adults' refusals and other negative responses.

So, even though the two- and three-year-olds are seeking independence—a must-have at this age—they still find it necessary to rely on parents and other adults for most of their needs. That alone produces much conflict—the children are trying to function independently but must actually depend on others for a normal life. The results are aggressive behavior in the forms of crying, shouting, hitting, demanding, and taking, and usually all targeted at adults—children rarely display tantrums when alone—even some by telephone by this age. What's a mom to do! Particularly, what's a working mom to do, one who, in addition to being a mother and wife, is responsible to a boss for performing a number of functions in her job. The answer increasingly has been to cave in, give up, let the child be in charge, or more precisely, let the marketer be in charge of the child. Her child is big now, aggressive, often mean-mouthed—as Mrs. Lawson termed her child, Lawrence—and in general, overpowering. And yet she loves that child more than life itself. So, she gives in, she buys whatever the child asks for, she brings it home from work, she asks others to provide it, and in a hundred ways she tries to pacify her big baby with things. Parents often mention to me—in the United States and China—that they spend more money than they wish to on cable TV—to bring in more viewing channels to their home—in order to keep their children happy, entertained, and calm. So, there is more of everything—more giving, more shopping, more TV, more eating out in those restaurants where children are appreciated—the ones that give them play items, playgrounds, play music, and TV. Of course, mom knows deep down inside that the more that is given, the more that will be asked for. But she knows also that when she says no, it can be an earthquake whether at home or at work or at the store. So, the answer to the terrible twos is usually to give in to it, try to quiet it, reduce its reverberations, and in general to acquiesce to its demands.

So, needless to say, by the time children and parents make it through the TTs, the children are firmly in charge of their household—they took it over by force. Dealing with the TTs through acquiescence lays down a pattern of behavior that most likely continues into school years and, to some extent, for the life of the child and into the next generation of children, thus confirming virtually every family as a *filiarchy* (McNeal, 1999). There are many so-called child-rearing specialists around who disagree with this approach to the terrible twos and who constantly write articles and books that tell mothers to just say no and keep saying no. In fact, I once read an article with exactly that title in *Reader's Digest*—"Just Say No" (Tyre, Scelfo, and Kantrowitz, 2005). But saying no frequently to a two-year-old, as mothers know, only precipitates more of the terrible twos' symptoms. Moreover, *no*'s also create much emotional turmoil in parents, who can handle only so much along with their many other emotional situations they experience. So, saying "Yes," "OK," and "I give up" appears to be the sane response to the children in this stage of life.

As a couple of side notes, one might wonder if the terrible twos is a time when bullies are born since bullies are primarily school-age children who take objects from others (consume) with force and without permission. If a two- or three-year-old consumer can bully mother around and win most of the time, a first-grader should be easy pickings. In China, there is also great concern about giving in to the two-year-old children constantly and therefore producing "spoiled brats" who may not become responsible citizens but continue to demand their pleasures from others—becoming bullies of sorts (e.g., Shao and Herbig, 1994).

Finally, as another side note, one might speculate that the behavior of children during the TTs may initiate childhood obesity. Their anger and disappointments often produce overeating and sitting around moping, which is a combination that can lead to a child's being overweight. Then, if the parents give in to the child with more fattening foods such as fast foods brought home after work, and more sedentary-producing products such as TV and video games, then overweightness is likely. And, of course, this overweightness will foster more eating and more sedentary acts.

STAGE THREE: SELECTING/TAKING

This selecting/taking stage of consumer development follows logically from the previous stage, stage two, in which children learned to look for and ask for those commercial objects for which they have developed preferences that began in stage one. In stage two, the children learn—and are taught—that asking is receiving, that mom and dad will give them just about anything they want and request. In fact, the parents have told the children many times that precise message: "If you want anything, just ask for it." One purpose of these instructions is to convey to the children that parents *love* them and will try to provide for all their needs. This is a major custom in developed and developing economies—expressing love with commercial objects. Another purpose of this declaration is to develop within the children an understanding of the concept of property. Children at age two or three cannot think abstractly and therefore do not yet process the notion of ownership. It has to be taught. Their egocentric nature subscribes to the adage of "What's mine is mine and what's yours is mine." Now, in stage three, which covers the time period of 24–48 months, the children are gradually becoming physically and mentally skilled enough—as demonstrated in the previous summaries of new physical and mental skills—to seek those favored objects, those that please them or have the appearance of giving them pleasure—and take them and put them into the uses for which they want them. Sure, children usually will ask for them; that is what they believe will please their parents who have taught them this tekram. But increasingly, as they move into this two-year time frame and beyond, they select those objects they want—they make some kind of decision in their mind that certain objects are desirable—and take them on their own—physically take possession of them. The selecting/taking process may be preceded by asking, begging, even demanding, but if negotiations do not turn out the way they want them to, the kids take matters into their own hands, literally, and take the items. Recall Mrs. Lawson saying, "I do have to watch it in the frozen foods." That is a bit of an indirect or polite way of saying that little Lawrence will take matters into his own hands and load the cart down with the ice cream products he wants. So, he is physically able to retrieve a six-pack of chocolate-coated frozen fruit bars from the frozen foods area of a store and get them to the shopping cart. Moreover, he is mentally able to do it; that is, he knows how, is determined to do it, and can usually anticipate the response of his mother.

As a side note, regarding Lawrence and kids his age and size, they can begin to read mom's face and her internal response to their requests. This ability begins somewhere around age 18 months, although some child development experts might say much earlier. But the point is that after a little practice, the kids in these early ages—in this consumer development stage of selecting/taking—can anticipate parents' responses to their requests and begin to develop appropriate requesting styles and appeals, as was mentioned in the discussion of stage two. The children develop these strategies to improve their batting averages, their effective asking rates (EARs), but also because they generate so much heat from physically taking the items. By the time they reach the end of this stage of consumer development around 48 months, they have perfected a lot of these requesting styles and appeals—their EARs are in the high range—and they will continue to improve on them throughout their childhood. Over the years I have observed these particular abilities of youngsters to use requesting styles and appeals, and it seems to me that they are important enough to single out in this third stage of consumer development where they get a lot of use. So, I have summarized them, named them, modified them somewhat, and placed them in "Requesting Styles and Appeals." Look them over; they are indicative of the consumer abilities that children develop around age two or three and use throughout their childhood. Are these requesting styles and appeals still valid since they have been observed over a period of years? Even more so, I think, as several generations of kids have learned them, honed them, and passed them on to younger children.

So, children at this age begin to perfect their asking skills that appeared in the previous stage of consumer development, but they are also preparing themselves to take what they want if they do not get it by asking. Most of them are now physically equipped to lift, carry, and release packages of cereal, ice cream bars, and most boxes of toys. And they are keenly aware of these abilities. They have performed these tasks a number of times; they have learned to do the "heavy lifting," so to speak, and have now plugged these tekrams into their minds and modified them several times, thus perfecting their related symbolic representations. The children's chests are much larger now than they were a few months ago, and their legs are strengthened by such activities at home as climbing stairs, pedaling a tricycle, and indeed lifting heavy objects such as the tricycle when their moms tell them to "Put up your tricycle and come into the house." Only recently, I witnessed a mother and child shopping together in a local Wal-Mart, and the child, whom I would judge to be three, was carrying a liter bottle of soft drink to the cart and making grunting sounds to draw attention to his newfound skills. If he can do that with a liter of soft drink, he can easily tote a box of cereal or "the biggest bag of candy," as Lawrence did.

Selecting/Taking in the Home Environment

All the asking that was learned in stage two of consumer development continues and accelerates in stage three and subsequent stages. So, why do we call it the selecting/taking stage? The consumer development stages described in this book are named after a significant behavior that first occurs in that stage, and in stage three the child begins to choose and take what he asks for either because it is not provided, or not provided at the time when he wants an object. Also, ever since the child was born, he has been practicing the act of taking through learning to reach out, grasp, crawl, and then walk to an object. By 24 months, the child has in place the body and mind to accomplish the taking. I have referred to this stage before as the "I can do it, I want to do it" stage because, in addition to having in place an adequate body and mind, the child at this time is exercising his desire for independence, to function on his own. This mind state, like the child's motor and cognitive skills, has been developing almost since birth. It fuses with the desire for new experience to produce exploratory behavior, and when attractive objects are discovered, they are wanted, asked for, and now that the child is age two or three, may be taken.

All this taking behavior begins at home, naturally, just as the previous two stages did. The two-year-old child who is playing in the floor at home sees a button that has fallen off dad's shirt and curiously picks it up and analyzes it by looking at it carefully and then tasting it by placing it in his mouth. He has the abilities to do this, and in this case he did not ask for the item; he just took it. He may follow this with a trip to his toy box and take a favorite toy from it and play with it, again, without asking. But if he cannot find his Milo (stuffed animal) in the toy box, he shouts to mother, "Where's my Milo?" When mother answers that it is on his bed, he then takes it. In this case, the child selected a toy from his mental repertoire of favorites, asked for it, and then took it. This is the standard procedure now at home in order for the child to obtain the pleasure-giving objects he desires. This is also a procedure that parents have encouraged and taught—asking and then taking—and have not intentionally taught their children to take without asking, as in the case of the button.

But, as noted, the muscles and mind are increasingly operating without parental permission. Children by age two have a mind full of object images that they like, and with their newfound abilities they look for, choose, and take those they desire. From a decision theory standpoint, the children do not go through a long series of steps in which they determine the best choice. They are not yet capable of this kind of thinking. Theirs is simple: Think, seek, take—think of something that tastes good, for example, look for it, and take it. Their most important need is play, so they are usually looking for play objects or the play potential in any objects discovered. Thus, mom's clothing, dad's tools, a cardboard box of facial tissue, a button, a spider—all fall into the domain of playdom. So, while a particular object may not look like fun to parents, it is the child who decides this. The example given in an earlier chapter of the children who received a gift for Christmas and also found play value in its box may not be easily processed by the parents who plunked down a hundred dollars for that Christmas gift—not for the box.

A daily routine of two- and three-year-old children at home is to wake up and then look for and play with a mentally recorded proven play item until they think of another item that has play value. Then they look for it. The other half of their routine is to explore the home for additional new play items. Now that they can walk, this means going from room to room seeking new fun. For example, rolling off the toilet tissue in the bathroom; putting on mom's make-up and wearing dad's shoes in their room; and then going to the kitchen, taking a box of cereal from the pantry, reaching in for a handful, and eating it while going to the living room to turn on TV and watch cartoons. That is one episode of household fun for a child—a taker—at this stage. The child has learned all of these tekrams of fun; none may involve the hundreds of play items that populate her room. All are performed without asking, without permission. If mom and dad are not at home, as they often are not, there is no asking or permission necessary; just do it. Most baby-sitters could care less as long as the child is contented. Grandma wants to watch her favorite TV program, and the high school girl who often sits with the child just wants to be alone with her cell phone and bag of chips. We can often witness the same pattern of behavior related to eating. When the child is hungry, she goes to the refrigerator and takes her bottle of juice, a piece of pie, and anything else that is sweet. She may be able to reach into the freezer at this point, also, and take a frozen sweet treat. She will likely choose some of the foods based on their play value, just as she does other objects. Of course, being both fun and sweet is the ultimate and might be found, for example, in a box of Froot Loops, according to its maker.

There are an upside and a downside to all of these new consumer behavior patterns that have developed concurrently with new motor and cognitive skills during the two- to four-year period. On the plus side this new independent behavior gives mom or another person a break from baby-sitting. Now that her baby can entertain himself, mom can accomplish some other things for herself and her family. Also, all this activity undertaken by her baby confirms that he is normal, that he is healthy and happy. Mom probably realizes that she is giving in too much to him and giving him too much rein, but his happiness comes first—and hers a close second. She is aware that her child is hard to get along with, that he is seeking his space, his life, and gets grumpy when he does not get it. She has heard about the terrible twos and understands that it is just a phase her child is going through, so cutting him a little slack makes good sense for the welfare of the household.

On the downside the bad eating and sleeping habits are becoming common. There are the dangers that the child is exposing herself to, such as picking up insects and even putting them in her mouth. Accidents are occurring more—falling down, slamming doors on her fingers, bumping her head. She is watching too much TV and being influenced too much by it. She is getting fat when she should be getting lean. But if she is not permitted to pursue her goals, she throws tantrums and in general behaves in an ugly manner. All of this and more worry mom and dad, frustrate them, even make them angry, and they find themselves blaming each other, the TV, a playmate, baby-sitters, daycare personnel, and definitely marketers. They also feel guilty for not spending more time with their child, which theoretically would make things better for everyone. Home life was better when the child was just a baby.

Selecting/Taking in the Market Environment

In the interview that began this chapter, Mrs. Lawson emphasizes that her 30-month-old son, Lawrence, will take things while they are shopping, so she has to warn him before leaving home and also during the trip to the store that he must not take things other than those agreed upon. She further notes that even though they have an agreement, he will violate it and take other things such as ice cream. Most likely, it is the same situation at home as it is in the marketplace. Add to the children's new improved motor and cognitive skills their terrible twos' temper and tantrums, and mothers have their hands full. Whereas Lawrence and other children used to sit in the seat of the shopping cart and ask for things mainly with gestures, they now walk alongside it and "dart off" and "grab" something such as "the biggest bag of candy" they can find, according to Mrs. Lawson. In fact, Mrs. Lawson reminisced a bit by saying, ". . . I wish he was in the seat still."

According to my research, American children start grabbing goods from the store shelf at around 24 months, and by 42 months over half of the children are selecting and taking on their own—with and without permission. In the case of Mrs. Lawson and Lawrence, the asking started at home before going to the store, and the two reached an agreement regarding what he could choose. In effect, he followed the asking, selecting, taking sequence. But once he was in the supermarket, he changed the rules and reversed the sequence—grabbing a particular bag of candy or some ice cream bars, putting them in the shopping cart and then asking if he could have them. Based on Mrs. Lawson's statement that "There's not much time for argument. I've got to get through the checkout with that frozen stuff and get it home," my guess is that Lawrence had thought it out and figured that the timing and the threat of a tantrum would permit him to keep both items.

At first it is food goods that American children select and take. But as their selecting/taking skills increase along with their negotiating skills, their shopping focus turns increasingly to what is really important—play items. Most U.S. supermarkets have a toy section, and mom takes the child there frequently when he is still in her arms. So, it is familiar territory. Also, mom has taken him to other toy sellers such as toy stores and mass merchandisers and bought him things that he requested. Finally, the child senses correctly that mom would rather cave in to a toy request than an ice cream request, so when the child is between ages two and four, play item requests increase as well as the EAR for them—the effective asking rate. Other items often taken without permission are various kinds of books. Again, mom is a sucker for these requests, wanting her child to learn to read in preparation for school—and he knows this well. And again, marketers know this too, and all kinds of stores stock books, particularly the expensive brand names such as those from Disney that line the shelf at the "always low prices" Wal-Mart.

All the selecting and taking that the child does in the marketplace are probably viewed by the child as a normal activity since it is something that parents do when shopping. We have noted before that many basic consumer behavior patterns of children are learned from parents through observation. So, some of the taking is a result of imitating parents and utilizing the imitation as a means of obtaining items that please. Probably many of the items taken are those that parents have purchased for the children before, thus giving the children a reason to take them without asking permission. Add to this thinking the knowledge that copying parents' behavior patterns often pleases the parents.

Finally, during shopping trips parents often have to use some of their precious time to lecture their children about "taking things that are not yours." This can be embarrassing to the parents and demeaning to the children. But most find it necessary. If the children are not corrected at the point of occurrence, their behavior could lead to what is termed *shoplifting* in later years. The little three-year-old girl in Photo 8-2 threw a tantrum in a small Chinese food store (convenience store) in order to get a frozen treat that her mother or grandmother often buys her. At the time of the photo, the mother is lecturing her about the tantrum and also the relatively high cost of the treat. If you look into the eyes of the little girl, you can see her response to mom.

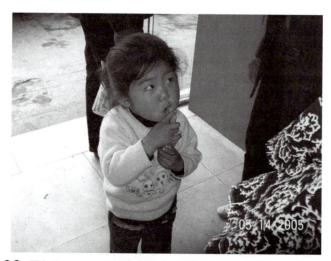

PHOTO 8-2   This three-year-old girl threw a tantrum in a small Chinese food store in order to get a frozen treat. The mother bought her the treat but lectured her about her behavior and the relatively high cost of the item.

We should note, also, that at age two and beyond the typical child is brand-minded with half of his noun vocabulary being commercial objects and many of these with brand names. Both increase greatly during this third stage of consumer development. The child learns the brand names from many sources—the parents particularly, who buy them and bring them home, but also TV, radio, videos and books, packages and stores, and friends. The child's using brand names is a convenient way to refer to products, so he uses them a lot for those items that he likes. For him, most of the time the brand is the product. The child senses, too, that mom likes for him to use brand names; it suggests a maturity that both are seeking. Also, mom feels more comfortable about knowing her child's specific likes when brand names are used. She plugs them in to her *evokked set*—the brands of products her child prefers.

By age four—the end of this stage of consumer development—most American children are routinely making selections and retrieving items from the store shelves and placing them in a shopping cart or basket—or consuming them in the store. Chances are the terrible twos have subsided and there is an unwritten agreement that as long as the child plays it cool—no mean mouth, for example—she can get just about anything. Many mothers at this point see this arrangement as providing desirable items for both the children and the adults. Mom and dad both work most likely, and this procedure speeds up the shopping process while minimizing the grief.

In the case of Chinese children, whom I have studied quite a bit, there is much less opportunity to take things from the shelves of stores since there is much less self-selection permitted in stores. Only in the last few years have supermarkets became a major player in food sales, and only in the past few years have department stores put items out on display so that children might select them. But the taking is happening now and at an average median age of 26–30 months, slightly younger than that of their American counterparts. Around half the time the selections will take place in a department store, followed closely with selections in the growing number of supermarkets. And most likely the selections will be play items, although not necessarily mom's choice because she thinks that her only child should be studying rather than playing. I think the selection/taking consumer behavior starts earlier in urban China than in America because of the one-child policy. Families are usually permitted only one child, so the parents and grandparents make sure that the child has every want met—the kid knows he can take the only seat on the bus ahead of his overweight grandmother. So, they often put their walking child down from their arms or a carriage and encourage him to select some item even if it is a toy. While choice by brand name is still much less of an occurrence in China than it is in the United States, brands names such as *Dove* (candies) and *Lego* (toys) are becoming household words in China and becoming common words to the children, who learn them mainly from parents and from store shopping.

CURRENT ISSUES IN CONSUMER DEVELOPMENT (#8)

Kids as Shoplifters

The National Association of Shoplifting Prevention (NASP), which gathers statistics on all aspects of shoplifting, says that around 25 percent of shoplifters are kids. And this consumer behavior begins during toddler years.

Parents (and other caretakers) give little children about anything they ask for and, of course, a lot that they don't ask for. So, why would the kids resort to stealing? The basic reason seems to lie within the parent-child relationship. When children start walking and talking, they begin to express themselves through commercial products; they rely on products to represent themselves to others. They learn this symbolic relationship mainly from their parents during the first two or three years of life. Parents tell children that these products will make you strong, these products are for boys or girls, these products will make you smart, and so on. As their motor skills develop, for instance, they want products that will heighten those skills—make them run faster, jump higher, throw farther. So, they seek out these products, often in accordance with advertising messages that emanate from the TV that mom has introduced to them when they were infants.

When toddlers see other children with these products, they may take those products from them. They still have not been taught right from wrong, so taking the products from others seems like a normal thing to do. After all, if they asked for them, parents would most likely provide them. If parents don't intervene with some moral lessons—"Don't take something that doesn't belong to you"—the children will continue to take—to steal. Of course, with most families being dual-working families, mom and dad may rely on others such as daycare personnel to teach etiquette and morals.

But even if parents do attempt to teach proper conduct, the children may continue to take from others—to steal—for any of several reasons. They may simply take something because it tastes good or is fun, or they would like to have something that other children have. One expert on this topic states that kids steal for such reasons as (1) to gain attention, (2) to get a thrill, (3) to get popular brand-name items, (4) to show bravado in front of their friends, or (5) they see their parents do it.

Shoplifting is a special case of stealing and often has more serious consequences than stealing from playmates or classmates. Shoplifting involves taking commercial goods from stores. Again, children begin taking things from retailers' shelves when they are toddlers. For instance, they may take a piece of candy from a bulk candy display and eat it, or they may take a bag of candy from the shelf and place it in mom's shopping cart—with or without her permission. Again, a lesson in proper behavior is necessary at the time the act occurs but is not always forth-coming due to mom's being tired and/or due to not wanting to create a scene in the middle of the supermarket. In these cases mom is very unlikely to do what is recommended by the experts—confront the child and, if it has happened before, take the child to the store manager or security department of the store and have them lecture the kid. This action is particularly recommended if the child is elementary school age.

Children's shoplifting must be dealt with sternly by parents before the stores' security personnel step in and take legal action. Most states today have introduced tough laws regarding shoplifting, and stores use these laws to try to catch the thieves in order to reduce the $10 billion in goods stolen each year from them. Getting caught is much more embarrassing to parents than a child's temper tantrum at the checkout.

Interviews with teens who were caught shoplifting confirm that this behavior usually begins in early childhood and becomes addictive. Further, most are not worried about getting caught. After all, only around 2 percent are detected and arrested. Thus, we are not talking about kleptomania in most cases. It's just out and out stealing for the thrill of it, to reward oneself, or simply to have something that the thieves or their parents cannot afford. Whatever the reason, this consumer behavior was probably learned during the preschool years and probably as a result of lenient or absent parents.

****
Sources: Berlin, 2006; Homeier, 2005; Vaughn, 2003.

Selecting/Taking at Daycare

Probably most two- and three-year-olds go to some kind of daycare system at least part of each day. It may be called many things—daycare, nursery school, preschool, or kindergarten—but it is a place where parents daily leave their children in the care of others. Taking is a normal behavior at these daycare centers, and it presents problems for their caretakers.

The taking at home and in the marketplace is transferred logically (to the children) to their daycare. In fact, often children select and take a play item to daycare from their collection at home. At daycare they take toys and books from shelves, and they may take similar items from other chil-dren. To deal with the problem, most daycare personnel offer some train-ing (lectures) for the children in the form of manners, etiquette, values, and virtues. They tell the children probably the same things the children's parents have told them regarding property and ownership. In the case of older children, meetings with their parents may be necessary. At some point the term *stealing* may be invoked as a matter of concern. Also, the notion of bullying may come up.

DISCUSSION

An observer in an American supermarket or superstore may perceive many three- and four-year-olds as seasoned shoppers. They have favorite stores, favorite store departments, and favorite brands, and they express these preferences in their product selections. They can be seen alone meandering up and down a cereal aisle, for instance, clearly making a selection based on the messages on the packages. The process may take several minutes, but at last they take a package of cereal from the shelf, usually the lower shelf, carry it back to the shopping cart that their moms are holding on to in another aisle, and drop it into the cart. The mothers usually thank and compliment their children, and they move on to another aisle while their children go to another. The children have reached this level of consumer expertise in four years or less, and much of it was learned on their own—watching and listening to others, trying out consumer tasks in their imagination, and then trying them out for real when permitted.

And children want to do more of it. Now that they have learned to ask for things they want, select them from a store display among several similar items, and take them in their arms and carry them to a shopping cart, they want to do it every day as a way of obtaining all those wonderfully satisfying products they have discovered in their short lifetime. As they fight their way through the terrible twos, they demand more consumer rights, more rights to find and take whatever pleases them—at home, at daycare, and at the marketplace. Mom and dad are so tired of the temper tantrums (TTs) and all that comes with them that they give in to their children's aggressive demands made with aggressive language only recently learned. Of course, this, in turn, teaches the children even more about how to fulfill their needs with certain asking styles and appeals. Boys are more difficult than girls since they seemingly have discovered that they are supposed to be. So much so, in fact, that several times mom has wished her son had been a girl. The major role of consumer behavior in creating and calming the terrible twos should not go unnoticed. Seeking and not receiving commercial objects produces emotional explosions. Then parents give the children more goods and services in order to quiet them. Thus, consumer behavior is on both ends of the TTs.

At 18–24 months—in stage two of consumer development—the typical children ask only for things that please them and usually do not take them. But within a few months more, they become like Lawrence Lawson, who, according to his mother, no longer allows a typical shopping trip. Thus, ". . . you don't know what to expect when you go anywhere with him." But this is not a result of just a change in a child's consumer behavior; it is a result of changes in physical stature, muscle growth, rapid verbal and visual language development, a new style of memory, and the appearance of a self-image that includes gender and physical abilities—and very permissive, cooperative, too-busy-to-matter parents. When the child is between two and four, a lot happens in child development that produces many changes in consumer behavior patterns. Without these changes in body and mind, there would not be major changes in consumer behavior. But the opposite is also true. Without new and more complex consumer behavior patterns, there would be little change in mind and body. They necessarily occur together like bees and clover blossoms.

It should be noted that not all the consumer behavior patterns learned in stage three between ages two and four are good ones or right ones. Learning to push parents around as part of consumer development is not a desirable attribute. As noted, while we have no way to prove it, such behavior is likely a precursor to pushing other people around later. Demanding and getting sweets on a regular basis do not make good eating habits although sweets are temporarily good for the children. Chances are, in fact, that such is a precursor to eating oneself to fatdom, particularly when combined with the TV habit that usually is encouraged by parents and other caretakers. Learning consumer behavior patterns that reinforce gender may not be in the best interest of the child, either. It may limit opportunities for the child, may mislead the child into believing she has certain superior qualities, and may even lead to some harmful consumption habits such as smoking and drinking. These observations are being made here about two- and three-year-olds to emphasize that, in this time period of consumer development, a lot of bad stuff may happen that will follow a child through life whether it is long or short and, in fact, may determine the length of it. Inattentive parents may underwrite some of this bad stuff and then blame it on the marketplace.

REQUESTING STYLES AND APPEALS

Starting around 18 months, toddlers begin to develop strategies to obtain those things they want but must be requested from parents. They gradually formalize styles of requesting and appeals to use to explain their requests. Through experience, they learn what works best for certain products they want and continue to improve on these skills.

Some of the major styles are as follows (in alphabetical order):

Demonstrative: This is perhaps the height in acting. In younger children, it means going stiff, holding their breath, or falling down on the floor screaming. Among older children, it may entail refusing to leave the store where the request is made or refusing to talk to or look at the parents wherever the request is made. Tears are often added for effect.

Forceful: Here, the children use loudness and forceful words such as "I must have it," "Nothing will stop me from having it," and "I will ask grandmother (your mother) if you don't buy it for me."

Persistent: In this case the child does not ask once or twice but repeats the request over and over, seemingly believing that there is a breaking point among parents that they will reach.

Pity: More acting takes place here by stating the terrible impact a refusal will have on the child. Parents may hear such sad results as "I will be the worst-looking kid at daycare if I don't have one," "None of my friends will talk to me if I don't have one," and the standard, "Everyone has one except me."

Pleading: This style usually contains such words as "Puleeze," "Please help me," "I'm begging," and they are often combined with the words, "Mother," "Dear mother," "I'll do anything if only. . . ."

Sugar-coated: This style relies on sweet words such as "love" and "wonderful," as in "I'll love you forever if you'll just get me one," and "Buying me one means you're the most wonderful mother in the world."

Threatening: This style is more intimidating than the forceful style; it dwells on the negative results that might occur if a request is refused. "I'll hate you forever if you don't buy it for me." "If I don't get one, I'm leaving home."

Some of the major appeals are these (in alphabetical order):

Economy: "In the long run it'll save you money."
Educational: A never-fail is "You want me to learn, don't you?"
Happiness: "Don't you want me to be happy?"
Health: "Don't you want me to be healthy?"
Security: "You don't want me to get hurt, do you?"
Time: "It'll save you lots of time."

REFERENCES

Berlin, P. (2006, May). *Why do shoplifters steal?* Retrieved from www.shopliftingprevention.org

Cole, M., S. R. Cole, and C. Lightfoot. (2005). *The Development of Children* (5th ed.). New York: Worth Publishers.

Eliot, L. (1999). *What's Going On in There?: How the Brain and Mind Develop in the First Five Years of Life.* New York: Bantam Books.

Gallahue, D. L. (1982). *Understanding Motor Development in Children.* New York: John Wiley & Sons, Inc.

Homeier, B. P. (2005, March). *My child is stealing.* Retrieved from Kidshealth/org/parent/emotions/behavior/shoplifting/html

McNeal, J. U. (1982). *Consumer Behavior: An Integrative Approach.* Boston: Little, Brown and Company.

McNeal, J. U. (1999). *The Kids Market: Myth and Realities.* Ithaca, NY: Paramount Market Publishers.

Payne, V. G., and L. D. Isaacs. (1999). *Human Motor Development: A Lifespan Approach* (4th ed.). Mountain View, CA: Mayfield Publishing Company.

Phillips Jr., J. L. (1969). *The Origins of Intellect: Piaget's Theory.* San Francisco, CA: W. H. Freeman and Company.

Piaget, J. (1963). *The Origins of Intelligence in Children.* New York: W. W. Norton & Company.

Shao, A., and P. Herbig. (1994). Marketing implications of China's little emperors. *Review of Business, 16* (Summer/Fall), 16–20.

Tyre, P., J. Scelfo, and B. Kantrowitz. (2005, May). Just say no. *Reader's Digest*, 36A–36F.

Vaughn, C. E. (2003, June). *Kids & shoplifting: What it means and what parents can do about it.* Retrieved from www.Parenthood.Com/Articles/html

9

STAGE FOUR OF CONSUMER DEVELOPMENT: CO-PURCHASE (48–72 MONTHS)

Carlos and His Mom Buy Paper for School and Ice Cream for Dad at the Supermarket

Arrangements were made with a South Texas kindergarten to conduct one-on-one interviews with its children. Each child was promised a "new Texas quarter" for sitting down at a table in a playroom and talking to an interviewer. The principal purpose of the interviews, which usually lasted 15–25 minutes, was to find out more about their behavior in the marketplace with and without their parents. One student who was interviewed was a five-year-old (who said he was "nearly six") named Carlos who seemed to enjoy talking to the interviewer. What follows is some key dialogue.

Interviewer: Carlos, would you please tell me about your last trip to a store with your mother.

Carlos: You mean me buy things, or you mean 'cause I had to go?

Interviewer: Either one. Whatever you wish to tell me.

Carlos: Well, the last time I went to the store with my mother we went to get me some [writing] paper. That was Sunday night. She took me to H.E.B.'s [supermarket] to get it.

Interviewer: What did you and mother buy at H.E.B.'s?

Carlos: Let's see. Just the paper, and we got some ice cream, and Mama got some milk.

Interviewer: You went to H.E.B.'s to get some paper for your school work. Is that right?

Carlos: Yes, I had to have it.

Interviewer: And you also got some ice cream too?

Carlos: Yes.

Interviewer: Tell me about the ice cream.

Carlos: You mean what kind was it?

Interviewer: Yes, what kind was it?

Carlos: It was Blue Bell [brand]. We buy Blue Bell ice cream. We got strawberry 'cause that's what my daddy likes. And I do too.

Interviewer: I see. You got Blue Bell strawberry ice cream because that is what your daddy likes. Who decided to get it, you or your mother?

Carlos: I did. While Mama got some things, I looked at ice cream and saw the Blue Bell was on sale. So, I told her we ought to get some for daddy since it was on sale. So we got some.

Interviewer: You say it was on sale. What does that mean?

Carlos: Yes, it was on sale. There was a sign there, on sale.

Interviewer: Do you remember the price?

Carlos: I think it was two for five dollars, I think. For the big one.

Interviewer: It was two for five dollars. Did you buy two?

Carlos: No, we just bought one.

Interviewer: Do you remember how much the one cost?

Carlos: I don't remember. I guess it was half of five dollars.

Interviewer: Do you know how much half of five dollars is?

Carlos: No, but they tell you when you check out.

Interviewer: Did you pay for the ice cream since you suggested it?

Carlos: No, Mama did. I just got it.

Interviewer: Did you pick out the paper and pay for it since it was for you?

Carlos: Mama paid for everything. She buys all my school things, but I sometimes do.

Interviewer: But you sometimes do?

Carlos: I sometimes buy pencils and things like that that don't cost so much.

Interviewer: So, you buy some things yourself. Do you buy them without your parents' help?

Carlos: I buy things all the time without their help. Mama just gives me the money and I pay for it.

Interviewer: I see. Do you buy things by going to a store without your parents?

Carlos: I could, but there ain't a store I can walk to except the 7-Eleven [convenience store] and my folks won't let me go there.

INTRODUCTION

This chapter considers the fourth stage of consumer development called *co-purchase*. In this stage children demonstrate a desire to make purchases, attempt to make purchases, and actually make purchases with the assistance of parents or other capable shoppers—like Carlos in the preceding interview who makes purchases with his parents and "could" make them on his own, according to him. Stage four follows logically from stage three, in which children learn to select and/or take commercial objects from store shelves and from storage locations at home and at daycare. These are normally products that they ordinarily ask for—as they learned to do in stage two—and parents provide them. However, as they gain physical capabilities and a good mental storage system, they shorten the loop in stage three and start taking things—as described in the preceding chapter.

Now, in stage four, covering the ages of 48–72 months—four- and five-year-olds—many children demonstrate a desire to try purchasing things on their own. After all, by age five, most children have made several hundred visits to the marketplace with their parents, made several thousand requests and suggestions for items they see and want, and during the past two years have selected and taken several hundred products from store shelves and displays. Thus, it follows that they may feel qualified to do their own buying. One can see these patterns of consumer behavior in the tekrams performed by Carlos. At home, he requests writing paper for his kindergarten; he goes to the supermarket with his mother, where he also makes a request for ice cream by brand after locating it in the store—presumably while his mother was locating the paper. Then the two pay for the ice cream, paper, and apparently a bottle of milk at the checkout counter. Carlos even showed some knowledge of pricing and signage that assisted him in his selection. He also reported that he could buy the ice cream on his own if his parents permitted, although there was some evidence that he has only a fundamental understanding of money. The school paper and the ice cream both could be considered co-purchases, but perhaps not the milk. Note what Carlos said when asked what he and his mother bought at the supermarket. "Just the paper, and we got some ice cream, and Mama got some milk."

The emphases indicate what was a co-purchase—"just the paper, and we got some ice cream"—and what was not—"Mama got some milk."

To put this stage in perspective, first let us examine briefly the physical and mental development of the children from age four up to age six, what is often called the preschool years that follow toddlerhood. Bear in mind that development is a function of time and that age is used as a measure of time but that it is an approximation.

PHYSICAL DEVELOPMENT

At age four, which marks the beginning of stage four of consumer development, children are around 40 inches in height. Thus, they can see the tops of most checkout and service counters in the marketplace, which average 38–39 inches high. During this stage of consumer development, covering the ages of four and five, children gain at least 2 inches more each year. Thus, at age five they will be around 42–43 inches, and by age six, approximately 45 inches tall. The rapid gains in height that were achieved during the first four years of life are not as dramatic during this four-to-six range, which tends to be a nodal period in the children's overall development before they start growing rapidly again.

At the beginning of this fourth stage of consumer development, children's average weight is between 36 and 38 pounds. During the years of four to six, they add on another 4 pounds per year, and by age six the typical kid weighs 46–48 pounds. Tragically, around a quarter of the six-year-olds are overweight, and perhaps 15% are obese—weigh at least 20% more than the average kid of this age and height. Pediatricians attribute most of this extra weight to overconsumption of fatty foods, such as the ice cream that Carlos bought, and to sedentary activities such as TV viewing and playing video games—all courtesy of good ol' mom and dad who probably learned the hard way during the terrible twos to give the kids anything they want. Ironically, children in stage four of consumer development—kids ages four to six—could easily be described as overactive, so it is hard to imagine that they can become overweight. At age four, children are well into the motor development stage called *fundamental movement abilities phase* in which the children put a great deal of emphasis on their motor skills. So, there must be a greater force on them than their determination to be active, one that often leads them to overweightness and obesity. There is. It is the fat-favorable environment fostered by overweight parents who act as models for the kids, along with the many favorite fat TV characters such as Barney, Teletubbies, and Pooh introduced to the children by their parents, and the commonly overweight actors in most sitcoms that the kids and parents often watch. The fact is that most four- and five-year-old kids are in pursuit of better motor skills in order to provide themselves a greater range of playing skills—playing is everything at this age—but being fat limits their activities, and it begins at this time to limit their social activities—a double whammy of sorts. By the way, parents rarely take responsibility for their fat kids, either denying that they are fat or blaming others, such as the fast-food restaurants to which they take their kids.

In the preschool period of ages two to six, children are going through the three stages of their fundamental movements abilities: initial, elementary, and mature stages (Gallahue, 1982). The initial stage usually occurs during ages two and three; the elementary stage, at ages four and five; and the mature stages, at ages six and seven. Thus, during the time period of the fourth stage of consumer development from ages four to six, children are experiencing mainly the elementary stage of fundamental movements. In the initial stage that usually occurs before age four, the children make their first goal-oriented effort at performing a fundamental skill. In the elementary stage that starts at around age five, children exert greater control and better rhythmical coordination of the fundamental movements. Finally, by age six the children are mechanically efficient, coordinated, and controlled in the performance of fundamental skills—unless they are significantly overweight. These stages of fundamental movements overlap, as might be expected, and the ages are only approximations, but they are identifiable and involve many tekrams of consumer behavior. But, in effect, they represent the children learning (discovering) body movements and perfecting them to the point that both boys and girls often boast about them. Let us consider some examples in order to get an idea of the change in motor capabilities of the child in this fourth stage of consumer development—between ages four and six—while keeping in mind that physical/motor development, cognitive development, and consumer development are inseparable and are dependent upon one another.

First, let us note briefly some changes in gross motor skills between ages four and six according to Gallahue (1982) and Payne and Isaacs (1999):

- **Walking:** Mature walking patterns are achieved between ages four and six. By age four, children's step length has increased from around 33 cm to 48 cm, heel-toe contact (compared to flat-footed contact) becomes normal, arms are gradually down to their sides, and out-toeing—pointing the toes out to the sides to gain balance—is eliminated, thus providing a narrow base of support. Of course, the heel-toe walking will wear out shoes faster, and thus the children will need new shoes more frequently, which they will most likely choose by this age, often choosing a brand that will help them "walk fast" and "take big steps." This normal walking skill also permits normal shopping activity, such as that done in a supermarket like the one that Carlos and his mother went to for his school paper and ice cream for the family.

- **Running:** Length of stride gradually increases until it is at its greatest at around age six. Flight—both feet off the ground at the same time—gradually appears at age four or five and becomes apparent by six. At first, the stride is stiff and uneven but gradually expands and smooths out. Speed triples between ages four and six as arms are leveraged to propel the body. Running shoes are now a necessity, according to the children, as well as matching socks, perhaps also a running suit. And walking through stores and malls may become running if parents don't put on the brakes.

- **Horizontal Jumping:** This motor ability requires coordinated performance of all parts of the body. At first, the arms do not initiate the jumping action, there is difficulty using both feet, and there is little emphasis on length of jump. But when children reach age five, arms initiate the jumping action, the preparatory crouch is assumed correctly, and extension of the knees and hips is more complete. When children reach age six, arms usually are swinging forward with force and are held high; there is complete extension of ankles, knees, and hips at take-off; and body weight is forward at landing. There is major emphasis on distance. Children may request some special shoes referred to as "basketball shoes" for this new capability. And when they go shopping with mom at the shopping center, the kids now have a tendency to jump out of the car and, once inside the center, try to jump over more than one tile at a time to demonstrate their newfound motor skills.

- **Vertical Jumping:** At first, for this motor ability, there is difficulty forming the preparatory crouch and taking off with both feet. Gradually, however, arms are coordinated with the trunk and leg action, and a two-foot take-off can be observed. Finally, when children reach age six or so, there is normally full body extension; forceful extension at the hips, knees, and ankles; and simultaneous upward arm lift. Landing is controlled so that it is very close to the point of take-off. There is a tendency for children to master jumping from a height at the same time they are mastering the vertical jump. Utilizing this new skill will take a basketball and accompanying equipment. And moms will have to hold their kids down at the checkout counters where they like to express their vertical jumping by getting an assist with their hands from the counters and railing.

- **Overhand Throwing:** The manipulative movement of overhand throwing action is at first mainly from the elbow, which remains in front of the body. Then the arm moves more so that the throwing object is behind the head and there is a definite forward shift of the body. Usually, there is a step of the foot on the throwing side of the body. Finally, around the time children are age six, the throwing motion starts with the arm being swung backward, the opposite elbow is raised for balance, the trunk rotates to the throwing side, and there is a step with the opposite foot. Concurrent with overhand throwing, children tend to learn underhand throwing. Now baseballs and softballs are a few of the requests prompted by this developed skill. And if moms don't control them, the kids will try throwing some packages into the shopping cart—just because they can.

- **Catching:** Catching is, so to speak, the receiving end of the overhand or underhand throw. A thrown object is stopped with the hands. At first, there is an avoidance reaction such as turning the face away and extending the arms as far as possible. The body is often used to trap the thrown object. Then the avoidance reaction is lessened, except for closing the eyes at contact; elbows are held at the sides; and on contact, the hands attempt to squeeze the object. Finally, when most kids reach age six, their avoidance reactions tend to be eliminated, eyes follow the thrown object, arms give on contact with it, and hands grasp the object in a well-timed motion. A couple of different baseball mitts will probably be requested. And sister and brother will play catch while shopping at the toy store with anything that can be thrown.

- **Kicking:** In the kicking action, the foot is used to impart force to an object directed to a goal. Movement of the kicking leg at first is very restricted, forward swing is short, and there is little follow-through. Preparatory backswing is from the knee. Arms swing in opposition to each other during the kicking action. Then the children learn to swing the leg from the hip, the support foot rises to its toes or leaves the ground entirely, and the trunk bends at the waist during follow-through. While walking and running seem to be easy to master, much time is needed to master the kick; it is not just a stepping motion as children first assume. In fact, at first children may opt to roll a ball after being frustrated by trying to kick it. But around the time children reach age six, kicking is becoming as routine as running. A new soccer ball is obviously on the minds of these children, and probably they will have to become members of some "little league" team and have team uniforms. Mom and dad may insist on it. And the kids may try out the soccer balls at the store if mom lets them shop alone.

Briefly, let us also note some developments in fine motor skills, that is, use of smaller muscles in more delicate efforts that take place in children between ages four and six, the fourth stage of consumer development. Most fine motor skills apparently have to await myelin production in the brain that raises the speed at which electrical impulses travel between neurons, and thus messages can reach the small muscles more rapidly and control them better. So, at ages four to six, children learn to accomplish many very important manipulation and language skills, the two often being intricately linked. Links between hand movements and language understanding are apparent in such efforts as word processing, writing, and drawing—all also very important tekrams to the children and their parents.

While attempts at drawing usually precede attempts at writing, both skills mature at about the same time—at around six to seven. Two- and three-year-olds begin their first drawing stage with scribbles. Then at four children are observed trying to draw shapes such as circles and squares, and maybe people. Interestingly, people and houses and cars have their origins in these geometric shapes wherein, for example, after making circles for a number of months, one becomes mom's face. At age five, children combine the shapes that they draw into pictures of objects such as houses, and once this is accomplished, although often accidentally, more pictures are pursued. By age six or so, the children are deep into the pictorial stage of drawing facilitated by increased myelination of the brain.

Probably drawing tools such as pencils and crayons facilitate writing efforts since they acquaint the children with marking instruments. When children are age four or five, writing with shoulders has progressed to writing with elbows, and in another year, with fingers and thumb. Likewise, holding the writing instrument improves from a supinate grasp at age three or four, to a pronate grasp a year later, until finally at age six or seven, the children learn the dynamic tripod grasp in which the thumb, middle finger, and index finger form a base for the instrument. At age four, the children usually can write some numbers and letters, but they cannot organize them yet into series and words. But by age five, most have mastered name printing in large, irregular uppercase letters. At six, they can embellish their name—the words—although in large letters. Then soon the height of the printed letters decreases, and there are some attempts at lowercase letters. It should be noted that learning to write letters and numbers during this four to six age range also facilitates understanding of advertising and pricing, such as the sign that Carlos saw offering two gallons of ice cream for five dollars.

Probably interrelated, during the time that children are learning to draw and write, they are learning some other fine manipulative motor skills. Buttoning and unbuttoning clothing; using scissors, spoons, and forks; and dialing the telephone are major examples. Perhaps the most related is the use of the computer keyboard and mouse. Not only are parents increasingly providing their preschool children with access to computers, kindergartens are doing the same. It is exciting to talk about these various fine motor skills that are developing, but we may forget that virtually all of them are also new consumer behavior patterns—drawing, writing, buttoning, dialing, and word processing.

At this point children's demonstrated drawing and writing skills have prompted mom to buy a lot of pencils, paper, and crayons—paper such as what Carlos had to have for his schoolwork. There are many kinds of drawing and writing instruments, and most likely mom will buy them all at one time or the other, often because her child asks for them and often asks for them by brand names that have been learned from the teacher and other students. (If you look at any list of required school supplies for kinder-garteners, chances are it mostly will be by brand name.) And these writing skills may appear in the children's shopping activities. We may witness a mom paying for an item at a toy store, for instance, and helping her preschooler sign the credit card receipt while the store clerk looks on with pleasure.

Speaking ability, a very important fine motor skill, develops rapidly during the four to six age period, with one new word spoken approximately every two hours. By the time the children get into the first grade at age six or seven, they have a vocabulary of around 14,000 words—compared to a maximum of 1,400 at the beginning of this consumer development stage. This tenfold increase in vocabulary is fostered by parents who read, write, and talk with their children and by personnel and children at daycare centers, nurseries, and kindergartens. But much of their improved speaking skills are a result of imitating TV program characters, older siblings, parents, and teachers. As they enter primary school, they will still have some trouble pronouncing some sounds, but starting particularly at age five, they are talkers, and the more talking they do, the more they correct themselves. At this point language production now catches up with language comprehension with the help of the children's schoolteachers. Chances are mom has bought many kinds of toys to promote her child's language development and most likely has graduated to some type of computer for her child. In China many stores sell what is called a "student computer" that all children seem to need and ask for—even before they reach elementary school—and be assured that parents provide them even though they cost a month's pay or more for most parents.

CURRENT ISSUES IN CONSUMER DEVELOPMENT (#9)

The Extreme Culture of Organized Youth Sports: Hurting Children by the Millions

Across the country, younger and younger athletes are injuring themselves in the relentless pursuit of sports achievement. There is a growing epidemic of youth sports injuries. Over 3.5 million children under the age of 14 are treated in hospital emergency rooms each year for sports-related injuries, with many more not being treated. For the most part these injuries are serious and, in fact, look much like those of professional athletes. They include broken bones, concussions, torn ligaments, frayed tendons, and lower back stress. An increasingly common injury is called "Little League elbow," in which the cartilage shears off the bone and requires surgery and much painful rehabilitation. Very important, also, many of these injuries will be with the children for life in the form of arthritis and other crippling diseases.

It's not just baseball or football producing these bodily injuries, but virtually every sport. Over 41 million children under age 19 participated in organized sports in 2005, and every sport claimed its serious injuries. Gymnastics and cheerleading lead the list for girls, while basketball and football took a heavy toll on boys.

What are the causes of so many sports injuries to children? From a physical standpoint, it is overusing bones and muscles that are still developing. Many of the children try to involve themselves in one sport all year—even more than professional athletes—and this produces repetitive movements that wear away unprepared body parts.

From a social standpoint there are many more causes of sports injuries. The culprits in this case are the major players in children's lives—parents, teachers, and coaches, and, of course, marketers including medical marketers.

- Parents have practically eliminated sports on a neighborhood basis because they worry about street crime including child abduction. So, gone are the sandlots and playgrounds where kids used to go for noncompetitive fun sports. Also, with both parents working, organized sports has become a place for their children after school. Many parents push their children into organized sports, hoping their children will be the next Michelle Kwan or Michael Jordon.
- Teachers, including coaches, often demand that the children practice a great deal, thus producing repetitive movements and consequential harm. Many elementary, middle, and high schools seek a reputation in sports, of course, at the expense of the children. This is equally true of the coaches, including those related to schools and those that operate independently. It is often the best athletes that are injured most because the coaches insist on playing them constantly in order to win—and contribute to their reputation.
- Marketers of athletic goods, marketers of professional and college sports, and marketers of sports training and sports medicine utilize all the marketing tools to drive the children to excel in sports. Movies and television programs demonstrate the "thrill of victory" and advertisements in children's magazines and on TV show the fruits of winning—great attention,

attracting the opposite sex, and money, money, money. The medical field, or what is called sports medicine, runs its marketing machine 24–7 glorifying the benefits of sports, offering training, and, of course, treatment. At least one hospital, for instance, gets the kids coming and going by advertising its fitness training as well as its treatment for injuries.

The only real losers in all this are the kids who listen to their parents, to their schoolteachers, and to the marketers who constantly shout at them to play and win. When one aims a critical eye at the situation, it looks as though a lot of people are trying to make money off the bodies of kids, bodies that are not yet ready for the task.

****
Sources: KidsHealth, 2006; Plancher, 2006; Weiss, 2006.

COGNITIVE DEVELOPMENT

During the previous stage of consumer development (stage three, ages two to four), children entered what Piaget called the *preoperational stage* of cognitive development (Phillips, 1969). In this stage there are several changes that take place gradually in the ways in which children think. Most important, children begin to represent objects and events in their minds in symbolic fashion. They do not discard the old way of storing in their memories objects and events upon which they acted—a sensorimotor memory or what might be referred to as a motor memory. Forming structures in the mind based on actions on them continues forever, but children seem to sense that memory based on representations—symbols, pictures, words—of objects and events is faster and more serviceable, so they migrate more to this kind of thinking. But at age two or three, when they begin to install this new way of thinking they are so egocentric, shallow in their perceptions, and unresponsive to the views of others that they are doing very little thinking in the technical sense of the word. Part of the reason is that they still do not yet have much to think with as compared to just a year later. For instance, they quickly make a mental note of the stinging feeling of a football hitting their hands as they try to catch it, and they may even begin to fear catching the ball—showing some reasoning. But they still record the result as a sensorimotor action and not as a relationship among the ball, its speed and weight, and the pressure it puts on their hands. Thus, much of their behavior at this time might be characterized as a butterfly flitting from one sweet thing to another while avoiding those that hurt, that are not rewarding, and making mental records of objects as one or zero, so to speak.

Now, in stage four of consumer development, which covers the ages of four to six, the children continue in the preoperational stage of cognitive development but grow gradually into the *concrete operational stage*, as Piaget called it, in which children can think and reason somewhat like adults (Phillips, 1969). Not overnight, of course, but over a period of years. In fact, they take on some of these grown-up characteristics at ages four and five, contrary to Piaget's research, which showed that such cognitive behavior did not occur until around age seven. (Piaget's theories of cognitive development have been challenged many times mainly on this basis—that is, that children today move through the stages of cognitive development earlier than those in his studies. Or, possibly, maybe they did also in Piaget's time, but his samples were so narrow that he may have been unable to detect this development.)

Let us consider briefly some of the dimensions of cognitive development that transpire during this time period between age four and age six:

- Children continue to reorganize their minds based on symbolic thinking of objects in addition to their actions on them. As they reach age four, they are aware of hundreds of objects and their names, and by the time they reach age six, they will be aware of thousands of objects. Each object is stored in the mind in symbolic form in addition to, or instead of, sensorimotor form. Thus, there is now much in the mind to play with, to imagine, to pretend to be, to want, to analyze. And as children think about objects, such as a football that hurts when caught, a network of attributes is gradually constructed. In fact, once the children begin to build networks around a particular object, they seem to want more information about it. These new networks prompt children in these ages to constantly ask why, what, when, and how, such as "What's that?" "How come?" and "Does it hurt their hands when they catch the ball going fast?"

- Although children's thinking is still egocentric, it gradually becomes more *social* mainly as a result of associating with an increasing number of children outside their home at daycare, nursery school, church school, and kindergarten. By age five or six, they often can sense the feelings of others with whom they interact regularly, such as those of children who cry when their mothers leave them at the school door or teachers who shout instructions to inattentive students. They also begin to realize that people have positions in society such as teacher, police officer, and store clerk. For example, they know by age five that there is a checkout clerk who "takes your money."

- Intuitive thought begins at age five or six and provides primitive explanations, although not always the correct ones, for why events happen or happen the way they do. Thus, children can intuit that pushing a button or two on the remote control somehow changes the pictures on the television set and that moving the computer mouse in a circle will move the cursor in a circle on the computer screen. Starting at around age five, they also reason that it takes money to get things in the marketplace although they do not know why. On the other hand, most likely they still think the moon follows them around, so some of their egocentric thinking is still in place.

- Attention span is gradually lengthened as children reach ages five and six. Perhaps it is due to the several years of practice watching their favorite programs on TV. Probably, too, there have been improvements in brain functioning. Whatever the reasons, they devote more attention to important matters—important to them— and thus become able to see more than just one dimension of an object. They now, for example, are aware that their favorite orange-flavored beverage comes in bottles of several sizes such as "big" and "really big." And with growing attention, they may learn a few simple little ditties from their favorite TV characters. Certainly, an improved attention span is necessary for children who enter formal education.

- School subjects that children encounter at ages four and five teach them much about counting, spelling, and writing. At age four, they begin to count, at first with glaring errors, but they count. By age six, they are rather accurate in this effort up to a point. They practice their counting frequently such as counting the tiles they walk on in a mall, the cracks in the sidewalk they ride their bikes on, and the coins they are accumulating in a piggy bank. From the books that mom reads them, and those read by the teachers, and the "show and tell" projects at nursery school and kindergarten, children gradually learn to read, although again, with many errors, and with very little comprehension. But the pretend reading that they have been doing since age three along with training and thinking are paying off. They still pretend to read, but they base much of their behavior on the pictures in books—they are so visual at this age. They seem to know that the words in the book describe the actions in the pictures. They can spell, read a few familiar words, and write or draw some of them. And they can discern many of the signs in a store and outside a store.

- Children's separation of objects is complete now. They now know that they are one among many social objects in their environment that includes parents, relatives, playmates, teachers, store clerks, and others. And they know the names of hundreds of physical objects with which they interact regularly, and they know the categories to which they belong. Very important, they recognize that physical objects belong to others (social objects); that is, they have a rudimental understanding of property, that all commercial objects are owned by someone. They understand that they own many things and that their playmates own many things. This is in contrast to two years ago when everything within reach was "mine."

- Children's self-image is becoming more accurate and more complex as they get feedback from their classmates at school. They are gradually developing a social self, one that reflects how others see them, as well as their personal self-image, which consists more accurately of how they look in certain clothing, how they walk or run, and how they perform certain activities such as eating and watching TV. Virtually all images are now gender-based, and there is a definite understanding that there are clothes and shoes for boys and for girls and they know which is for them. In fact, they emphasize the difference in their language—"Girls do that" and "Boys do that." There are still many exaggerations—the children sort of delude themselves much like many adults do—as they see themselves as better than, faster than, smarter than some of their classmates. Many products are now cataloged as either for boys or for girls, and for older or for younger children.

- One of the noticeable characteristics of children in this stage of consumer development is their ability to reverse their thinking, which becomes apparent at around age five or six. Reversibility allows the children to get to one point in their travel, their counting, their play, and then return. Symbolic representation that is now regularly taking place in the minds of children at age four and on produces networks of information. And as they think about something such as shopping at a supermarket, they can trace their thinking through these networks. For example, children can envision entering a supermarket door, doing some shopping, and then leaving through the same door. Now, at five or six, the child who has made many forays into stores begins to envision doing it on her own, which necessitates getting there and getting back. Reversibility is really difficult for most children at this age range, and they fear, for example, losing their way and not being able to return—a feature of separation anxiety that still remains. Piaget (1954) indicated that reversibility is not common until the child reaches age seven, but as in the case of several of his theories, it appears that reversibility does take place, at least to some extent, by age five or six, as shown in our research. Perhaps reversibility first appears in salient situations such as shopping for a favorite cereal and less so in meaningless tasks such as adding and subtracting that were often the concerns of Piaget.

ZONE OF PROXIMAL DEVELOPMENT

One explanation for why children, at least in the consumer role, seem to defy Piaget's thinking is provided by Vygotsky's (1978) thinking. Lev Vygotsky, a Russian developmental psychologist, showed that the culture in which children are reared makes a difference in what, when, and how the children learn culture-imposed tasks. He introduced the concept of the *zone of proximal development* (ZPD) to refer to the level at which children can almost, but not quite, perform a task on their own, but can do so with the help of a more capable person such as an older child or adult. Thus, the ZPD reflects both physical and mental abilities in combination. Vygotsky recognized that the culture in which children were born made a difference due to the extent and kinds of help, training, provision and use of cultural tools, and parental thinking that were present in the culture. Vygotsky grew up, academically, in Marxist Russia almost at the same time Piaget grew up in Switzerland. Different information begets different results in child rearing is the way Vygotsky would see it. When children in the ZPD are exposed to more information about what they need to know to accomplish some task, they learn it faster and better. Thus, their parents, their teachers, their friends, and the tools that each provides can be instrumental in moving children through the learning of a task such as cooking or shopping. (Shopping was not a task of interest of Vygotsky or Piaget.) The help that children receive from their society to support their learning and problem solving is termed *scaffolding* because it is not unlike the supporting scaffolding used by workers in constructing a building (Woods, Bruner, and Ross, 1976). Parents and older siblings help children to perform in the consumer role. In-store observations, for example, have shown parents assisting their little children to place items in a shopping cart, to carry items purchased, and to check out with purchases. As an interesting side note, contrary to Vygotsky's thinking, when self-service was first introduced in the 1930s, some supermarkets used trained bears and chimpanzees to show customers how to use the system. When both Vygotsky and Piaget were doing some of their best work in the 1920s and 1930s, there was no way that they could envision the influence of media such as radio and television on children's learning, much less the marketplace in general. None of the children whom they studied were members of a market-driven society to the extent that children are in the studies reported here. Moreover, probably most of those children were not in daycare, nursery school, and kindergarten between ages two and five. And very important, neither thinker could imagine that children could be "head of the household" and what this would mean for their learning about their environment—the topic of both theorists. Thus, four- and five-year-old children today may be big enough and smart enough to make purchases, but still usually need help with the sequencing and, of course, the money— obtaining it and counting it.

MOTIVES

Reasons for wanting and seeking more objects—commercial or natural—rapidly expand when children reach the four to six age range. Their needs for food and sleep are practically put on automatic as they turn these physiological needs over to parents and dwell more on doing things. Exploration characterizes their waking moments, looking in new places for objects to have any time there is an opportunity. They want to look outside, in their parents' room, in the cabinets, trash cans, and the storage areas of the house. They want to look in the neighbors' homes and yards, look in other children's pocket and bags. They are extremely curious about nature's objects—bugs, birds, cats, and dogs, and all the plants around them—as they begin to realize that these objects have life like people. They also watch more TV and change channels more frequently. And all of this exploratory behavior is accompanied by the basic exploratory question: "What's this?"

Play is as equally important as the exploration need. In fact, play is probably the main explanation for exploration. It does appear to be the most predominant motive (need) to be satisfied, just as it was a year ago. Not only are play objects now sought for satisfaction of the play need, but also foods, beverages, and many adult products such as mom's clothing and dad's shaving cream. As noted previously, at age five or six, children make improvements in many motor skills, and they begin to seek achievements with those skills. Thus, they merge the play and achievement motives to win contests, to appear to be better than playmates and classmates at running, jumping, drawing, and writing. And they seek challenges. They even attempt to compete against one or more parents in some physical activity, participation in which is often encouraged by the parents.

Also, starting at age four or five and certainly by age six, children begin a childhood practice of looking up the age range for commercial objects belonging to older children—mainly because they want to be older, to be like older children, to relate to older children. That is, in addition to exploration, they are looking to older children at school, church, neighborhoods, and in the marketplace for information, for guidance in proper consumption—what might be called conspicuous consumption. Thus, older children, mainly those in school, become reference groups for the younger children, and when these younger children are making decisions about, for example, what to wear, they more often turn to older children for clues. Until this time the children were pretty much satisfied with what parents provided them. But seeing the property of other children, particularly older children, gives the children more reasons to want more commercial objects. Thus, those things of other children that are conspicuous—that can be seen and stand out—become objects to know about and want. It is at this time, for example, that shoes and clothing become more important to children, particularly as they represent the children's self-images to others.

At ages four and five, most children are being thrust into some kind of formal schooling with other children—perhaps even as early as age two. Thus, they are gaining some autonomy, some freedom from parents, which they started seeking at walking age. Also, they begin to want to be with other children, to express the need for affiliation, even though they are still very much centered on themselves. Usually, at this time the children have at least one friend who they like to be with and from which they seek information and affiliation in addition to that obtained from parents. The affiliation motive also drives four- and five-year-old children to create relationships with inanimate objects, imaginary objects, and pets.

In addition to the psychological explanation of motives, a neurological explanation for the children in this stage of consumer development to begin thinking more clearly, reasoning more about objects and situations, is the brain development that takes place in this time period. Eliot (1999, p. 414), a neurologist, called age six "the dawn of reason" and a time period "when most children regardless of their cultural experience reach a new level of intellectual functioning" as a result of frontal lobe development. Since the frontal lobes are the slowest part of the brain to mature, according to Eliot, they limit children's cognitive development, particularly their attentive abilities. There are several reasons why the frontal lobes are so slow to develop—slow development of the neurotransmitter, dopamine, and slow myelination in the region. But the main point is that children are not able to reason very well or very fast—to think on their feet—until the frontal lobes are in place. Thus, much of children's working memory and attention have to await this neurological development. In the meantime they keep seeking objects and asking lots of questions until they are able to reason out the answers on their own.

STAGE FOUR OF CONSUMER DEVELOPMENT (48–72 MONTHS)

Consumer Behavior Patterns at Home

Most of children's consumer behavior takes place at home in stage four—eating, sleeping, bathing, dressing, playing, to name a few of the basic ones. There are at least two or three notable home-based consumer behavior patterns that take on significance at around age four or five.

Accumulating and Collecting Objects

One of the most apparent consumer behavior patterns at home is collecting objects, usually commercial objects. This activity typically starts around age two or three and usually with noncommercial objects such as rocks, flowers, and bugs, and gradually includes commercial objects such as Christmas cards, toys, stamps, and coins. The collecting activity seems to be part of the "terrible twos" that apparently all children go through and thus may be explained by the two-year-old's strong desire for independence— for having his own domain to control. Weinstein (1985. p. 21) said that "collecting objects is a form of power for young children, a way in which they can organize and control at least one small part of the world." While the practice may begin among two-year-olds, it becomes more organized and purposeful around ages four or five. At this time the children tend to focus on commercial objects more than nature's objects, including some of nature's objects that are purchased in the marketplace such as goldfish and turtles—and thus become commercial objects. Usually, the commercial objects are play items such as dolls, miniature cars, marbles, and construction toys. Money—mainly coins—also tends to be a commercial item that is collected usually with the assistance of parents and relatives who want to teach the saving practice.

At first, children's collections can more accurately be described as accumulations motivated by the "sheer number and mass" that the collection represents (Acuff and Reiher, 1997, p. 15). But as the children are able to discern special characteristics of each item in their accumulations, they clearly become collections. This discernment is a result of children's being able to focus their attention on more than just one characteristic of objects. For instance, a four- or five-year-old girl can begin to see the differences in Barbie clothing and want to collect many different sets. Or a five-year-old boy takes more interest in miniature cars as he is able to discern different models and brands. Thus begins formal collections of what marketers often term *collectibles* such as baseball cards, stickers, stamps, coins, dolls, and doll clothing. The list is endless and mainly extended by marketers who try to dream up new items for the children to buy and collect and may be sold separately or in tandem with other products such as cereal, gum, and fast foods.

There are many explanations for children's collections of commercial objects. As noted, initially the needs for control and independence may explain such activities. Then it appears that additional motives for collecting, such as achievement, come with age of the children and the suggestions of marketers—"Be the first in your school to own all twenty!" Reflecting and maintaining one's self-image seem to be a significant explanation— being cool, being a cool boy or girl, or just being male or female. In this case the children usually can be seen showing their collections to others, maybe at show-and-tell at nursery school and kindergarten. It does seem that an additional explanation for collecting is children's copying their parents and/or older siblings. At least a third of adults have a formal collection of objects, often a collection that started in childhood. Interestingly, and often at odds with their children, parents may collect children's play items but may not permit their children to play with them—just look at them. Adults' collecting play items is mainly driven by economics—hoping that a developed collection will eventually have substantial value. Of course, the items must be in good condition; therefore, their children and grandchildren usually are not permitted to play with them. For instance, one of the reasons some parents go to specific fast-food restaurants is to collect the latest toy collectibles (for kids), which today may have substantial value. (See, for example, *Tomart's Price Guide to Kid's Meal Collectibles* [Clee and Hufferd, 1994].) Never mind that such efforts may contribute to their children's obesity as well as their irritation (from not being able to play with the items). In fact, such behavior on the part of parents may create a competitive atmosphere in the household, even an adversarial atmosphere that likely will lead to problems and strife between parent and child. In a sponsored research project, one 10-year-old girl told us about her mother's collection of expensive dolls. She related to us that her mother kept the dolls on display in glass cases, and neither she nor her little sister was allowed to go near them. She said she considered her mother "mean" when asked about her feelings about the doll collection.

Money Collection, Use, and Meaning

Economic motives also may drive children's collection of money, although a slightly different kind of economics. Around age four or five— in stage four of consumer development—children begin to understand the purpose of money, as well as how to count it, so the accumulation (e.g., piggy bank) of coins from the past year or two gradually takes on more value to the children because they want to use the money to buy things. Thus, the saving concept kicks in, but gradually, as the parents and children together plan and count and save the children's money. Once children in this stage begin to attempt purchases—with the aid of parents and other caretakers— and the price of things therefore enters into the children's commercial world—their collection of money takes on much more significance, including the counting of it.

Children's accumulations of money may be in jars, piggy banks, purses, or boxes, but it becomes a significant matter to children beginning in this stage of consumer development. Its significance is due to several factors. At home there is often talk of money among parents and other adults such as relatives and neighbors. Also, parents and others give the young children money and tell them to save it. Probably, the idea is to teach the children the saving practice as well as "the value of a dollar." To the child, the concept of saving at this time is more of a sensorimotor matter than a symbolic matter. It consists mainly of the action of putting coins into a container of some sort from which they are taken out from time to time to be part of play. For instance, when the weather is bad outside, a four-year-old plays in his room, and one of the things he may do is pour out his money and examine it. He gradually learns denominations although he tends to use size as a determinant. This means that dimes are confusing since they are smaller than a nickel but worth twice as much. As part of his examination, the child may ask mom or an older sibling, "How much is this?" or "How many is this?" His questions are probably prompted by observations of money use by parents at home (pay for the delivered pizza), in the car (take money from a storage drawer and pay road toll), and at the marketplace (buying a newspaper at the nearby convenience store). The parents paying this much attention to money gives money more significance beyond being play objects.

As a side note, about the same time that children indicate that they understand the purpose of money—"to buy things with," is how one preschooler described it—parents do more encouraging of saving money. One of the actions that some parents take when their children are around age five or six is to introduce them to formal savings plans at banks of various kinds. Parents may know of a bank—probably the one they use— that welcomes saving accounts from children. The parents take the children to the bank and, through bank personnel, introduce the children to the concept of the bank savings plan, which often has a special name such as "kids savings" and "kids banking." Some forward-looking banks have rec- ognized the potential of children as a future market and have aggressively sought out children as banking customers. The banks may develop the program, put someone in charge of it who understands the concept of growing customers, advertise the program, implement in-bank services to the children such as a special teller to serve children, provide free gifts with large deposits in order to attract those accumulations at home, and even mail statements to the children—these banks know that children just love receiving mail. In sum, they try to form a relationship with the children that they hope will last a lifetime.

At age four, children are learning how to read numbers and *count*— learning on their own, learning from parents and nursery school teachers. When children reach age five, particularly, counting becomes a major cog- nitive activity as they count the items in their accumulations, pages in a book, peas on their plates. The counting probably is not accurate, such as 1, 2, 5, 6, but it improves quickly at age five. The act of counting money accel- erates at this time, being prompted by its frequent use in the household and the frequent mention of price related to the marketplace. For example, Carlos was aware of the price of a big container of ice cream as a result of reading the price (numbers) placed on the in-store freezer. By age five, chil- dren often will examine their accumulation of money, place some in their hands, and ask their mom, "What will this much buy?" Such a question indicates at least some understanding of money as a means to obtain objects—a basic requirement in becoming a buyer. Collecting money as a hobby or for its future value usually is not a practice of children until they reach at least age eight or nine. For now, it is a commercial object that moves from a play item to a purchase item that reflects the price of an object in the marketplace. As noted, when children begin to attempt a purchase, their understanding of money comes to the forefront of the situation and increases the significance of it.

Helping at Home

Starting at around age four, maybe five, children begin to sense the feelings and concerns of others. At this time they also possess a pretty good sense of the impact of their actions on the feelings of others, although they have trouble articulating the relationship. Putting the two together, children, even though still quite egocentric, begin to try to help others. Mom is the main recipient at first by receiving help with putting away the laundry, putting away toys, and cleaning fruits and vegetables for meals, to name a few tasks. These efforts may be sought by moms, and/or they may be volunteered by the children. Mom may suspect that some of the helping is manipulative behavior by her child, and she may be right. As noted in the two preceding chapters, children at this age specialize in techniques that support their requests to parents for more commercial goods.

Four- and five-year-olds may also help younger siblings in order to give some relief to their moms, and also to try out the role of father or mother as they seek identity. Such sibling help may include feeding, walking, entertaining, and even reading to them, although it may be pretend reading. And children at this age offer help to grandparents, whom they now recognize as needing it. This is particularly the case where grandparents sit with the children while parents work—commonly the case in China.

Finally, children in this stage of consumer development help out with the household pets—those of the children, such as gerbils and goldfish, and those of the family, such as cats and dogs. If the children can take over the feeding, for example, of the family pets, moms and dads are also the beneficiaries. Caring for pets may be driven by nurturing behavior, particularly of girls who may wash and groom the pets and even dress them as babies.

There is a tendency at this time in the lives of children to begin to provide all this help for a price. As noted, children in this stage of consumer development are beginning to understand the value of money. Therefore, they and/or their parents may relate their helping in the house with pay. Many parents use money as a motivator of the children to perform household tasks, and parents also may try to relate money and work as a first step in teaching their children the value of money—and its purchasing power. At first, parents may offer a fixed sum of money to children to do some work (to help out). "I'll give you a dollar to clean your room." Later, when their children are age five or six, parents may offer a weekly allowance to them that may be tied to chores in the house such as cleaning, feeding the pets, and emptying the trash cans. It should be noted, also, that the money-for-work idea may originate with the children who want to accumulate more money to buy more things. When their children are around age five, many parents often introduce the allowance system as part of their value teaching and also to slow down the requests for money from those children who are learning to use money as a purchasing mechanism. At first it may be difficult for the children to understand since it is a rationing system of sorts related to the children's wants and getting them satisfied by parents—as they have always done. In any case a new source of money for the children—in addition to gifts—is instituted, and just in time for the growing need for money to buy things in this stage four of consumer development.

Consumer Behavior at School

Sometime during or shortly after the "terrible twos," children may be placed in some kind of formal schooling. This schooling may go by many names—daycare center, nursery school, preschool, pre-K, enrichment program, and kindergarten, and specialized teaching programs such as music school or language school. By the time they reach the fourth stage of consumer development around age four, the children are usually in some kind of school that goes beyond baby-sitting—three-quarters of American mothers work and need care for their babies—and into formal teaching.

Going to school requires some new consumer behavior patterns for children—sitting at desks, writing and drawing, using papers and writing/drawing instruments, having lunch at school, carrying a backpack, wearing special clothing. There are also some consumer behavior patterns that parents and children invent in addition to those that are a part of the schooling. They include fixing and/or buying special foods and beverages, buying athletic gear of various sorts, and buying and wearing certain clothing chosen by parents and kids. Also included are the show-and-tell items chosen by the parents and children, such as collections mentioned previously, books, photos, and musical instruments. In any case consumer behavior at school is the first significant consumer behavior performed outside the home other than the marketplace. (Actually, schools, particularly those before primary school, are just another element of the marketplace but are treated here as having separate stature.) The tekrams performed at school are sometimes "firsts" for the children and therefore may be remembered for a long time—writing with chalk on a chalkboard, taking the teacher a gift such as a piece of fruit, and storing school items in a locker or other storage unit.

Consumer behavior is not intentionally taught at these preschools—formally called consumer education—but some school subjects intersect with consumer behavior. For example, drawing and coloring may include pictures of restaurants, homes, and cars—sometimes companies provide teaching aids such as coloring books with the companies' names and/or brands on them. Math lessons may involve buying two apples or counting money according to their pictures in a math book. And reading may reach into many areas of consumer behavior, such as items about agricultural products, manufactured products, and retailers. The point is that there is indeed consumer behavior being taught in addition to that required for attending school. Consequently, on any given day at school during a four-hour session, children may perform several hundred tekrams—many more in an eight-hour session that occurs in primary school and some kinder-gartens. By the time children reach the fifth and final stage of consumer development—somewhere around the third grade for most of them—they are performing hundreds of tekrams daily at school and a similar or larger number at home and in the marketplace that are school-related. These new consumer behavior patterns take center stage when children enter primary school and are discussed in detail in the next chapter.

Consumer Behavior in the Marketplace

Stage four of consumer development, called co-purchase, begins children's functioning in the purchase phase of consumer behavior. Until now children have performed in the prepurchase phase and the postpurchase phase. Learning the purchase act in this stage and in the subsequent stage five is the final step in becoming a bona fide consumer.

By age four, children have made several hundred visits to the market-place—supermarkets, malls, convenience stores, toy stores, clothing stores, restaurants—they have made several thousand purchase suggestions to parents while visiting the marketplace, and they have made several hundred product selections for themselves from shelves and fixtures in the market-place. It follows, then, that the children at this time may want to try to make their own purchases. They have some cognitive skills that were absent just a year ago such as some means-ends understanding of money's role in consumer behavior. They have observed hundreds of times their parents' use of money in the marketplace, and not only that of parents but also of other family members, friends, and many other consumers present in the market-place. Just notice how a five-year-old will watch intensely the selection and purchase actions of other children.

Let us look briefly at the previous three stages of consumer development from the perspective of the marketplace. Observations mark the first stage, in which children assimilate products and their packages that are on display, the shopping and purchase behavior of parents and other consumers present in the shopping setting, and the use of money in the exchange process. The second stage is characterized by children's request-ing of specific products usually by brand. Requests also may be for money as children develop an understanding of its role in obtaining the observed items that are desired for their satisfaction. The requests may also be for assistance in obtaining the desired goods and services, and may extend to seeking permission to make a purchase. In stage three, products that are observed and asked for are physically selected from their displays and placed in a shopping cart or given to parents for purchase. They also may be placed on the checkout counter so that parents will be sure to buy them. At this point children are only a click away from making a purchase on their own. The trouble is they are not able to make the purchase without substantial assistance from parents or other co-shoppers. That is the essence of this stage four of consumer development—co-purchase.

As we noted earlier, four-year-old children have developed a fascination with money, particularly coins. They accumulate them as they receive them from parents and others. At some point the coins go from being playthings to being purchase means. Usually, at this time money also takes on meaning to children as a result of work in their households. When the children reach age five or six, the two are fitted together in the minds of children—earn money, use it to make purchases of satisfying goods and services.

One of the first co-purchase acts involves vending machines. Four-year-olds ask their mothers if they can take some of their money to the marketplace and buy something from the vending machines that can be found there. For example, children are introduced to vending machines each time they enter and exit a mass merchandiser such as Wal-Mart. They see not only the devices at the entry/exit, but also other children obtaining candy and gum and an endless number of bright, shiny trinkets from them. And chances are mothers show their children how to use them. By the way, many of these vending machines are just a pull away from being gambling devices not unlike slot machines in Vegas (that children supposedly cannot use). For example, in some vending machines, children insert their money and then attempt to manipulate a device to grasp an object such as a stuffed animal and drop it into a vending chute. Probably most often they are unsuccessful, and this failure motivates them to spend another quarter and another. Vending machines of some kind are also in other locations such as malls, drugstores, barber shops, dry cleaners, and schools.

Mom may utilize the vending machines to make a deal with her child in order to control her behavior at the marketplace. "You can spend a quarter in the vending machines and get whatever you want while I buy the things we need." Or, "Here are two quarters. You can buy something from the vending machines while I check out." Often, as Opdike (2005) observed, "If (mothers) can buy a little peace and give pleasure to (their children) for just a quarter, it seems like a no-brainer." For many parents, too, they see the quarter spent as a big savings compared to a $5 toy, for instance, that their children constantly scream for. Thus, many parents rely on vending machines to give them and their children a great deal of satisfaction.

Children's first vending machine purchase, wherever it may take place, alerts the children to other vending machines in other locations and to other kinds of gifts and confections available in other vending machines—and a thousand trinkets. This co-purchase behavior is soon routinized by the children who begin to carry some coins with them when they go to the marketplace with their parents—usually two or three times a week at this age. Using their coin accumulations to make regular purchases from vending machines is only a step away from making purchases in stores—although a giant step.

Making a purchase in a store requires selecting the product from the store shelf—the sort of thing that children learned to do in stage three—transporting it to a cashier, standing in line, paying the cashier, and taking the bagged product out of the store—functions found in stage four, discussed here, and in stage five, discussed in the next chapter. Unlike a vending machine purchase, products in the store usually are not at coin denomination prices—1 cent, 5 cents, 10 cents, 25 cents. Instead, they are usually psychologically priced such as three-for-a-dollar or 39 cents. While such pricing may be appealing to an adult, it is confusing to a child. Remember Carlos knew ice cream was two for five dollars, but he was not sure how much one container cost. Such pricing, which is normal for all retailers, means that children need a greater understanding of numbers than that required for purchasing from vending machines.

Another important point: Products in a vending machine represent a small selection of one or a few items, but the same items on the shelf usually are part of a much wider variety, thus adding more confusion to that resulting from adult pricing. Look at Photo 9-1 to see this confusion firsthand. A five-year-old girl is shopping in a Chinese supermarket with her grandmother and has been told she can buy one snack from a display containing

PHOTO 9-1   A five-year-old Zhengzhou girl selects a snack from a supermarket display while her grandmother stands nearby giving her advice and waiting to pay for her selection.

PHOTO 9-2   The five-year-old girl and her grandmother walk to the supermarket check-out to pay for the snack she has selected, and in her haste to sample her choice, she opens it and begins to consume it—before paying for it.

over two-dozen choices. She has also been told that she can only spend one Yuan (12 cents). After several minutes of agonizing over the options with the two limitations set by the grandmother, the child chooses one. In a self-service environment such as that in which the little Chinese girl is shopping, it is necessary to take the product to a pay station of some kind in another part of the store, stand in line with giant-size adults, and then pay for the selected item. We adults forget that, once children have made a selection, they want to consume it now, or at least get out of the store and get home with it as soon as possible. So, in Photo 9-2 the little girl can be seen short-ening the loop and opening and eating the product before she or her grand-mother pays for it. This process is complicated and intimidating at first, not necessarily fitted to the thinking of children, and requires substantial prac-tice to get right. Therefore, much assistance is needed from co-shoppers, usually parents.

Just what kind of purchase assistance children receive from parents depends on the shopping setting, the attitudes of the parents, and, of course, the actions of the children. Assistance of the parents actually begins at home before parent and child enter the marketplace. Parents and children prob-ably will reach some kind of agreement as to how much money the chil-dren may take with them, for instance. If a particular child has taken a quarter with her on trips before and purchased something from a vending machine, then the agreement may be on one or two quarters. If the amount is more, perhaps to buy a birthday gift for a playmate, mom will have to help count it as well as suggest how much the gift will cost. There likely will also be an agreement as to where and when the child will actually make the purchase. If the shopping trip is a major one for mom, she may not want to spend time helping her child with a first purchase. She knows that there will be some time necessary for finding the candy or gift, choosing one, and then paying for it. Mom may want to simply include the purchase in with hers rather than separate them. But she knows that if her kid has asked several times to make the purchase on her own, then she must prepare to spend time and energy with her child's purchase.

Some moms are reluctant to give permission to their children to make a purchase (other than the minor purchases from vending machines). But most moms, based on my research, recognize the first real purchase— although it is a co-purchase—as a milestone for the child and therefore its importance to the child. Consequently, most moms will be ready to assist with the in-store tasks of selecting and paying for the item. The typical self-service environment always requires standing in line and paying for selected products. Mom will likely find it necessary to calm her child during waiting; some children just cannot wait as the little girl in Photo 9-2 demonstrates. Once at the checkout, mom will have to assist with the money to make sure the sum given and the change given back are correct. Mom may want to do some debriefing, also, after the purchase in which she reminds her child of the waiting time and not to open the package or consume the product until it is paid for. She may even advise her child to look for the shortest line, that there are express lines in most mass merchandisers and supermarkets.

Children's first co-purchase may be made in a convenience store near home when parents buy gasoline or some other item such as a newspaper. Since the parents' purchase is usually small in number, they can devote more time to helping their children with their purchase. Also, the line is usually for the cashier, which surely will appeal to both—although the child should be prepared for a counter that is often above his head at a convenience store—and cluttered with many products not suitable for children. Learning to make a purchase at a nearby convenience store has some other advantages. Usually, less time is needed for selections because the shopping space is much smaller than the typical supermarket, for example, and the offering of each product is narrower. Single parents particularly like for their children to learn to make purchases at nearby stores so that the children can eventually make some independently (stage five) for the household and save the parent a shopping trip.

Children's first assisted purchase (co-purchase) usually takes place between ages four and six—the time frame for stage four—with the median age being 64–66 months for American children. It may be in a convenience store or supermarket, but most of the time it is in a mass merchandiser such as Kmart. The most common co-purchase is a toy of some sort, usually for the purchaser but perhaps for a playmate. Another common co-purchase is a snack item such as candy, gum, or a drink.

Children in China normally make their first co-purchase somewhere between 36 and 48 months with a median age of 42 months—much earlier than American children. Usually, the children's first purchase is a play item of some sort, although not necessarily what mom or dad would prefer. But both parents seem eager to get their child—there is usually only one—to participate in the purchase process as soon as possible. The parents are not so interested in their child gaining independence, as is the case in the United States. Instead the Chinese parents see the purchase act as part of the child's education, which is a major concern—making choices, using money, interacting with store personnel. Incidentally, most stores in China are still not self-service like they are in the United States, and you might think, as I do, that having to select a product with the assistance of store personnel would slow things down, delay the first purchase effort. But actually many store clerks are willing to help a child with his first purchase. Also, mom and dad often carry their child in their arms while he tends to the first purchase. I think this physical closeness gives the child a boost in confidence that will get him past his shyness in dealing with adults (strangers). And it sure helps at the very tall cashier counters that are found in department stores and others. It appears that at this median age of 42 months, Chinese children know little more about money than American children, and further, both are equally shy at this age. But the substantial help of the parents and that of the store clerk, who is almost always a woman, make up for these shortcomings.

American children seem more motivated, more excited by their first assisted purchases than Chinese children. American children seem to want to do it again, to earn more money at home, and therefore to spend more and more frequently. I think the fact that Chinese parents rarely say no to their children's requests for anything, whereas no is more common among American parents when their children are this age, gives the event less significance to Chinese children. It, in effect, tells American kids that they can start getting more of what they want since they do the buying.

In Photo 9-3 a Chinese mother shops the open marketplace with her four-year-old son. While the boy sits in a seat on the back of the bicycle—the family transportation—he makes requests for certain products, he recommends certain products, and he gives his approval or disapproval to purchase suggestions of his mother. Once his mother has decided on a product, usually with her son's advice, she bargains for it, purchases it, places it in the bicycle basket, and heads for another vendor. While the boy may not leave the bicycle seat, which serves as an observation post much like the seat in a supermarket cart, he still often has a great deal of influence on the purchases the mother makes—enough so, in fact, that some of the purchases could be called co-purchases.

PHOTO 9-3   A Chinese mother shops street vendors while her four-year-old son sits comfortably in the seat on the back of the family bicycle. He makes suggestions and recommendations, gives approval to some of his mother's purchases, and in sum, together they make some co-purchases.

DISCUSSION

In this chapter we have described children's first purchase with the assistance of parents—the co-purchase—and the conditions that make it possible. The selecting/taking in stage three is now replaced by a purchase—not just taking the product and consuming it, but taking it, paying for it, and then consuming it. This major milestone of co-purchase in the children's process of consumer development takes place usually between age four and age six. At this age, children are reasonably equipped with the cognitive and motor abilities to deal with the complexities of making a purchase. They are big enough and strong enough to reach a checkout counter, a product on most shelves, and maybe push a shopping cart ahead of them. Cognitively, they have reached a point at which they understand, at least at a rudimental level, the purchase act, the use of money, and the exchange system. However, they still cannot make a purchase without a lot of help from their parents or some other skilled consumer. Even though they understand the basics of a purchase—asking, selecting, buying with money from a store clerk, consuming the purchased product after it is purchased—they still cannot conceptualize the entire process of exchange and its sequences. So, making the first purchase often takes a lot of talking with parents and getting guidance from them—it is a co-purchase; the child is a co-purchaser.

While first co-purchases are usually of very small value, such as that from a vending machine, they are major to the children who make them. It is an adult thing they do; it gives them an even greater feeling of autonomy as consumers than when they first started selecting and taking products from store shelves. It is something that they talk about with others, and it is something they want to do a lot more of. It motivates them to obtain (earn) more money so that they can repeat the act. A co-purchase, a purchase with help, follows logically from the several years of tekrams that preceded it. Discovering products to want (stage one), seeking and asking for those products (stage two), and selecting and taking products from store shelves for parents to purchase (stage three) naturally lead to the child's "doing it myself" when he has the money and the know-how.

How much parents actually train their children to be consumers has been debated for years (e.g., Ward, Wackman, and Wartella, 1977; McNeal, 1987). But when it comes to the first purchase, parents provide much help, without which the purchase would surely be delayed. As noted, Chinese parents give their children more assistance than American parents give theirs. The results are that the Chinese children average making their first co-purchase almost a year earlier than American children. Another way to look at the difference in age of the first co-purchase is that American children have to learn more consumer behavior on their own, and therefore the process takes more time. An exception is that in households where there is only one parent. In those households, American children make their first co-purchase at least six months earlier than kids in two-parent households (McNeal, 1999). The acceleration of the process appears to be due mainly to the one parent putting pressure on the child to grow up faster—somewhat like Chinese parents do.

I would note at this point that this first co-purchase milestone probably goes without any knowledge of it or concern for it by the retailers. Somehow I see it as some kind of award to the retailer by the child, that she would select that store for her first purchase effort. But retailers in general do little to assist children in maturing in the consumer role and, in fact, are just as likely to put deterrents in the way, such as out-of-reach products and checkout counters. Thus, as noted here and in previous chapters, children learn much consumer behavior on their own.

This first co-purchase is a motivator to the children and will be repeated many times over the next several months. During that time the children will learn more money math, learn how to earn more money, and learn how to save money. Then, as described in the next chapter, they will make that final act of an independent purchase. Making this purchase is like taking the training wheels off their bicycle.

REFERENCES

Acuff, D. S., and R. H. Reiher. (1997). *What Kids Buy and Why*. New York: The Free Press.

Clee, K., and S. Hufferd. (1994). *Tomart's Price Guide to Kid's Meal Collectibles*. Dayton, OH: Tomart Publications.

Eliot, L. (1999). *What's Going On in There? How the Brain and Mind Develop in the First Five Years of Life*. New York: Bantam Books.

Gallahue, D. L. (1982). *Understanding Motor Development in Children*. New York: John Wiley & Sons, Inc.

KidsHealth. (2006, April 14). Preventing children's sports injuries. Retrieved from http://www.kidshealth.org/parent/fitness/safety/sports_safety.html

McNeal, J. U. (1987). *Children as Consumers: Insights and Implications*. Lexington, MA: D. C. Heath and Company.

McNeal, J. U. (1999). *The Kids Market: Myth and Realities*. Ithaca, NY: Paramount Market Publishers.

Opdike, J. D. (2004, June 6). Love & Money: If a quarter will buy happiness, why not? *Wall Street Journal* (Eastern Edition), 2.

Payne, V. G., and L. D. Isaacs. (1999). *Human Motor Development: A Lifespan Approach* (4th ed.). Mountain View, CA: Mayfield Publishing Company.

Phillips Jr., J. L. (1969). *The Origins of Intellect: Piaget's Theory*. San Francisco, CA: W. H. Freeman and Company.

Piaget, J. (1954). *The Construction of Reality in the Child*. New York: Basic Books.

Plancher, K. D. (2005). Spike in children's sports-related injuries. Retrieved from www.emediawire.com/releases/2005/3/emw213379.htm

Vygotsky, L. S. (1978). *Mind in Society: The Development of Higher Psychological Processes*. Cambridge, MA: Harvard University Press.

Ward, S., D. B. Wackman, and E. Wartella. (1977). *How Children Learn to Buy*. Beverly Hills, CA: Sage Publications, Inc.

Weinstein, G. W. (1985). *Children and Money: A Parents' Guide*. New York: New American Library.

Weiss, M. J. (2006, April). The agony of victory. *Reader's Digest*, 134–141.

Woods, D., J. S. Bruner, and G. Ross. (1976). The role of tutoring in problem solving. *Journal of Child Psychology & Psychiatry & Allied Disciplines*, *17*, 89–100.

10

STAGE FIVE: THE INDEPENDENT PURCHASE (72–100 MONTHS)

Jimmy and His Pal, Chris, as Independent Consumers

In an open-ended interview with a third-grader, Jimmy, outside a small-town convenience store, it was determined that he had income from an allowance, from chores around his home, and some from door-to-door selling. Further, he confidently stated that he routinely made purchases on his own. What follows is some of the dialogue from that interview taken from the notes of a trained interviewer.

Interviewer: *How often do you come to this store to buy something?*

Jimmy: *Me and my buddy, Chris, ride down here about every day after school.*

Interviewer: *Is Chris a classmate?*

Jimmy: *He goes to the same school with me, but he is in the fourth grade. I'm in the third. When we get out of school, we ride our bicycles home together and then usually come here after we check in. Chris lives across the street from me.*

Interviewer: *What do you mean by check in?*

Jimmy: *I go home, call my mom, then put up my books, grab a snack, and head out.*

Interviewer: *When you go home, you call your mom. Is that right?*

Jimmy: *Yeah. She works at Celanese [chemical plant] and she likes for me to call her when I get home. Chris does the same thing. His mom works there.*

Interviewer: *Why do you choose this store in which to buy things?*

Jimmy: *I can be here in five minutes from my house.*

Interviewer: I see. When you come to this store, what do you usually buy?

Jimmy: About everything. I usually get a Slurpee (self-serve soft drink), candy, lots of things.

Interviewer: What is a Slurpee?

Jimmy: It's good. You get to mix it yourself with different flavors, and sometimes I put together a dive bomber. Then we sit outside (the store) on the bench and drink them.

Interviewer: What's a dive bomber?

Jimmy: It's good. It's all the flavors in one big cup and a little ice.

Interviewer: Sounds good. You said you buy candy. What kind?

Jimmy: Me and Chris like to get a big Butterfinger and crush it up in the wrapper and eat it a little bit at a time while we ride our bikes.

Interviewer: That sounds good, too. Anything else you buy here?

Jimmy: I bought a kite here.

Interviewer: A kite? Tell me about that.

Jimmy: It's a Humming Bird. They're the only ones that sell Humming Birds. It cost $1.98. I bought one and my buddy, Chris, bought one. And we flew them up on the school ground.

Interviewer: $1.98. That's quite a bit. Where do you get your spending money?

Jimmy: I work for it. I mow our lawn and some others. And I sell greeting cards. And I get an allowance every week.

Interviewer: Do you ask your parents first if you can buy expensive things like the kite?

Jimmy: No. I buy whatever I want to with my money. Just like Chris does. It's my money.

Interviewer: Do your parents know you come here (to the convenience store) often?

Jimmy: Sure. I guess.

INTRODUCTION

The final stage of consumer development, stage five, transpires during children's primary school years and specifically covers the age range from 72–100 months—from 6 to around 8 1/2—as many children would say. The

100-month age—I sometimes call it the 100-month line—marks the time when most U.S. children have achieved *independent purchase*. (We will give some consideration to children beyond the age of 100 months for the sake of putting the topic of consumer development in full perspective.) The developmental psychologist Erik Erikson (1968) labeled this age of children, and specifically the age range from 6–12, as the *industry vs. inferiority stage*. During this time, according to Erikson, children are working hard to develop their skills and abilities so that they do not feel inferior when they compare themselves to other children—or when others such as parents compare them to other children. Notice how Jimmy compares himself to his friend, Chris, who is older and a grade ahead. He points out that he does some of the same things as older children—"Just like Chris does," he states as if to emphasize the fact that he performs at a higher level.

Now, at ages six through eight, children gradually construct a new reality of their environment and how they fit into it basing their assessments on their own reasoning, which is becoming somewhat adult-like, and on information received from parents, schoolmates, teachers, and marketers. Like adults, they also rely on the marketplace—advertisements, television programming, promotions, packaging, and products that are targeted to them and to youth in general—to understand who they are and how they should behave. Thus, at this stage children are more outward-looking, more aware of the feelings and thoughts of others such as parents and peers—as Jimmy is of his mother and his "buddy" Chris.

This stage of consumer development is marked by independent purchase that follows from the co-purchasing efforts that began in stage four discussed in the preceding chapter. These co-purchases continue in this stage just as all the learned consumer behavior patterns from the previous stages continue in every subsequent stage. It is this cumulative development—accumulation of consumer knowledge, skills, and abilities over time—that matures the child into a *bona fide consumer* in this current stage discussed here. The term *bona fide* is used to describe child consumers at the end of this fifth stage of consumer development because they are performing in the consumer role at an effective, although usually a minimum, level—performing prepurchase, purchase, and postpurchase functions. This is in comparison, for instance, to children's functioning as pretend consumers as they did in their imagination over the past several years, or as partial consumers as they did in the previous stage when parents and other experienced consumers had to assist them by providing some of the skills and knowledge necessary to complete the transactions. At this point, then, children are observers discovering satisfying objects (stage one), seeking out and asking for those objects that arouse them with potential satisfaction of their needs (stage two), choosing and taking those objects that are most desired (stage three), buying some of the selected object(s) with the assistance of others (stage four), and finally, buying them on their own without any noticeable help from others (stage five). These patterns of consumer behavior will continue for the rest of their lives as they become tweens, teens, and adults, improving their consumer skills, faltering at some, failing with others, but in general performing at a rewarding level of consumership. As one reads some of Jimmy's remarks, one can almost feel the satisfaction he derives from performing tekrams on his own and together with his pal, Chris. He is a bona fide consumer.

In order to examine this last stage of consumer development, we will briefly look at the consumers themselves including their physical and cognitive status, as we have done in discussions of previous stages, recognizing that consumer development is dependent on physical and mental development. But first we will analyze the children's environment that suddenly expands into a very important factor in their consumer behavior starting around age six or seven and continuing through adolescence.

ENVIRONMENT EXPANSION: SCHOOL

We need to step back a moment and look at this final stage of consumer development from the perspective of the *environment* of six-, seven-, and eight-year-olds. The environment dramatically expands in this stage, perhaps much more so than in any of the other stages, but somewhat comparable to the time when children began to walk during stage two. We stated in earlier chapters that children's consumer behavior is a function of their person (P), which includes their physical and mental characteristics, and their environment (E), which includes their physical and social domains. Entering *school* full-time greatly expands their environment, particularly their *out-of-home environment*, including both the physical and social dimensions; and this, in turn, has a dramatic effect on children's developing consumer behavior patterns. When children enter the first grade, they normally enter formal education on an all-day basis for the first time. It is true that most have been in some kind of preschool that helps prepare them for the first grade, but there is much difference between the two. Preschool in its various forms ordinarily is on a half-day basis, often not much more than baby-sitting even in many kindergartens; most of the participants are still considered toddlers; and most of the day is spent singing, playing games, and being read to much like mom does nightly. Thus, up through stage four of consumer development, children, for the most part, can be characterized as homebodies who may experience brief spurts of formal education away from home. But starting with the first grade, children begin to "live and breathe" school from the time they get up in the morning to the time they go to bed at night. School is now a full day of what is often characterized as *drill-and-kill*, as the children are suddenly cast into a structured life in which they are told to act grown up. In fact, first-grade teachers may reference kids in grades 2–5 as models of maturity. First-graders can be over-heard talking about what they are learning and how much they are learn-ing. They also speak of some of the special subject matter they like and classmates who are friends. They also can be heard complaining about their homework, about a teacher, about other children, as well as not having enough time to play—probably using kindergarten as a reference point. Often these complaints are justified, but like that first independent purchase discussed here, going to school is an exhilarating experience for most. Kindergarten children will tell a researcher, "I go to kindergarten," while the elementary school student will say, "I'm in the first grade." The big difference is *being in* rather than *going to*, and the children are quick to espouse the difference. So a perceptual difference as well as a physical difference is noticeable in most children in this last stage of consumer development.

But the main point here about primary school is its sudden and rapid expansion of the children's environment that produces a parallel and lasting impact on their consumer behavior patterns. To this point in most children's lives, no events have had such a dramatic effect on them as enter-ing school. Let us briefly elaborate on this significant event in children's consumer development while bearing in mind—as set out in the first chapter—that the child's life is now mainly a consumer's life. The child will measure success, happiness, friendships, achievements according to con-sumer behavior patterns.

Children's *physical environment* in which they spend much of their day changes substantially upon entering school. The school building, its walls, stairs, floors, and grounds are most likely quite different from most chil-dren's homes where they have been playing, sleeping and eating, and learn-ing to read and write. And the surroundings are probably unlike anything in preschool. Logically, such new surroundings are noticeable to six- and seven-year-old discoverers and most likely overwhelming—not necessarily in a good or bad way, just overwhelming. The floors, for example, look much different from those in a child's bedroom where he has been playing for years with his toys. The floor at school is for walking only—no running—and it does not look like it would be a fun place to play. There are no pictures or posters on the gray or green walls to remind him of people he likes, admires, emulates; only a faded photo or two of a political or religious figure—and perhaps some graffiti. Certainly, there is not the interesting and entertaining wallpaper that is in his room at home. And there is not just one floor like there is at home; there are three or four or more connected by stairways, and some of them are mysteriously off-limits to first-graders such as him, and certainly none is for playing.

The *object* environment is perhaps most startling, although some of the children will be somewhat familiar with some of it due to their attendance in kindergarten. There are many new objects, however, in the hallways such as lockers, fire extinguishers and fire hoses, big doors, although maybe not on the restrooms like there are on the classrooms, and the restrooms have no bathtubs or showers to play in. The only space for playing, in fact, is outside, where children seldom are permitted except for a few minutes a day in good weather. There is a library with seemingly many volumes, but rarely do the children go there either. The cafeteria is next to the library, but it is also off-limits most of the time to children and their classmates. The computer room near the library also is not a place that children are allowed to go without being marched there once a week. Thus, with all this environmental newness, there are also some new rules that may seem a bit startling to the child, also. We will say more about them later.

In addition to the objects found in the hallways, there are the more interesting objects in the classroom where the children spend most of their time. There are the desks, one for each child, although some classrooms have desks that accommodate two children. At the front of the room is the very large teacher's desk on a step-up platform and, like many other physical facilities, it is generally off-limits or by invitation only. Inside the classroom are many items that the children may observe, some for the first time. There is a large map globe made of many interesting colors; the letters of the alphabet are plastered across the top of the chalkboard; and a child can see, on a daily basis, many books, magazines, papers, marking instruments, and art materials that belong to the teacher and to classmates. Virtually all of these physical objects are also commercial objects, and most of them possess brand names. The classroom even has a unique and memorable odor, which the children will soon realize is mainly the odor given off by crayons, and an odor that they probably will remember warmly for a lifetime. Thus, the children's commercial world expands as a result of school including many more tekrams—observing and handling all these objects, buying or asking for them by description and/or brand name, bringing money to school to pay for some of them, and wanting more of some, less of others. It is not a far stretch to say that children at this point have entered another commercial environment—in addition to home and marketplace.

As an extension and continuation of the new physical environment of the school, the children experience a transportation system—a system of tekrams for the most part—that is specific to the school. Now many of the children ride those big orange buses that they have seen many times before and that their parents told them they would one day ride to school. The buses are not as colorful on the inside as they looked last year on the outside, but they are interesting because of the noises they make and the children who sit in them and play in them—and the driver who frequently shouts instructions. Some of the children now ride to school in a car that may not be their parents' car but that of another person who is part of something called a car pool. In fact, this car is likely an SUV that the children like better than the sedans owned by some of their families. But it is not like riding with mom and/or dad. The children have to greet the drivers with a title such as Mr. or Mrs., for instance. A few of the children who live close to school get a new bicycle just to ride to school, and they feel very proud and showy. Some of them ride together, and they can see some of their classmates walking and looking enviously at them and their new bicycles. Typically, during the trips to and from school, the children observe stores, perhaps stores they have not seen before, and there is an increase in the number of visits to these stores for school supplies and snack items.

The children's changing *social environment* due to entry into elementary school probably has as much impact on their consumer behavior patterns as the new physical environment. Their social environment is rapidly expanded with the number of new adults and new children. The new children are classmates with whom the children now interact and many more older students in higher grades whose behavior patterns are immediately of interest to the first-graders. The adults are, of course, mainly the *teachers*, but they also include school administrators and custodians, and *visitors* to the classroom—businesspeople, athletes, religious figures, and government officials (particularly those running for election or re-election). This burst of social objects will have a parallel effect on the children's consumer behavior. Count on it.

First, the mere observance of the adults and other children in the school environment will produce consumer behavior patterns. Additionally, the typical activities at school, such as eating, reading and writing, using chalk and board, and sitting at their desks, provide the new students directions for consumption of many new objects. For example, seeing the teachers or students write or draw on the board and erase the writing is a new set of tekrams for the first-grade children to learn. Also, both the adults and the children put their belongings on display—their clothing, school supplies, foods and beverages, and jewelry, for example. Or, noticeably, some hide them from the view of teachers in the case of gum and candy but show them to classmates. The mere perception of these items constitutes important tekrams as the children observe them, learn about their purposes and how to use them, and in many cases to want them. More tekrams will follow as the new children seek some of these items from their parents and from the marketplace.

This entry into school, then, marks the real beginning of *peer influence* on children. Actually, such influence may start as early as age two or three when children attend daycare, then nursery school, and kindergarten. They may notice the toys and clothing and school items of the other children, but at preschool age, most children are so self-focused that they tend not to give much attention to possessions of others even though they sit and play side by side. But peer influence grows with age (Hartup, 1979), and by elementary school age—the focus of this stage of consumer development—the children have firmly in place the practice of copying the behavior of others—other children, their father or mother, their siblings, their neighbors, even their pets. Some of this duplicating behavior supposedly started even before preschool, according to some developmental psychologists, when they were just infants, and through imitation, pretend behavior, and curiosity, they continued to develop these skills (e.g., Meltzoff and Moore, 1989). In fact, children teach themselves many consumer behavior patterns prior to going to elementary school by copying consumer behavior patterns of others. So, in this uncertain new environment called school, they often look to other students for guidance in what to wear, eat, draw with, and even what words to speak. It should be noted that the children tend to look up, to take guidance from older children for how to behave as students and as consumers. For example, Jimmy was quick to mention that his friend, Chris, is in the fourth grade—a grade ahead of him—but both practice similar consumer behavior patterns such as buying the same brand of kite at the same store. It is quite possible that the kite buying was Chris's idea more than Jimmy's.

There are those developmentalists whose research shows that peer influence is even more important than parental influence (e.g., Harris, 1999) in all phases of life. My best guess based on studies of children's development over many years is that peer influence among school-age children is twice as powerful today as a generation ago. Moreover, peer influence on school kids is probably greater in pounds and ounces than that of parents (even adults in general) simply due to children's greater accessibility to other children through daycare, preschool, elementary school, gathering at shopping malls (settings), participating in group sports with their peers, and seeing more of their peers in television programs and advertising as well as in other children's media. And I know there is decreasing accessibility to parents who both work, work longer hours, and also spend additional time away from their kids because of work-related social obligations—lunches, dinners, meetings, retreats, and additional education. Prior to the mid-1980s, I think the opposite was generally the case. Again, the combination of much more accessibility to peers and much less accessibility to parents logically explains the major interpersonal influences on kids' consumer behavior.

Regarding peer influence among kids, it is not just any children influencing other children, but usually children of the *same gender*. This is logical. Most first-grade girls, for instance, normally are not interested in what kinds of jeans boys in their class are wearing or what kinds of soft drinks boys are consuming. Prior to and probably up through the second or third grade, children have little interest in the opposite sex—not even in an older sister or brother. In fact, most studies show that at least up through the end of elementary school, peer influence is almost always gender specific: Boys influence boys, girls influence girls. Thorne's (1993) research, in fact, demonstrated that from preschool years through adolescent years 95 percent of children's friendships are gender specific, and the other 5 percent between boys and girls has sexual overtones. Moreover, not only is the transfer of influence normally between the same genders but most often between popular students of the same gender. Popularity—possessing good social skills and being liked by large numbers of other peers—directs much consumer behavior. Children want to be like popular students, so they copy much of their apparent consuming patterns, including regrettably many of their bad habits such as smoking. (Tobacco companies learned many years ago from such research that if they get popular students to smoke, they can easily win over others.) By the time children reach the third or fourth grade—by the time they become tweens[1]—they routinely and even unknowingly check with popular peers, including celebrities, before they make major purchases of *conspicuous* items such as bikes, shoes, clothing, backpacks, jewelry, hair styles, and soft drinks. Interestingly, such behavior is just as likely in China even though there is more reverence for adults (which, according to my observations, is declining rapidly). In some interviews in Xiamen, China, with working mothers and their children, I asked a mother and her eight-year-old son how the child decided on his unusual haircut. He answered that he styles his hair like his best friend at school does. His mother answered with a qualification. When he sees a hair style on certain popular boys, he asks her if he can have the same. She responded further that if she said no he might stop studying—one of the frightening threats that Chinese children use to help them get what they want from parents.

School-age children do learn consumer behavior patterns from adults, particularly their elementary school teachers, whom they usually admire and respect and see as credible—although the younger the teachers are, the more respect they receive in America (less so in China). For instance, the children learn new consumer behavior patterns from the teachers' lectures and from their teaching materials. They also learn new consumer behavior patterns from after-school teachers such as their coach or music teacher. And they learn from the adult visitors who are invited to their classrooms— most of whom are in a marketing role of some sort. It should be noted, also, that children learn from adult-designed in-school promotions—advertising, publicity, product placement, and selling. In addition, of course, there are

---

[1] I am not sure who originated the term *tween* or when. I started using it in the late 1980s, early 1990s, after borrowing it from a 1938 movie, *Love Finds Andy Hardy*. In the movie Betsy Booth (Judy Garland), a nearly 13-year-old, falls in love with Andy Hardy (Mickey Rooney), who just turned 16, and while she sees herself as a teen, he sees her as a child. She sings a song about her torturous love affair in which she says, "I'm too old for toys, too young for boys, I'm just in between." I took the *tween* off the *between* only after referring to 10–13-year-olds for a while as *betweens*. Today the term *tween* is routinely used to refer to kids 8–13, who may also be called *preteens* and *preadolescents*. I once referred to tweens as "a state of mind" rather than an age, noting that it is as much a psychological as a biological phenomenon, and this seemingly is even truer today (McNeal, 2001).

adults in the roles of retailers that locate as near to the school as possible just to sell the students foods and beverages, school supplies, and tobacco. For example, in China a government-blessed tobacco store is usually located just outside the front gate of each school.

Let us take a moment to highlight some of these major adult influences on elementary school students' consumer behavior patterns (besides parents):

- **Teachers' Lectures:** Most teachers use consumer behavior examples to teach math concepts (buying two apples for 15 cents each), as social science subject matter (the free enterprise system and how it benefits society), and as health and nutrition matter (learning to read the labels on food packages). These tekrams may be their own thoughts—" an apple a day will keep the doctor away"—they may be from their own education, or they may be from recommendations handed down by the school administration. They certainly can be expected to be derived also from the teachers' own daily consumer experiences.

- **Teaching Materials:** Many teaching materials used by elementary schools contain consumer behavior examples such as in a storybook in which a child flies on an airplane to visit her grandmother, or in a math book in which a certain number of products are bought for a certain price. In addition, some companies provide teaching materials in order to get their names and products before the children. For example, around 1990 the AT&T Company developed some teaching modules on how to teach children to use the 911 emergency phone number—and also how to recognize the AT&T logo. A local bread bakery developed map books and distributed them free to its city's elementary schools. And teachers loved them even though they showed in three colors a loaf of the bread on each page. Elementary school teachers often give children samples of products such as soap and toothpaste (provided free by their makers) in order to teach health and hygiene.

- **Visitors to the School:** The children's classrooms may have many visitors, most of whom are marketers bringing suggested consumer behavior patterns with them for the children. Some I have witnessed are a supermarket manager, a restaurant manager, and a theater manager—all soft-selling their retail outlets and their brands. In addition, these visitors may include insurance salespeople, stock brokers, and attorneys, to name a few more who are promoting their services. There are salespeople who actually come to the classroom to sell the children books, magazines, and student newspapers. Then come the politicians, religious leaders, police officers, and firemen, and members of the armed services selling their wares and in some cases some products for the children's health, safety, and spirituality. And finally, many charities come selling the children on the idea of giving money and giving their time to a "worthy cause."

- **In-School Promotions:** The term *promotion* is used here to refer to all personal and nonpersonal commercial messages (as it usually is in marketing textbooks). Several personal sellers and PR (school relations) people were mentioned in the preceding description, but we would add to that list advertising executives and many, many marketing researchers. The nonpersonal side of promotion includes advertising, product placement, and premiums. Often there is advertising in the classroom, in the restroom, in the cafeteria, on bulletin boards, and in buses. Product placement refers to insertions of a product and/or its brand into children's books and printed materials, movies that the teachers show, and recorded TV programs such as newscasts and sitcoms that may be seen in the classroom. Premiums are gifts given to the students for academic achievement, health achievement, and any other kind of achievement the teacher and/or school administration can think of to distribute commercial products into the classroom under the guise of "motivating the children." For example, coupons for pizzas are given for reading accomplishments, samples of toothbrushes and toothpaste for oral health, and bar soap for cleanliness. (When I was in elementary school, my favorite was a big red box of pencils and crayons with Coca-Cola embossed in gold on it, an award that was given for perfect attendance.) Most national brands and sellers that target children are in the classroom in some way to help educate the children and, of course, to sell their products. (We will not take up the debate over the benefits of these to the school, the children, their parents, and, of course, the marketers. This debate can be found in many sources, including some of my writings.)

CURRENT ISSUES IN CONSUMER DEVELOPMENT (#10)

Consumer Education for Children

Following up on President Kennedy's Consumer Bill of Rights, President Nixon turned it into an Executive Order (#11583) in 1971. Since then all consumers—"all" includes children—have these rights:

The right to make an intelligent choice among products and services;

The right to accurate information on which to make a free choice;
The right to expect that the seller of goods and services takes into
    account the health and safety of buyers;
The right to complain, to register dissatisfaction regarding sellers,
    and their products and services.

These rights are so basic that it seems logical that they should emanate from the President of the United States because people, including children, spend more time seeking, buying, and using products and services than in any other activity. However, when these rights were established and legalized by Executive Order in the early 1970s, their implementation was not commensurate. President Nixon concurrently set up the Office of Consumer Affairs (OCA) in the White House and staffed it with only a director and a small staff to enforce these rights. The OCA's director—at that time, Virginia Knauer—saw the solution to effective implementation of the Consumer Bill of Rights as *consumer education* beginning in kindergarten and extending to every year of school.

Consumer education was expected to provide appropriate information to children and their parents so that the parents could make good choices in the marketplace for their children until the children were able to do so. Thus, under the notion of consumer education, such topics as financial education (using money as consumers) and media education (consuming media) were subsumed. For instance, the American Academy of Pediatrics for years has called for media education of children and their parents recognizing that mass media provide both health risks and benefits. Further, media education should result in young people becoming less vulnerable to negative aspects of media exposure.

Broadly speaking, consumer education as proposed by Mrs. Knauer was supposed to prepare each person in the skills, concepts, and understandings that are required for everyday living. Thus, the focus was primarily on providing information about sellers and their products and services that facilitated everyday living. Just how adults (parents) were expected to receive such information was never clear. Some community projects developed under the notion of adult education were supposed to reach special groups of adult consumers, but none were ever nationalized. As for the children, daily consumer education classes were supposed to start in kindergarten and go through high school. Topics taught in school were supposed to be the result of committees made of volunteers from all walks of life and appointed by the Office of Consumer Affairs.

But there were no teachers in the 1970s qualified to teach this broad range of topics to kindergarten and elementary school children, and there were no university programs to turn out such teachers. So, for the most part, public schools have winged it. Now, 30 years later this is still pretty much the case. In fact, it may be worse since few teachers want to teach such topics, and not many parents want them taught: parents prefer basic academic topics be taught instead. In the interim many teachers invited businesspeople to their classrooms to expound on certain topics that they, the teachers, knew little about. This approach had a down-side—often the visits became sales visits for products, companies, and industries.

So, today—in this new millennium—relatively little is being taught in school about the people's most important activity—being consumers. The Consumer Bill of Rights that originated with the President of the United States has pretty much faded from public thought; the rights seem no longer to be rights. For example, the right to expect that the safety and health of the buyer are taken into consideration by sellers is surely obscured by the national concern for the obesity epidemic that exists and is blamed on the food industry and media. And the calls for the right to register complaints about businesses and their offerings are now taking the form of lawsuits and threatened lawsuits against busi-nesses that failed to provide enough information about their products or show enough concern about consumers. In the meantime children are assuming more responsibility for consumer behavior decisions in their households and are doing it with no increase in information on which to make those decisions. If parents want to choose the most important topic to be taught to their children in preschool, they should choose—demand—consumer education. Through that topic, children can also be prepared for primary school by corollary learning of the "3 R's."

****
Sources: American Academy of Pediatrics, 1999; McNeal, 1987; Villani, 2001; Woolley and Peters, 1999–2005.

PHYSICAL STATUS OF CHILDREN

Now that we have discussed the major changes in the children's physical and social environments (E) in stage five of consumer development, let us turn to the children themselves and look briefly at their person (P) that interacts with the new environments. Their body and mind growth is very important and necessary for them to perform the purchase function.

Children at ages 6, 7, and 8—those in stage five of consumer develop-ment—continue to grow at about the same rate as they did from ages 4–6, which is a lesser rate than that at ages 2–4 (Payne and Isaacs, 1999; Gallahue, 1982). They add on approximately two to three inches of *height* each year, which easily accommodates their *weight* increases annually of around four pounds. Compared to a typical 39-inch checkout counter, a

6-year-old averages around 45–46 inches tall; a 7-year-old, 48 inches; and an 8-year-old, around 50 inches; and by the time they leave elementary school at age 11, their average height will approach 58–60 inches, or around five feet tall.

As for weight, the kids at 6 weigh in at around 48 pounds; at 7, 52 pounds; and 8, at 56 pounds; and by age 11, they probably weigh close to 70. We often hear moms say of their elementary school children that "they're as big as I am." And this may be true, at least as it pertains to weight, since perhaps a sixth are obese, grossly overweight for their height. As noted in the previous chapters on consumer development, overweight children—OWs—are a serious health problem and a serious consumer behavior problem. And this is at a time when children become very concerned with their body features and their general physical appearance. Thus, some of the OWs will begin to experience lower self-esteem as they compare themselves with others and as they are recipients of name-calling.

Development of Gross Motor Skills

At the time that children enter elementary school, their motor skills take on much importance to them as well as to their parents and teachers. During the preceding two years, children have been perfecting their fundamental movements. Now their *gross motor skills*—use of major muscle groups—of walking, running, jumping, throwing, catching, and kicking are showing a form very similar to adults. As they enter primary school, they also enter what motor skill experts call the *sport-related movement phase* (Gallahue, Werner, and Luedke, 1975). In this phase of motor development, the fundamental movement patterns are refined and combined with one another to form sports skills. For example, locomotive skills of running, leaping, and jumping are combined with manipulation skills of throwing, striking, and catching to produce baseball skills. And kicking may be added to the combination of these locomotive and manipulation skills to produce soccer skills, or they may be combined with volleying and bouncing skills to produce basketball skills. The net result is that children may undertake sports of many kinds in early school years at the encouragement of both parents and schoolteachers, and, of course, indirectly by sports stars themselves to whom children of this age are responding with awe and envy. Also, specific sports such as baseball and basketball each have major marketing organizations representing them that seek out children as markets as well as future participants.

The list of possible sports in which young children may participate is endless, and since children are seen as potential markets for the sports industries—as spectators of football and basketball, for instance, on TV, or better yet, at the stadiums and arenas. For example, Major League Baseball and the National Football League both have programs to attract children to the stadiums to watch professional games. Of course, once the children begin attending, they will need special clothing—particularly caps—and baseballs, footballs, and all the equipment that goes into the games. (And to fit in at the games they eventually need to learn how to drink beer and gorge themselves with fatty foods.) And practically all indoor and outdoor sports—ping pong, badminton, golfing, bowling, fishing, camping, to name a few—try to recruit children into participating in some way.

Along with this pulling by the various sports associations is the pushing of the parents. Often the parental pushing may be the result of personal motives. Some parents may see it as a social opportunity for themselves, some may want to demonstrate how involved they are with their child-rearing as a result of feeling guilty about not spending much time with them, and some may hope that their children's athletic potential—as identified by a physical education teacher—will one day support them financially. This parental pushing also may be partially for the children's benefits. Some parents may want their children to learn to be competitive, they may want to build the self-esteem of their children, or they may simply want to put their children on display as representatives of the family, its BMW, so to speak.

The net result of all of the sports activities is that many schoolchildren become participants in the "sport of the season" for the rest of their school life as they try to please all the adults involved, impress new friends, and feel pleased with themselves—build self-esteem. This flitting from one sport to another requires a lot of consumer behavior on the part of parents and children—buying gear, uniforms, special protective clothing, even boats, cars, and coaches. Summer camps may be chosen according to the sports that are taught there, and of course, the sports celebrity that attaches his name to them. And underlying all of the sports will be sponsorships by the beer and tobacco industries that remind the children of some other items on which they can spend their money once they learn to consume these products from attending games at the stadiums or watching them on TV.

Virtually every boy and girl in this stage of consumer development will give sports a try. It seems to be a call of the body, to take its abilities and combine them into some kind of sport. Maybe it is also the yelling of the parents. Maybe, too, it is the ballyhoo of all the sports on television. Perhaps it is due to schoolteachers and parents recognizing that a happy, healthy body produces similar results in the mind. However, a majority of the children will move away from organized sports by middle school. Further, the "sports bug" does not bite all the children in spite of the pushing by parents and teachers and pulling by the sports associations and the life-like portrayals of superstars in the fast-food restaurants. By the third grade, many children are electing not to participate in sports, or at least to minimize their participation. They instead are choosing other activities of interest—mind rather than muscle activities such as reading, word processing, writing, painting, studying science, or just listening to music during the times that other children are involved in sports activities. Whether these options are in their wiring, so to speak, or these children are embarrassed by their clumsiness or perhaps their overweightness, they begin to march—or sit—to a different drummer. By fourth grade, a majority of elementary school children, in fact, are sitting or lying down around 18–22 hours of each 24-hour day, and thus probably not taking sports seriously. But it usually is at this time—in the first few years of elementary school—that the next generation of sports superstars is identified and selected by parents and others, and they begin to perform many sports-related tekrams a day.

Development of Fine Motor Skills

The smaller muscle groups of the typical child go through a lot of refinement in the preschool years, but will go through much more in their early primary school years as *fine motor skills* are honed by and for the formal education system. Some of this refinement has to wait for more myelination of those parts of the cortex that control attention and information processing, two very necessary cognitive skills that will help the children respond to all-day teaching. The crude drawing and writing skills learned in preschool years are now fine-tuned in the first and second grades. Also, the children are introduced in these years to coloring such as that used in map making. And in the field of arts, children learn to utilize their fine motor skills in clay modeling, painting, paper cutting, and perhaps sewing. Usually, by the time children enter the second grade, they are taught to use computers, which require special fine motor skills in which children use each hand independently. This ability does not mature until around age seven or eight.

Starting the first year of school, particular emphasis is placed on writing, marking, drawing, and painting. Of course, these tasks include how to hold marking instruments properly. For example, Chinese children are taught to hold marking instruments approximately 90 degrees to the paper as compared to American children, who are taught to write and draw at a smaller angle. Marking instruments include pencils of all kinds and shapes, ink pens of various styles, crayons, and brushes. And the children have to learn about the many kinds of writing pads, writing paper, and art paper that may be used in marking, writing, drawing, and painting.

Actually, the children are usually unaware that they use some of these fine motor skills in other tasks at home and in the marketplace. Using a spoke wrench to tighten the spokes in their bicycle, playing video games, and winding and setting watches and clocks are just a few examples. Some fine motor skills that are developed and put in place at this time include personal hygiene matters such as brushing teeth and hair, cleaning eye glasses, administering medicine to themselves, and dressing themselves. All of these, of course, in addition to being fine motor skills, are tekrams— units of consumer behavior—that most likely will be repeated throughout life.

A very important set of fine motor skills still under development as kids enter the first grade are those that underlie *speaking*. (Some first-grade teachers would tell you there is an opposite problem—of how to get the kids to shut up.) But many children at six and seven are still learning pronunciation, and a major percent have speech impairments or other impairments (visual, hearing, for example). Plus, many are still dealing with shyness that affects their talking to a teacher or to a retail clerk. So, there are a number of small muscles in the head, neck, and chest whose development will assist speech development.

On the positive side of their speaking, with increasing myelination at this time, the children have a fantastic ability to learn more words and to correct their spoken words themselves, and they keep adding new words at an extraordinary rate once in school for the full day. They come to school with a vocabulary of 14,000–15,000 words, and most of the children are eager to use them all. Just how many of these are commercial words— words for products, brands, stores, spokescharacters, and other marketing objects—is hard to say. Certainly, according to my measures, at least 200–300 brand names are included and at least 10 times that many words for commercial objects—e.g., cereal, juice, football, coat, and cap. And it seems as though children often can speak these words better than they can the words in their textbooks. Perhaps this is due to hearing them over and over on their TV set, because of the advertising in the school environment, their use by other students and their teachers, or simply the increased frequency of experiencing these products.

Correct speaking—and singing—will be part of the responsibility of the elementary school teacher, who will deal with those troublesome sounds of children at age six or seven. Consumer behavior is a partner to the child in learning to pronounce words. Asking for desirable products as concepts (candy, gum, spaghetti) or brand names is great practice for children. Hearing the words spoken, for example, on the TV, in the stores over their public address system, and by others—and particularly in a jingle—helps children learn to pronounce correctly as well as gives them confidence in saying the words. As noted several times throughout this book, performing tekrams helps build bodies and minds. (In some of my research, I ran across a middle school teacher who used the incorrect grammar of TV ads to teach children correct grammar—and to remind the children of this bad practice in advertising.)

COGNITIVE DEVELOPMENT

Perhaps more important than children's physical/motor development are the changes in cognitive development that occur at ages six to eight and make it possible for the children to perform as bona fide consumers. The children in this independent purchase stage require some basic under-standing of the purchase act, money, and the exchange system, all very complex concepts for a first-grader and all placing substantial learning demands on the children.

Prior to the first grade, children learned mainly from observation and participation—from watching others and from trying something, doing something, involving themselves in an activity. Now, school fosters more *learning-from-teaching*, which the children have experienced very little except maybe from a small number of parents who utilize classroom methods to teach their children subject matter, and maybe from some exceptional kindergartens. So, what the children first experienced in kinder-garten will be amplified and modified in elementary school, and will become a model for lifelong learning through the education system. Elementary school is a formalized program designed mainly to teach the three *Rs*— Reading, 'Riting, and 'Rithmetic. Whereas prior to elementary school, the children learned pretty much on their own by exploring and gulping down units of knowledge, now the children are expected, for the most part, to simply sit with their mouth open and let the teachers fill it each day. This is particularly true for China's schools. The emphasis is on knowledge more than on understanding. For example, in reading, the emphasis is on learn-ing words, how to spell and pronounce them, more than how to understand them. In arithmetic, the emphasis is on counting—adding, subtracting, multiplying, dividing—more than on the meanings of numbers and their combinations. And writing, like reading, tends to focus on how to write letters—what they look like in certain forms such as lowercase, uppercase, and cursive—and less on their meanings. So, the child in formal education is being taught a new way to learn, which is mostly passive as compared to the active learning she has been performing since birth. As noted, for most children some kind of preschool helps them prepare for this new system of learning, but it still produces a lot of boredom with the system by the sixth grade, and consequently dropping out.[2]

Of course, the children will continue to learn through observation and participation. This is their mindset that has been established since the begin-ning of life. But, what I am calling *formal education* has an enormous impact

[2] A few states—New Mexico is the first—are adopting a year-round kindergarten system called Kindergarten-Plus that is supposed to deal with these problems by preparing the children better for the structured learning model of elementary school (Toppo, 2005). This system appears to be particularly beneficial for children in impoverished families, one-parent families, and families whose native language is not English.

on the cognitive world of children, with its emphasis on memorization— learning of many words and numbers, using these symbols in such activities as reading and writing, and testing for their existence in memory. In fact, as the children surprise themselves with how much they are learning, they will begin to adopt this learning method to other situations such as board games and card games. Let us briefly look at cognitive development in this fifth stage of consumer development that occurs between 72 and 100 months, or roughly ages six through eight.

Self-Image

First, let us reconsider the image children hold of themselves and some of the changes that occur due to entering the formal education system. During the previous stage of consumer development from ages four to six, children developed a self-image based mainly on their physical appearance and to some extent their physical performance according to them, perhaps according to their parents. Now in this next stage from ages six through eight, children add much more complexity to their self-image. In effect, it is partitioned into several selves. Particularly important is the *social self* that develops as a result of interacting with many new peers. It consists of the responses of the child to others and the responses of others to the child. It is articulated with some terms as *popular*, *good friends*, *buddy*, and *liked by*. The social self becomes increasingly important as children reach age eight when they are *in* or *out* of small groups of peers, and being *in* is essential at all costs. The social self is based in part on the *physical self* of children and on a growing new self-image, the *academic self*. The academic self is a result of performance in school—spelling, reading, writing, memorizing, answering the teachers' questions, and study habits—and the responses of teachers and students to the children's academic performance. Now a child compares herself with others not only in terms of physical performance— "I can run faster than any girl in my class"—and academic performance— "I am the fastest reader in my class"—but social performance—"I have more friends than my brother." Note again the comparison with others—a behavior pattern that will determine an enormous number of tekrams on a daily basis. In effect, the children are looking at their new self-image through introspection and comparing it with the images they hold of other individuals. While it is egocentric-based during the first year or two of elementary school, the self-image does help children appreciate the viewpoints of others through the comparison system they utilize.

Logical Thinking

Logical thinking becomes standard fare in this stage of consumer development starting at age 6 or 7—Piaget (1954) would say 7. Beginning about the time children enter the first grade, they show signs of logical thinking about concrete objects such as numbers, words, things, and people. Using the thousands of symbolic representations in their minds, including the many new ones being introduced at school every minute of the day, children now can *analyze* objects that they encounter beyond just a single characteristic. They can describe classmates, teachers, and their desk, and they have much more to say about marketing objects such as stores, advertising, and brands. They also have improved their *reversibility* thinking so that they can see the reverse of an action such as walking to school (coming home from school), going to the lunchroom to eat (coming back to the classroom after eating), and going shopping after school (returning to home or school after going to the store). They also can operate on numbers and words better as a result of the reversibility in their thinking. For example, when the teacher puts a problem on the board such as $3 + 1 = N$, the child gradually figures out (reasons) that $1 + 3$ also equals N and that $N = 3 + 1$, and so on. Related to reversibility, children at this age also practice *conservation* of objects, numbers, and shapes. Rather than centering their attention on one characteristic of an object, children can now see multiple characteristics at the same time. Through this ability, children learn that a soft drink is the same no matter if it is sold in a four-pack or a six-pack, a one-liter or a two-liter bottle, whether one is poured into a six-ounce glass or an eight-ounce glass, and whether it is served cold or hot. (Of course, much of this seemingly improved knowledge may be just a function of branding and labeling.) To what extent children can think logically about specific objects is in great part due to their experience with those objects and their salience. For instance, in counting and sorting and classifying objects, a child at this time usually can perform better with coins than with buttons and beads. By age 8 or 9 (Piaget would say 11), children can anticipate the responses of a store cashier to their presentation of money at the checkout. They can also envision the reduced level of coins in their savings after spending the money. By second grade they probably know how much money they have in their piggybanks; in fact, they may be able to tell you how many of each coin denomination they have as their memorization skill is applied to banking.

Symbolic Representation

As compared to sensorimotor representation in the mind, symbolic representation is now the norm for the child of six or seven. That is, all the thousands of objects the children are learning about through experience, particularly the school experience, are stored in the mind in symbolic form—in words, pictures, numbers, and combinations of these. As children apply logical thinking to these objects and their experiences with the objects, they gradually build networks of objects and their attributes. For example, as they interact with (experience) their first-grade teacher, they learn more about her and use what is learned to build a mental image of her. This mental image is a hypothetical construct consisting of a network of her attributes as interpreted by one child, and it changes as the child ages—and as the child describes her to others. But probably 20 years from now that same first-grader who is completing graduate school can recall some salient attributes of the teacher that were assigned to her in the first grade.

To attempt to capture some of these networks—to see what they look like—we asked first-, third-, and fifth-grade children to "draw a cereal box"—a common object to most children these ages (McNeal and Ji, 2003). This meant that the children sitting in their classrooms had to select a cereal box (a commercial object) from their mind—if there was one in their mind—and draw and color a picture of it. Results? All of the children drew a cereal box in the normal vertically rectangular form reminiscent of a typical ready-to-eat cereal box. On the front panel of the box that was drawn—some who could express depth drew more than one panel—98 percent of them showed a brand name and 82 percent showed a picture of the actual cereal product under that brand name. But there were substantial differences in complexity by age of the artist. Briefly, 92 percent of the youngest children, the first-graders, included a brand name; 100 percent of the fifth-graders. Just over 62 percent of the youngest and 82 percent of the oldest included a picture of the cereal. And 53 percent of the youngest and 78 percent of the oldest drew a bowl and/or spoon demonstrating the purpose of the product. From these and other measures of their drawings, we constructed an associative network of cereal boxes (not cereals) that we believed existed in the minds of most of the children. Figure 10-1 shows a composite network based on all the children's drawings. Notice the relative complexity for this concept in the minds of these children. We might conclude that the high level of complexity is due to the age of the older children, and that would be technically correct. But it probably would be more logical and probably more accurate to suggest that the level of complexity is due to the greater level of experience of the older children. Also, the older children have had more experience at symbolically representing objects in their minds and thus know more about how to organize them and their attributes.

Bear in mind that the hypothesized mental structure shown in Figure 10-1 is but one of thousands of networks existing in the memories of elementary school children. For example, we might have asked a group of third-grade boys to draw a football—an object that many of them are interested in and probably own. My guess is that many would have included a brand name like they did on the cereal boxes since at this time they are so brand conscious. But it might be difficult for them to express (draw) other major attributes such as "heavy," "shaped for passing," "may hurt your

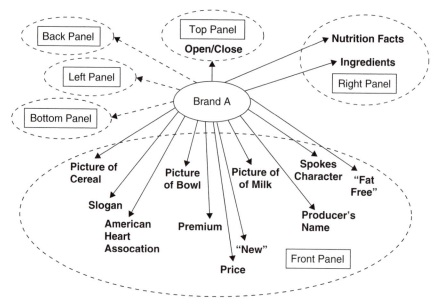

→ Indicates that a link between brand name and the elements on the panel was observed

- ▸ Indicates that no link between brand name and the elements on the panel was observed

FIGURE 10-1   *Associative network of children's memory of cereal box.*

hands when you catch it," and "expensive." Perhaps the reason for the difficulty in representing the physical aspects of the football such as weight, size, and pain when you catch it are likely recorded via sensorimotor representation rather than symbolic representation. Thus, finding the right research procedures to reveal the mental structures holding these images is necessary, and the drawing procedure mentioned here is but one of a number of techniques that might be used (McNeal, 1992). Attaching some postperformance interviews to children's drawings has been found useful in some cases. For instance, we asked eight-year-old boys and girls to draw a pair of shoes. Afterward we asked the children to talk about their drawings—which they usually like to do probably due to their egocentric nature at that age. One of the things we found out was that the numbers, such as 64 and 88, several of the boys had drawn on the shoes were not the prices as we thought, but the designated numbers of some professional athletes— a brand name of sorts—but usually were in addition to the brand name.

Moral Reasoning

Parents have been teaching their children moral reasoning—right and wrong—since they were born. At first the teaching is, for example, through holding the baby's hand and saying, "No-no." Then as the infant begins to walk and talk, more words are added to the teaching such as "Bad boy" and "Cannot" and "Should not." Then, when the child is around age two or three, parents begin to teach their children basic values such as understanding property, being kind, being honest, and respecting others. For instance, one of the morals that all parents have to teach their children is that they do not take something from others—from other children, from a store shelf, from the daycare center—a common tekram that appears during stage three of consumer development.

Prior to entering school, most children are egocentric and think little of the feelings of others or the perspectives of others. But by the time children are well into the first grade, the parental teaching of morals has been reinforced by teachers' putting the subject matter into the classroom. When the children reach second grade, there are signs that they are abiding by these rules and the many additional rules imposed by school as the children enter what Kohlberg (1984) called the *conventional level of moral reasoning*. At this level the children tend to take the rules literally—taking something from another is wrong, using drugs and smoking are wrong, and there are no exceptions. They know for sure that they have to pay for something when they take it from the store shelf. Not only teachers push such messages, but also visitors to the children's classrooms such as police officers often underline them. By the end of the third grade, most children know right from wrong and apply this thinking to their everyday consumer behavior. In fact, most third-graders are so intense about their moral thinking that we might wonder when and why their thinking about bad consumption practices such as drug use and smoking change and these behaviors become more acceptable. Perhaps some of these behaviors start so early in their lives that they accept it as normal. For instance, one study among two- to six-year-olds found that when the children pretended to be adults and shopped at a store set up in a behavioral laboratory for "a social evening for adults," three-year-olds purchased not only the things they liked, but 36 percent also purchased cigarettes and 71 percent purchased beer for the adults, suggesting that they see these items as normative (Dalton et al., 2005).

STAGE FIVE: INDEPENDENT PURCHASE (72–100 MONTHS)

By age six—the beginning of the independent purchase stage—children have been witnessing the purchase process for several years—really since sitting-up time around six months. Thus, they have watched their parents and others make hundreds of purchases in all kinds of stores. By the time they reach the co-purchase stage of consumer development between ages four and six years, they understand the rudiments although not the fine points of the exchange process. So, in the co-purchase stage, children intend to make a purchase, want to make a purchase, and vocalize this desire to their parents, but they do not yet possess enough skills and knowledge to consummate a store purchase alone. So, at some point they join with more competent consumers, probably their moms, to attempt the act. During the children's early school years, co-purchases that probably started when they were around age five continue—just as all stages of consumer development continue—and increasingly become an independent act. By 100 months of age, most children have undertaken purchases on their own on a regular basis.

As noted also in the discussion of the co-purchase stage, children may make some relatively independent purchases during that stage but only in vending machines. For example, with a quarter taken from their money accumulation, they may buy a ball of gum or a trinket from a vending machine at the mall or some store; malls, for instance, have large clusters of vending machines placed strategically throughout them to attract those young purchasers to spend their quarters. But as also observed, a vending machine purchase is far different from a purchase in a store. There is less complexity, there are no store personnel with whom to interact such as checkout clerks, and there is virtually no mathematics or logistics involved in a vending machine purchase. But vending machine purchases move the children a step closer to making a purchase in a store.

Vygotsky's (1978) theory of the zone of proximal development (ZPD) set out in the preceding chapter on co-purchasing has more application in this purchase stage of consumer development. The theory says that there is a point in time in children's development when they reach a level at which they can almost, but not quite, perform a task such as a purchase without help from someone who is *competent* to perform the task. Once children get into school, they enter a broader social situation in which a number of competent people around them can help them with specific purchase tasks—provide information, provide guidance, provide aid regarding the purchase of certain products and services. These people, in addition to the children's parents, include teachers, classmates who have performed in the purchase stage, neighborhood children who share the path to school—like Jimmy and Chris—and, of course, a few retail personnel who work at the increasing number of stores the children patronize, particularly the convenience stores along the path to and from school. Children say they sometimes develop a first-name relation with some of the convenience store clerks.

In Photo 10-1 two Beijing boys—one a third-grader, one a fourth-grader—are purchasing snacks at a convenience store. The younger boy makes a purchase in this photo, while his older, taller, and more competent friend stands beside him ready to help out if needed. Thus, like Jimmy and Chris, these two encourage and support each other in many tasks including purchasing.

Stage five, the final stage in consumer development, flows naturally, then, from stage four, the co-purchase stage. In the co-purchase stage, chil-

PHOTO 10-1 A third-grader and a fourth-grader purchase some snacks together in a Beijing convenience store. The older and taller boy in the background appeared to guide the selection and purchase of the younger boy.

dren find products that they want, ask their parents for them, retrieve them from store fixtures, and take them to a pay station where parents help buy them. The children still do not have the competence to complete certain purchases on their own, except maybe at a vending machine, and therefore parents or someone must help them. Now, however, as they enter elementary school, they become surrounded with competent people who can help them, mainly other children who have various degrees of purchase experience. Also, they are a year or so older and have gained more purchase knowledge and skills, perhaps enough to make the purchase on their own. Once they begin making purchases on their own, they are considered bona fide consumers who perform in the prepurchase (search, ask for), purchase (use money, consummate the exchange), and postpurchase (use, consume, dispose of the product) stages. Let us examine this final stage of consumer development from the standpoint of the necessary three *m*s—money, motives, and methods.

Money

Children begin to accumulate money around age three, and by the time they understand its purpose—somewhere around age five—they usually have a substantial cache of it. Additionally, parents provide money to their children often without the children's asking for it—to contribute to the children's accumulation, and as gifts and perhaps as allowance. Chinese parents, for instance, as well as other relatives give children money as gifts

PHOTO 10-2 Two children in rural China help out in their household by doing the laundry as a way to earn a bit of money. The 10-year-old girl beats the wet clothing with a paddle while her 8-year-old brother takes a break and snacks.

at Chinese New Year and other celebrations. It is usually new money given in a red envelope and therefore called *Hong Bao* (red wrap). It may be a substantial amount, and the children are expected to save most of it. American children also receive money as gifts and handouts, particularly when they reach the age at which they understand its purpose. By the time American children begin attending elementary school, parents normally provide money through an *allowance*—a periodic distribution of money to children that is often tied to children's performance of household chores. Jimmy, for example, has an allowance, he has income from doing some work around his home such as mowing the lawn, and he even earns some money selling greeting cards door to door.

In Photo 10-2 in rural China, a 10-year-old girl and her 8-year-old brother work outside helping parents with housekeeping in order to earn some money. The girl is using a paddle to beat the soapy clothes clean while her little brother is snacking on one of his rewards given him for helping.

So, by the time kids reach the co-purchase stage, at around age four or five, they have some basic understanding of money, often can provide their own money for many small purchases, and may use it as leverage in order to promote a purchase—"If you won't buy it for me, can I use my money to buy it?" or "You pay half, and I will pay the other half with my money." When they actually get into the purchase stage, they often carry money with them that they may use for snacks on the way to school, at school, and after school. In fact, carrying money in a wallet or purse or in a pocket of a back-pack is a symbol of maturity for elementary school children. Sometimes it is the money that separates a co-purchase from a purchase. In-store requests may be made to parents, with the child expecting the parents to pay for it and therefore accompany him through the checkout. This would be a co-purchase. On the other hand, if the child takes money with him, asks to buy something and the parents agree, and he pays for the object at the checkout while the parents wait, that is an independent purchase—even though the child and his parents shopped together. Actual use of money for a purchase is one of the stopping points in children's consumer behavior, and they usually must have help with the mathematics of it for a year or so after their first co-purchase. One gets the impression that Jimmy has a good understanding of money that probably was gained from accumulating it, working for it, and spending it. Also, it has probably been a topic of some of his school subjects.

Motives

Motives drive purchases and all other human behavior (except reflexes). We could list many *motives* or *needs*, as they also are termed, that theoretically may be satisfied through purchase behavior, but we will note those that most direct early schoolchildren to obtain products and services through asking for them, or co-purchasing them, or independently purchasing them. Besides the physiological needs, as the motivational psychologist Abraham Maslow (1943) would call them, that drive children to seek food, clothing, and rest, many psychological needs push children to the purchase act through either their own abilities or those of caretakers and friends. When children are at school age, the predominant needs that drive their purchases include autonomy, affiliation, achievement, and play, and often one or more needs are fused together that more accurately determine a purchase (Murray, 1938; McNeal, 1992). In addition, most purchases are filtered through the children's self-image. Thus, maintaining a self-image also could be considered a major motive that explains the purchase of certain products such as long pants or product features such as brand, style, model, and price.

Affiliation—the need for cooperative relationships with others—takes on much importance in school as children desire to develop relationships among equals. In order to do this, they try to purchase products that are similar to those consumed by peers, such as clothing and school items. They also begin to purchase items that they can share with others—video games, foods, and beverages. And they begin to share their families' homes, cars, and travels with their close friends. Notice the relationship between Jimmy and his older friend, Chris, and how this relationship drives their consumer behavior. For example, Jimmy states (with poor grammar), "Me and my buddy, Chris, ride down here [to the convenience store] about every day after school." There is a good chance, in fact, that Jimmy would not ride to the store alone, but the togetherness with Chris gives life to the purchases he makes.

Autonomy—the need to act independently—is responsible in great part for children's wanting to purchase on their own during the first few years of school. This need to show independence has been pushing kids since they were age two—it is partially responsible for the terrible twos—and it grows stronger as children enter elementary school. It drives them to want their own money—an allowance, for instance—at least some source of money over which they have control. It also pushes them to seek money for work, such as offering to perform some task around the house for a certain amount of money—like Jimmy apparently does. Their striving for autonomy reaches fruition when they make their first independent purchase. Even the purchase and use of some products are a way to put space between children and their parents. Music players with earphones, their own email address, and a good bicycle are just a few products that give children more autonomy. Notice how a bicycle gives Jimmy and Chris freedom from their parents. "When we get out of school, we ride our bicycles home together and then usually come here . . ." is how Jimmy described using his bicycle to get away from the home environment and into the shopping environment. When fused with play, for instance, autonomy encourages the purchase of hand-held video games—or kites in the case of Jimmy and Chris—so that the children can have fun while logically ignoring parents. Most parents receive requests from their third-graders for "my own TV," and many say they understand that the children want their privacy (independence) and deserve it.

Achievement—to accomplish something difficult—takes on much more importance in elementary school. Being able to accomplish in athletics and being able to accomplish in academics are two ways that children distinguish themselves among their peers and build self-esteem. This need for achievement also pushes kids to excel in some activity without parents' assistance in order to demonstrate to parents their maturity. Some other achievements may include scoring high on hand-held video games or/and on certain games at video game parlors, and having good knowledge of music such as the words to popular songs and advertising jingles. In all cases the children are driven to purchase achievement-related items such as basketballs, skateboards, and video games, or symbols of their accomplishments such as certain shoes, clothing, and books. Many parents understand that their son wants a new bicycle so that he can "race it" or a new pair of shoes so he can run faster.

Play—fun for the sake of fun—is another important need of children in elementary school, although perhaps not as important as it was in preschool times. Increasingly, play is fused with the affiliation need to provide fun with others, with the achievement need to compete with others such as in athletics, and the independence need to separate children from their parents. Jimmy's kite gave him play with a friend, play without parents, and a chance to demonstrate achievement while playing. In fact, it is not difficult to see how Jimmy *fused* the play, autonomy, achievement, and affiliation needs into one major purchase of a $1.98 Humming Bird kite—and he probably sensed that the kite would satisfy all those needs and more, for example, the exhibition need. As a side note, learning how to satisfy several needs with one purchase is an important measure of consumer skill. For instance, a child may want to buy an item out of a vending machine just because it is colorful, maybe because it looks like it would be fun to play with, thus to satisfy one need. Eventually, the child develops more maturity in consumer behavior by analyzing a purchase and intuiting how to satisfy multiple needs with one purchase as Jimmy did with the kite.

Methods

Armed with the money to facilitate purchases and the motives to encourage them, it is only a matter of applying the know-how—the procedure or process for independently obtaining commercial objects. There is no way or no need to try to list all the motor skills and all the cognitive skills necessary to make a purchase because they differ depending on the commercial object and the store in which it is purchased. For instance, being able to slide open a freezer chest door and retrieve a frozen ice cream bar is much different from being able to put ice into a cup and draw a soft drink from a soft drink dispenser, particularly a "dive bomber" as Jimmy concocted. And buying food items in general is much different from buying clothing items or school supplies. In all cases, the ability to read prices and the knowledge of both money and where to pay for an object are necessary, but procedures related to each item must be learned. These procedures usually are assimilated by watching others perform them (observation) and then the children's actually trying them (participation). Those skills and knowledge that are missing become apparent either through reasoning or trial and error, and at first the children rely on others to provide these (co-purchase)—a taller, more dexterous person to obtain the drinks from the drink dispenser, for instance.

The act of paying for a product is no easy feat for most first-graders, and the procedure is different at different kinds of stores—convenience stores, mass merchandisers, specialty stores, and department stores—and at different kinds of direct sellers such as street venders in China or the "ice cream truck" that hawks frozen treats in the neighborhood. In addition to knowledge of money and prices, knowledge of logistics is required for each store. Children usually find it relatively easy to pay for something at a convenience store, more difficult at a mass merchandiser with its multiple checkout lines, and usually very difficult at department stores. Most store clerks do little to help the children, and in fact many ignore them. So, most of the time the onus is on the child to perform appropriately. For instance, in some research a third of eight-year-old boys and girls told us in their own words that they wanted to do more of the buying of their clothes but did not fully understand how they were sized, how to try them on, and whom to pay. All together, this is a complex purchase effort made doubly difficult by dressing rooms that are locked and, perhaps worse, dressing rooms that do not have instructions on how to lock them once inside.

Independent purchases mean much to children. The act is a rite of passage to adulthood. Most of the time, first purchases are made at stores that are most convenient—where parents take them and where their travels take them. This means, then, that most first purchases are likely made near home or near school. Any type of store may be the site of a child's first purchase, but my research shows that a convenience store in a city or a food store in a small town usually receives half of first buys. The other 50 percent are at stores conveniently located near home or school such as supermarkets and mass merchandisers. And at least half the time, the first purchase is a snack item—soft drink, candy bar, frozen treat, chips. Sometimes it is a play item for the child, probably one popularized by classmates, such as a kite. Age-wise, about a quarter make their first purchase before entering first grade, half make their first purchase in the first or second grade, and the final quarter are third-graders. The median age is 96 months plus or minus 4 months. By 100 months, most American kids have made their first purchase.

Chinese children, on the other hand, make independent purchases earlier than American kids. Usually, by the time they enter primary school, Chinese children have made their first purchase on their own. Thus, the median age of their first purchase is somewhere around 54 months, with 75 percent performing independently by 70 months. And the first purchase is most likely a snack item, also. For instance, it is not uncommon to see a mother or grandmother in Beijing pause on the way to kindergarten or primary school and let her child step up to a fast-food restaurant's serving window and buy an ice cream cone or a fried vegetable pie, and eat it on the way, perhaps on the back seat of a bicycle.

Interestingly, in both China and America, boys usually make first purchases earlier than girls, typically around six months earlier. And if the children live in a household with only one parent, regardless of gender, they make first purchases at least six months earlier than the median. In the case of single-parent households, children simply are put to work performing household tasks earlier than in two-parent households. In the case of gender, in China and the United States, boys are seen by parents as a bit more mature than girls at school time, and thus are permitted to make purchases earlier. By 100 months, however, boys and girls normally are performing equally in the consumer role, and in fact, at this time girls may be viewed by parents as more skilled consumers.

CONSUMER BEHAVIOR PATTERNS: OUT-OF-HOME

As observed, entry into all-day formal education has a great impact on the lives of children and particularly on their consumer behavior development. It has substantial effects on what they and their parents buy, where they buy, and when they buy. For example, in the preceding chapter a kindergartener, Carlos, and his mother were in a big supermarket at night buying writing paper for his schoolwork—not something that was ordinary in the consumer behavior patterns of Carlos or his mom, but nevertheless, an action that was required by schooling. Such unusual tekrams become usual as Carlos and others his age enter elementary school. Let us look a little closer at the children's purchases, first those out-of-home and then those at-home.

What They Buy

Six-, seven-, and eight-year-olds in this last stage of consumer development continue to want and buy those things they have observed, asked for, selected, and co-purchased before—foods, clothing, play items, and room furnishings, particularly. While they buy very few of these things with their own money—their 5 to 10 dollars of weekly income for American children—they ask for the money when they see things they want or simply ask their parents to buy them. But within these categories, there are changes in the nature of many of the items, of *what* is asked for and bought. For example, children in this stage still ask for and moms still buy them a variety of play items, but now they may ask for different brands that they learn about at school, and different styles such as in shoes and shirts, even different room furnishings such as lamps—now, for instance, they need a reading lamp. Going to school makes many children feel grown up, and therefore they must have grown-up things, not kiddy things—not a miniature football but a full-size one, not a Snoopy cap but a New York Yankees cap, not short pants but long ones, for instance.

But many new items that children need, want, and wish for are a result of their going to school. Of course, there are new school supplies—the usual paper and pencils, but special kinds just for first-graders or second-graders. Now they need a backpack or a bigger one than they used in preschool and a branded one. While all schools prescribe the school supplies, many also prescribe the types and brands. The children seek these and replacements for them as they progress through school. But they also discover that in addition to what the schools require, some of the children bring other brands and other kinds, and these may become requirements of sorts for some of their classmates. Maybe it is the beginning of "keeping up with the Joneses," but most likely these additional requirements can be explained by "seeing and wanting," just like at home when children see a new product on TV and want it. In any case, these additional school supplies that a few popular children place in the mix may become models for other children. Children often tell their parents that certain items or brands of items are required for school. Parents may disagree, particularly if the items are relatively expensive, but at the end of the day they usually cave in and buy them. Parents buy practically all of the school supplies used by children in the United States; the children tend to expect it. In China most elementary school kids spend some of their own money on school supplies.

In addition to school supplies, there are new foods and beverages required by entry into school. These items may be at the suggestions of the schools, at the suggestions of moms of older children, but likely they are new requests of the new students. Popular brands of prepared foods and beverages are tops on the lists of "gotta haves," and even though they are relatively expensive, often fattening, and low in nutrition, they become requirements. Also, these requirements may change weekly as the children learn about other products from other children in the lunchroom or walking/riding to and from school.

The most conspicuous items, shoes and clothing, are at the top of the list of things to buy during the back-to-school (BTS) sales. Certain brands, definitely, of certain styles are presented to moms before they and their children head for the mall or specialty stores. Store brands usually will not do, and hand-me-downs—what older brother or sister wore last year—are out of the question. "I won't wear them" is the standard response and a negative that makes moms and dads cringe. But as noted earlier, appearance has become very important to the children who are in school, particularly by third grade.

Where They Buy

Now that the children are in school and much older than they were a few months ago, at least in their perceptions, they are much more aware of what peers are consuming, and *where* the school-related items are bought matters. Children in the second and third grades are able to discern good and bad characteristics of stores, and they share them with each other. Some stores earn a bad reputation with many kids at this time. As noted previously, store brands are often a no-no, and particularly if they are recognizable as being from certain stores in the children's shopping area that are on a negative list verbally circulated at school. They may be national chains or locally owned stores, but they are not the place to buy certain products or certain brands for certain children. So, many children tell their moms not only what brands and kinds of things they want, but also where to get them. Again, this is particularly true for conspicuous items such as clothing, backpacks, and those items consumed for lunch at school or in restaurants the children patronize.

Additionally, now that children are in school, some of their wants and purchases go to stores located near school or on the way to school. This is particularly the case for snack items and maybe a few school supplies. Convenience stores now become more important retail outlets to children and possibly to their parents since they often are located on the route to and from school. Self-serve soft drinks, candy bars, chips, and frozen novelties are just a few of the treats that children buy at convenience stores themselves and may share with classmates. Convenience stores are also good places to get a pencil or a pack of paper when there is a short memory operating or a short supply at home—where moms normally keep backup stock. In China, for instance, and probably most Asian countries, the kids typically walk to school, and making small purchases of snacks both on the way and on the way back is standard fare. And in China, stopping by McDonald's for a quick breakfast is considered cool by the children and convenient by the working parents.

When They Buy

We have already given several examples describing when children and their parents buy that is a time when they probably did not buy things last year. On the way to school and on the way home are just two examples. Late at night when they finally remember that they need paper or a protractor, or some kind or brand of juice for their lunch box, the children and parents head for a mass merchandiser, a supermarket, or drugstore that stays open until midnight or all night.

Also, the children buy a number of things at school, from the school, that are merchandised by the school. Sometimes the schoolteachers sell the kids anything from candy to computers at the "school store" or in the classroom. These items may be merchandised as helping to buy books for the library or build a new wing onto the school, or a hundred other causes. In addition, as noted previously, the kids are sold various charities, and at a certain time of day they practically have to buy into these by giving donations to the teachers who ask for them. By the way, the teachers often ask the children to sell these charities to their parents, neighbors, and relatives, ". . . and the one that sells the most wins a new bicycle" or some other premium. Finally, there are all the foods for sale in the lunchroom that not only are "nutritious" but also may contribute to that new building wing or library. These foods and beverages may actually be questionable for their nutritious benefits or their prices, but they are a normal part of the school system that the children are now in and must accept.

As mentioned earlier, BTS—back to school—is a special time now that the kids are in school. It means new jeans, new school supplies, and many other school-related items. It also means taking time from summer play to go shopping, often for many, many hours. Usually BTS time is July and August, although now it increasingly goes into September and then may start up again in January or February thanks to the incessant shouting of merchants. This is normally an exciting time for the kids, maybe their parents, and certainly for the merchants and makers of all the school-related items that spend hundreds of millions of dollars promoting them. If we can believe the ads, BTS now even includes expensive items such as cars and vacations. Some states with high sales taxes such as Texas even have passed laws that allow the merchants to sell such products for a few days without collecting the sales tax. While parents certainly welcome this benefit, it is most welcomed by the merchants who sought it from the lawmakers. In any case, it is a stimulation to purchases (sales) and to the excitement that goes with them.

CONSUMER BEHAVIOR PATTERNS: IN-HOME

The consumer behavior patterns in the home—the location of most tekrams performed by children—have been described to some extent by default in the preceding discussion of out-of-home consumer behavior. Each day that children come home from school, they seem to bring a list of wants ("Can I have some?") and needs ("I have to have it"), and when their parents arrive home, the list is articulated during the next couple of hours. In addition to asking for many things and often using the school as justification for them, with the advent of co-purchasing and independent purchasing, children now are asking such questions as, "Can we go buy it tonight?" or "Can I buy it tomorrow on the way to school?" And a whole new set of questions has arisen regarding money—"Can I have a dollar to buy one?" and "Can I have more allowance?" So, the basic consumer behavior patterns are still in place—eating, sleeping, bathing, playing, watching TV—but as noted, they have been modified by school life and more tekrams related to school have been added.

School brings on more purchase requirements for the home environment, particularly after a year or so in school. New furniture and furnishings for the children's room, for example, have to be purchased. These items include lamps, desks, chairs, bookcases, and even a double bed—if the child is still sleeping in a single bed. Since children are now having other children in their room to study, visit, watch TV, and sleep over with friends, certain items such as bedspreads and rugs have to be replaced; the Snoopy rug has to be replaced with an NFL team rug, for example.

Some changes kids seek in the home environment are expensive. Installing a basketball goal can cost hundreds of dollars, a skateboard ramp at least that much, and a new SUV thousands. But these are just a few of the items that a second- or third-grader may request. Many, perhaps most, of these items are referred to here as *school-related*, but really many of them are a result of having new friends and seeing what they own. As noted previously, invidious comparison is now normal behavior and can be expensive behavior.

Around the time of entering the third-grade, children are expressing their independence from their parents as they grow more attached to friends. Yet, they are still very dependent on parents for most of their wants and needs—and the money to satisfy them. So, much conflict arises from this situation, with children and parents often arguing about the children's independent actions, including particularly their consumer behavior patterns. And parents are hearing more of the children's rebuttals, "Everybody does it," and "Everybody has one." "Everybody" in this case is, of course, classmates, and "it" or "one" may be any action or object of which the parents disapprove, such as watching certain TV programs, eating and drinking certain foods and beverages, and taking part in dangerous practices such as smoking. The net result is often that the parents do not want to buy some things for their children, and in response, the children want to buy them on their own—the topic of this chapter. Thus, I bet if one could somehow analyze all the parent-child conflicts—at any age—most of them would be consumer behavior-based.

Somewhere around the third grade, children begin to exhibit an increasing amount of negative, socially undesirable consumer behavior. They start experimenting with alcoholic beverages, tobacco, and drugs that are often available in the home. As third-graders see or hear about older children consuming these items, these items become desirable. In addition, their respective industries promote these product categories to the children in many ways. And all of these products are available in the marketplace from which children may obtain them or, worse, steal them.

CONSUMER BEHAVIOR PATTERNS BEYOND 100 MONTHS

In the movie *The Natural*, actress Glenn Close portrays a baseball groupie and girlfriend who tells Robert Redford, a successful late-blooming baseball star, "We have two lives: the one we learn with and the one we live with." That statement somewhat conceptualizes consumer development "stage theory." The stage theory of the development of consumer behavior patterns that has been described in these chapters suggests that at 100 months or so, children are functioning independently in the consumer role with at least minimum proficiency. Thus, we can anticipate a significant increase in consumer knowledge and skills in subsequent years that result from children's expanding performance in the consumer role. But the basic consumer procedures are in place at 100 months, and no new functions will occur—just improvements in all three phases—prepurchase, purchase, and postpurchase behavior—that result from continued physical and cognitive growth of the individual and particularly from consumer experience. Thus, approximately the first 100 months of tekrams constitute the consumer life "we learn with," and what follows then is the consumer life "we live with."

If one analyzes the hundreds of studies of consumer behavior of youth published in the journals, one finds that general maturity in consumer behavior occurs between ages eight and nine. This is an age when first purchases are made, when there first appears to be a basic understanding of marketing messages, and when children demonstrate a fundamental understanding of the exchange system. From this point on, the consumer funnel widens and deepens—widens with more purchases and more purchases of different products and deepens with an increasing understanding of the players in the exchange system.

During the preteen years of 9 through 12, children are accumulating thousands of tekrams of experience weekly. They begin to see their mistakes, perhaps because it increasingly is their money that is involved, perhaps because they are so concerned with how they and their behavior appear to their peers. But mainly their cognitive abilities mature so that they have a good understanding of others—of their parents, their friends, and, very importantly, marketers. Somewhere around the 100-month mark, kids acquire a pretty good understanding of marketers and their motives—retailers, advertisers, promoters. At the same time, that understanding brings with it caution about trusting these marketers, their products, and their messages. Children now know they are being sold, that the selling often comes with dishonesty, and that these marketers do not have sincere concern for them—like, at least to some extent, their parents have. In fact, there becomes a general distrust of adults as the children approach adolescence, and it becomes an us- versus-them social environment. This means a general mistrust of all institutions—not just business, but government, religion, family—since all are managed by adults (them) who seemingly do not care about youth (us). Thus, preteens can begin to think in the abstract, to hypothesize about social and economic relationships, and to form opinions as a result of their more analytical thinking. If there was some way we could compare the consumer thinking and behavior of a 100-month-old tween and a 150-month-old tween, we would mainly use the word *more*. We would see that the 12-year-old knows more stores, products, brands, and more about each concept than the 8-year-old. Most of these differences are due to more experience with these concepts—more store visits, more purchases, and more usage—which result from having more money to spend and knowing more about how to spend it. But we would unlikely find any essential differences in the consumer behavior patterns of the two age groups. Probably the 12-year-olds, for example, are beginning to want a credit card and want to buy online, whereas the 8-year-olds are aware of both of these tekrams but just do not yet utilize them. Probably the 12-year-olds are more knowledgeable of health matters but unlikely spend any more money on them than the 8-year-olds. And probably the 12-year-olds are more cynical about marketers, in general, and mistrust them a little more than 8-year-olds, but both are easily duped by them. So, all of these new abilities gained between 100 months and 150 months, for instance, are improvements over those gained from 0 to 100 months, and we generally could term the older child more effective as a consumer. But neither is what we could call a highly skilled consumer and probably will not be until she reaches what we might term a *seasoned level* at around the beginning of adulthood.

DISCUSSION

In this chapter we have considered the final stage of consumer development: the independent purchase that usually transpires between ages 72 and 100 months—the early school years. Entry into school dramatically changes the children's environment and thus their consumer behavior patterns. It is not just the school itself, but it is everything about school that impacts the child consumer. It is the time spent daily in a formal learning environment building mind and body, the teachers becoming new authority figures to the children, marketers presenting their wares to the schoolchildren in many forms and disguises, and the peers who become compelling figures in the lives of the children. While the teachers actually teach some of the necessary consumer skills such as reading, counting, and speaking, it is the peers who set the standards for the new consumer behavior patterns learned in this time period. Adults, however, might question some of the standards, such as the concoction of soft drink syrups that Jimmy called a "dive bomber," but to kids they are normal rites.

Now, it all comes together for the children at around age six or seven—the physical development including the brain, motor skills, cognitive skills, and the acquired money, motives, and methods—to produce independent purchase behavior. Reaching this point is not an overnight matter, as we have shown, but an accumulation that happens to mature concurrently with the children's entry into elementary school. This development has been going on since their birth and has developed logically stage by stage until, in stage four, there are purchase attempts with the assistance of more competent consumers. These attempts become legitimate purchase actions in this final stage of consumer development with the children's new consumer skills and knowledge fostered by school life and by more competent consumers. By 100 months, the children begin stepping up to the checkout counter to make their purchases, such as the young man in Photo 10-3 who is confidently making a purchase of a book at a bookstore. He is nine years old, and he said that he had purchased two other books before at this particular bookstore that is near his home. So what we see here is a new consumer who has more market potential than any other adult since he has all of his purchases ahead of him, and we can also see the pleasure in his face from making an independent purchase as well as the pleasure in the face of the store clerk who welcomes his business.

PHOTO 10-3 A nine-year-old boy in Wuhan, China, makes an independent purchase of a book at a small bookstore near his home. He said it was the third purchase he had made there with money provided by his parents.

Some children undertake independent purchases before entering the first grade simply because circumstances require it. But most American children are not labeled bona fide consumers until sometime in the first two years of school; that is, they are not functioning adequately in the consumer role until then. Thus, at this point they can plan a purchase, make the purchase, and use the purchase—all three phases of consumer behavior—in a satisfactory manner. They have the backup of millions of tekrams behind them that have been performed since birth. They have the help of many adults and peers, and they have the physical and mental abilities to be full-fledged consumers.

Of course, all the consumer behavior patterns children developed in all the stages will continue throughout their lives, with many new ones added and many old ones modified. But the consumer behavior patterns learned in the first 100 months of life will set the stage for all future consumer behavior patterns. The skills, knowledge, and practices learned in this first consumer century will be the foundation for the next and the next. They may be faulty, bad, incorrect, or dangerous consumer behavior patterns as judged by others. For instance, overeating and sedentary consumer behaviors learned (taught) in preschool years are likely to be accepted and practiced throughout life and produce another overweight, unhealthy person. Others may question such practices, but the answers are now in the consumer wiring, so to speak, having been learned and reinforced during these formative years.

Back in the early 1970s, I worked with the Department of Education examining consumer behavior practices of people of all ages, including children. The idea was to use research to develop a program that taught children good consumer behavior patterns as well as to recognize bad consumer behavior patterns. For instance, we documented some bad consumer behaviors practiced by central city families, and we showed how these behaviors could be corrected and life greatly improved for the children of these consumers. Then the plan was to cast these principles into consumer education modules that would be taught each school year starting in kindergarten, and consequently reduce the number of faulty tekrams practiced by kids and carried into adulthood. It seemed like a good idea then, and now, but it never came to be. Everybody from the president to members of Congress to state legislators to school board officials stepped forward at one time or another and found something wrong about it.

So, by stage five of consumer development, there seems to be a layer of consumer schemes constructed in the minds of children that generally determine the next layer and the next and so on. With parents ceding much of their consumer teaching rights to marketers, and, of course, to the children themselves who do much of their own learning from many sources, we might logically expect a lot of errors in the mental structures of today's child consumers. And if history repeats itself, and it usually does, there are likely to be a bunch of politicians to step forward in some way at some time to make sure those bad consumer behavior practices I am calling errors stay right where they were put—in advertising, in stores, and in the forefront of children's minds.

REFERENCES

American Academy of Pediatrics. (1999). *Media education.* Committee on Public Education. Retrieved from http://aapolicy.aappublications.org/cgi/content/fullpediatrics

Dalton, M. A., A. M. Bernhardt, J. J. Gibson, J. D. Sargent, M. L. Beach, A. M. Adachi-Mejia, L. T. Titus-Ernstoff, and T. F. Heatherton. (2005). Use of cigarettes and alcohol by preschoolers while role-playing as adults. *Archives of Pediatrics and Adolescent Medicine, 159,* 854–859.

Erikson, E. H. (1968). *Identity: Youth and Crisis.* New York: W. W. Norton & Company.

Gallahue, D. L. (1982). *Understanding Motor Development in Children.* New York: John Wiley & Sons, Inc.

Gallahue, D. L., P. H. Werner, and G. C. Luedke. (1975). *A Conceptual Approach to Moving and Learning.* New York: John Wiley & Sons, Inc.

Harris, J. R. (1999). *The Nurture Assumption: Why Children Turn out the Way They Do.* New York: Touchstone.

Hartup, W. (1979). The social worlds of childhood. *American Psychologist, 34,* 944–950.

Kohlberg, L. (1984). *The Psychology of Moral Development: Essays on Moral Development* (Vol. 2). San Francisco: Harper & Row.

McNeal, J. U. (1987). *Children as Consumers: Insights and Implications.* Lexington, MA: D. C. Heath and Company.

McNeal, J. U. (1992). *Kids as Customers: A Handbook of Marketing to Children.* New York: Lexington Books.

McNeal, J. U. (2001, April 16). It's not easy being a tween. *BRANDWEEK,* 22.

McNeal, J. U., and M. F. Ji. (2003). Children's visual memory of packaging. *Journal of Consumer Marketing, 20*(5), 400–427.

Maslow, A. H. (1943, July). A theory of human motivation. *Psychological Review, 50,* 370–396.

Meltzoff, A. N., and M. K. Moore. (1989). Imitation in newborn infants: Exploring the range of gestures imitated and the underlying mechanisms. *Developmental Psychology, 25*(6), 954–962.

Murray, H. A. (1938). *Explorations in Personality.* New York: Oxford University Press.

Payne, V. G., and L. D. Isaacs. (1999). *Human Motor Development: A Lifespan Approach* (4th ed). Mountain View, CA: Mayfield Publishing Company.

Piaget, J. (1954). *The Construction of Reality in the Child.* New York: Basic Books.

Thorne, B. (1993). *Gender Play: Boys and Girls in School.* New Brunswick, NJ: Rutgers University Press.

Toppo, G. (2005, August 25). Constant kindergarteners: A year-around program in New Mexico shows promise. *USA Today,* p. 6D.

Villani, S. (2001, April). Impact of media on children and adolescents: A 10-year review of the research. *Journal of the American Academy of Child and Adolescent Psychiatry, 40,* 392–401.

Vygotsky, L. S. (1978). *Mind in Society: The Development of Higher Psychological Processes.* Cambridge, MA, Harvard University Press.

Woolley, J., and G. Peters. (1995–2005). *The American presidency project.* Richard Nixon, Executive Order 11583—Office of Consumer Affairs, Retrieved from www.presidency.ucsb.edu/ws/index.php?pid=59092

PART V

ROLE OF PARENTS
AND MARKETERS
IN CONSUMER DEVELOPMENT

The two main sources of influence on children's consumer development are parents and marketers. Chapter 11 will examine and summarize the role of parents in their children's consumer development. Chapter 12 will detail the influences of marketers in their many forms on children's consumer development.

This watercolor of old China's children flying a kite was done by Chen XueMei of Chengdu, China. This consumer behavior pattern of children was encouraged by the parents, who often gave a small amount of money to their children to buy kites from local merchants. The kites, called *fengzheng*, were often designed as many kinds of birds and insects that were given the winds and the skies to live and play in.

11

ROLE OF PARENTS IN CONSUMER DEVELOPMENT

A Father's Thoughts about His Schoolchildren's Field Trips to Retailers

Parents were interviewed at a Parents' Night event held by an elementary school in a West Texas city. The topic of the interviews was parents' attitudes about their children going on field trips to local retail outlets. A father, Mr. Ed Bentley, agreed to talk to an interviewer about this topic in regard to his two children, Bobby, a first-grader, and Betty, a second-grader at the school. He described both of his children as "earning high marks in school" and "in love with learning," and both "liked their teachers." Mr. Bentley told the interviewer he and his wife were accountants at an accounting services company in the city, and both of them grew up there. "Can't imagine living anywhere else" is how he characterized the city. Following is a portion of the dialogue taken from the interviewer's notes made on an Interviewer Guide.

Interviewer: Has either of your children gone on a field trip to a store of any kind?

Mr. Bentley: Yes, both of them went on a field trip this fall term. They both went to Gafford's supermarket, although at different times. [Gafford's is a large independent supermarket located near the school that the children attend.]

Interviewer: Could you tell us your children's opinions of the experience as far as you know?

Mr. Bentley: They both liked it. Like I say, they went to Gafford's at different times, but each one came home excited by the visit. They both said their classmates were still talking about it. We sometimes take the kids shopping with us at Gafford's, so they knew the supermarket. But they received a better understanding of it from that field trip. Betty told her mother that she believed she could now do the grocery shopping since she learned so much about the store. Bobby said he liked watching them unload the trucks in back of the store.

Interviewer: *What are yours and Mrs. Bentley's opinions about the field trip to that supermarket?*

Mr. Bentley: *We signed off on the permission forms that the kids brought home, so that is an indication that we think it is a very good idea. I think it teaches the kids a lot about business operations, and my wife feels the same way. You know, it's not often that young kids get a chance to learn about business operations. In fact, that is something they may not be taught until later in high school or college. Yet, it's valuable information. I'm glad McClanahan [elementary school] does that sort of thing.*

Interviewer: *I'm curious. Do you or Mrs. Bentley feel that the field trip is a kind of advertising by the stores?*

Mr. Bentley: *It can be, but so what? Kids are surrounded by advertising nowadays, but if it is educational like this field trip was, then I'd call it good advertising.*

Interviewer: *Do you think that Mrs. Bentley would agree with you about that?*

Mr. Bentley: *I'm certain of it. I remember she was telling people at work about the benefits of Bobby's field trip to the supermarket. She particularly thought the view from the back end of the store was helpful to the children's understanding of store operations. You know, like shipping, storing, and breaking bulk.*

Interviewer: *One more question: Do you think the field trip is a way for the stores to get new customers?*

Mr. Bentley: *I'm sure it is, just like advertising attempts to build new business. But it is also a good way for children to learn about the business community in which they will participate in some way for the rest of their lives. So, as I see it, it's a win-win situation for the stores and for the kids. Our family is already customers of Gafford's as I told you. And as far as I know, we will continue to shop there. I'm sure the kids will want to. As I said, Betty wants to do more of the family shopping there since she has a better understanding of the store and its layout.*

Interviewer: *I understand, but do you think Gafford's is trying to build customer relations with your children?*

Mr. Bentley: *Yes, I expect they are. But that's just good business practice.*

Interviewer: *Then, do you think your children are old enough to realize that?*

Mr. Bentley: You mean to realize that Gafford's is trying to get them as customers?

Interviewer: Yes.

Mr. Bentley: I think they are. They're constantly bombarded with marketing of some kind. So, they know what is going on. And I don't think that Gafford's is trying to hide the fact that they are always seeking new customers. Like I said, that's good business. And if my kids can learn about business at the same time, then I think it is a good trade-off. The coupons they received from their field trip to the store are an obvious effort to bring in business. So, like I say, I don't think they are trying to hide their intentions.

Interviewer: Another question then that is prompted by your comments is: Do you think it is the responsibility of the school or the parents to teach the children about business practices?

Mr. Bentley: As I see it, it's the responsibility of both. The school is supposed to be teaching the children to enter the real world. Parents also should prepare their children for the same thing. There's a lot more to school than just the three Rs, you know. They've got to teach the kids how to function in today's world.

INTRODUCTION

Socialization literature contains frequent discussions regarding influences on children's behavior and specifically their consumer behavior patterns. Since practically all human behavior in an industrialized society is consumer behavior, it should be apparent to any student of consumer behavior that *parents* play a major role in their children's consumer development just as they do in their children's overall development. In fact, practically all the books with the term *child development* in their title focus primarily on the parents as sculptors of their children. And virtually all consumer behavior writings do the same. Yet, it should be emphasized that converting children into bona fide consumers is not a formalized process designed by parents. As I observed many years ago:

> We know that the spare bedroom (at home) is rarely turned into a classroom for teaching marketplace behavior. . . . We know that the children are not graded on the bargains they bring home or the money they save by comparison shopping, and we know that there are not pop quizzes over Saturday morning television advertisements. (McNeal, 1987, p. 16)

The point is that while parents teach many specific consumer behavior patterns such as how to put on a pair of shoes or push a shopping cart, most tend not to have a goal regarding their children's development as consumers. That is, they do not report in research among them that they hold certain expectations of their children performing in the consumer role by certain ages. Further, to underline the lack of formality in teaching their children consumer behavior, parents tell us that they expect their children to develop many consumer behavior patterns by watching them function as consumers and copying these actions. Moreover, they often say that they assume their children observe and copy their consumer behavior, and when asked about the source of some specific consumer behavior pattern, the parents are quick to say their children probably learned it from them. Finally, the parents may add that they frequently apply corrective actions to their children's consumer behavior patterns to make sure they do it right and likewise are quick to disclaim responsibility for some of their children's consumer behavior patterns.

Through many discussions with parents, it appears that they are not aware of how much consumer behavior they teach their children, or their children learn from them, particularly in the children's early years. In fact, either through research error—not asking the right questions, for example— or through narrow parental conceptualization or both, parents often focus on purchase behavior and less on prepurchase and postpurchase behavior when they are asked about their teaching of consumer behavior patterns to their children. Yet, some of the most fundamental tekrams—acts of consumer behavior—are taught to children before they can walk or talk, such as sleeping in a certain manner (e.g., in the prone position), eating food in a certain manner (e.g., drinking beverage from a bottle), and playing various games in a certain manner (e.g., hand-to-hand such as patty-cake). Moreover, many more basic tekrams are taught to the children after they learn to walk and talk, such as choosing products and retail outlets by brand name.

The actual consumer behavior patterns that parents teach their newborns ordinarily depend on the *culture* in which the parents live and rear them. As the famous Harvard anthropologists Beatrice and John Whiting (1975, p. 66) said, cultural features "presumably determine the learning environments in which children are brought up, thus influencing their behavior." Thus, parents are *agents* of the culture, and the culture assumes that enculturation is primarily a function of the parents. However, the customs and values that children inherit from their culture often are derived not just from parents but also from those socialization agents chosen by parents to participate in their children's rearing. During the 1970s and 1980s in the industrialized world, the majority of children's mothers joined the children's fathers in the workforce and, through necessity, introduced others into their children's enculturation. Additionally, the basic mother-father family type changed dramatically during these two decades to the point that today millions of children are reared by *several* parents, whereas millions of others are reared by *one* parent, who also, by necessity, brings other adults into the child-rearing process.

As we look back among the pages of this book, we find many other major players in children's consumer development in addition to their parents. We see that peers, teachers, and marketers determine much consumer development in childhood. For example, all three of these social units were active in the Bentley children's development of knowledge of store operations through school field trips. In fact, theorists such as Judith Harris (1999) strongly proclaim that virtually all behavior patterns of preteens and teens are a result of peer influence rather than parents' influence. This seems to me to be naïve thinking, however, since such basic consumer behavior patterns as brand choice and shopping at a mall almost always originate with parents very early in childhood—before children are concerned with—or know how to be concerned with—the views and behavior of other children. Specific brand choices and specific store choices at a point in time indeed may be a function of peers and others, but usually not until elementary school age when such basic choice tekrams are set in cement.

Just which children's specific consumer behavior patterns are derived from persons other than parents depend to a great extent on how early parents relinquish their child-rearing responsibilities to others. Parental yielding of child rearing to others—which certainly includes teaching consumer behavior patterns since they are the most common human behaviors—has been a growing concern of child developmentalists since the 1970s. For example, almost with signs of disgust, distinguished psychology professor Urie Bronfenbrenner (1973, p. 99), who for many years studied the relationship of economic development and family behavior, tried to summarize this relinquishing of parental responsibilities to others in one statement in the early 1970s by cynically but seriously declaring: "Children used to be brought up by their parents." But again, like Harris, his research efforts tended to focus mainly on middle and late childhood and not so much on the first few years of life when many basic consumer behavior patterns are formed. During the past two decades, particularly, parents have increasingly brought others into their children's rearing, and brought them in at an earlier age. The late Professor Bronfenbrenner would have been even more appalled by such recent findings regarding child rearing. For example, many children today are taken daily to various kinds of preschools even before age two, thus letting others such as peers and para-parents do much of the teaching of consumer behavior patterns such as eating, reading, exercising, and playing games. And most of today's parents invite marketers into the children's nursery shortly after birth, for instance, through television programming and advertising and through brand markings on clothing and transitional foods. Accountant Ed Bentley, for example, said that the elementary school had joint responsibility for teaching children "how to function in today's world," which to him included understanding operations of stores. This shedding and shifting of parental responsibility for child development surely determine how much and what kinds of influence parents have on the consumer development of their children. We will take a refresher glance at these matters on a stage-by-stage basis.

PARENTS' PARTICIPATION IN CHILDREN'S CONSUMER DEVELOPMENT

Let us summarize briefly parents' role in their children's becoming consumers on a stage-by-stage basis. For more depth, the reader may want to look back at the respective chapters that treat each stage.

Stage One: Observation (0–6 Months)

Stage one is the age of *discovery* for newborns in which they first become acquainted with their new environment, its social and physical components. At first the environment mainly consists of mom, and the baby quickly learns her sounds, smells, and the feel of her skin and clothing—some of the baby's first tekrams. Very soon, though, the baby begins exploring the physical environment that the parents have established—the one that contains all the things parents purchased for him such as wallpaper, furniture, bedding, clothing, play items, lights, sounds, and temperature—and the one that will permanently replace the womb. Once babies move beyond the random observation stage during their first six to eight weeks, real consumer behavior begins in which choices are being made among these environmental elements and communicated in some manner to parents. By six months—at the end of this first stage—babies are sitting up and taking in greater portions of their environment and performing hundreds of tekrams a day—eating, drinking, sleeping, playing, and sensing hundreds of commercial objects that constitute their environment.

Note, then, that the new baby's *parents have predetermined his environment, its features, contents, and atmosphere.* In effect, parents have determined every kind of product that the baby will consume at least until he can express his likes and dislikes. These products become normalized for the child, what the child accepts and lives with, and what the child will grow up believing is the standard package necessary for living and growing. If the home smells like baby powder, fried food, or cigarette smoke, that is normal to the newborn. If the home contains the sounds of rock music, a computer, or a TV set, that is normal, too. The baby will begin to make choices (through gestures and sounds), as noted, among what exist, and what is given, and the parents likely will respond with more of what the baby chooses, seems to like, and makes good sounds about. For example, around six months, when the baby is placed on the floor to play, the floor becomes a normal place to play, and the baby demonstrates this to mom with signs of happiness. As the baby sleeps soundly in the crib provided him, parents interpret this as happiness with the bed. And mother's body sling or cradle becomes a normal mode of transportation from which the baby emits sounds of satisfaction—which are satisfying to the parents. Displeasure with some situations may not be easy for the baby to communicate, such as the smoke and smells in the room, and therefore by default they become acceptable to babies who have no other situations in their memories for comparison—what they see is what they get. So, if dad and/or mom smoke, so does the baby by default. The Surgeon General, Vice Admiral Richard Carmona, would label the baby an "involuntary smoker" (Department of Health and Human Services, 2006).

Most moms are likely to quickly recognize those play items that contribute to the physical and mental development of their children, and they will shop for more of the same or similar items—replace those consumed. Moms will also figure out on their own that the TV set is a play item of sorts that entertains and keeps their babies happy and contented and therefore acts as a convenient baby-sitter. Of course, if moms spend little time with their new children, and/or if they can spend little or no money on them, then the children will probably suffer in their development from the social and physical deprivation. Thus, under normal circumstances the children's development is the sole responsibility of mothers at this time, who must utilize the marketplace properly to fulfill this responsibility. *Very importantly, moms' knowledge of the marketplace and their performance in it on behalf of their babies will have a direct impact on their babies' development.*

When babies are two or three months old, most parents take them to the marketplace and in effect *introduce them to the source of all the commercial objects* that make up the home and specifically their room. It is not like the baby woke up one day at two months old and said, "Mom, let's go shopping." Going shopping is part of the standard package provided by most parents in an industrialized society—what we usually call a market-driven economy—and it also becomes a normalized dimension of the baby's environment. By six months, most children are acquainted with the marketplace, hold preferences for many features of it, and begin to build it into their repertoires of good things to want.

In this first stage of consumer development, the infant learns from parents the simple but basic principle (tekram) of wanting something satisfying and expecting to receive it from parents. The infant also learns to adapt to the less satisfying elements of her environment. This consumer relationship with adults is totally dependent, and its outcomes are completely determined by the sensitivities and perceptions of the parents. I once asked some new parents if they thought it was all right that the father smoked in their little apartment around their new baby; it was a very small and very smoky apartment. The mother defensively responded quickly with several statements indicating that the father did not smoke in it everyday and that the baby did not seem to mind when he did. "I have never heard him (the new baby) cough when his father is smoking," the mother added. And seemingly as an afterthought—and perhaps a hint to her husband—she said, "In fact, I think the smoke bothers me more than it does the baby," while she patted her own chest. The father also suggested that some of the smoke in the apartment was due to cooking and a lack of a working ventilator in the kitchen.

Stage Two: Requesting (6–24 Months)

The second stage of consumer development may be viewed as two substages: the first, from 6–14 months before talking and walking fully develop; and the second, from 14–24 months, when both of these motor skills are routine. At this time, many physical and mental abilities develop hand in hand with the development of consumer behavior patterns. During stage one, the observation stage, children learn to sense out those elements of their environment that give pleasure, form a motor memory of them, and look for them again. *Requesting* these pleasure-giving objects marks this second stage. At first, requesting starts with body language, growing in sophistication with increased use of arms, legs, neck, even the whole body, and accompanied by some sounds but not actual words. As children begin to comprehend words, they use them in their memory, along with pictures of action to represent objects, mainly desirable objects. Soon, around 10–12 months, the children begin to speak some of these words as tools for requesting objects. Of course, parents welcome children's talking even if it most often is used to request things. In fact, *the novelty of verbal seeking tends to cause parents to honor virtually all requests*, a response path that usually leads to spoiled-bratdom.

Observing objects continues and intensifies as the children in this second stage develop new facilitating motor skills. At the end of stage one, children learned how to sit up, thus permitting new vistas of objects. Six months later in this stage two, children learn how to stand up and, soon after, to walk. The standing and walking abilities multiply by many times the number of items in the child's environment that can be observed, wanted, and requested. And, as speaking concurrently develops with these motor skills, many requests spew forth. By the time the children are 24 months old, they are making between 50 and 100 requests a day in some form, and again, parents tend to respond positively to most of them.

What we see in this stage is a *great expansion of children's physical environment* due to their new cognitive and bodily abilities—walking, talking, symbolizing—and due to *parents adding objects to the environment as a result of the children's requests*. Consequently, the seeing-asking-receiving consumer system is normalized, as are the elements of the social and physical environments. For instance, a full refrigerator and pantry are standard, along with a toy chest and bookshelf. If children are aware of something missing— they now see objects separate from themselves—they speak for them and often in such brand forms as "Where's my Oreos?" and "Where's my Mickey?" Virtually all their waking hours are spent as consumers, and in fact, getting the children to cease their tekrams and take a nap or go to bed usually requires additional tekrams such as hugging their teddy bear, being read to, and listening to music or TV. There should not be any doubt at this point that parents are sculpting their children to be 24/7/360 consumers.

And, in addition to parents, siblings and grandparents are now primary parts of children's social environment. The now egocentric children see all people in their household as sources of desirable items to whom requests are to be made at any time. It takes only a few requests to discover the most generous giver, and the children then revere this person—*just as tekrams are a basis for love from parents and other caretakers, tekrams are a basis for love from the children.* Thus, all social objects at this point in children's lives tend to be givers knowing that the giving contributes in various ways to the pleasure and contentment of the children—and to the givers.

In stage one, the children were first taken to the marketplace by parents, and this practice continues on a regular basis in stage two. As the children gain their walking and talking abilities, they request to go shopping and are taken to the marketplace more. Also, like at home, the children make more requests once in the marketplace, and they use their new motor skills to lead parents to objects that they want on store shelves. Gradually, these *requests are made by brand name,* thus constructing their consumer memory in a form that is much like that of adults. *Parents encourage and reinforce this practice by frequently mentioning brand names and often praising the children for doing the same.*

Bear in mind that from 6–24 months, children do not choose the objects that populate their environment, although they are responsible for many as a result of their requests. But most stuffed animals, toys, foods, and beverages, for example, are the choices of parents. For example, "fat" stuffed animals are preferred and first selected by parents and other adults, usually not by the children. The point here is that these fat stuffed animals probably contribute to normalizing fat and indirectly contribute to the children's becoming overweight—OWs (because it hurts). Neither do the children choose the other members of their households, although these other persons are appreciated for what they can provide. The children do not ask for a fat mother and/or father, but the mere fact that parents are fat, again, contributes to the normalization of fat. And making a snack stop while shopping is the choice of the parents. Thus, *fat gets okayed in many ways very early in children's lives,* and by the time they have mastered this requesting stage, they routinely are imitating parental consumer behavior and asking for those satisfying things that have been introduced and normalized by the parents. So, when they say to their parents, for example, "I want some French fries," it is unlikely that the parents will respond, "No, they will make you fat," since they introduced them to the kids and purchased them several times before. Besides, *refusals to honor consumer behavior patterns that have been established will only produce confronta-*

tions that most working parents try to avoid—the normal response of new-millennium parents to a parent-child conflict. In sum, the children's requests have already been blessed many fast-food visits ago, and certainly by the two-year birthday party that parents recently held at a fast-food restaurant.

In this second stage of children's consumer development, parents have firmly established the seeing-asking-receiving consumer system in their households. They have taught their children that asking is receiving, that asking for what has been provided before is definitely receiving, and that asking for anything is normal behavior. Furthermore, in this stage, the practice of identifying and asking for products and sellers of products by brand name has been put in place. Also, in this stage the children have learned not only to ask for things they want, but also to ask certain caretakers for certain things with certain asking styles. Those asking styles that work are retained and perfected in the next stage.

Stage Three: Selecting/Taking (24–48 Months)

During the third stage of consumer development, two- and three-year-old children learn to *select and take* satisfying objects from their physical environment. Their body grows from 30 pounds to around 40 pounds, and their height increases at least 6 inches, reaching around 40 inches by the time they reach age four. Thus, they have the necessary physical abilities, which are accompanied by very improved cognitive abilities—the children now represent all objects in their minds with words and pictures and can recall them at any time. Children also begin to sense and think more about the feelings of others. Thus, the asking that began in stage two now is reaching a new level of sophistication in which the children craft requesting styles and appeals that they feel work best with parents in getting what they want—made possible by a vocabulary that grows from around 200 words at the beginning of the stage—age two—to 1,200 words by the end of it—age four.

Children regularly demonstrate in this stage of consumer development that they are master copy-cats. *Imitation* of consumer behavior patterns of parents, characters on TV, preschool teachers, and playmates becomes standard fare; it has been encouraged and rewarded by parents many times in many ways. It is difficult at this time to say what CB is taught by parents and what CB is learned by children through their own efforts of observation and participation. For example, in the Dalton et al. (2005) study of preschoolers' role-playing, 36.5% of three- and four-year-olds pretended to purchase cigarettes, and 71.2% pretended to purchase alcoholic beverages for an evening social. The researchers' conclusion: Children are simply copying their parents. During this stage, a majority of children are placed in some kind of preschool, where they gradually learn to take consumer cues from other children, particularly older children, and imitate these

PHOTO 11-1   A Chinese mother selects and buys fresh vegetables while her three-year-old son observes. Within a few years the child will imitate his mother by performing the same act in the same manner.

strangers, thus adding a new layer of copy-cat consumer behavior to that resulting from parent-child interactions.

In Photo 11-1 a Chinese mother selects and buys fresh vegetables while her three-year-old looks on with interest. The child stores this image of his mother in the selection and purchasing mode and will one day repeat—imitate—the action by attempting to purchase on his own.

Parents are faced with a major change in the disposition of their children in this stage that produces what is often called the "terrible twos"—TTs—in which children are unruly, aggressive, and often out of control. Parents really do not know how to deal with this situation. Perhaps that is why so many books and articles are written about it. This behavior seems to be fostered by children's consumer demands that are not answered as they wish by parents, thus producing frustration and anxiety. Hannaford (2005) said that all the theatrics of the TTs are simply *exaggerations of behaviors copied from parents* as part of the children's development. In any case, busy working parents often tire of trying to figure it all out and just give in to the behavior by granting more consumer freedom to the children—letting them have their way, letting them choose whatever products they want, letting them take whatever they want. Of course, parental nourishing of this aggression—it is worse among boys than girls—only leads to more of the same. At some point the children seem to have the parents trained with their manipulative language, aggressive behavior, and theatrics. The results: Children get their own consumer world with the products and brand names they like sourced from their growing list of favorite stores, their favorite TV programs, their peers, and from parents at the ready to provide more of these when asked. Thus, the TTs almost always work in favor of marketers, thanks to parents.

During this period most parents have their two- to four-year-old children in some kind of preschool, where the children are introduced to more products and product uses. They also are introduced to some new consumer behavior patterns that are expressed by other children, particularly in their play. The results are often conflicts among the egocentric children—usually over commercial objects—that are often resolved by parents buying their children more of what other children have. The lesson the children often learn is that conflicts with parents or with peers may be rewarded if the children make enough noise about the conflicts. Moreover, turning requests into demands usually has good payoff for the children—and marketers.

When children are at the end of this stage—at age four—a number of basic consumer behavior patterns are pretty much in place, and it can be assumed that most have been learned from parents. These patterns include identifying and asking for products and their sources by brand names, taking the products if asking does not work, obtaining product information from mass media, acknowledging retailers as sources of goods and services, comparing one's products with those of others, and viewing parents and peers as model consumers. To this point in their consumer development, most tekrams practiced by children originate with their parents, and while this general consumer behavior pattern will continue, it will be compounded by more influence from peers and the mass media.

Stage Four: Co-Purchase (48–72 Months)

In stage four of consumer development, which embraces four- and five-year-olds, children make attempts to undertake purchases and finally, around age five, *make first purchases with the assistance of parents and other competent consumers.* Thus, it is called the co-purchase stage. Between ages four and six, children develop a rudimentary understanding of the parts of the purchase system: Discover the product—want the product—select the product—pay for the product—consume the product. This means that their minds can now understand the idea of a purchase and that they have filed away some purchasing schemes in their minds based on shopping and buying with parents. Also, they have watched other purchasers—including other kids—in the marketplace where they go at least once a week, usually more—and their growing independence says they want to try it on their own. They have an accumulation of money at home in a piggy bank or some similar kind of depository—thanks mostly to parents—but counting it and using it are still tasks to be learned.

Children already know about the products and their brands available in certain stores that they have been patronizing with parents practically since they were born. Now they are learning about many products and their brands from their schoolmates and from the mass media, mainly TV. At age five—in the middle of this stage—kids have a vocabulary of probably a thousand products and at least 10 percent are known by brands and many by multiple brands, and they usually know which stores offer these products. In fact, they have asked parents to buy them hundreds of items before in these stores, and their parents have accommodated them most of the time. *Whether planned or unplanned, most parents have led their children to this point in their consumer development where they want to make their own purchases—by taking them to the marketplace regularly, buying them something on every visit, asking for their recommendations, talking to them about some of the purchases, and even letting them hand the money to the cashier to pay for something they requested. Chances are, too, the parents have let their children make purchases in some of the vending machines that are always open for business at all the malls, mass merchandisers, and many other retailers, including hotels and transportation terminals.* This is good practice for the children to prepare them for the more complicated (to the children) purchases from the shelves and fixtures of stores. Finally, *parents have provided the means—the money—to the children so that they can make the vending machine and store purchases.* So, ready or not, each set of parents has groomed another child to be a purchaser of potentially satisfying goods and services.

In Photo 11-2 two mothers at a shopping mall in Wuhan, China, co-purchase some entertainment for their stage four children from vending

PHOTO 11-2   Two mothers at a shopping mall in Wuhan, China, give their children a ride in a vending machine that vends entertainment. This is a co-purchase since the children ask for it, ask for money for it, and put the coins in the device.

machines that provide the children a few moments of fun. The children ask to ride in the vending machines, the mothers give the children coins, and they insert them in the machines. Soon, in stage five, the children will be able to make the purchase without help from parents.

As a side note, most retailers are not aware of these purchase trials by children, and most do not care about them. They like for children to badger their parents for purchases of big bags of candy and two-liter soft drinks, but they really prefer that the children do not clog the checkout lines with their slow and uncertain attempts to buy, even with mom standing by for help when needed. This first purchase, even though with parents' assistance, is a very big deal to the kids, but it is strictly a parent-child thing. Even the parents may not be enthused about their kids' first co-purchases; parents are generally too busy to be concerned with many matters that are of major concern to their children. But sometimes accidentally, sometimes almost unknowingly, parents lead their children through the co-purchase act that puts them on a straight line to their first independent purchase—another major step in consumer development fostered by parents.

Stage Five: Independent Purchase (72–100 Months)

All the children's consumer development in the first four stages from birth to six years old culminates in *independent purchase behavior* in stage five. Independent purchases usually take place after children enter elementary school between six and eight years old. School itself adds many tekrams to the children's consumer repertoire as they observe, ask for, select, and maybe try to buy school-related items and products they see in the possession of other children at school. The parents, of course, send their children to elementary school knowing that they will have new consumer requirements and knowing that they will want to copy the consumer behavior of other children, particularly older children. Parents—at least parents in a developed economy—also know and expect that, as their children grow older, they will want to perform in the consumer role more frequently. This behavior is a major part of children's quest for independence in general. In stage four, they attempt purchases with the help of parents, who usually give it gladly. So, it follows that, *as soon as the parents think the children are mature enough, they allow them to try purchasing products on their own.* Approximately a third of American parents are single parents, who often encourage their children to make independent purchases even before entering school as a way of helping out in the household. The outcome of this stage is a functioning consumer utilizing many consumer behavior patterns learned from parents. Another outcome, from a marketing standpoint, is a group of functioning consumers with a great deal of market potential, theoretically more than that of their parents since they have most of their purchases ahead of them.

To become independent consumers, children must learn much from their parents about the purchase act—the use of money, the role of the retailer, the nature of the exchange system. It is not possible to separate the many tekrams in the purchase act and say which ones the parents taught and which ones the children learned from their parents and others. And when focusing on the purchase itself, one can easily forget all the steps that parents took their children through to get to this point—their postpurchase use of thousands of products and the prepurchase initiation of thousands more. Suffice it is to say that at the time of first independent purchase, children are performing several thousand tekrams a day, and most originate in the parent-child relationship.

PARENTS HAND DOWN BASIC CONSUMER BEHAVIOR PATTERNS TO THEIR CHILDREN

As we have shown in the pages of this book and specifically in this chapter, parents hand down to their children many basic consumer behavior patterns beginning in the first year of life. Moreover, those CB patterns are not randomly selected but are representative of the culture in which the children are born and live. Parents in a developed economy do not convey to their children that they must not act like consumers or must not act like other consumers. Quite the contrary. From birth, the children are introduced into a commercial environment—their home and their community and its marketplace—and actively taught how to function in it, including copying the tekrams of others. Naturally, all of this is done at a pace that is commensurate with the physical and cognitive development of the children. *It should be emphasized that teaching consumer behavior is tantamount to child rearing since most human behavior in a developed economy is consumer behavior.* Let us briefly note some of these consumer behavior patterns passed on to children from an evaluative standpoint.

Good Consumer Behavior Patterns

Classifying the consumer behavior patterns handed down to children by parents as good or bad may seem presumptuous since the parents generally have a right to teach their children or have their children taught whatever they (the parents) want. But from a theoretical perspective, there are good and bad consumer behavior patterns. *Good consumer behavior consists of tekrams that promote the welfare—the health and happiness (H&H)—of the children and do no harm to others. Bad consumer behavior consists of tekrams that do harm to the children and likely do harm to others.* We will not list all of either group but try to summarize them. And when we use the term *teach* as an action of the parents, we are referring to showing children how to perform in the consumer role by training them in consumer behavior patterns as well as by acting as a model for consumer behavior patterns.

Fundamentally, parents hand down two groups of good consumer behavior patterns to their children: (1) those culturally approved uses of commercial objects, and (2) those that lay a foundation for effective consumption of commercial objects, the term *effective* meaning those that provide H&H for the lives of the children. Naturally, these two have some overlap since the classification is intended to embrace all consumer behavior.

Teaching culturally approved uses of commercial objects starts at birth with teaching the babies to nurse, sleep, and engage in other sensorimotor activities such as watching, feeling, and listening to physical and social objects present in the environment. This practice continues as the children develop their cognitive and motor skills under the premise that parents know pretty well what consumer behaviors promote the maturation of body and mind. Thus, training newborns in ways to consume mother's milk, sleep in a bed designed for them, and stay warm in the clothing purchased or made for them is basic enculturation. Later, when the children are able to sit up, then stand and walk, parents teach the children to play with objects that foster their motor skills and the accompanying cognitive skills. Shortly following, the children will be shown how to use wheeled goods—tricycle, bicycle, skates, skateboards—and educational objects such as drawing tools, books, and videos. These parenting practices—child rearing—continue throughout childhood, in fact, usually through teenhood, when parents teach children how to drive a car or boat, for example. If parents are unable or unwilling to perform these teaching tasks, they may assign them to others such as grandparents and schoolteachers, but they are the parents' responsibilities. In China, for instance, both mother and father work in around 80 percent of households, and grandparents often tend to the children and therefore assume a lot of the child-rearing responsibilities.

Photo 11-3 shows a kindergarten teacher demonstrating to a five-year-old how to use a knife and fork. The kindergarten in Beijing has assumed responsibility for teaching children Western consumer behavior such as this.

Teaching children consumer behavior patterns that lay a foundation for effective consumer behavior might sound like teaching survival, and it is, but it is much more. It is showing children how to utilize the marketplace to satisfy their needs—to become all they can be. It reminds me of that adage: Give a person a fish and you feed him for a day; teach him how to fish and you feed him for life. There are only a few foundational consumer behavior patterns for children to learn from parents (and other caretakers), but each one consists of many tekrams.

A. Depend on parents for appropriate consumer behavior patterns.
Children learn to depend on parents for teaching them how to survive and grow, although they are not conscious of this fact until

PHOTO 11-3   A Beijing kindergarten teacher shows a student how to use a knife and fork. Teaching children Western consumer behavior patterns is becoming standard fare in Chinese schools.

parents become separate objects from the children. However, the children enter the "I want to do it myself" stage between ages 2 and 4 and tend to want to rely on themselves more. This is logical development and parents usually foster it, and should, but not at the expense of learning bad habits. One teenager I knew began experimenting with smoking when he was around 10. His father, who was a smoker, let him experiment, believing that it would make him sick and he would not try it again. Of course, just some basic parenting reasoning would tell dad that the boy was trying to be like him. And the child kept trying and trying until he succeeded. He was a "pack-a-day man" at 16—"just like his father," according to his mother.

B. **Effectively utilize the marketplace.** Most parents teach their children that the marketplace contains all the products and services that make life good, that foster body and mind development, and that help them grow into the adults they dream of being. But, as noted a couple of times in this book, the marketplace—stores, schools, transportation, athletic events, Internet, on and on—also contains all the bad products and services that marketers can bring together. It is not for us at this point to try to figure out why. We will do that to some extent in the next chapter. Suffice it is to say that marketers are inclined to live their lives on an incline, so children must be trained in *effectively* using the marketplace in order to separate the good from the bad. This means attentively reading packaging and labels of products, it means carefully evaluating advertisements and other promotional messages from marketers, and it means understanding the intent of all marketers with whom they interact. That is a tall order for parents to fill but absolutely necessary for children to succeed in the marketplace. It means that the children should receive a lot of consumer education from parents, but regretfully, many do not, or do not receive enough. They may learn some consumer behavior patterns from schools to which parents send them. This was the case with the Bentley children and was expected and appreciated by these parents. In such cases it behooves the parents to be observant about what their kids are learning at preschool and elementary school and provide them with evaluations of these tekrams.

C. **Efficiently utilize the marketplace.** Children should be taught how to get the most from the marketplace with the least effort. They can learn a couple of important tekrams from parents to accomplish this. *Use proven brands.* Assuming that the children or their caretakers have read and analyzed the marketing messages of particular brands of particular products, and have used them and received satisfaction from them, they should continue to buy and use those brands. If the makers and/or sellers of those brands of products guarantee them and do not change them without informing the consumer, then through choosing those brands of products and services, the consumers are getting about as much satisfaction from the marketplace as they can. Related to the satisfaction received from specific brands is *good price knowledge* of them. Satisfaction usually comes from "getting the most for your money," an idea that parents often teach. So, buying brands by price usually is the most efficient way to operate in the marketplace. Most parents know that successful brands are copied with slight variations by other marketers—supermarkets for example, copy the packaging of well-known national brands—and the child consumers who have been trained to watch for and assess this practice are miles ahead in satisfaction. It is assumed that the children have been trained, as noted earlier, in *understanding the intent of marketers* with whom they interact directly and indirectly. Parents should also teach their children that *many retailers sell the same product*—same brands, sizes, and prices—and should utilize those outlets that give the most satisfaction from price, store location and layout, and customer-oriented personnel.

Many products purchased are not branded, and children must be taught to deal with these products separately. Fundamentally, children must be taught that *goods and services that are not branded cannot be provided in a consistent manner* and therefore require a much keener shopping effort. They must learn to see the unbranded items as sellers' brands and make some decisions about the quality of these products and intent of those sellers.

As a side note, all these appropriate consumer behavior patterns may also be taught in public schools that the parents choose for their children. It is likely, however, that the practices described here are taught in only a few elementary, middle, and high schools and may be taught by unqualified teachers. Thus, teaching these principles is mainly the parents' responsibility, but with so many parents both working and working long hours, they may not have enough time to do it properly. Part of this responsibility could be fulfilled by parents working through parent-teacher organizations and petitioning kindergarten and elementary schools—maybe the local school boards—to teach these principles to their children.

Bad Consumer Behavior Patterns

The marketplace, as observed, is replete with all the bad—unhealthy, dangerous, socially undesirable—products that one could possibly want or want to avoid. Consuming them is bad consumer behavior. If the products and/or brands and their sellers do not serve the health and happiness of the children, they are bad. Many, for example, may make the children happy but unhealthy, such as fattening foods. And if the products and/or use of them results in harm to others, they are bad. Permitting children to smoke will hurt other children who copy the behavior, for instance, and will harm other persons who involuntarily breathe the secondhand smoke (Department of Health and Human Services, 2006). Parents teach a lot of bad tekrams to their kids, such as the use of bad products, the abuse of some, and the avoidance of some that are good for the children. Some of such teaching is due to ignorance, some is done through thoughtlessness, and some is done unknowingly. Parents themselves demonstrate many bad tekrams in front of their kids—overeating, smoking, drinking, playing with guns, to name a few—then often say they expect their children not to copy such behaviors. But most parents also tell us that they expect their children to copy their behavior. So, what reasons can we give for such conflicting, naïve thinking and behavior? Regardless of the reasons, the outcomes are the same—negative impact on children's H&H.

Two very *bad* patterns of consumer behavior that parents regularly teach their kids is *how to get fat* and *how to be violent*, with each having corollary bad tekrams. Both usually have their roots in the terrible twos (TTs), and therefore both are somewhat related. The time period of the TTs is somewhere between age two and three and is characterized by rage and destruction that are also learned mainly from parents. TTs seem to result from the children's encounter of obstacles that get in their way of conquering their expanding environment and getting the things they want. *Violence* is one of the results of the children's being thwarted in their attempts at independent consumer actions. Violence may take many forms but at this early age is manifested in screaming, bad-mouthing, hitting, and breaking things. Much of the violence is aimed at parents who are away or who say no, and in either case prevent their children from obtaining whatever it is they want and has been previously provided by parents. Parents also become frustrated and tend to give in to their frustrated children by giving them what they want, giving them more, and in many ways appeasing them. Such actions, of course, reinforce the notion that violence pays. That message is also present in many of the TV programs children are watching, programs increasingly provided by parents ironically to bring peace to the household—to calm and quiet their children. It may be, too, that this violence is demonstrated in later years as bullying, another kind of bad consumer behavior that some children direct at their classmates.

Getting fat is another result of appeasing the tots during the TTs by giving them more to eat, especially snacks, and more sedentary consumer behavior such as TV viewing, which usually contributes to getting fat. Thus, in order to reduce the ranting and destruction of the children, their parents give in and give—give in to their demands and give them whatever they want, and more. Parents literally turn the house over to them—turn it into what marketers call a *filiarchy*—and starting at this time, the children pretty much control the things purchased for them as well as for the household that they have hijacked. The net result is more of those good-tasting foods— salty and sweet snacks—to have while watching TV and playing video games. Ironically, this consumer behavior pattern occurs at a time when play is the most important thing to children. In fact, it is hard to believe how children can get to a point where eating and sitting are more desirable than playing. It takes a lot of training by parents—training that takes place in a fat-favorable environment—to accomplish this. A fat-favorable environment results from one or more fat parents who, in addition to the giving and the giving in to their kids, treat overweightness as normal. They show favor to fat characters who have their own TV programs—Barney, Pooh, and the like—buy these fat characters' products—dolls, videos, toys—and bring home many fattening products to eat—pizza, fries, and two-liter nondiet soft drinks—to be consumed by both parents and kids often while watching TV together. The parents even pack high-fat processed lunches that are "fun to eat" for the kids to take to preschool and later to elementary school. "Fun" is what the marketers call it—"fat is fun" seems to be the theme of many of their messages—whether it comes from Barney or Pooh or the many fat stars that populate many of the sitcoms that parents and their children watch. So, together moms and marketers march the kids off to fatdom, that is, until the kids can hardly march. The fatter children get, the less they want to do and the more they want (need) to eat.

CURRENT ISSUES IN CONSUMER DEVELOPMENT (#11)

Parents Create Fat-Favorable Environment for Their Children

Thanks in great part to inattentive, conflict-avoiding, time-strapped parents, one-third of U.S. children are overweight, and by 2010, this number will be one-half. Reams have been written about the resulting lifetime damage to the minds and bodies of children who get fat.

Child-rearing experts in the medical and social sciences explain that children are overweight mainly due to their consuming fattening foods and engaging in sedentary activities. That appears to be true. But their analyses should not stop there if they are seriously interested in averting this dangerous trend. They should ask specifically how the children obtain the products that fatten them since the children don't buy most of the products on their own. The answer, of course, is that the products are forthcoming from a fat-favorable environment created by parents and other caretakers chosen by parents. This fat-favorable environment consists primarily of four parts.

Part one is the direct *supply* of potentially harmful products given to children by parents. For instance, take TV, the most sedentary-demanding product in the home. It is usually introduced to the children before they can walk or talk, and certainly before they know about it or can ask for it. At first—while children are in infancy—the TV is used as a baby-sitter/entertainer, particularly to give caretakers some personal time. Then by the time children reach toddler age, it is used also as a reward—for not crying, for being good, for helping mother. Also, starting at about this time, it is employed as an educator—to teach the alphabet, science, music, and other academic topics claimed to be a benefit of certain TV programs. So, the older the baby becomes, the more she watches TV because there are more reasons to watch it. However, according to the President's Council on Physical Fitness, the more the children watch TV, the more likely they will become overweight. It should be emphasized that advertisers, of course, are grateful to parents for early installation of a TV in children's rooms and in other rooms—and for the invitation to come into the household so that they can daily hold down the children and stuff them full of sales messages for more fat-producing products.

What about the fattening foods that the children snack on while watching the TV? The sweet and the salty ones? The ones advertised on TV? Once again, these products are provided by parents. For instance, parents may hold their baby's first or second birthday party at a fast-food restaurant, bring fast foods home when life is too demanding to fix a meal, and may pick up some fast foods at the drive-through as they head out on a family weekender. So, all those chips and colas that children never knew about but now love and demand are furnished by their loving parents. In fact, we usually find that specific kinds and brands of these products are favorites of mom and dad.

So, most likely all the fat-causing products consumed by children were put in place in the household by parents. And as if to assure the children that these products are parent-blessed, parents also consume them with the children—as they probably did before the children arrived. As one professor of pediatrics stated, "I never see a child who has better eating habits than his parents." So, part one of a fat-favorable home environment is the supply of fat-producing products and services by parents beginning when the children are born, and the variety and quantity are increased as the children mature.

Part two of a fat-favorable home environment is parents' perceptions of fatness. "Show me a fat kid and I'll show you at least one fat parent" is now standard thinking among pediatricians. Research shows that one overweight parent doubles the risk that a child under age 10 will become an obese adult. About two-thirds of adults are overweight—although they may not agree—and overweight parents make the home environment more fat-favorable. A major percentage of these overweight parents are unlikely to see themselves as significantly overweight and, more frightening, unlikely to see their fat children as overweight. In one study, adults reported that 90 percent of their friends were overweight, but only 40 percent of the respondents saw themselves as overweight. In another study, one-third of moms and one-half of dads who were overweight rated themselves as about right. Regarding overweight children, only one-third of their moms and 57 percent of their dads saw them as overweight. And in another study, 79 percent of fat mothers failed to recognize when their preschoolers were too heavy. Add to these figures the number of parents who hold such stereotypical values as "a fat baby is a healthy baby" and that "overweight is better than underweight," and you have an environment in many homes that welcomes fat.

By the way, some of these parents who create a fat-favorable home environment belong to organizations that actually promote fat thinking. For example, the National Association to Advance Fat Acceptance (NAAFA) believes that everyone should accommodate overweightness. Such groups promote the fat-is-fate notion with such slogans as "fat by nature, proud by choice." They also believe that children should decide how much they eat as well as determine to a great extent the foods they eat.

Part three of a fat-favorable home environment is the *positive attributes* assigned to other fatties by parents. There is a tendency for parents who are overweight to find a lot of good in others who are fat and in various ways pass on these evaluations to their children. They praise fat entertainers such as "Idol" Ruben Studdard, Oprah Winfrey, and Rosie

O'Donnell and the many other fat performers in virtually every sitcom. They applaud most fat people on TV who perform well in spite of their added weight, such as professional football players—pick any one since the majority of them are overweight—and those in other athletic fields. And they like fat politicians such as Senator Ted Kennedy and Vice President Dick Cheney, and they usually see nothing wrong with law officers being fat. Parents also tend to choose fat characters as "playmates" for their children, such as Barney and Winnie the Pooh, and tend to disfavor thin characters such as Barbie and her friend, Ken. So, in the eyes of parents, particularly fat parents, fat is fine in others.

Part four of the fat-favorable home environment is its *extension* to other environments of the children. Many parents over the years have voted to eliminate playtime—recess, physical education—at school and put in its place more academic subjects. Add to that reduction in physical activity the fact that most children under age 12 are required by parents to ride to school—by car or bus—and most are not permitted to go out and play after school, and you have pear-shaped kids in the making. As if to make sure of that shape, parents pack the kids school lunches with fat-laden foods—often prepackaged lunches that advertise to moms their convenience and time-saving preparation and their contribution to happy kids. These products supposedly will hold them until they can get back home in the afternoon to the TV and the snack-laden pantry and refrigerator.

If there is a fifth part of the fat-favorable environment constructed by parents, it is their attitudes toward child rearing. Busy parents often are not attentive enough to their children, their mind being instead on their job and its problems and opportunities. To the extent they do show special interest in their children, it is usually through giving them things—showing thoughtfulness through things—and taking them to special places like theme parks and fast-food restaurants, and shopping. Since they don't have as much time with the children as they would like, they tend to avoid conflicts, again, by letting the children have what they want when they want it.

****

Sources: Associated Press, 2006; Grossman, 2003; Hellmich, 2003; Laliberte, 2003; Serdula et al., 1993; Tyre et al., 2005.

Many other bad consumer practices often originate with parents. Purchasing without evaluation (impulse purchasing), purchasing from endcaps (end-of-the-aisle displays), and purchasing on the basis of convenience are a few of them. The point, however, is that children in their early formative years learn both good and bad tekrams from their parents even though the parents—not the children—have a choice as to what is taught.

As another side note, most marketers know that children learn many of their consumer behavior patterns from their parents. So, they target a great deal of advertising and promotion to parents on behalf of kids' products. In the case of fattening products, the marketers often appeal to the parents to please and reward their children with their brand of products and imply it is a parent's obligation—"you owe it to your children" and "make your child happy by giving him or her our brand of product."

PARENTS HAND DOWN A CONSUMER GENE OR SOMETHING LIKE IT TO THEIR CHILDREN

The basic nature of human beings is to consume objects for the satisfaction of their needs. In order to consume objects for need satisfaction, they must be acquired—produced or purchased. Production of satisfying objects is common to purely production-oriented or undeveloped societies. Acquiring through purchase—with money and money substitutes—is common to consumer-oriented or developed societies and fosters what we call *economies* in which humans are motivated to work in order to provide the means for supporting consumption. Thus, people in a purely production-oriented society cannot imagine giving money to others (if they have it) for goods and services or going shopping for one's necessities at a store for such items that are produced by many others, none of which are personally known. These people would say, "You grow what you eat, you make what you wear, you build what you live in, you treat your own maladies, and you teach your children the necessary knowledge for succeeding in life as you know it." People in a consumer-oriented society—the primary focus of this book—cannot imagine doing all those things themselves instead of buying them. They would consider it *primitive*—the term we often use to describe the consumer behavior of people living in undeveloped societies.

Humans are also inherently motivated to pass on their consumer skills and knowledge to their offspring—as shown in this and previous chapters. Such child rearing is so basic that it is built into virtually every aspect of a developed society, along with the culturally approved products to satisfy specific needs. Newborns in a developed society must learn patterns of consumer behavior necessary to obtain objects to satisfy needs. This practice, as we have shown, begins at birth since it is so fundamental to human nature. Of course, the children's inability to perform as purchasers in the consumer role during the first several years of life places the responsibility on parents to do the purchasing for them. And they do, while the infants develop cognitively and physically in order to gain the equipment necessary to be complete consumers. Parents buy all the commercial objects they deem necessary for their children's development and have many of them ready for them when they are born. Many more are forthcoming as children's needs and wants change. Further, parents teach their children how to perform in a commercial environment—how to consume the objects and express their wants for more.

Concurrently, children learn consumer behavior patterns on their own through observation (discovery) and participation (trying out objects through imitation or actual use). Children learn not only through observation of parents but also through observation of friends and public role models as they are encountered. Thus, children's performance in the consumer role at any point in time is a result of a joint effort of parents and children—one eager to teach consumer behavior patterns and one eager to learn them. And we can predict with certainty that when the children grow up and marry, they will introduce their newborns to the consumer role and its elements in much the same manner as their parents did. Life in the United States is perpetual consumer behavior.

When we step back and look at child rearing in a developed society such as the United States specifically, it is clear that parents are driven to convert their children into competent consumers. It is clear, too, that their children are driven to learn to be consumers and, in fact, learn to be consumers from anyone. Why? What is the force that produces 10,000 tekrams a day by a competent child consumer and at least that many by her parents? Is it survival? Is it a cultural requirement? Or, as often suggested by consumer protectionists, is it a result of marketers making children and parents want and buy things? Or, alternatively, is it a joint effort of parents teaching children how to be consumers and marketers taking over parenting and making the children buy specific things? And bear in mind, seeking to be consumers is not the vision of a few, but of every child born in the United States. That is why we are often called a *mass market* by marketers.

It does appear that the root cause of consumer behavior is something that lies inside each child and that comes with his wiring since it starts at birth. Parents are already practicing consumers when their children arrive, and they use their consumer skills and knowledge to prepare a consumer environment for their new arrivals. It appears that the consumer environment—room, bed, food, clothing, music, play items, controlled temperature—is instinctively constructed by the parents much as nests are constructed by parenting birds. Then, beginning the first day of life, infants are shown how to utilize the environment—where to sleep, what to wear, what to eat, what to play with—and this consumer education continues and expands rapidly. As soon as practical—at two or three months—parents begin introducing their newborn to the marketplace where objects in his current environment were obtained. It is almost as if the parents are saying to their babies that this is where all your environmental objects come from, and you must eventually learn to replace them and embellish them on your own through utilization of the marketplace. Thus, parents as practicing consumers seek to sculpt their newborns into their likeness. It is the nature of people of all ages in a developed society; that is, each has a *consumer character* that is passed on from generation to generation.

This thing inside people that drives them to perform in the consumer role and to help others perform in the consumer role has usually been explained as a need, motive, drive, or propensity by psychologists. In the late 1930s, Henry Murray (1938) and his colleagues at the Harvard Psychological Clinic explained such behavior as we are describing here as caused by needs and particularly the acquisition need. The *acquisition need* was defined as the need "to gain possessions and property, to grasp, snatch or steal things, to bargain or gamble, to work for money or goods" (Murray, 1938, p. 80). Murray further said that the acquisition need is one of 20 to 30 psychogenic needs that are learned in order to satisfy a person's dozen or so viscerogenic (bodily) needs with which he is born. The key to understanding why people want and buy certain products—from Murray's theoretical perspective—is in the concept of *need fusion*, that is, the joining together of two or more psychogenic needs that are satisfied by one act. For example, a mom buys (acquisition need) a signature brand of clothing for her two-year-old to protect the child and also to impress others, what Murray would call the *exhibition need*. The same child asks mom (acquisition need) for a Spiderman shirt to be liked by a friend at daycare who wears that shirt, what Murray would say is satisfying the *affiliation need*— the need to have cooperative relationships with others—as well as the exhibition need. In both cases the clothing is also intended to provide warmth (viscerogenic need). Murray would also say that the child probably learned that particular fusion behavior from parents. He would also predict that such a pattern of consumer behavior would be continued throughout the child's life, that it would characterize the person the child becomes. Thus, whatever consistent behavior patterns in satisfying needs that are demonstrated by a person are what Murray and a number of other psychologists would call the person's *personality*—a term that we have avoided throughout this book because of its elusive nature.

While the notion of needs as a basic explanation of human behavior, including consumer behavior, has persisted since Murray's time, it often has been challenged much like any other psychological theory that utilizes a hypothetical concept. Today, with many more analytical tools, there is an increasing tendency to explain human behavior patterns with more scientific documentation—to utilize explanations that you can hold in your hand, so to speak, rather than just in your faith. Much human behavior, and thus consumer behavior, today is being explained by a relatively new field of study called *behavioral genetics*. The behavioral geneticists (BGs) in this field have backgrounds in genetics, molecular biology, neuroscience, psychology, and psychiatry. This discipline attempts to delineate behavior patterns that are inherited through *genes* as compared to the behavior that results from the environment in which children are reared—often simplified as *nurture versus nature*. To explain much human behavior, BGs hold to the theory that genes have a direct influence on people's personality, or character, which, in turn, has a direct influence on their behavior. Thus, BGs would say personality characterizes their behavior. Genes are the basic units of genetic information that are composed of sequences of DNA (deoxyribonucleic acid) molecules that ". . . determine every cell in the body and how it will function" (Feldman, 2000, p. 48). One of the noted BGs, Dean Hamer, who is Chief of Gene Structure and Regulation in the Laboratory of Biochemistry at the National Cancer Institute, said it this way:

> Your thoughts, fears, hopes, reactions, behaviors, and dreams all come from your core personality. . . . [M]any core personality traits are inherited at birth, and many of the differences between individual personality styles are the result of differences in genes. (Hamer and Copeland, 1999, p. 6)

The notion that we inherit our physical characteristics such as blue eyes, red hair, or long legs has been around forever, and thus we often hear remarks about babies looking just like their father or their mother. In addition to physical features, behavior patterns of children once they reach toddlerhood and beyond also may be noted as being like those of their father or mother. Today, scientists who study genes explain and confirm such observations. Thus, BGs see parents passing on their genes to their kids, those genes producing personality traits in the kids, and the total personality producing consistent patterns of behavior in the kids throughout their lives.

The notion of gene-directed behavior does not violate the basic premise of this book—that is, that behavior is a function of the person and the environment: B = f(P, E). In fact, this notion fits right in since genes are a fundamental element of the person (P) that directs the cognitive and physical development of the person. Also, BGs recognize that the environment (E) of the child starting at birth can foster or can deter inherited proclivities and that often the behavior patterns a child demonstrates are almost solely due to the environment. For example, as noted in previous chapters, parents provide practically the entire environment of infants and toddlers, and in one extreme this may be an impoverished environment devoid of little stimulation. Also, parenting styles can buffer the expression of gene-directed behavior through permissiveness and strictness. As also noted throughout the book, today's parents tend to be very permissive, thus permitting the genes to function almost undeterred in designing and directing behavior patterns. Moreover, we have noted that children learn a lot of consumer behavior patterns on their own, and we might expect that what they learn is predetermined to a great extent by their genes.

Some of the most revealing studies on gene-directed behavior can be found in the studies of twins. We have all noticed how parents of twins dress both exactly alike in colors and styles, even give them similar names such as Mary and Cary, and buy them the same item such as a bicycle or ice cream bar. Thus, we would observe that the consumer behavior of each twin is very much alike. But what if the twins were not raised by the same parents and were in fact raised by parents who differ greatly in their lifestyles? This is often the case when twins are put up for adoption at birth and placed in separate homes. Now, what if the behavioral patterns of these separated twins were studied and many of their consumer behavior patterns were found similar? What would we say then? These are the kinds of questions being answered by those who study twins, and particularly by the Minnesota Study of Twins Reared Apart at the University of Minnesota that was begun in 1979 (e.g., Bouchard et al., 1990). Twins who participate in the Minnesota study are given 50 or more hours of medical and psychological assessments that look in detail at personality, occupational interests, rearing environments, life history, lifestyles, and contents of households. So, consumer behavior patterns make up an important part of the characteristics of twins who are studied. (Remember, though, the alert that was presented in other parts of the book: Psychologists rarely use the term *consumer behavior* or claim that they study consumer behavior, and that is the case in these twin studies.)

Consider a few of the findings regarding consumer behavior of identical twins reared apart from one another:

> Two identical twin girls were reared apart and met for the first time in their late 30s at the Minnesota twin study. "The manicured hands of each bore seven rings . . . each wore two bracelets on one wrist and a watch and a bracelet on the other . . ." (Identical Twins Reared Apart, 1980, p. 1323).

> Two identical twin boys reared apart who were brought together in the Minnesota twin study in their late 30s also showed similar consumer behavior patterns. "Both vacationed in Florida, both drove Chevrolets . . . both had dogs named Toy . . . and both had almost identical drinking and smoking patterns . . .—both smoked Salem cigarettes and drank Miller Lite beer" (Identical Twins Reared Apart, 1980, p. 1323; Hamer and Copeland, 1999, p. 22).

> Two identical twin boys reared apart in two different countries and studied at age 47 showed the following similarities in consumer behavior. "Both were wearing wire-rimmed glasses and mustaches, both sported two-pocket shirts and epaulets . . . both like spicy foods and sweet liqueurs . . . both flush the toilet before using it . . . store rubber bands on their wrists, read magazines from back to front, dip buttered toast in their coffee . . ." (Identical Twins Reared Apart, 1980, p. 1324).

Regarding these and other behavioral findings of identical twins reared apart, one of the principal investigators concluded, ". . . what we see is pretty much the same as in twins brought up together" (Identical Twins Reared Apart, 1980, p. 1324). That is, identical twins who share exactly the same genetic inheritance behave pretty much alike regardless of environment. Hamer and Copeland (1998, p. 301) concluded that "[v]irtually every aspect of how we act and feel that has been studied in twins shows genetic influence . . ." and that genes play a "decisive role in behavior." Thus, it is not a stretch at all to suggest that genes also play a decisive role in some consumer behavior of people in a developed society. Following the theory of behavioral genetics, we might expect that various combinations of genes produce various combinations of personality traits, which, in turn, produce various combinations of consumer behavior patterns. Contrarily, we might expect that this genetic influence posited to function in developed societies does not exist in undeveloped societies. China is still two-thirds rural, and among these 800 million rural people, my observations show that there is a majority mass that does not seek to perform in the consumer role, views it as confusing and capricious, and generally avoids it. It would be easy to argue the chicken-and-egg model and suggest that these people do not act as consumers because marketers do not seek them out with products and services. And marketers would say, as they have to me, that there is no need to seek out these people as customers; they have little or no money to spend and what they do have is mostly used in production necessities. (For an analysis of consumer behavior of rural and urban China, see Chan and McNeal, 2006.) Interestingly, this same discussion could have taken place in the United States in the early 1700s when most of the country was rural. Also, in deep rural China, as in the early rural United States, there is a lack of infrastructure—electric power, water pressure—to facilitate much consumer behavior. Finally, it should be noted that a society's philosophy may foster or discourage a consumer orientation. Moreover, a society's philosophy may have a genetic origin according to Jerome Kagan and his colleagues (Kagan, Arcus, and Snidman, 1993), who speculated that a genetically determined underlying temperament of a given society will predispose its people to a certain way of thinking.

Thus, it seems undeniable that many consumer behavior patterns are a result of genetic forces. Perhaps over the history of our country, a consumer gene—a C-gene—or something like it has evolved just as other genes have evolved and now are evolving in China. We are, after all, ". . . the product of generations of evolution, countless bits of information collected over millions of years, focused, narrowed, and refined . . ." (Hamer and Copeland, 1998, p. 7). Parents (and their parents) who are driven by the C-gene pass not only this gene on to their children but also many consumer behavior patterns that it has fostered and stored. Children learn many of these behavior patterns on their own through people and objects, and this is possible only because of predetermined networks that mature in their minds. These behavior patterns—tekrams—give direction to body and mind development that, in turn, makes more tekrams possible. Marketers, in turn, respond to this consumer drive by providing products and services to match the tekrams performed by both parents and children. (We will talk about this issue more in the next chapter.) Thus, as parents give their children sweets to please them, calm them, reward them, and children seek out more of them, marketers, through their research, define this behavior in terms of wants and needs and come up with endless variations of sweets to satisfy them. On the other hand, marketers do not respond this way to people in undeveloped societies with a production orientation.

We have noted several times that consumer behavior in the United States occurs 24 hours a day, 7 days a week, in all dimensions (360) of life. In fact, very little behavior occurs that could not be classified as consumer behavior, suggesting that the C-gene is a dominant gene that makes the consumer role the dominant role, as illustrated in Chapter 1. This C-gene directs much of our behavior in all social roles—student, worker, lover, friend, and so on. Its results are not all positive, depending on the personality characteristics of a person. It may produce crimes against others, such as robbery, bullying, and cheating, and may restructure one's personality so that he becomes addicted to some consumer behaviors such as gambling, narcotic use, and overeating—behaviors less likely to be found in an undeveloped society. The C-gene serves and directs physiological needs such as food, air, water, sex, and health as well as the many psychological needs such as achievement, aggression, and affiliation. So, when parents tell their children, "All you ever do is want, want, want," the children may logically respond with, "Of course, that's my heritage talking."

PARENTS MAKE CHILDREN RICH IN MARKET POTENTIAL

If one reads between the lines of what has been said here and in preceding chapters about children's consumer development, it should be apparent that parents create much market potential among their children. In fact, by the time children reach 100 months, they possess more market potential than their parents! How is this possible? Starting as soon as their babies are ready, parents let them choose the products from which they get the most satisfaction. At first, these choices are in the form of body language, but by the time children are a year old, they are also in the form of spoken language. The children's choices are made not only at home, but also in the marketplace, where parents take them starting around the time they can express their wants through body language. Thus, children become an *influence market* determining much of what parents buy for them and for the household in general. The amount of influence grows rapidly as children learn how to talk and express their vocabulary of products and brands. When children reach age two, estimates of their power over parents suggest that they directly and indirectly influence around 45–47 percent of routine purchases of their households (McNeal, 1999). How much is this in dollars? The figure is a moving target that has been growing at a rate of around 10–15 percent a year since the early 1990s. Marketers know they can go to government statistics on household spending and calculate these figures for all spending and for specific spending. For specific industries such as furniture or fast foods, there are also estimates by the industry trade associations and by many marketing organizations that are involved in the kids market, such as advertising agencies and marketing consulting firms. Usually, the estimates are divided into direct and indirect influence, mainly for the benefit of marketing strategies targeted at family members. *Direct influence* consists of requests made to parents—what the kids ask for, hint for, and demand. It may also include requests made to other household members such as grandparents in the case of China (McNeal and Yeh, 1997, 2003). *Indirect influence* is essentially the likes and dislikes of children represented in the minds of their parents in what earlier was termed the *evokked set*. The evokked set consists of the products and brands that children have asked for before and parents remember; the extra *k* in the spelling of *evoked set* stands for *kids*. It allows the parents to buy what their children prefer without actually shopping with the children. Dollar-wise, it is at least as big of a figure as direct influence, probably bigger.

As children become older and get more marketplace experience, they attempt to buy things on their own—stage four of consumer development. By the time they reach 100 months, they are regularly purchasing items for themselves—stage five. Concurrently, parents provide most of the money to make these purchases possible through handouts, gifts, and payment for work around the household. Thus, children as buyers become a *primary market* for such items as confections, soft drinks, and play items. Later, by the time they enter middle school, they are a major primary market for clothing, sporting goods, and entertainment. The amount of their own money that they spend is substantial to some industries. Some clothing stores, for instance, target children of a certain age and gender. As primary markets, children are targeted with marketing strategies to attract their spending—just as they are as direct influence markets.

Finally, beginning in childhood, children represent a *future market* for *all* consumer goods and services. Starting at least by the time children begin making their own purchases, they are viewed as future purchasers of certain commercial products—soft drinks, for example. Thus, parents through training, modeling, and encouragement have blessed their children with enormous market potential—as an influence market, a primary market, and a future market. In total, this is more market potential than that of their parents since, in addition to being primary and influence markets, the children are future markets that have all of their purchases ahead of them—more purchases than those of their parents. While this description may sound a bit airy-fairy, believe me, it is not to a fast-food chain, for instance, that estimates that if it can win over a four-year-old, it probably will get $50,000 in business from that one child over his or her lifetime. This type of marketing is called *growing customers* and many industries practice it in one form or another. And bear in mind there are around 4 million children in the United States entering the consumer market each year and 10 times that many worldwide.

The net result of parents' providing their children with so much market potential is that millions of marketers are trying to reach them, target them, sell to them, and convince them to want their products. And whether parents realize it or not, they help marketers in these efforts. Parents introduce the marketers' brands to their children before they can read or speak and show them how to utilize them. Parents take their children directly to the marketers on a regular basis while they are still babies and show them how to perform in the marketplace. And, parents invite marketers into their children's homes through TV, other media such as magazines and the Internet, packaging, and branded products, and show their children how to use these items. Then most parents turn over their children to preschools and schools that link the children with more marketers. So, in sum, parents impart in their children more market potential than they, the parents, have, show the children how to express it, and then bring marketers and their children together to make it easy for the marketers to extract this market potential.

DISCUSSION

It is logical to question where and from whom children learn consumer behavior patterns. And it is easy to speculate about the "pounds and ounces" of influence on children consumers by parents, peers, schools, and marketers in their many forms. The plain fact of the matter is that it is virtually impossible to observe a specific tekram by a child and conclude where she learned it. Situations change so much in the environment of children that what might have been a correct assumption last year is incorrect this year. Family life for children is changing, school life for them is changing, and marketing's role in children's consumer life is constantly on the move. However, the research that forms the basis for much of what is said in this book is ongoing and therefore makes a few generalizations possible.

From children's birth to the walking and talking stage, their CB is pretty much in the hands of their households. This means that most of children's tekrams—certainly most of their primary tekrams—are a result of parental teaching/modeling. For example, identifying products by brand name, which begins around 18 months, is a primary tekram that is learned from parents and, in the case of China, also from grandparents. Secondary tekrams such as learning the brand name of a specific product like a toy or a cereal also are a function of parents at this age but may result from TV programming and advertising, packaging, and store visits. Likewise, the primary tekram of viewing the marketplace as a source of satisfying objects starts with parents when children are at the walking/talking stage, while secondary tekrams at this time of identifying certain products with certain retail outlets is a function of parents as well as the specific retail outlets.

However, once the parents allow more marketing into the household through more media, products, and packages, and once they cede the children's socialization to others such as preschools and the social and marketing objects found at preschools, they share the teaching of tekrams to their children with others such as peers, teachers, and marketers. So, starting when children are around age two to three, the influences on their consumer behavior patterns widen and expand beyond that of the their households. Part of the consumer influence at this age is a function of the children who make choices about information sources such as peers and in-school marketing. Thus, in addition to consumption messages coming in to the children, such as those directed at them by marketers, children are also reaching out to other sources for information besides parents. At this point in time, parents can be judged only as a major influence on their children's consumer behavior—a guesstimate of 50 percent parents, 50 percent others, such as peers, teachers, and marketers. By the time the children enter elementary school, parents are still very influential in their children's consumer lives through teaching purchase behavior and its elements. But other influences are also very great and, in total, are likely to be more than that of parents who are quickly yielding their schoolkids' learning to many others. From this point on, children obtain more of their consumer behavior patterns outside their household instead of inside.

REFERENCES

Associated Press. (2006, April 10). Daily PE class a remnant of the past? Schools struggle to provide exercise programs as child obesity grows. Retrieved from www.msnbc.msn.com/id/12255239

Bouchard Jr., T. J., D. T. Lykken, M. McGue, N. L. Segal, and A. Tellegen. (1990, October 12). Sources of human psychological difference: The Minnesota study of twins reared apart. *Science*, 223–228.

Bronfenbrenner, U. (1973). *Two Worlds of Childhood: U.S. and U.S.S.R.* New York: Pocketbooks.

Chan, K., and J. U. McNeal. (2006). Children and media in China: An urban-rural comparison. *Journal of Consumer Marketing*, 23(3), 77–86.

Dalton, M. A., A. M. Bernhardt, J. J. Gibson, J. D. Sargent, M. L. Beach, A. M. Adachi-Mejia, L. T. Titus-Ernstoff, and T. F. Heatherton. (2005). Use of cigarettes and alcohol by preschoolers while role-playing as adults. *Archives of Pediatrics and Adolescent Medicine*, 159, 854–859.

Department of Health and Human Services. (2006). *The health consequences of involuntary exposure to tobacco smoke: A report of the Surgeon General.* Washington, DC.

Feldman, R. S. (2000). *Development across the Life Span* (2nd ed.). Upper Saddle River, NJ: Prentice Hall.

Grossman, J. (2003, November 24). The perils of fat acceptance. *National Review*, 34–38.

Hamer, D., and P. Copeland. (1999). *Living with Our Genes.* New York: Anchor Books.

Hannaford, C. (2005). *Smart Moves: Why Learning Is Not All in Your Head.* Salt Lake City, UT: Great River Books.

Harris, J. R. (1999). *The Nurture Assumption: Why Children Turn Out the Way They Do.* New York: Touchstone.

Hellmich, N. (2003, January 6). If parents lighten up, then so will the kids. *USA Today*, p. 6D.

Identical Twins Reared Apart. (1980, March 21). *Science, 207*, 1323–1327.

Kagan, J., D. Arcus, and N. Snidman. (1993). The idea of temperament: Where do we go from here? In R. Plomin and G. E. McClearn (eds.), *Nature, Nurture, and Psychology* (pp. 197–210). Washington, DC: American Psychological Association.

Laliberte, R. (2003, September). The big issue. *Parents*, 141–144, 278.

McNeal, J. U. (1987). *Children as Consumers: Insights and Implications.* Lexington, MA: D. C. Heath and Company.

McNeal, J. U. (1999). *The Kids Market: Myth and Realities.* Ithaca, NY: Paramount Market Publishers.

McNeal, J. U., and C. H. Yeh. (1997). Development of consumer behavior patterns among Chinese children. *Journal of Consumer Marketing, 14*(1), 45–59.

McNeal, J. U., and C. H. Yeh. (2003). Consumer behavior of Chinese children: 1995–2002. *Journal of Consumer Marketing, 20*(6), 542–554.

Murray, H. A. (1938). *Explorations in Personality.* New York: Oxford University Press.

Seerdula, M. K., D. Ivery, R. J. Coates, D. S. Freedman, D. F. Williamson, and T. Byers. (1993). Do obese children become obese adults? A review of the literature. *Preventive Medicine, 22*, 167–177.

Tyre, P., J. Scelfo, and B. Kantrowitz. (2005, May). Just say no. *Reader's Digest*, 36A–36F.

Whiting, B. B., and J. W. M. Whiting. (1975). *Children of Six Cultures: A Psycho-Cultural Analysis.* Cambridge, MA: Harvard University Press.

12

ROLE OF MARKETING IN CONSUMER DEVELOPMENT

One Family's Attempts to Protect Its Children from Marketing Messages

Two one-hour interviews were conducted with a Houston, Texas, family to determine the nature and extent of the influence of its children on household purchases. A research firm chose the family in a cluster sample of households and requested a confidential interview with its members about their "daily consumer behavior." The family lived in a modest four-bedroom home where it had resided for eight years. Both husband and wife were educated; Mr. Soper held a master's degree in aerospace engineering, and Mrs. Soper held an MBA. Mr. Soper worked at a major oil refinery. Mrs. Soper had held "a good-paying job" at the same firm for which her husband worked but elected to be a homemaker after their first child was born. During the first interview held in the home, it was discovered that Mr. and Mrs. Soper believed that they should try to protect their three children—three girls ages 4, 5, and 6—Sarah, Mary, and Ruth, respectively—from marketing communications and particularly advertising messages because, according to Mrs. Soper, "It [advertising] often teaches kids the wrong values." A second interview was requested to discuss the ways in which they try to protect their children from advertising messages. The interviewer agreed to donate $25 for each interview to the Soper's favorite charity. What follows are excerpts from the second interviewer-respondent dialogue.

Interviewer: *The other night you told me that you did not own a television set. Is that correct?*

Mrs. Soper: *No, that's not correct. We own a television set, in fact two, but shortly after our second girl, Mary, was born, we decided to unhook it. So, technically we still have two sets, but none is hooked up. We use them to watch movies sometimes.*

Interviewer: *Do you remember when you decided to disconnect the TV and what prompted you to do it?*

Mrs. Soper: Sure. That was the summer of 97, Ruth was a year old or so and Mary was around three months old. I sometimes watched cartoons with Ruth and Mary, which I had developed a habit of doing with Ruth. It was intended to keep them laughing. But I kept seeing those commercials for all the sugared products, you know, like cereal, cookies, and candy, and how much fun they supposedly were for kids to eat, and I just suddenly realized that that wasn't good information for the babies to be hearing. As you know, they use lovable cartoon characters to sell all that stuff to the kids—and Ruth just loved watching them. So I knew it was soaking in, even at that early age. As a matter of fact, I think she liked the ads as much as the cartoons, probably because they usually were for foods. So, one day I just said, "That's it."

Interviewer: Did you agree with your wife's decision to unhook the TV, Mr. Soper?

Mr. Soper: Yes, indeed. In fact I really didn't care for the TV. I seldom watched it except for an occasional ballgame. And I agreed that it wasn't good for the kids.

Mrs. Soper: As a matter of fact, we talked it over one night, and the next day I called the cable company and told them to come out and disconnect it. We both agreed we didn't need it, and while the girls had fun watching it, it was bad for them.

Interviewer: Let me ask you both to explain what you think is wrong with your children watching television.

Mr. Soper: The main thing is it is trying to sell the kids stuff that is bad for them including bad ideas and bad values. It's as simple as that.

Interviewer: By sell, you mean the advertising?

Mr. Soper: Sure, advertising, but all TV—the news, movies, cartoons. Don't get me wrong. Some of the toys and things they advertise would probably please the girls, but we don't need advertisements to tell us what toys the kids like or should have. We can decide that ourselves. They're just companies with products they have to sell, and they will do anything and say anything to sell them—to sell them to little kids.

Mrs. Soper: It's mainly the sweets they push and push. It's just empty calories that taste good. I bake cookies; Ruth even pitches in and helps me since she wants to learn to cook. But we don't eat sugared cereal like they shout about or any of that other junk food. Advertisers seem determined to make the children unhealthy, but not mine, not if I can help it.

Interviewer: When you watched TV with your children, did you ever watch commercial-free TV with the children?

Mrs. Soper: Come on. There's no such thing. Those programs on public television that teach the kids the alphabet and so forth are mostly just one long ad for toys. You may call them commercial-free, but they're not; they're selling the kids something every minute.

Interviewer: In what ways does commercial-free television sell?

Mrs. Soper: All the cute characters in the programs are really just kids' products! Go into any toy store, and you can see shelves full of them.

Interviewer: I see. That's very interesting. Any other thoughts?

Mrs. Soper: Have you read the new book, Saving Childhood, by the Medveds?

Interviewer: No, I haven't.

Mrs. Soper: If you are interested in researching children's consumption, you should read that. It pretty well sums up our views about the dangers for our children from the TV.

Interviewer: You mentioned, Mrs. Soper, that you watch movies on your TV. What kind of movies?

Mrs. Soper: We have a good collection of old movies that John [husband] and I sometimes watch, and we have a collection of probably all the Walt Disney movies that we show to the kids. And, yes, before you say it, I know those movies are just ads for Disney dolls and things, but they are ones we choose just as we choose the toys the kids get.

Interviewer: I'm curious. Do you buy any Disney items for your girls?

Mrs. Soper: We have. We went to Disney Land and we bought each of the kids a doll they picked out. And we will probably buy them Disney movies from time to time.

Interviewer: Do you take the children to movie theaters to see some of the children's movies with them?

Mrs. Soper: No, those movie houses try to sell the children everything including bad health and bad movies. We would prefer to buy the movies the girls want to see and have them here at home. It's a much better environment for them than the typical movie house. And they like to watch them again and again. And I like to watch them with them.

Mr. Soper: You might be interested to know that we don't have any Internet hookup here at our home for the same reason we don't have a TV hookup. We don't want to link our kids to trash.

INTRODUCTION

In the preceding chapter, we summarized the role of parents in children's consumer development. In this chapter, we will look at *marketers'* role in children's consumer development. The term *marketers* is used as a generality for all organizations that attempt to sell products, services, people, and ideas to children and their parents and includes for-profit manufacturers, retailers, packagers, promoters, and advertisers as well as not-for-profit organizations such as governments, schools, churches, and charities. The two together—parents and marketers—appear to constitute the majority of the sources of consumer behavior patterns that children learn in early childhood (0–100 months).

While business and economic textbooks praise modern marketing for providing for the needs of all consumers including children, we often hear and read that marketers are responsible for a great deal of undesirable consumer behavior among children that harms the children and their societies in which they live. For example, according to press reports over the past decade or two, fast-food restaurants cause children to eat too many fattening foods; TV advertising causes children to want things that are not good for them, to nag their parents for these things, and to encourage sedentary behavior among children; many marketing messages are directed to children without the children's (or parents') awareness of them through product placement in children's movies, video games, and TV programming; many harmful products are marketed to children, including overly fattening, highly sugared, heavily salted foods and beverages, and dangerous tobacco and alcohol; and media, in general, partner with those who deliver socially undesirable products and services to children.

However, as observed in the preceding chapter, both parents and marketers often are jointly involved in influencing children's consumer behavior. For instance, parents bring marketers' products and brands, along with the media presentation of them, into the nursery in the very early life of their children, and it is the parents who introduce their children to retailers—including fast-food restaurants—that may target them with undesirable products and services. Moreover, parents and marketers are often jointly responsible for children's learning of consumer behavior through a third party, for instance, the school, church, and children's organizations such as athletic teams and scouting where parents take their children and marketers come to greet them with messages about their offering. So, it is sometimes difficult to describe marketing influences on children without noting the active participation of caretakers. Even marketers' use of mass media to influence children usually has at least tacit approval if not direct involvement of parents and other adults—unless parents such as the Sopers take action to limit mass media from the presence of children.

From the standpoint of trust, parents generally have a good reputation in society for being trustworthy teachers of children's consumer behavior, whereas marketers generally have an untrustworthy reputation as teachers of children's consumer behavior. Probably both are stereotypical to a great extent rather than actual. We have already shown in the preceding chapter that parents introduce their children to some bad consumer behavior patterns. Marketers do, too, but offer many good products and services along with the bad ones. Neither party seems fully trustworthy to direct children's consumer development.

WHY DO MARKETERS TARGET CHILDREN AS CONSUMERS?

As mentioned, we hear and read a great deal about marketers' efforts among children as consumers. There surely is not a consumer goods industry that does not target children, and probably a majority of companies in each of the industries aims some kind of marketing efforts at kids—target marketing always begets competition. Since marketers ordinarily are charged with making money or some kind of gain for their organizations, in some manner their targeting of children must have a significant payoff in order to be justified. It thus makes sense to ask why so many marketers develop strategies and tactics that target children as consumers.

Two answers to this question were already mentioned in Chapters 1 and 11. First, *children consume products and services 24/7/360*; that is, they perform in the consumer role constantly from the day they are born. Each tekram—each consumer act—performed by children makes them a potential market for many businesses. For example, a four-year-old who takes a bath—with or without parental help—is viewed as a member of the bath soap market, the water toy market, the shampoo market, the bath towel market, the bathroom rug market, and the underclothing market—to name a few. And you can bet that there are at least 10 marketers in each of these industries who define the child as a member of their markets and target specific marketing efforts—advertising, branding, product development, packaging, retailing, displaying, sales promotion, publicity, public relations, pricing—at him. Here's one more example just to make my point. When this same child eats a bowl of cereal in the morning in front of the TV, he is viewed as a member of the ready-to-eat cereal market, sure, but also the milk market, the sugar market, the fruit market, the cereal bowl market, the spoon market, the TV viewing market, the TV program market, and the furniture market. Now, if you think about the many toys played with during the day, the media attended to, the bedroom items used, the clothing items worn, the bicycle rode, the car in which he rides to school and to the marketplace, and of course, the many other foods eaten as snacks, lunch, and dinner, one can begin to understand why this one child is targeted by hundreds if not thousands of product marketers—and advertising agencies, packaging designers, public relations firms, and marketing research groups. This child is a target for marketing 24 hours a day, 7 days a week, in every activity he performs—sleeping; eating; playing; going to school; helping mom with household chores; going to the marketplace, church, the baseball game, the little league meeting; and visiting with the next-door-neighbor's kid. Thus, consumer behavior 24/7/360 begets 24/7/360 marketing.

What we have been describing so far are markets based on children's use of products designed and produced primarily for them. But children are also a target of marketing efforts for products they use very little or none at all but will use later in life. Thus, the second reason children are targeted by so many marketers is that in total *they have more market potential than any other demographic group*—more than teens, more than adults, more than their parents. The explanation for this fact is that all children are viewed by marketers as three markets in one (McNeal, 1991, 1998). They are a *primary market,* starting as early as age 4, that buys and consumes a large number of products designed particularly for them (and their budget)—for instance, snack foods, soft drinks, bubble gum, candy, toys, movies, and some clothing items. Children ages 4–12 spent somewhere around $40 billion of their own money on such items in 2005. Additionally, children constitute an *influence market* for products and services ranging from autos to zoos. These are all the products that they cannot afford to buy themselves but suggest to parents, request from parents, or even demand from parents. Parents and other caretakers purchase these products for children's use—for example, TVs, computers, bedroom furnishings, shoes, apparel, many foods and beverages—and for general household use—for example, furniture, cars, boats, vacations. Children become an influence market very early in life when they signal to mom that they like something by cooing, by ceasing their crying, by shaking their body, and when they develop language ability, asking for certain items. In this sense, kids ages 2–14 are a direct influence market who caused parents to spend at least $350 billion in 2005. They are also an indirect influence market in the sense that moms have registered in their minds—in their evokked sets—what their kids have asked for before and consider these items (usually brands of items) when they make purchases for their children. Indirect influence accounted for another $350 billion or more in 2005. (See McNeal, 1992 and 1999, for a more detailed explanation of these expenditures.) Marketers know children of certain ages request a wide range of products and services and therefore target both kids and parents with messages about these items. Additionally, children are a *future market* for all goods and services, for many goods and services that they do not yet use but will, and therefore are targeted today as tomorrow's consumers. For example, preschoolers are targeted as future consumers by soft drink companies, elementary school children are targeted by computer manufacturers, and tweens are targeted by automobile makers and stock brokerage firms. And children logically have more future purchases ahead of them than anyone, than teens or adults. So, altogether—as primary, influence, and future markets—children have more market potential than any other demographic, and astute marketers—not all marketers—know this and target

PHOTO 12-1   Teens (in their school uniforms) line up at a Beijing McDonald's after school. In interviews with middle school and high school children in China, 100% said they had been eating at McDonald's since they were little children—just as McDonald's planned it in its customer growing strategy.

them early in life. Why do you think soft drink logos are on babies' bibs, cereal brands are in their books, and toothpaste brands are on their bulletin boards at school? This marketing is called *growing customers* (see Photo 12-1). Think about it from a marketer's standpoint. Where does a company get new customers? After some successes and failures, most soon figure out that there are only two sources. Either a company switches them from competitors, or it grows them from childhood. And if a business firm— or a school, church, or charity—hopes to survive and expand, it targets kids of all ages as primary, influence, and/or future consumers. When you combine these two basic reasons for targeting children as consumers—they are consumers 24/7/360 and they are three markets in one—you get millions of marketers targeting children of all ages worldwide, day and night, everywhere they go, in everything they do.

MARKETERS' PARTICIPATION IN CHILDREN'S CONSUMER DEVELOPMENT

For two very, very important reasons, then, marketers target kids as consumers beginning in the birthing center and throughout childhood and adolescence. In a variety of ways, a variety of marketers are involved in all the consumer development of children, but principally as a source of the commercial objects that populate the children's environment. (Bear in mind that many services marketers, such as television and radio broadcasters, and many nonprofit marketers, such as churches and charities, also target children of all ages as consumers, and they are subsumed here under the general title of *marketer*.) As the children's environment expands through the stages of consumer development, marketing participation in consumer development expands with it.

Stage One: Observation (0–6 Months)

When newborns arrive home from the hospital or birthing center, marketers are already there greeting them with a dazzling array of their products and services courtesy of parents and other caretakers. Thus, children are born into a mostly commercialized physical environment in which they are expected to quickly learn to function as consumers. Most of the elements of the physical environment, aside perhaps from the structure itself, can be recognized by the brands that are attached to most of them—brands that the children will likely prefer and be able to articulate within 24 months or less. They include brands of stuffed toys, diapers, facial tissue, lotions, bedding, and transitional foods. This is probably the smallest number of commercial products that will ever surround the children, and that number will grow faster than the children thanks to parents and grandparents who are targeted by marketers in every medium that reaches new parents—parenting magazines, books, email, direct mail, retail displays, packaging—on adult products as well as children's products—to name the most important ones. For instance, the parenting magazines that moms turn to for guidance in child rearing are principally sales messages in the form of publicity and advertising for marketers' products and services—including, of course, those of the magazines.

During approximately the infants' first two months, most of their consumer behavior patterns consist mainly of approach and avoidance reflexes. But apparently these tekrams produce some kind of memory so that by the end of two months the infants are routinely seeking out those items that please them through sensorimotor activities such as sucking, twisting, and grunting. Then, between the ages of two and six months, the babies take on an exploratory character in which they seek contact with many more objects in the environment and begin to make choices among them. Parents respond to the children's consumer behavior by providing more of what is liked, less of what is not liked. Thus, marketers' products such as stuffed toys and formula that are first made available to the children through the parents are now claimed by the children through expressed preferences.

Somewhere between the age of two and six months, children are taken to the marketplace by parents—in China and other Asian countries by grandparents, also—where they are introduced to actual marketers with whom they sensorially interact for the first time. During these marketplace visits, parents buy many things for their children, but the children are mainly aware of the sweet things and play things purchased. Soon the young consumers establish a perceptual link between these pleasure-giving items and the marketplace. Or said another way, producers of goods establish channel of distribution links to new consumers—from producer to retailer to parents to children. Thus, a relationship between the children and marketers begins that will last a lifetime. At about this same time parents introduce their children to television programming—an electronic marketplace—and another marketing-child consumer relationship is established. For example, the children may show liking for a program—including "commercial-free" programs, which, as observed by Mrs. Soper in the chapter introduction, are not really free of commercials. These programs are "selling the kids something," as they usually are built around one or more cartoon characters that may also be brands for many products that the children may see and want in the marketplace. Thus, during the infants' first six months of life, many marketers and most newborns form relationships—even if some parents such as the Sopers try to prevent it.

Stage Two: Requesting (6–24 Months)

The relationships children and marketers form in stage one are confirmed and expanded with words and actions in stage two. By the end of stage one, around 6 months, children are sitting up and taking in much more of their environment. They begin stage two not only sitting up but also doing some crawling. And they are making a lot of sounds that probably they intend to be replications of what they hear in their environment. During the latter half of this stage—starting around 10 to 14 months—these sounds are turned into words, some of which represent products and their brands. In fact, the majority of their vocabulary at this time consists of products and brands as nouns. Thus, by the end of this stage, children are talking and walking consumers in many relationships with marketers. For example, children at this age often start a relationship with one or more of their stuffed animals, which are used as mother substitutes. These transitional toys often are brands of cartoon characters—some from commercial-free TV—so in reality the kids have an indirect relationship with marketers of the transitional characters. Other products with these cartoon characters' brand names—found in both the physical and electronic marketplaces—take on more appeal because they are a member of the family so to speak, and perhaps even have the credibility of moms.

Since the children can now talk, they can ask directly for a range of products—ask parents, grandparents, and other caretakers. Relationship marketing practiced by makers of kids' products now takes on more meaning as a result of the children actually talking to the marketers through the TV set, through products that they own, and through other media such as movies and videos. Unlike adults, children do not feel silly talking to inanimate objects such as toys and movies; and therefore, they strengthen the relationships they have with marketers, who talk to them via advertising, programming on TV and radio, and in books, magazines, and packaging. (Dad does talk to or even shout at baseball players; he will teach his children to do this when he takes them to a game.)

During this stage, children develop their walking ability and therefore observe and interact with many more commercial objects. And with their newfound speaking ability, they ask parents for many of these objects, and most parents gladly oblige. Parents like that their kids can now actually express themselves and hold what might be called "intelligent" conversations; they talk about products by brand names, which are now egocentrically fronted with "my" as in "my Mickey Mouse." Parents are now regularly taking their 12–24-month-olds shopping with them where they talk about the stores and the products in the stores, both of which encourage their children to ask for things. Moms, in effect, become agents for marketers and do some of the talking for them to their kids. Of course, this activity bonds the kids to the marketers—retailers, products, brands—whether or not the parents realize it. The result is a good relationship between marketers and kids that may have started in stage one but is now formalized with words and motor behavior in stage two. Brand names now are part of day-to-day conversation in the children's households—and a normal part of TV and movie viewing as well as reading and radio listening. So, marketers and children have a lot in common in this stage and routinely begin to communicate. The results of these communications are passed on to parents in the form of requests for more of the marketers' products. Marketers know that if they can get their products' names in the sensory neighborhood of children, the children will ask for the products if they seem appealing—if they have kid appeal. As most marketers know, kid appeal is mainly the fun that any product provides, and if the product really isn't fun, marketers say that it is: Medicine is fun, going to special schools is fun, shopping at XYZ Mall is fun, every food and beverage item is fun, and even fat is fun.

Stage Three: Selecting/Taking (24–48 Months)

In stage one of consumer development, children start scanning their environment for things that they like, and this behavior continues throughout childhood. In stage two, children learn to ask for those things they like and want, and as their environment expands through sensorimotor activity, their asking naturally expands. Parents tend to fulfill all the children's requests in some way; in fact, parents try to anticipate what their children will want and provide it ahead of time. But, alas, most parents are unable or unwilling to respond to every request, forcing the children to become innovative in their asking. Now, in stage three, at ages two to four years, children are in possession of the brains and brawn to take what they ask for if they do not receive it or do not receive it quickly enough. They have perfected their asking strategies in order to counter the many *no*'s they are receiving from parents, but even with new asking skills, they still are turned down more frequently at this point in their lives. So, increasingly they physically take items from their home, such as food from the refrigerator, items from other children such as play toys, and items from store shelves such as bubble gum at the supermarket checkout.

There are some other features of this stage in addition to their selecting/taking things they want. Children have become self-centered as a result of asking and receiving so much so often. They believe that the moon follows them around and that the world revolves around them, including the family world and the commercial world. They are unable to take the perspective of others no matter how much others try to reason with them. And they increasingly encounter obstacles to getting what they want—all the *no*'s from parents and other caretakers, the absence of parents, which prevents them from responding to their children's requests, and their inability to obtain pleasure-giving items from the marketplace on their own. The results: the terrible twos (TTs). This year-long malady of sorts affects just about every child around age two—the beginning of this stage of consumer development—and can be identified by moodiness and tantrums. Busy parents have trouble coping with this stage and tend to deal with it by giving in and giving more to their children. The children can have what they want, can watch more TV, can eat what they want, can play or sleep more, whatever will please them and "shut them up." It is at this point that the children's households become identified with them as much as or even more than with their parents. Rather than the mother (*matriarchy*) or father (*patriarchy*) being in charge of the household, the children (*filiarchy*) are in charge—they make most decisions about their household's purchases. The children gradually take over the responsibility for getting what they want for the household, for them personally, and thus what is purchased.

A filiarchy is a marketer's dream, and more of them are rushing to live it. Three-year-olds are taking over their homes to which marketers have been invited in many ways, and many times by the parents. Now, with most parents working, and most ceding routine consumption decisions to the kids, marketers can pretty well decide what products will enter the children's homes. Marketers have been targeting the kids and parents since the kids were born, and now this effort is paying off. Most brand marketers who target kids as influence markets are in the homes in some manner—products, packaging, children's books, children's coloring books and school supplies, all advertising media such as TV and radio, product placement in videos and TV programs, and, of course, in public television, where marketers of kids products practically rule all broadcasting to them. When the children are at preschool, the marketers are there, too, and when the children go shopping with parents, the marketers guide them with eye-level displays and child-sized shopping carts. Concurrently, many of these marketers are targeting the kids' parents in parenting magazines, books, and videos—advising the parents about how to deal with the terrible twos usually by buying more of their products for the children and spending more time with the children, which, of course, many parents cannot do. Thus, rather than parenting magazines, books, and videos, they might properly be called *marketing media*, particularly since through them marketers are doing much of the advising of parents about child rearing.

Now that the children have a vocabulary of somewhere around 1,000 words by the end of this stage—most of which are nouns and most of which are commercial products—they can articulate the products and brands of all these marketers and put in memory information about them as provided by marketers and parents. And now that they are three to four feet tall and weigh 30 to 40 pounds, they are big enough to retrieve the marketers' products from the lower shelves of the marketplace and place them in a shopping cart, particularly one designed for them. At this point, competition among marketers for children's shelf space and media space—and mind space—gets intense, as measured in part by the slotting fees (rent of sorts) that producers pay retailers for shelf space.

Stage Four: Co-Purchase (48–72 Months)

In stage four of consumer development, children are four and five years old and have made hundreds of trips to the marketplace with parents, made thousands of purchase suggestions to parents, and have selected and taken several hundred desired products from shelves and fixtures. They have also stood beside their parents hundreds of times while their parents made purchases and have watched many other store patrons make purchases, including older children, who are becoming reference groups. Now that they are in kindergarten, they see some of these older children and compare possessions with them, which is now becoming a common consumer practice. Thus, children at these ages are increasingly interacting with retailers and with the products they sell.

At home, children in stage four are routinely asking for products and receiving them, and in fact have their parents trained so that the parents keep the household—refrigerator, pantry, toy box, bookshelves—stocked with products they anticipate their children will want. Children are also collecting certain commercial objects such as books, Christmas cards, marbles, toy cars, dolls, and videos. And they are accumulating money. Starting around age three, children are beginning to "save" money, with help from their parents and grandparents, and by age four and five, most have a piggy bank full of coins.

Now, with much shopping experience, much observation of parents' purchases, and much money accumulated at home, four- and five-year-old children are ready to try purchasing on their own. They are probably 45 inches tall, so they can reach most service counters in stores, they have learned to count at kindergarten so they have some money management skills, and they are getting a lot more *no*'s as responses from parents to their product requests.

At first children are permitted to spend some of their money in vending machines—mechanized marketers—that are in every store and mall that they visit with their parents. Parents usually show them how to make this kind of purchase and give them the coins to insert in the vending machines. Thus, a vending machine purchase is usually children's first co-purchase with their parents—and their first purchase interaction with marketers— with many marketers of kids' products. It serves as a precursor to more complex co-purchases of snack items and play items. These co-purchases, in turn, are just a click away from making independent purchases in stage five of consumer development.

Co-purchases, by definition, are purchases children make with more experienced and more skilled consumers—consumers who understand the exchange system and the use of money. Usually, co-purchases are made with parents and grandparents, but not uncommonly are made with an older sibling or older friend. The point is that the older co-purchasers make up for the purchase skills that the young children lack. As soon as the children gain the additional basic purchase skills of the older co-purchasers, they will attempt their own purchases alone. In the meantime, somebody older is bringing the children and marketers into a closer relationship, a kind of bonding that approximates that with parents.

Most of these co-purchases are made in self-service stores such as mass merchandisers and supermarkets, with a few being made in toy stores and convenience stores. Thus, the children usually interact with the typical minimally educated, minimally trained checkout clerks who often demonstrate that they despise their job—and most customers—and are mainly concerned with what time it is and what time they get a break. Consequently, there is little understanding, little sympathy, and little help for these new purchasers—co-purchasers—who report that they often feel very uncomfortable with the undertaking. Frequently, in fact, observations show that the checkout clerks are angered by the co-purchase attempts—angered at the children for not knowing the details of how to make a purchase, and angered at the children's parents for bringing an unskilled consumer through the checkout line. This is probably the first of many unpleasant purchase experiences children will have with retailers. It is ironic that often this type of person is one who greets the most powerful consumers in the world.

In the meantime, at home marketers are trying hard—24/7/360—to influence children's wants, requests, and purchases. Their brands are scattered in every part of the children's home; their sales messages are in every media with which children interact; and they are in the lunches, books, and bags that children carry to school, where children also are regularly targets of sales messages. Of course, children do not understand that they are the subjects of hundreds of sales messages daily, and to the extent they sense it, they are probably overjoyed that they would be the focus of anyone's efforts to please them. Children are gradually learning to read in this stage and therefore are able to understand some of the messages that marketers direct at them not only on TV but also in their books and on the many packages with which they interact. There is no way to overstress the influence of package messages to the children beginning at this point in their consumer lives. Packages give a visual "sales talk" to children in the store, and then children take the packages home, where their sales presentation may continue. Packages that are not thrown away until their contents are used up, such as cereal boxes, toothpaste tubes, and shampoo bottles, repeat their messages each time they are handled. In this manner, children learn many brand names and their attributes. Also, at this time children are able to read the billboards that line the highways of their family vacation, and they are also able to read the brand names on the hotels and restaurants that they patronize. Marketers often talk to these about-to-purchase children through jingles that children easily remember and often repeat for years.

Stage Five: Independent Purchase (72–100 Months)

Somewhere around six or seven years old, most American children make their first purchase without any help, thus giving their prepurchase and postpurchase consumer behavior patterns new meaning: They now think about buying something to consume (prepurchase) and/or consuming something they buy (postpurchase). Children's cognitive and physical developments have reached a point where they can operate independently in the marketplace. While they have had much preparation for it since birth, the first purchase is a big deal to them, a rite of passage, so to speak, to adult life. They have been earning and/or accumulating money for the past couple of years, they have been learning about its uses, and, of course, they have had thousands of marketplace experiences in which they have witnessed the exchange of money for goods and services. Finally, during the past year or so, they also have been making co-purchases with parents and other older consumers. So, this behavior all comes together usually during the first year of school where they are learning other independent behaviors such as reading, writing, and counting—all behaviors that support the consumer role. Chances are the first purchase is at a convenience store near home or school—because it is convenient and because it is comfortable due to its proximity to home and classmates. And chances are the first purchase at the convenience store is a soft drink and/or candy bar that is packaged and displayed to catch the eyes of children—although unlikely displayed as prominently as the store's bountiful supply of tobacco and beer that are promoted heavily throughout the selling area. Within a short time, children will transfer their convenience-store purchasing experience to other stores, perhaps those visited with parents such as supermarkets and toy stores with which children are familiar.

Now, in addition to children's perceptions of products and their brands held prominently in their minds, they are quickly forming thoughts about stores—specific stores and specific store types. The reactions of the stores—actually, the store personnel—to children will play a major role in children's opinions of them. As noted earlier, the disrespectful behavior of many checkout clerks keeps children from forming warm relations with the particular stores even though children are looking for these kinds of unions, perhaps much like they have with their parents since the stores are becoming parent surrogates of sorts. Store personnel lend little if any significance to these first purchases of children, thus too often making the children feel equally insignificant in those stores, perhaps much like they do in their first-grade classroom where teachers are too often there "to do a job" and less for the kids. Of course, there are many other results—good and bad—from children's good and bad store experiences. Good experiences will bond children to a store, its name, and its brands, and thus they are likely to make many more purchases there, perhaps for life. Store management that understands the concept of "growing customers" will see these first purchases of children as a chance to "get a customer for life." McDonald's, for example, is a master at this, although some of its badly managed restaurants—such as those in the central city—that we probably have all experienced undo some of these ties. Even where children have good experiences—such as at some convenience stores where they often learn the names of store personnel—management may not sense it and try to form relationships with them. Where children have bad experiences in their first purchases, the stores will unlikely have a chance to grow them into life-long customers of the stores and their brands. This, in my opinion, is what happened to Kmart—at one time the largest chain of stores. Its top management, with whom I worked in the early 1990s, only gave lip service to children as customers and allowed its store personnel to make children uncomfortable and feel unwanted. Pretty soon, it ran short of new customers since it was dependent almost solely on switching customers from competitors—including Wal-Mart and Target—rather than growing them from childhood.

While most stores where children make their first purchases in the United States are self-service, the situation is commonly the opposite in

PHOTO 12-2 This Chinese retail clerk was apparently having a bad day. The children who wanted to buy the yummy candies and cookies on display in and behind the counter had to cope with her attitude in order to obtain them from her.

China. As shown in Photo 12-2, products desirable to children are often displayed in and behind glassed-in counters that may be very high, and children must interact with the salesperson, who often is also the person who is paid for the product purchased. In such a case, children must also contend with the mood and manner of the clerks. The lady clerk in Photo 12-2 apparently was having a bad day when the picture was taken—she later told the researcher she had a cold—and children who were wanting to buy such treats as candies and cookies had to cope with her attitude in order to obtain them. Some children probably did not even approach the adult-high counter, and those who did may never again if they have a choice.

In stage five of consumer development, store marketing has a major impact on children. As noted, the treatment of children is paramount in turning them into customers. Interestingly, most of the time the stores at which children make early purchases are those introduced into their lives by their parents. Thus, the stores have the parents to thank for bringing the new customers to them, but probably most stores do not see it this way. In some ways, then, the stores' displays, branding of many products, attempts to sell special products, and various promotional programs can be lost in the bad relationships that may form with children as new customers. Probably the clerk in Photo 12-2 will not be responsible for building store relations with many new consumers and, like most store clerks who are hourly workers, couldn't care less.

At the same time, this is the stage in which children learn to rely on shelf/fixture information and packaging for assistance with purchases in self-service stores. Now that children are an additional market—a primary market for certain products that they buy with their own money—more point-of-purchase advertising will be aimed at them. Astute marketers that are advertising to children, for instance, on TV and the Internet in this stage, usually attempt to lead children to certain stores and to specific product displays. In such ads the sellers are sure to emphasize their packages—perhaps showing them on the store shelf to give children visual directions—and may mention the names of the stores in which they can be found—in order to link the potential customer to the products on display in the stores. At the stores themselves, in-store advertising (point-of-purchase or point-of-sale advertising, as it is more often called) placed in the ceilings and on the floors may lead the way to the products. Thus, marketers at this time in children's consumer development target the kids "coming and going"—coming to the advertised product message and going to the source of the product.

By the time children reach 100 months—in the United States, currently 4 million of them per year—most are bona fide consumers, having made purchases on their own and having asked parents for adequate money to make these purchases. Concurrently, children at this century mark have made thousands of requests to parents for products and services and received them. And in total, children at this age are performing somewhere around 10,000 tekrams—consumer acts—per day, including those hundreds related to their own purchases. From this point on these 10K consumers are viewed by marketers as three markets in one—primary, influence, and future consumers—and are targeted in some manner by most major marketers of children's products 24/7/360.

Summary of Marketing Efforts Targeting Children

By the time children make their first purchase in stage five—around age six or seven—virtually every major marketer of consumer goods is targeting them as primary, influence, and/or future consumers with numerous products and services ranging from automobiles to zinnia seeds, from airlines to zoos. The approximately 4 million new consumers born each year in the United States are recognized by business organizations (and nonprofit organizations, too) as having more market potential—are responsible for more purchases—than any other demographic group. Moreover, a majority of businesses recognize that their very existence and success rest with these new consumers, who may become their new customers. They have figured out that every business must have a steady flow of new customers; as noted, there are only two sources of them for any business: Either the business switches existing customers from competition, or it grows them from childhood. Switching customers from competitors is the typical short-term strategy used by most retailers and producers. It is apparent, for example, in advertisements of business A (retailer, producer) comparing products and/or prices with those of business B to demonstrate to potential customers the benefits of buying from business A. However, businesses gradually become aware that a switching strategy is not very profitable and, in fact, may become unprofitable and therefore must be strategically combined with a growing strategy. That is, fast-food restaurant A, for instance, can easily switch a family from, say, fast-food restaurant B by offering more attractive premiums for children, but B can do the same by applying one-upmanship—offering a more attractive premium, for example. (Using an advertised premium to switch a child who will bring his or her family to the restaurant through requests technically may triple the size of the restaurant purchase of just one person.) The net result is that each marketer temporarily "buys" new customers from the other. But at the end of the day, the cost of switching another customer who will probably switch back as a result of some promotion may be more than the gross margin from that customer. (The fast-food restaurant chain has to buy the millions of action figures, for example, that it "gives away" after it has made a costly contract with the movie studio that licenses them; then it must advertise them in the media and at the point of purchase.) Of course, restaurant A's management can claim that it will keep that new customer switched from B with its superior products, but B can claim the same thing. But each must admit that once the premium offer is over, its business falls off—consumers buy less and/or go back to one or more competitors. An underlying point is that mom and children often go from one brand of fast food to another for the premiums that are intended to switch them. Thus, they may show little loyalty to any restaurant—or supermarket or superstore or auto dealership—because a switching strategy usually does not produce loyalty among children or adults. Incidentally, a switching strategy does not have to be between retailers. It also is common among producers of kids' products such as candy makers and cereal makers as well as adult product manufacturers such as auto makers and computer makers. Just go to the cereal aisle, for instance, at a supermarket and note how many cereals offer some kind of premium for children, hoping to clinch the sale at the point of purchase. I should add also that the temporary bump-up in sales of a retailer or manufacturer due to a promotion such as premiums may give a bump-up in rank to a brand manager or product manager, but this increase is almost always temporary and must be repeated over and over. I would add also that the various kinds of promotion programs that involve "buying" new customers do not always produce a lot of new business, and in that case it may be necessary to dump thousands of premiums, perhaps along with a brand manager or two.

On the other hand, a growing strategy that targets children from their earliest years is likely to produce loyal customers who have a tendency to buy more not only when short-term strategies such as premiums are in place, but also when they are not. That is, even when other competitors institute switching strategies, loyal customers tend to stay with one brand of product or service. The marketers and children have formed a relationship in a growing strategy that becomes a normal part of children's consumer minds—their evoked sets—from the time that children become practicing consumers. Those retailers and producers that recognize this relationship have both strategies working simultaneously. Let's continue with the fast-food industry as an example. Along with a switching strategy, some restaurants also have in place a growing strategy made apparent, for example, by its attractive children's play areas in most of its restaurants. Those extra amenities cost a lot, but they keep new customers coming back by producing good memories for the tots who seek them again and again. I would add that families would not come back for just the benefits to their children if it were not also for other features of the restaurant chain. My research in China shows that "good food" is the fourth or fifth reason given by parents for bringing their children to McDonald's (as compared to other fast-food restaurants) after mentioning features such as cleanliness, including clean restrooms, well-lighted space, fixed prices, and a no-smoking environment—all unusual features of restaurants in China and, in combination, rare. And, yes, the McDonald's restaurants in China provide premiums for children perhaps with even greater frequency than the company's U.S. restaurants as they compete short-term with KFC and others for the Chinese family business.

The switching and the growing customer strategies of businesses that target kids are marketing strategies that, as noted, often begin when the children are infants and follow them into adulthood. As observed in previous chapters, parents first introduce marketers to their children by buying the marketers' products for them when they are babies. Thus, many products and their brands and packages are a normal part of children's environments by the time children can first detect objects. Also, while children are still babies—typically around two to three months old—their parents take them to the marketplace and introduce them to many more marketers. And before children are a year old, parents likely have turned on the TV and introduced their infants to even more marketers. Thus, many marketers get entry into newborns' lives through parents (and other caretakers) who tend to act as agents for specifically preferred retailers and manufacturers. Once in, marketers operate 24/7/360—day and night in all dimensions of children's lives—to sell children (and their parents) on their brands and products.

Marketers use what might be termed *surround selling* to reach each child with messages about a specific brand of a specific product. Marketing academicians may refer to it as *integrated marketing communications* (IMC), a notion that I introduced as the *promotion mix* 40 years ago (McNeal, 1966) and refined by Professor Shultz and his colleagues and students at Northwestern University (see, for example, Schultz,

Tannenbaum, and Lauterborn, 1993), in which all marketing communications through all personal and nonpersonal media are coordinated so that they most effectively and continuously reach a body of consumers—in this case, children of certain ages. Mothers are definitely a major media through which to target messages to children, but they are only one of many. The product itself is a major channel through which to reach children, so the brand name is placed on the product wherever possible. If not placed on the product, then it is placed prominently on the package, and as many times as the producer can. In addition to the products and their packaging, the brand and its message are combined in all advertising and programming on radio and TV, magazines, and many other media such as race cars, bulletin boards at preschool, clothing and uniforms, shoes and bibs, books and book covers, and in movies and video games. The general message, if aimed through parents, usually is that the product is in some way good for children—good for their health, their minds, their bodies—and definitely fun. Therefore, the parents owe it—the product—to their children in exchange for their health and happiness (H&H). In China, for instance, messages aimed through parents for all kinds of children's foods and medicines often claim to make children smarter; they may guarantee 100 percent on school exams after regular usage of some products (Chan and McNeal, 2004). With marketing messages targeted directly to children, they usually boil down to simply "It's fun" in order to appeal to children's insatiable need for play—cereal is fun, crackers are fun, candy is fun. If the marketers are doing their job effectively according to modern marketing principles, parents and children are never far away from these messages; they surround the family. Every time the TV is turned on, for instance, it is a marketing moment.

It should be emphasized that these marketing efforts are not just nonpersonal such as the brand presentation in books and magazines, displays, packaging, and advertising. They are also personal by funneling them through parents, teachers, peers, salespeople, and the endless number of celebrities that make their living in this manner in such media as movies, TV and radio programming, magazines and newspapers for children, books, and billboards as well as stores (point-of-purchase ads and personal appearances), schools (buses and bulletin boards), and events (athletic meets, fashion shows, and science fairs). There is a tendency among consumer protectionists to be concerned with the power of TV advertising messages to children, but actually those messages inside the programs are probably more powerful due to their personal nature—the actors wearing, eating, drinking, playing with, riding, and driving various products. Figure 12-1 shows a model of surround selling (or IMC) that focuses on children. As one looks at the many elements of surround selling as suggested in Figure 12-1, one senses that the brand and its message are never far away from any one child or parent.

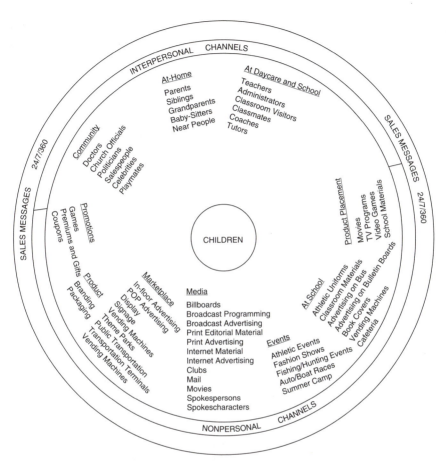

FIGURE 12-1 *Surround selling that targets children.*

Naturally, all this surround selling costs a great deal of money, but again, bear in mind that children have more market potential than any other age group, so they are worthwhile from an accounting standpoint. I estimate that total identifiable marketing dollars spent annually on targeting kids through childhood—through age 12—is well above $1 billion a month. This may seem like a hefty amount, but U.S. children of this age group are probably responsible for around $60 billion in household purchases per month.

CRITICISMS OF MARKETING TO CHILDREN

We frequently hear certain complaints about marketing to children, particularly about advertising, one of marketing's many messaging tools. The criticisms of marketing to children are really a reflection of the criticisms of marketing in general that have existed at least since the time of Plato's writings—at least over two thousand years. Criticisms of marketing have been made more specific as conditions change in an industrial society such as ours. I should mention also that the criticisms of marketing can be found worldwide—I bumped into them in various forms in Beijing, Hong Kong, London, Toronto, Mexico City, for example—thus seemingly validating those that are common in the United States and were common in the ancient world. Worldwide negative judgments of marketing existed before U.S. marketing practices were globalized, so we can assume that they are not the results of exporting them from America. Criticisms of marketing aimed at children began seriously in the late 1980s and early 1990s as business organizations poured more resources into the children's market (McNeal, 1999). Today, the many criticisms of marketing in general and marketing to children specifically can be boiled down to one word: *unethical.*

I remember around 1967 an article titled, "Would you want your daughter to marry a marketing man?" by Richard Farmer in the then-prestigious *Journal of Marketing.* The article took up the issue of marketing ethics—a first for this journal. Starting around this time—and continuing today—the topic became a normal part of many marketing textbooks. For example, the most respected writer in the field of marketing, Professor Kotler (1967) at Northwestern, included a separate chapter on the topic in his first marketing management book that examined modern marketing. The chapter was entitled "Social, Legal, and Ethical Issues," which probably established the practice of treating the topic of ethics jointly with the topic of legal issues since the two intertwine. As a side note, the topic of ethics in the marketing textbooks was intended also to remind the many thousands of students who take a marketing course each year how they should behave as future marketing practitioners.

Today we might take Farmer's lead and pose a similar question to his: Would you want your kids hanging out with a marketer? *The fact is that today most kids are in the company of marketers in some form more than in the company of their parents.* Both parents usually work, as do the single parents with whom nearly one-third of kids live. So, the kids are turned over to another party much of the time for child rearing. While at home, the kids are quickly placed in the hands of marketers in the form of media, products, brands, and packaging. And when the kids are placed in the care of others such as nurseries, preschools, kindergarten, elementary school, and specialized schools, usually they are exposed to even more marketers, including, of course, many of the caretakers themselves. So, in one way or another, most kids are reared in the company of marketers and are expected not only to accept this environment but to be glad to have it. Parents here and in other countries tell us through research that they give their kids much more than they had as kids—*more*, meaning more commercial products—and often add that the kids do not act grateful. Most working parents—most parents—tell us also that much of their giving to their kids is due to trying to make the children feel happy and secure because they are away from them so much. So, marketing in its many forms is doing much of the baby-sitting of kids who have to manage on their own. And according to the *Home Alone* movies, the kids are doing a pretty good job of it. Many parents see to it that by the time their children reach toddlerhood they can function to a great extent on their own—use the telephone, dial 911, work the remote control on the TV and VCD player, even operate the microwave oven—and they brag about these feats. Look carefully at the child in Photo 12-3. He is nearly three years old and has been taught to use a cell (mobile) phone to talk to parents and grandparents. His parents say that they are proud of him for learning to use the phone, and it makes them feel better about being away from him so much. The plain fact of the matter is that he is also in a relationship with the phone maker whose name—not the parents' name—is displayed prominently on the phone every time he uses it.

PHOTO 12-3 This three-year-old Chinese lad is being taught to stay in touch with his family by mobile phone. He is also being taught to stay in touch with the marketer of the phone whose name—not the family name—appears prominently on the cover.

Starting in the 1980s, a number of child-rearing authorities began asking if children are growing up too fast, if they are being put in charge of their lives too soon, if they are being deprived of their childhood too early. (See, for example, *Children without Childhood* by Marie Winn [1983], one of the first books on the subject.) It would appear that in spite of the advancements in technology enjoyed by children, we have, to some extent, taken childhood back to the Middle Ages when ". . . children were thought to be able to function without mothers or nannies at about the age of 7 years and they moved immediately into the adult world of work and play" (Grusec and Lytton, 1988, p. 4). Working parents tell us that many of their elementary school children prepare, or help prepare, their own meals, help prepare supper for the family, do housework such as cleaning and laundry, "and still have time to watch too much TV," reported a working mom. (When asked how much her third-grade daughter studies each day, she did not know, but she assumed "as much as she needs to.") So, with the help of many marketers that parents bring home with them from the birthing center, introduce the children to in the marketplace, and let in through the TV and other media, children are pretty much in charge of their households. This is such a standard pattern of family life today that we even posited in the preceding chapter that it may indeed be a function of genetics. The point is that the thousands-year-old reputation of marketers as ". . . fast-buck artists, con-men, wheeler-dealers, and shoddy-goods distributors" (Farmer, 1967, p. 1) seems to be somewhat ignored by many parents, who in various ways utilize marketers as baby-sitters, pals, partners, friends, companions, and socialization agents to their children.

Today's marketers are not your mother's marketers. They have always lived on the edge, handsomely rewarded when they can sell something, or more of something, to someone who does not seek it and who may even try to avoid it. But today marketers are armed with more sophisticated selling techniques, including scanner data to tell them what is selling at an exact moment in an exact location to whom, data mining methods to obtain names and addresses of the most significant buyers, and promotion with pinpoint accuracy to convey their sales messages to potential buyers. Most of these marketers are delighted to be included in mom-made relationships with children who are in charge of their households. It's like receiving the key to the bank's front door *and* the combination to its vault.

The one word that summarizes marketers' bad reputation—*unethical*—can be broken down into several, somewhat separate categories. First, probably the most common complaint against marketers who target children is there is *too much of it*, at least too much advertising. Advertising to children has been under attack ever since I can remember, and part of the reason is that it is everywhere and in great quantities. That is one of the reasons that Congress passed the Television Act of 1990, which placed limits on the amount of advertising time on children's television to 10.5 minutes on weekends and 12 minutes on weekdays. Given the fact that children have more market potential than any other demographic, it is unlikely that there is too much advertising aimed at them, at least from a business standpoint. There is, however, too much *inappropriate* advertising—and marketing— aimed at them that logically and deservedly garners many complaints from parents and consumer protectionists. Some of these major criticisms— besides the charge that there is too much advertising and marketing—are that advertising is often (1) untruthful, (2) deceptive, (3) in bad taste, and it targets young children—usually those under eight—who (4) cannot understand its purpose and therefore (5) cannot defend themselves against it.

Looking at the latter criticisms first, it is generally true that most preschool children have trouble understanding the purposes of advertising for the same reasons they have trouble understanding the purposes of parenting, retailing, or most any human behavior: They are so self-absorbed that they cannot take the perspective of another. However, we should recall from previous chapters that three-year-olds are able to defend against the repetitious *no*'s of parents (adults) by understanding the parents better— reading their faces and anticipating their refusals to requests—and developing and improving appeals to parents. Thus, they gradually learn to see the views and intentions of others as they experience them over and over and as they are taught them over and over by others. This is probably one of the payoffs of being sent to preschool very early: Children learn the perspectives of other children and other adults at an earlier age. For example, around age three, children learn that taking toys from other preschool children is wrong, that the toys are the property of others, and that taking them makes the other children—and the teachers—angry. Probably most of this learning results from simple repetitious responses by playmates and teachers—one of the major learning models also used by advertisers. In much the same manner, preschool children can learn—be taught—the primary purpose of advertising in its many forms—that is, selling products, services, people, and ideas—and be able to better defend themselves against it. But the likelihood of parents and preschool personnel actually spending time teaching this fact to children is small, particularly as a concerted effort among parents and teachers. The net results are frequent calls for halts to advertising to young children rather than media (consumer) education.

Children's understanding of advertising messages improves with age, just as Piaget would have predicted (Chan and McNeal, 2004). Probably self-interest motivates them to take an interest in advertising presented through, for example, the medium of television. As they become aware of the many satisfying products in the marketplace during preschool years, they take more interest in ads for these products. By the time they reach elementary school age, they begin to have an understanding that the ads— and the people behind the ads—are trying to promote the products to those who are interested in them. Thus, they tend to understand the ad messages and their purpose simply because they are repetitiously talking about products of importance to children. On the other hand, children will not understand many ads simply because they contain words, actions, and symbols foreign to them. Thus, in general, the more experience children have with products at home and in the marketplace, the more they understand the messages about them in the media.

In its typical form, advertising targeted to very young preschool children probably should be presumed to be deceptive, even untruthful, because children often cannot or will not take the perspective of others and therefore do not know that the advertisements are intended to sell them a product, service, or idea. However, it is possible for children-oriented advertising (and marketing, too) to be designed so that it is legitimate and can be understood by children. Then the too-much complaint would probably subside. First, *warnings* of advertisements and their intent could be designed in *children's language* and signs in all media so that children could understand and learn them—through the repetition of the warnings as well as those from adults. For instance, we have known for many years that television programming disclaimers—for example, "partial assembly required"—and separators—for instance, "this show will return after these messages"—can be understood by children if they are constructed in children's language (Liebert, Sprafkin, Liebert, and Rubinstein, 1977; Stutts et al., 1981). In addition to the warnings, various visual and verbal language could be used—or prohibited—within the ads so that preschool- and school-age children could grasp the messages in the ads (McNeal, 1992). Surely, the "creatives" on Madison Avenue could create these "rights" as easily as they can create the "wrongs" in advertising. And they should be applied to other marketing communications efforts such as packaging, publicity, and product placement.

Probably the worst offense and the most widespread criticism of marketing, including advertising, is *deception*. (Other legal terms might also be used, such as *misrepresentative* and *misleading*.) Even though forbidden by the Federal Trade Commission Act since 1937 and by similar state laws (Stern and Eovaldi, 1984), marketing deception in its many forms is rampant today—in media and point-of-purchase advertising, in packaging, in pricing, in the product itself, even in the brand name. And it is targeting kids and their parents. Marketing messages that deceive parents about products for their kids often can be found, for example, in parents-oriented magazine articles, many of which are more publicity than editorial content—sales messages for certain branded products that are presented as news. Moreover, often in the same magazine that contains articles embedded with sales messages, ads are made to appear as magazine articles. These same deceptive practices may be found in magazines for kids, and none is necessary for selling kids' products and services.

It should be emphasized that *deceiving parents* about a product for their kids may *indirectly deceive their kids*. For example, a recent lawsuit against makers of sunscreen products specifically for children alleges "that parents have been misled into believing their children are protected [from the sun's UVA and UVB rays] as a result of claims in labels" of these products (Beasley, 2006, p. 1). What the lawsuit did not mention, and in theory makes the message more dangerous, is that the parents pass on this information to their children, who then probably believe the brand claims also since they came through their parents. Related to the sunscreen deception, there is a sort of double deception in some pharmaceutical ads that target parents with prescription drugs for their kids. Drug makers who sponsor research that compares their products with those of competitors almost always win in the sense that "systematic bias favors products which are made by the company funding the research" (Lexchin, Bero, Djuibegovic, and Clark, 2003). Then ads that show the biased results may be directed to parents and their children by the sponsoring (winning) firm.

Marketing communications through advertising, packaging, and point-of-purchase presentations for kids' products that are directed to parents (and therefore to their kids) are often presented by *spokespersons* paid to make certain positive statements about a branded product. As in advertising, using paid spokespersons (and spokescharacters) on packaging to praise the product—particularly, cereal packaging—is standard fare. So, at any moment parents may find these people pictured in a fast-food restaurant, and kids can peruse the cereal aisle or any other aisle offering kids' products in their favorite supermarket and find paid football players, race car drivers, ice skaters, and movie stars gracing the front panels of some of the packages—as if they sincerely favor the product and want to tell children about it. To underline this point, I will note that last year the sports news announced that The University of Texas had won the 2005 national football championship and the team would be pictured on a cereal box. Why are these celebrities paid to be pictured on packages of products for kids and in their advertisements? Simple. To deceive kids into thinking that the product must be good if famous people say it is, and further that the kids also can be like those persons if they consume the packaged product. Many professional athletes make more money with their endorsements than they do from their salaries—as long as they are willing to deceive kids.

Another way that marketers deceive, and one of the most blatant ways, is the use of very *small print* in media advertising—and in the case of TV, very small, *fleeting* print—to present important information. Ditto for the use of *asterisks* that are often used in combination with the small print. Asterisks are used so often to mislead that one cartoonist, Joel Pett, in *USA Today* (2006, p. 12A), referred to the United States as an "asterisk nation." A beguiling brother of small, fleeting print in TV ads is the doubling of *speaking speed* by the voiceover. One might ask why spokespersons speak so fast or get rid of the small print so fast, and the answer surely is to deceive. By the way, children report they are amused by this fast talking and seem to see it as marketing humor. There is more. In print and broadcast ads, there is the frequent use of *limiting words* such as *just* and *only* as in "just $19.95" and "only $19.95" when they are not true. In fact, the full price often is 30 to 50 percent more than just or only the stated price. (I believe the Federal Trade Commission found these limiting terms used in this manner deceptive practice years ago, but. . . .)

In packaging—another means of conveying printed marketing messages—deception is just as common as in advertising, particularly among those for kids' products. Packaging of cereal—kids' favorite product and moms' favorite product for their kids—may employ many means of deception. One of the worst—recognizing how visual children are—is featuring a picture of the cereal product that is not really like the actual product inside the package. Then in very small print, usually in a barely visible black color, there is a statement, "Enlarged to show texture." Using untruthful graphics along with the small black print seems to show determination to deceive. And let's face it, it is not necessary to show the texture of the product or to exaggerate it.

Another deceptive technique used on packaging and one that often seems downright mean to kids as well as to their parents is the improper use of the word *free*. *Free* is a term that kids love since they can use it to justify to their parents the purchase of the specific brand; we get not only the cereal, they reason, but also a free toy. The word *free* is usually in shouting form on the cereal packages, when in fact there is often a catch (the deception): The free item is not free unless mom buys three more boxes of cereal—free "with four proofs of purchase." Or the cereal is free with the purchase of a one-year subscription to some magazine. Or it is free if mom mails in a form printed on the inside of the box that must be cut out and filled out, and then mom and child must wait "four to six weeks." Compare that to the noise that mom gets when she says her child can open the cereal purchased but must wait five minutes until they get home. It should be noted that many of these free offers can also be found in media advertising for the products, sort of doubling the deception.

I could easily give a hundred more examples of deception through marketing messages. Product placement—the placing of branded products in movies, TV programs, video games, and storybooks without the viewers/users/readers being warned—is another blatant attempt to deceive. Another deception is giving the product a brand name that is misleading, such as including the word *fruit* as part of the brand name when the product contains no fruit. Or, even more deceptive, is showing a certain fruit on the package when there is very little or none of that fruit in the product—perhaps just the flavor of the fruit. On and on and on it goes. But the point is that deception is unethical and seems to me to be illegal in most cases. One may ask why the Federal Trade Commissioners do not do something about such rampant deception. And, to me, the simple answer is they are political appointees, and businesses are the strongest supporters of political appointers. One might also ask why marketers of good products find it necessary to use deception at all in their commercial messages about the products. That one I cannot answer except to say that marketers generally feel compelled to deceive and, in fact, usually get rewarded for it if done well enough. When I have asked some marketers directly why they practice deception, every one irresponsibly answers the same: Competition does it, so we have to. I should add, also, that deceiving a kid is easy; even the least experienced marketer can do it and therefore really should not be rewarded for it.

Another kind of criticism of marketers is the unethical practice that Mrs. Soper mentioned in the introductory vignette—". . . trying to sell the kids stuff that is bad for them including bad ideas and bad values." Marketers take advantage of their unregulated deceptive powers over children to persuade them to do just about anything—to consume their products and to consume them in great quantities. In the process of selling children— directly and through their parents—marketers too often *teach children (and their parents) bad values*. What bad values are we talking about here? The list of bad values marketers teach kids is at least as long as that of their deceptive techniques. So we can only generalize here and maybe point out a few of these missteps.

One of the bad values that originates with marketers and is passed on to children (and their parents) is the notion that *fat is fun* (FIF) in spite of the fact that daily we read in the press about the increasing numbers of overweight children—OWs, as we called them in an earlier chapter, because it hurts; it hurts the children's physical and psychological health. Virtually every TV *program* that targets kids demonstrates in some way that fat is fun—surrounding fat people and fat characters with fun actions including loving others and being loved by others, portraying fat actors as happy, the hit of the party, the focus of fun. And FIF is a message not just in TV programs but in all media—movies, videos, and magazines, particularly. And in addition to editorial and programming, virtually every advertisement with people in it contains at least one fat person as if to be politically correct— from a voter's or an audience's standpoint, they are correct. These kinds of marketing messages normalize fat. Actually, fat is normal in the United States like smoking is normal in China—and fat is quickly becoming normal in China, too. The role models of children—TV and movie stars, athletes, political leaders, policemen, parents, grandparents—present themselves or are presented by the media as fat as if to underline the notion that fat is fine; it goes with stardom and leadership. Fat moms may even belong to a fat-favorable club that boasts of the benefits of fat and whose members are targets of all kinds of fat marketing. This elevation of fatdom by marketers and moms is naturally passed on to the kids.

Corollary to the fat is fun value are others that are harmful: It is fun to relax in front of the TV or computer and with the telephone and other communications devices; it is fun to overeat, to gorge oneself, to eat or drink large quantities; it is loving and caring for parents to overfeed their kids; it is cool to cheat on exercising; and fattening foods are sociable, best-tasting, preferred by others, including children in the family. A fat-favorable environment has been created by marketers—and fostered by many parents— for children, and in many ways is promoted by virtually every marketer that targets kids and kids' parents. Of course, such a notion is injurious to children and their parents—the Federal Trade Commission Act seems to suggest that deceptive marketing should also be injurious to consumers in order for it to be adjudicated—and it benefits only the marketers.

ISSUES IN CONSUMER DEVELOPMENT (#12)

Fat Is Fun: Marketing Pigs and Pears and Teddy Bears to Kids

When we look back at marketing to kids and their parents over the past 10–15 years, one message stands out: Fat is fun. Supporting messages include the following: Fat is fun-loving, fat is love, fat is cute, fat is good, fat is cool, fat is friendly, fat is happy, fat is strength, and, of course, fat is huggable and snuggly. All these positive characterizations of fat were targeted to kids and to moms for their kids at a time when two-thirds of adults and one-third of kids became overweight, and resulting health problems were being described as an epidemic.

These fat messages can be found throughout TV programs for children—including "noncommercial" programming—and in magazines that parents supposedly look to for guidance in rearing their children. Moreover, they are interlaced with hundreds of messages saying that eating and overeating are fun; that moms who provide their children with calorie-laden foods are kind, loving, thoughtful, and cool; and that parents and children who eat calorie-laden foods together are a happy family that is full of love.

Most of these fat messages are passed along to kids in ads, programming, and editorial content through fat characters that are favorites of kids and moms, including Barney, Winnie the Pooh, Teletubbies, Big Bird, Cookie Monster, Pikachu, Babe, and many teddy bears of many brands. These characters are used presumably because they are credible with both moms and kids; they are fun and loving and honest. Along with these messages, these characters are shown having lots of fun, particularly through eating and drinking. In addition to food goods, they are also paired with such product categories as medicine, clothing, bedding, and, of course, play items.

Take a stroll through the past several years' worth of various parenting magazines and you will see hundreds of these messages mainly targeting mom on behalf of her kids. Here are a few examples:

1. An ad features fat Big Bird and four of his pals representing Sesame Street Snacks in which four different snack packages and a dozen snack items are shown along with the headline, "Characters so cute you could just eat them up," suggesting that fat is about as good as it gets.

2. Mom and obese Barney are tossing a two-year-old in a blanket, and one headline with an arrow pointing to Barney reads, "This is a beloved friend"—not just a friend, but a *beloved* friend who can be identified by his obesity.

3. An infant is nursing from a fat Pooh bottle holder with the headline, "Some friendships require no words," implying that even though the baby cannot yet talk she is learning who her friends are, including very friendly (and fat) Winnie the Pooh.

4. A big bottle of Gummy Vites (vitamins) is shown including the label with fat Gummy Bear and two preschool children, and accompanying headlines say, "Gummy Bear Vitamins A complete vitamin & mineral formula in a fun gummy bear!" The message: Take vitamins from healthy, fat Gummy Bear whom you can trust, and have fun doing it.

5. An ad for Barney Music (CDs) shows four preschoolers happily listening to fat Barney's Greatest Hits and a headline, "Everything You Love about Purple All in One Place . . . ," leaving no doubt about the many things to love about fat characters, including all kinds of music.

6. A full-page ad from Toys 'R Us shows a little girl holding a very fat teddy bear that is as big as she is, and the copy says, "Take home a furry friend . . . They're warm and huggable . . . and, oh so snuggable!" Of course, the fatter they are, the more huggable and snuggable they are.

7. An ad for Get Better Bear Sore Throat Pops from Dimetapp shows a sucker on a stick that is a fat purple teddy bear, and the headline says, "Lick That Sore Throat." There also is a package showing Get Better Bear Sore Throat Pops with the slogan "Soothing Relief for Child's Sore Throat." The message: Mom and kids can trust the bear for medicine because he is fat—healthy.

8. In a rather complex ad, the top half shows a page from a Winnie the Pooh children's book. In it, fat Pooh jumps from the

page and becomes a spokesperson for Keebler Rumbly Grahams. Two packages are shown in the lower half, along with Pooh in the form of a cookie. The copy says, "Kids have always eaten up his stories, but never quite like this," followed with some smaller copy that explains this snack is being introduced and is "shaped like your favorite Winnie the Pooh characters." Presumably, the ad is attempting to connect the warm emotions parents and babies have with fat Pooh books to the snacks.

Following are a few examples of ads from these magazines that glorify moms for feeding and overfeeding their children lots of high-fat-content foods:

1. An Oscar Mayer hot dog ad shows a five-year-old girl rubbing her tummy with one hand and eating an Oscar Mayer hot dog with the other, and there is a big, beautiful smile on her face—just as mom would want. The headline reads, "My tummy's very happy."
2. An ad for Snickers candy bars shows a kitchen scene in which mom is standing beside the refrigerator beaming with pride while her three kids have opened the door showing the refrigerator is stuffed full of bags of Snickers Miniatures and the kids are each grabbing the bags. No other food is shown in the refrigerator, but many food items litter the floor, presumably tossed aside for all the bags of candy. The headline reads, "A Cool Way to Help Celebrate National Kids Day on August 5th." The signatures at the bottom of the page include National Kids Day, Boys & Girls Clubs of America, 4-H Clubs clover symbol, KidsPeace: The National Center for Kids Overcoming Crisis, and Snickers brand.
3. A very interesting ad in the form of editorial content has a small, one-word notice at the top that it is an advertisement for the National Dairy Council and specifically for chocolate milk. The ad consists of hundreds of words and several parts. One part has the headline "Research Study Reveals the Truth" and a smaller headline, "Kids Love Chocolate Milk." Then that part of the copy goes on to provide data from a study among children ages 8–13 by McDonald Research, Inc. For instance, it states that "39% of kids agree, 'I would drink more milk if it were chocolate,'" and "52% of children say, 'Chocolate milk taste better than white milk.'" Another part is labeled "Chocolate Milk Myths" and explains away such myths as "Chocolate milk is high in sugar and causes hyperactivity" with "fact: Chocolate milk has two fewer teaspoons of sugar per 8-ounce serving than colas." And "Chocolate milk isn't good for

CRITICISMS OF MARKETING TO CHILDREN   **385**

kids' teeth" with "fact: According to the American Academy of Pediatric Dentistry, it's less likely to cause cavities than sticky foods." Finally, there is a recipe for "Double Chocolate Milk Shakes."

4. A Nabisco ad shows in black-and-white a five-year-old boy hugging his mom's skirt and a multi-pack of cookies and copy in four-color. The little boy has a big, loving smile on his face and mom is placing her hand on his head acknowledging his love. The package of Mini Oreo Bite Size, Nutter Butter, and Chips Ahoy cookies is prominently displayed with the bold message: "Makes moms happy. Makes kids happy. Finally, snacks that can multi-task." And in smaller print, "With Nabisco Multi-Packs, kids get all the snacks they love and mom gets an easy way to serve them. Nabisco Multi-Packs. Everybody wins." Implied from the skirt that mom is wearing is that she is a working woman, and the message tells her that the Multi-Pack is an easy way to feed her kid.

Finally, there is a type of fat message that comes from food marketers to families that says, in effect, eat as much as you can of our products—such as that in the Snickers ad noted here. The products may not be fattening in normal use but are fattening in overuse. For instance, supersize your fast-food order, get two pizzas for only a dollar more than one or a bigger pizza for only a dollar more, or come to our restaurant and get "all you can eat" for one low price. And perhaps the ultimate, "kids eat free." And at the supermarket, you can get 10 for $10, or buy one and get one free. In other words, increase your portion size and eat to your heart's content.

Marketers not only use advertising and publicity to push fat, but they also often package labeling of food products to hide fat, suggesting that they are aware of people's concerns about it but are still determined to sell it. A *Wall Street Journal* article stated that "Many shoppers rely on food labels to help them pick nutritious and low-calorie foods, but a closer look at labels shows many are misleading, making products seem far healthier or less fattening than they are."

Marketers also praise famous fat people as well as fat characters and often use them as spokespersons. For example, professional football game announcers boast about certain players weighing 300+ pounds by describing their skills and agility without mentioning their bad health. TV programs such as *Cops* may focus on law officers who are fat but fast and can outrun crooks. Every sitcom has fat characters who are shown to be good, loving, fun, smart, good friends and imply that being fat helps them receive high pay as actors. And speaking of actors, the movies feature many fat ones who are just as attractive, active, and successful as thin ones. And if fat needed any more legitimacy, it receives that legitimacy through Wal-Mart ads showing fat children and adults modeling its clothing and other products mailed to all households.

It should be noted that all those ads described here contain strictly one-sided messages, and there is no mention of fat as dangerous, of overeating as unhealthy, and of snacks not providing a wide range of needed nutrition. Apparently, the marketers rely on parents to convey the other side, the dangerous side. But as noted in the preceding chapter, parents are often creating a fat-favorable home environment that is not likely to present the negative side of fat.

It should be added that presenting the negative side of fat has been turned into a big marketing opportunity. A whole new set of marketers are targeting the kids and their families with sales messages about how to get rid of the fat. Concurrent with the fat-is-fun messages are messages from the many arms of the medical industry saying you should be unhappy with your fat and get rid of it with their products and services—dieting medicines, surgery hospitals, and psychological counseling. This is the growth part of the fat market, but others are innovating new products and services to serve fat and capitalize on it. Perhaps the furniture industry is the best example, with stronger sofas and chairs, more suitable seats in cars, and bigger, stronger beds in hospitals. And for the children, there are new exercise and athletic programs offered by private tutors, videos, and hospitals. Fat-is-fun marketing has really paid off for many marketers, but, of course, it has severely hurt children.

****
Sources: Dixon, 2006; Parker-Pope, 2003; Strauss Pollack, 2001.

Another bad value that marketers offer to children in abundance is *violence*, often in the form of violence is fun, good; it often serves a good purpose. Like fat, violence has been normalized for children in all media and in many marketing messages. These messages tend to reinforce the violent nature of children during the terrible-two period in their lives and make it more acceptable beginning in earliest childhood. So, in addition to being fat, movie and TV stars are often shown to be violent—and their violence is respected or at least can be laughed at. Much violence that is okayed by marketers' messages is violence with firearms: shooting an adversary is a quick and easy way to deal with him. Related to the notion that violence is good in some way is the notion that life ought to be full of *risks* including risks that are created by the individual—fast driving, bungee jumping, cliff climbing. Between violence in its many forms and fat in its many forms that are normalized, children are increasingly being placed in harm's way. Then, ironically, marketers offer up many products—medicines, exercise programs, active toys—to cope with fatness and violence. So they are winners coming and going. They make money contributing to the problem and then make money solving it.

As noted, the list of bad values touted by marketers is endless, but a few more deserve mentioning. Most of them could fit under the classification of *dishonesty*. Two that seem to go together, *lying* and *stealing*, are common themes of many marketers' messages. Movies and TV programs, video games, as well as commercials often show lying as a normal means for children to cope with parents—to get parents to buy them what they want. Stealing is actually shown in some ads for kids' products as virtues of sorts; that is, it may be necessary for children to steal a product because it is so good, *so good* for them. Related to stealing a product is getting violent if necessary in order to obtain the product. Tied into the stealing and violence sometimes is the notion of *revenge*—getting even for someone who steals from you or hurts you—à la Clint Eastwood and Charles Bronson. I would add *greed* as another value that is related to violence and to fatdom. The message "greed is good," like revenge, received a running start into the lives of kids through the pushing of Hollywood (e.g., Michael Douglas as Gordon Gekko in the movie *Wall Street*). Of course, all these actions underlie crimes that may occur in later childhood, including bullying.

Would the executives in companies that target kids agree with what has been said here about them being unethical? A Harris Interactive poll was taken among a large number of marketers in the youth marketing industry, and two-thirds of them felt their ethical standards were higher than those of the industry as a whole—whatever that defensive response means (Geraci, 2004). Most characterized the ethical climate in the youth marketing industry as being on par with that of other industries—whatever that defensive response means. However, they do feel that ethical standards among youth marketers are not as high as they once were—whatever that defensive response means. Regarding specific issues, they said that they felt it appropriate to begin marketing to kids at age 7, but also said that most young people cannot view advertising critically until an average age of 9.1 and cannot make intelligent choices as consumers until an average age of 11.7. So, the ambiguous nature of their responses regarding their ethics seems not too distant from their actual marketing practices.

A FINAL NOTE ABOUT MARKETERS' ROLE IN CONSUMER DEVELOPMENT

Marketers have a featured role in children's consumer development. They are responsible for teaching children about the uses of their brands of products, where and how to obtain those products, and, of course, the products' benefits to them. Children need and seek this kind of information, which will help them develop mentally and physically. Children are constantly in the learning mode, yet they are so gullible. Tell or show a five-year-old that a certain cereal or beverage will prepare him to leap over tall buildings, and he will request the product from mom and pick out a building to test it. But why would marketers tell children that their products have such benefits if they were not true? The answer is often called *puffery*, *exaggeration*, and other terms including *deception* and *misrepresentation*, and seems to be in the nature of marketers to do that sort of thing—in spite of the likelihood that children will take the messages seriously, particularly if they are from the mouth of a superstar. And particularly if the messages are presented in every medium, every day, everywhere—through surround selling (integrated marketing communications). To the point that marketers resort to deception, there are laws—plenty of them—at the federal and state levels to contend with such practices. The laws are rarely utilized; therefore, more deception is encouraged. Whenever laws are used to threaten marketers, and particularly advertisers, the accused usually resort to what all marketers in their many forms, including politicians, say: We will police ourselves. But self-regulation—through various company documents such as a Code of Ethics, self-regulation organizations such as the Children's Advertising Regulation Unit of the Council of Better Business Bureaus—has never thwarted marketers' unethical efforts as far as I can tell, but invoking it usually fends off the accusers. Since neither regulation nor self-regulation seems to work, some consumer protectionists resort to lawsuits. For example, during the past couple of years, several major marketers have been threatened with lawsuits to get them to change their marketing practices aimed at children. These attempts seem like desperate measures and are unlikely to be successful in their goals. But if legal recourse is the answer, then theoretically it should be aimed at government and business CEOs and heads of families that foster marketing-child consumer relationships.

In this age of "relationship marketing" (e.g., McKenna, 1991) and "consumer-oriented marketing" (see any basic marketing book), it is hard to understand the prevalence of unethical marketing. But some of my colleagues tell me that it is simple: It is condoned and practiced by the highest levels of government and business—it makes headlines daily—and therefore is okayed for the public. We live in a "culture of corruption," they add journalistically. Whatever the explanation, competition or corruption, children pay a high price for being the brightest stars in the consumer constellation, for they attract it all—the good, the bad, the ugly.

As noted, 24/7/360 consumer behavior begets 24/7/360 marketing. Marketers usually do not spend money unless they believe they can make money. So all that constant marketing to children is intended to have good financial results. But does it produce too much marketing to children in spite of their great marketing potential? Probably there is not too much marketing; as noted, there is too much *unethical* marketing—marketing laced with deception and bad values. There is concern among consumer protectionists that there is too much advertising to children—or that there is too much advertising to children who cannot yet understand it or defend against it—at least children under a certain age, usually under 100 months. But asking marketers not to advertise—or package or display or promote or sell—to children under a certain age is asking them not to do what is standard marketing practice—marketing to markets. Again, marketers do not overspend technically. Their spending is supposedly commensurate with the payback. As households cede their decision-making power to the children in residence, they automatically cause marketers to target children—the decision makers. Thus, the thousands of tekrams performed by children simply keep growing in number as they assume more functions in the consumer role at an earlier age, and this makes them even more attractive marketing targets.

To borrow an overused phrase, "the system is flawed." Perhaps better said, modern marketing, which knows how to accurately satisfy a market target such as kids, has inherent flaws in it. Marketing develops a product to satisfy a set of needs of kids and then, through surround selling that is coordinated by the likes of a brand manager, persuades children to buy it in large quantities. The more bought, the more the brand manager will be rewarded. Thus, marketers try to sell as much of the product as they can to a market. They have no idea how much one child consumes of their product or how much one child consumes of similar competitive products. They apparently assume that caretakers will intervene to prevent the child from consuming too much. But busy working parents have put their children pretty much in charge of their own consumption levels. If children ask for more, they get more. The net results are too many children taking risks, getting fat, becoming unhealthy, not studying enough, not sleeping enough, and, in general, endangering themselves through overconsumption. There was never a needier time for the rebirth of children's consumer education programs that were proposed and implemented by Presidents Kennedy, Johnson, and Nixon. I believe those consumer education efforts would allow children to continue safely in their regal role as the most important consumers in society.

REFERENCES

Beasley, D. (2006, March 30). Sunscreen makers sued for misleading health claims. Retrieved from news.yahoo.coms/nm/20060330/usn_msunscreen

Chan, K., and J. U. McNeal. (2004, March). Children's understanding of television advertising: A revisit in the Chinese context. *Journal of Genetic Psychology, 165*, 28–36.

Dixon, K. (2006). Hospitals prepare for growing ranks of obese. Retrieved from http://news.yahoo.com/s/nm/20060602/ts_nm/bizfeature_obese

Farmer, R. N. (1967, January). Would you want your daughter to marry a marketing man? *Journal of Marketing, 31*, 1–3.

Geraci, J. C. (2004, April–June). What do youth marketers think about selling to kids? *International Journal of Marketing & Advertising to Children*, 11–18.

Grusec. J. E., and H. Lytton. (1988). *Social Development: History, Theory, and Research*. New York: Springer.

Kotler, P. (1967). *Marketing Management: Analysis, Planning, and Control*. Englewood Cliffs. NJ: Prentice Hall, Inc.

Lexchin, J., L. A. Bero, B. Djuibegovic, and O. Clark. (2003, May 31). Pharmaceutical industry sponsorship and research outcome and quality: Systematic review. Retrieved from bmj.bmjjournals.com/cgi/content/full/326/7400/1167

Liebert, R. M., J. N. Sprafkin, R. M. Liebert, and E. A. Rubinstein. (1977, Winter). Effects of television commercial disclaimers on the product expectations of children, *Journal of Communications, 27*, 118–124.

McKenna, R. (1991). *Relationship Marketing: Successful Strategies for the Age of the Customer*. Reading, MA: Addison-Wesley Publishing Co.

McNeal, J. U. (1966). Promotion: An overview. In J. U. McNeal (Ed.), *Readings in Promotion Management*. New York: Meredith Publishing Company.

McNeal, J. U. (1991, May/June). Planning priorities for marketing to children. *Journal of Business Strategy*, 12–15.

McNeal, J. U. (1992, August 31). Marketing to children means communicating in a special language. *Advertising Age*, p. 21.

McNeal, J. U. (1998, April). Tapping the three kids' markets. *American Demographics*, 37–41.

McNeal, J. U. (1999). *The Kids Market: Myth and Realities*. Ithaca, NY: Paramount Market Publishers.

Parker-Pope, T. (2003, July 15). A "fat-free" product that's 100% fat: How food labels legally mislead. *Wall Street Journal*, p. D1.

Pett, J. (2006, May 22). Forum page, Asterisk nation. *USA Today*, p. 12A.

Schultz, D. E., S. I. Tannenbaum, and R. F. Lauterborn. (1993). *Integrated Marketing Communications*. Lincolnwood, IL: NTC Business Books.

Stern, L. W., and T. L. Eovaldi. (1984). *Legal Aspects of Marketing Strategy: Antitrust and Consumer Protection Issues*. Englewood Cliffs, NJ: Prentice Hall, Inc.

Strauss, R. S., and H. A. Pollack. (2001, December 12). Epidemic increase in childhood overweight, 1986–1998, *JAMA*, 286. Retrieved from jama.ama-assn.org/issues/current/rfull/jbr10287.html

Stutts, M. A., D. Vance, and S. Hudleson. (1981). Program-commercial separators in children's television: Do they help a child tell the difference between "Bugs Bunny and the Quik Rabbit?" *Journal of Advertising, 10*, 16–25.

Winn, M. (1983). *Children without Childhood*. New York: Pantheon Books.

SUBJECT INDEX

Voluntary observation, 27–28, 166–172
Vygotsky, Lev, 259, 300

W
Walking
  autonomy and, 200
  developmental features of, 106
  by five-year-old child, 249
  by four-year-old child, 249
  heel-to-toe, 249
  learning to walk, 192–193, 197–200
  marketplace visits and, 198, 214, 362
  object seeking after, 214
  by six-year-old child, 249
  studies of, 112
  by two-year-old child, 219

Weight, of newborn, 98
Whiting, Beatrice, 322
Whiting, John, 322
Word comprehension, 108–109
Writing skills
  of six-year-old child, 253
  of two-year-old child, 225
  in Stage Five, 292

Y
Youth sports, organized, 253–255

Z
Zone of proximal development, 259,
  300